1951–2001
Made in Italy?

Project by
Luigi Settembrini
(*Contemporary Cultural Engineering*)

Belvedere
by Achille Bonito Oliva

coordination
Manuela Gandini
exhibition design
Pierluigi Cerri

Memory
by Gae Aulenti and Luca Ronconi

installation by
La Fura dels Baus

Brockenhaus
by Oliviero Toscani

Flavours
by Gaetano Pesce and Andrea Pezzi

Allegory
by Pier Luigi Pizzi

video-installation by
Enrico Ghezzi

Project by

Graphic design
Studio Cerri & Associati

Editing
Marco Abate

Translations
Tim Stroud
Per Language Consulting s.r.l.:
Robert Burns
Lucian Comoy
Barbara Cooper
Cristopher Evans
Daria Kissel
Liam McGabhann
Marco Migotto
Leslie Ray

*The publisher is at the
disposal of the entitled
parties as regards all
unidentified iconographic
and literary sources.*

Printed in March 2001
on behalf of Skira,
Geneve-Milan
Printed in Italy

The exhibition is promoted
and organized by Cosmit Spa
with the patronage of
Federlegno-Arredo,
Federazione Italiana
delle Industrie del Legno,
del Sughero, del Mobile
e dell'Arredamento

**1951–2001
Made in Italy?**

TRIENNALE DI MILANO
Palazzo della Triennale
4th april–13th may 2001

COSMIT

President
Rosario Messina

Vice Presidents
Enrico Pirovano
Rodrigo Rodriquez

Franco Arquati
Paolo Boffi
Giampaolo Ferretti
Francesco Forcelli
Paolo Lombardi
Roberto Moroso
Giuseppe Origlia
Riccardo Sarfatti

Managing Director
Manlio Armellini

In collaboration with

 RegioneLombardia

Under the aegis of

Ministero per i Beni
e le Attività Culturali

Comune di Milano
Cultura e Musei
Settore Musei e Mostre

General Curator
Luigi Settembrini

Artistic Director
Franco Laera
(*Change Performing Arts*)

General Coordination
Laura Lazzaroni
and Francesca Sorace

Corporate Identity Image
Studio Cerri & Associati

Belvedere
Curator
Achille Bonito Oliva

Coordination
Manuela Gandini

Exhibition project
Studio Cerri & Associati
with the collaboration
of Fabio Bertola
and Dario Zannier

Memory
Curators
Gae Aulenti
and Luca Ronconi

Contributions by
Vanni Pasca for furniture
and industrial design;
Paola Acquati, Cristina
Brigidini, Aurora Fiorentini
for fashion;
Paolo Mereghetti
for cinema;
Paolo Murialdi and Guido
Vergani for news stories

Sound's dramaturgy
Luca Ronconi

Exhibition project
Gae Aulenti
with the collaboration
of Chiara Costa, Vittoria
Massa and the coordination
by Milena Archetti

Grafic design of "Vele"
Carola Reverdini

With an installation by
La Fura dels Baus

Brockenhaus
Curator
Oliviero Toscani

Flavours
Curators
Gaetano Pesce
and Andrea Pezzi

Video production
Bibop Research Int. S.p.A.

Allegory
Curator
Pier Luigi Pizzi

Exhibition project
Pier Luigi Pizzi
with the collaboration
of Luca Rolla

Video installation by
Enrico Ghezzi

Production

Change Performing Arts
Izumi Arakawa,
Laura Artoni,
Elisabetta di Mambro
Franco Gabualdi,
Yasunori Gunij,
Patrizia Mangone
Marta Peloso
and Andrea Petrus
Lighting design
A.J. Weissbard
with the collaboration
of Virginia Manoni
*Sound design and original
compositions*
Peter Cerone
and Stefano Scarani
Technical director
Pierre Houben
Construction manager
Massimiliano Peyrone
*Video installations
coordinator*
Sabina Uberti-Bona
with the collaboration
of Cristina Proserpio
Exhibition materials research
Anna Congiu,
Maria Gabualdi,
Petra Lossner
(Advertising
and Management)
Installation coordination
Laura Scarani
with the collaboration
of Daniela Balsamo
and Sue Jane Stoker
Technical team
Claudio Bellagamba
and Marco Zecchini
with Francesco Caggianese,
Alessandro
Montemaggiore, Roberto
Morello, Dario Nicali

Editing
Roberto Rosati

Iconographic research
Paola Richetti
and Orio Vergani

*External relations
and Press office*
Advertising and
Management
Consultants
Cristina Brigidini
Silvia Martinenghi (Regia)

Secretary
Isabella Gaspardo

Constructions
Agorà srl
Delfini Group s.r.l.
Morini & Mancinelli s.n.c.
Way spa
Xilografia Nuova s.r.l.

*Lighting and sound
equipment*
Volume s.r.l.

Video equipment
Eletech sistemi video
Stand By s.r.l.
Vigorelli Servizi

Video editing
Dropout Officina
dell'immagine

Transportation
Gondrand s.p.a.
Zust Ambrosetti s.p.a.
Smontini Trasporti

Insurance
Axa Nordsten Art
CEBI Assicurazioni

Ninety years in two; as time goes by you can be rejuvenated

Two anniversaries in one, fifty years of fashion and forty of the Salone Internazionale del Mobile. Ninety years in two, yet no one would dream of calling either of them "old", a sign that in some dimension – such as this one, of design and things project-related – with the passing of time you can even be rejuvenated. As regards the Salone del Mobile, in 1961, the year of its foundation, it was simply proposed as an exhibition space for the production of furniture, yet, in just a few years, it became the chosen venue of Italian design, acting as a catalyst for and driving force behind all the creative energy that constitutes the great success of Italian design.

When I began the entrepreneurial trade, twenty-five years ago, I would never have imagined myself having to celebrate forty years of the Salone del Mobile as President of Cosmit. It is a great honour, which I feel I must share with those who work in this mighty exhibition machine and, even more, with those who have preceded me in the construction of a fair system that the whole world envies, firstly with Manlio Armellini, managing director of the Salone del Mobile and its general secretary and reference point for twenty-seven years, in a certain sense the father of the show.

In 1961 the Italian furniture industry, as such, did not even exist. Today, at a distance of eight quinquennia, it has a turnover of 46 thousand billion lire, 17 thousand of which for exports. To say that the quota of exported products, in forty years, has grown by 220 thousand per cent (Italian furniture exports, in 1961, amounted to 9 billion lire) is arithmetically obvious; behind this, however, lies the intelligent and stubborn effort of whole generations.

Many will note that, as the operators of fashion, we furniture dealers too tend to use and in some case misuse the term "culture". It is because we consider that many ingredients of quality meet in furnishing, and not only industrial: history, taste, art in all its forms. The furnishing project is indeed the result of a series of moments of civilisation. Perhaps the awareness of this has prompted us Italians to commit ourselves in the production of furniture much more than others have done; and this perhaps explains why Italy has long been the number one world exporter of furniture, though not being the top producer of furniture. In many homes in every country there is a piece of Italian furniture, recognised as such; rather, often acquired precisely for that reason.

Yet we have our first customer here at home: it is the Italian industrial world as a whole. The furnishing industry in fact consumes 40% of the wood, 22% of the metal, 12.5% of the chemical products, 8% of the fabrics, 1.5% of the glass produced in Italy. The wood-furnishing sector (64 thousand billion in turnover, of which 22 thousand for exports) gives work to almost 450 thousand families. And in all this, the Salone del Mobile in Milan is what attracts the largest audience, talked about by more than one hundred specialist magazines in over 50 technologically developed countries.

These are not things that we have discovered today; the Salone del Mobile has already celebrated some important recurrences with great pomp and ceremony; I am thinking of the great 1991 exhibition at the Triennial in Milan, entitled *Italian Furniture 1961-1991. The Various Ages of Languages*, on the occasion of the thirtieth anniversary of the Salone del Mobile; or the recurrence of 35 years (1996), also celebrated with many festivities and a major book on the history of the sector.

But we wanted to insert an innovation into the celebration of this year: forty years of the Salone del Mobile, that is, forty years of Italian design, are combined with the other great event that occurs in this special year of 2001, fifty years of Italian fashion. Tradition has it, as is known, that the birth of Italian fashion – and perhaps also of products "Made in Italy" – is dated February 12th 1951, when Giovanni Battista Giorgini persuaded some taylors to parade together in Florence for American buyers. It was then, say the chronicles, that Italian fashion, the other great phenomenon that illustrates our creative genius throughout the world, was born.

It is from that moment that the evolution in forms and tastes proceeded along the same seam. Some even consider that it was lucky – paradoxically – that Italy lost the Second World War. In the years immediately following the end of the conflict, in fact, there were a large number of architects who, finding themselves without jobs, agreed to design small objects. And Milan, a city with a large middle class, its many architects and its strong industrial tradition, knew how to take this opportunity in a special way. Was there a moment when this process was formalised? I would say yes, in 1972, at the Museum of Modern Art in New York, with the exhibition *Italy: The New Domestic Landscape*. The exhibition not only revealed the inventive capacities of Italian design in the field of furniture but also revealed the very concept of a domestic landscape that reflects the changes and evolution of society. It was a full-blown revolution, which consecrated Italy as the country of taste and the project or, if we prefer, of the project of taste.

Today the differences between the fashion system and the design system remain, and do not allow the two systems that constitute the skeleton of products "Made in Italy" to approach each other if not in an evocative manner. The world of furnishing, to name but one, remains considerably fragmented, while the world of fashion flies towards major concentrations (the ten main groups of the fashion industry in Italy make up 79% of the sector's turnover; the first five are worth 56% of the market), just as we find profound structural differences in the financial structure of the two systems. But what unites them is no small thing: the ability to continually invent the new – in form, materials, technology – and the capacity to remain on the international markets.

Increasingly often, we tend to blend fashion with design. And why this is intimately true can be explained better than anything by a sentence of Stefan Lengyel, a lecturer in industrial design and a designer himself: "Industrial design is at all levels of development one of the most important factors for the creation of objects that belong to people's everyday lives, from the simplest tools in common use to the complex systems of the industrial and public sectors. A good design is always the optimal adaptation of the technical, economic and social elements to an objective reality, since the design influences the forms of use, it also influences human relationships. In other words, the design is a socio-cultural phenomenon of great significance."

If this is true – and I sincerely believe it to be – then allow me to say that the Salone Internazionale del Mobile, which is a point of departure and fundamental arrival of the design system, is a socio-cultural phenomenon of great significance. Congratulations to everybody!

Rosario Messina
Cosmit President

Acknowledgements

If you think that *Made in Italy?* was told it would be given an exhibition venue in Milan only on 18th December last year, one can appreciate the tremendous commitment and self-sacrifice of all those who helped to organise an event of this importance and size in such an incredibly short time. Therefore, my thanks are far from being a mere formality. First of all, I wish to thank the directors of the Salone del Mobile (Furniture Fair) who, through their decision to back the mounting of an exhibition around the theme of 'Made in Italy' (and not just in terms of design), have evidenced an understanding and *political intelligence* that are very special in a country where out-of-place self-centred interests and patriotism are commonplace. I do not wish here to provoke a sterile controversy but rather write an invitation so that other fundamental components of the 'Made in Italy' industry begin to reflect upon the great institutional strength, and great strength in absolute terms, as well as the impact of the image and advertising, that projects able to represent the entire system would have.

These far-sighted friends are Manlio Armellini, managing director of Cosmit, who daily shared the selections and decisions concerning the project, and solved an infinite number of problems; Rodrigo Rodriquez, president of Federlegno-Arredo, who was generous, constant (and at times providential) with his help during the entire project; Rosario Messina, president of Cosmit, who was one of the first businessmen in the sector to understand the importance and usefulness in broadening the availability of information to a vast, transverse public that was not made up solely of trade operators and experts; Giulio Castelli, to whose dedicated work we are indebted in large part for the solution of the problem of exhibition space, as well as other aspects, which *Made in Italy?* had to face and resolve in the "Cesarini quarter", even thanks to Augusto Morello, president of the Triennale di Milano, David Rampello, director of the Triennale, and Andrea Cancellato, president's personal assistant.

Naturally, my thanks go also to all the great professionals who accepted our invitation to curate the five nuclei into which the exhibition is divided:

Achille Bonito Oliva (together with whom my thanks go to Pierluigi Cerri for his helpfulness in solving space problems; Manuela Gandini for her invaluable, unswerving work; the Italian and international artists and gallery managers who lent us the works on show. A special thanks goes to Mrs Xu Min, to Lorenzo Fiaschi and Gian Enzo Sperone);

Gae Aulenti and Luca Ronconi (together with whom I also thank, in particular, the Fura dels Baus and Carlos Padrissa for the sets they created which are one of *Memory*'s focus points, and, for their significant contribution: Paola Acquati, Cristina Brigidini, Aurora Fiorentini, Laura Lazzaroni, Vittoria Massa, Paolo Mereghetti, Paolo Murialdi, Vanni Pasca, and also Milena Archetti, Chiara Costa and Vittoria Massa of Studio Au-

lenti, and Carola Reverdini for the graphics of "Vele");

Oliviero Toscani;

Gaetano Pesce and Andrea Pezzi (together with whom I also thank Bibop and its managing director Gabriele Gresta for their understanding and the enormous help they gave the project);

Pier Luigi Pizzi (together with whom I'd also like to thank Enrico Ghezzi for the – as always – unusual, amusing and intelligent editing of the video input for *Allegory*, and Luca Rolla for his help in the preparation).

My affectionate thanks, of course, go to Franco Laera, the project's artistic director, who has been helping me in my work with great intelligence, quality and patience for a number of years now. Together with him, I thank Francesca Sorace, my irreplaceable assistant in all my activities and general co-ordinator of the exhibition.

Thanks also to Contemporary Cultural Engineering and to Roberto Rosati for assistance in drafting the ideas for the project and to Change Performing Arts, impeccable as always in their management and handling of the production of the entire event. For the co-ordinated image, our thanks go to Studio Cerri e Associati.

A special, heartfelt thanks goes to Guido Vergani, the editor of the historical part of this book, who showed extraordinary generosity throughout the project.

Thanks to *Nonsolomoda* and the cordial and understanding assistance of its director, Fabrizio Pasquero; to *Show Biz* and Armando Bolzoni for allowing us to use their archives.

Thank you also to Anna Del Gatto and *Rai Educational* for excerpts from *Lezioni di Design*. For the Rai archive material my thanks go to Anna Cammarano of *Rai Teche* and Marilena Avola of *Rai Trade*. Thanks to Paola Richetti and Orio Vergani, true thoroughbreds, for their invaluable iconographic research. Thank you, too, to the management, employees and consultants of Cosmit for all the help they gave. Among them, my special thanks go to Giovanni De Ponti, managing director, Petra Lossner, production administration co-ordinator and Isabella Gaspardo, organiser's office.

My thanks to Titti Santini for his idea of using Andrea Pezzi's exuberance to celebrate Italian gastronomy. My special thanks go, lastly, to Valeria Magli who agreed to present *Tutte come una* (*All like one*) – the show drawn from Lina Sotis' book *Una come tutte* (*One like all*) – an intelligent, invaluable friend.

Luigi Settembrini
General Curator

Contents

The Exhibition   *edited by Luigi Settembrini*

(Pre)Conceptions of an Exhibition
Luigi Settembrini

Gio Ponti
(Publifoto/Olympia)

Roberto Rossellini
(photo: Apis/Coatsaliou/Ledru/
Sigma/Grazia Neri)

At the end of the war what was left of Italy's image abroad? Not very much. The yellow jerseys worn by Bartali and Coppi, champions of the Izoard and Tourmalet passes, the reputation of the odd professional. That of Gio Ponti, for example, who at the end of the forties was the most famous Italian in the world (along with the pope and Arturo Toscanini). Architect, designer, artist and founder of *Domus* (1928), Ponti designed everything: from churches to sewing machines and from furniture to fabrics to jewelry to the Pirelli skyscraper (1955). It was with Gio Ponti that Italian design was born, one of the first strong signals of the metamorphosis the country was about to undergo. But in the meantime something else was rearing its head: fashion. While the extraordinary neorealist films of those years – *Roma città aperta* was made in 1945, *Sciuscià* in '46, *Ladri di biciclette* in '48 – shared in the reality of a country on its knees, fashion was dreaming about a quite different reality. And in so doing anticipated what came to be known years afterward as the *Italian miracle*. The magic of the Sala Bianca in Palazzo Pitti, where the new Italian fashion was put on show from 1951 onward, enchanted American buyers. Its inventor, Giovan Battista Giorgini, wanted it to be fresh, modern, colourful and accessible, in contrast to French fashion, which was classical, stiff and too expensive. And so Italian products of quality and image began to appear in the shops and department stores first of America and then of Northern Europe.

These were the years of the first Festival of Sanremo (1951, master of ceremonies Nunzio Filogamo, winner Nilla Pizzi with *Grazie dei fiori*), the first Miss Italy (1947, which put the spotlight on, among others, Lucia Bosé, Gina Lollobrigida and Silvana Pampanini), and the first *Lascia o Raddoppia?* presented by Mike Bongiorno (1955), the greatest success of black and white TV along with *Carosello*, which came two years later. The phrase "to bed after Carosello" entered into common use, as the latest possible time mothers would allow their children to stay up. The first issue of *Il Giorno* came out in Milan, on April 21, 1956: taking its inspiration from the modern newspapers of the English-speaking world, its language (in its columns on politics or sport, the theatre or the cinema, current affairs or literature, or even in its cartoon strips) was aimed at an open-minded reader.

The sixties were ushered in by *La dolce vita* (1960) and brought to a close with the revolution of 1968. In the middle, the economic boom. *Paparazzi* in pursuit of stars and colonizers in a Rome still inhabited by "poor but beautiful" people, although already teeming with creative ideas and new talents: from Flaiano to Sordi, from Mastroianni to Garinei, from Sonego to Risi, from Moravia to Pasolini. The state-run TV monopoly, not having to worry about audience ratings above all else, offered drama and produced quality shows like *Studio Uno* (1961), on which Mina became an international star and the Kessler twins sang and danced the *Dadaumpa*.

That decade went by without Italy noticing Anita Ekberg's bath in the Trevi Fountain or the conquest of space, woman as sex object or the beginnings of feminism. The dream was of a more powerful automobile, of travel, luxury, vacations: a weekend in "Swinging London" perhaps, with the Beatles, Carnaby Street and Mary Quant's miniskirts. People indulged in the first true – and at bottom more than legitimate – consumption of non-essential items since the war. But Antonioni had already made *L'Avventura* (1960), *La Notte* (1961) and *L'Eclisse* (1962) and was speaking to us about existential malaise and the inability of the *nouveaux riches* to communicate. A few years later the director, with that explosion of the symbols of prosperity shot in slow motion by seventeen cameras to the music of the Pink Floyd, not only produced the highly emblematic finale of a film (*Zabriskie Point*, 1970) but confirmed the end of an era: an end that had already been announced a year earlier with the carnage in piazza Fontana.

A prominent figure in the fashion world and jet set since the fifties, Emilio Pucci, marchese di Barsento, was an anomalous personage in that still not very cosmopolitan Italy. Elegant, cultured, at home anywhere in the world, he spoke English so perfectly that Americans had a hard time understanding him. Female buyers from the United States (and women everywhere, really) adored him. He once rode down Fifth Avenue on a white horse, dressed as a captain in the historic Florentine soccer game of *Calcio in Costume*, for he understood that this was the metaphor of aristocratic Italy, rich in beauty and tradition, for which Americans with few roots and no crown yearned.

Movies like William Wyler's *Roman Holiday* (1953, with Audrey Hepburn, Gregory Peck and the Vespa) and Antonio Pietrangeli's *Souvenir d'Italie* (1957), relaunched Italy,

province of the empire, as a tourist paradise and land of love, just as was suggested by the highly ambitious United States ambassador in Rome, Claire Boothe Luce, wife of the owner of the *Time-Life* publishing empire. Such figures as gondoliers, the Latin lover in the style of Rossano Brazzi and fascinating noblemen like Louis Jourdan (Negulesco's *Three Coins in the Fountain*, 1954) and Vittorio Gassman as the Sienese prince who seduced Diana Dors in *La ragazza del Palio* (Zampa, 1957) entered the imagination of women all over the world. Clichés? Of course. But it was an excellent way of exorcising the memory, by now embarrassing even for the Americans, of bombing raids, bicycle thieves, shoeblacks, emigrants, waiters and Mafiosi who had not yet been rendered charming and at bottom even rather nice by Mario Puzo and the films of Francis Ford Coppola.

Pucci was the perfect testimonial to the new image of Italy and the great leap forward that the country made in those years. But Pucci was not just about folklore: no one could claim to have understood the woman of the sixties and her desire for modernity and a new lifestyle better than he did, just as few people can be said to have grasped the changes underway at the time better then Zanuso or Colombo, or to have foreseen the absurdities and malaise of the end of a very short and happy age as did Fellini and Antonioni.

While Pucci was a forerunner of ready-to-wear, another leading figure of the sixties, Valentino, remained firmly anchored to a vision of woman as woman, of woman as queen. By dressing everyone from Farah Diba to Jacqueline Kennedy and the great actresses of those years, he gave *made in Italy* a much more glamorous and international image. In the panorama of fashion, Valentino remains a distinct phenomenon, a talent who has been able to go on imitating himself for over forty years. Owing to this fidelity to models, values and images that any sociologist would regard as obsolete (and perhaps even "discreditable"), his style has stood the test of time. It is curious to note how much similarity there is between one of his dresses from thirty years ago and one from his most recent collections, as well, in all probability, as those of the future. For him, history is an optional. There is a story about him that may be apocryphal, but nevertheless rings true. In an interview a journalist asks Valentino: "What comes to mind when you think about 1968?" And he answers: "My extraordinary collection in black and white."

But 1968 was not just a collection. On the contrary, it changed the world and its values. Sartre and Marcuse preached new ideas and the young, from the Sorbonne to Berkeley, demanded new values, a life without compromises and lies. These were the years of great hopes, of great struggles by the workers, of the crisis of the family, of the open relationship, of group work and group exams, of the rejection of consumer society.

But the world awoke from this grand dream into a very serious identity crisis. Experts scared the public by announcing that global oil supplies were almost exhausted and forecast a chilling dark age to come. Petrol was rationed: not for environmental reasons, but because it was thought to be running out. On alternate Sundays, only cars with license plates ending in odd or even numbers were allowed to circulate, and sometimes none at all.

In the meantime *jeans* and the *parka* became the uniform in progressive circles. Formal dress, suddenly considered reactionary, was banished. The GFT group (Facis, Cori, Sidi, Marus), the largest manufacturer of clothing in Italy, saw its profits collapse. The company signed a contract with an almost unknown stylist.

The unknown stylist, a former window dresser at La Rinascente department store and employee of Cerruti, was not even an up-and-comer given that he was already in his forties: his name was Giorgio Armani.

The miracle happened: out of the synergy between Armani's talent and the GFT's production and distribution capacity was born modern fashion and what would be the first authentic, planetwide *made in Italy*, capable of dressing millions of people all over the world in clothes of the same quality and with the same image. Armani or democracy then: with the stylist was born politically correct fashion, symbolic of the new mode of thought.

Just as in fashion, politics entered into industrial design as well, or rather a "political way" of thinking. These were the years of the debate between "establishment design" and "radical design". The former viewed design as an activity capable of proposing solutions and collaborating with companies more sensitive to the problem; the latter emphasized, often through the autonomous production of objects intended to serve as manifestos, the need for reform and for social and political engagement. Enzo Mari is perhaps the figure who epitomizes this period of transition: in 1974 he designed *Metamobile*, a range of "low-

Ladri di biciclette,
by Vittorio De Sica, 1948
(Team/Grazia Neri)

Claire Boothe Luce, 1958
(photo: Carlo Riccardi/Team/
Grazia Neri)

Emilio Pucci at the annual
parade of "Calcio in costume",
Florence
(photo: Andrea Bazzichi)

cost" furniture, for Gavina. Dino Gavina was a difficult, arrogant and brilliant man, a scholar, businessman and student of history and art. Friend of Roberto Longhi, Marcel Breuer, Duchamp, Man Ray and Fontana, he was the entrepreneur who encouraged Carlo Scarpa and who was the first to produce his designs. He was one of the founders of Flos and got it off the mark with the operation *Ultrarazionale* (1968), typified by Scarpa's *Doge* table, which was followed by *Ultramobile* (1971), with furniture designed by artists.

After the malaise came tragedy. Italy slid into the spiral of terrorism. In 1972 the dead body of the publisher Giangiacomo Feltrinelli was found on a mined electricity pylon at Segrate: descendant of a wealthy Lombard family, he was a Communist and friend of Castro who had decided, against the wishes of the party, to publish the book *Doctor Zhivago*.

But the most dramatic images that spring to mind are those of the urban guerrilla warfare in Milan between the police and armed men, their faces covered with balaclavas. And then come those of Aldo Moro, held prisoner and murdered by the Red Brigades (1978).

This was the very time when the ex-window dresser of La Rinascente, in a case almost unique in the history of fashion, ended up on the cover of *Time* and was dubbed "Gorgeous Giorgio." Once again the international image of *made in Italy*, now a runaway, worldwide success, was helping to create a more positive image for the country.

The reaction to austerity and to the "years of lead" came in the eighties, in the form of a genuine restoration. Men started to wear the tuxedo again after its apparent demise and those who went to La Scala were able to do so without fear of being pelted with rotten vegetables and eggs. The national soccer team won the World Cup in Spain in 1982. *Azzurra* aroused Italians' enthusiasm for sailing and the America's Cup. Good humor, hedonism and yuppies were all the rage and the glossy magazines made a fortune out of it all.

Finance became a fundamental component of life, the politics of worldliness. The dominant figure on the scene was Bettino Craxi. The self-referentiality of the powerful was stepped up, but by now, after so much minimalist correctness, who felt like renouncing the whiff of oxygen that came from a bit of unsophisticated vulgarity? The feminists who had burned their bras in public were now replaced by women who wore padded bras, career women who wanted to be loved as women, but respected as managers. Suntanned, fresh from the hairdresser, the masseur and shopping: the eighties were all for them. And for the men? Not much. It was they who were for the women.

And who more than Gianni Versace was the poet, the interpreter, the d'Annunzio of these heroines? Gianni Versace understood the "woman of the Restoration" better than anyone else, grasping her need to be aggressive, her need for ostentation and even vulgarity. He knew what her home should look like, what sort of ashtrays and cushions it should have. And what sort of glasses, T-shirts or shorts her men ought to wear.

Another protagonist of those years was Ettore Sottsass, who opened the decade with *Memphis* (1980-81): a "master of industry" decreed the end of *form follows function* and cleared the way for free design. Sottsass's vision of the world was not the same as Versace's, but it was equally colourful, liberating, superfluous. Versace *was* "vulgar" by nature: Sottsass was very good at *feigning* it.

And the nineties? The memories have not settled yet. Certainly, Miuccia Prada's little knapsack is not enough to make us forget the films of Carlo Vanzina, the violence and madness of the soccer stadium, the lack of planning on the left, the conventionalism of the right. The impression, however, is that vulgarity in Italy has become stratified: in the eighties it was a game – though a game that revealed its limits and its risks – while today it appears to belong more and more to popular culture.

***

These scattered memories constituted the brief for *Made in Italy?*, an exhibition and at the same time a multidisciplinary event with which COSMIT is celebrating the 40th anniversary of the foundation of the Salone Internazionale del Mobile, the highest Italian expression of the culture of furnishing. In fact the first of these events, eventually to become the most important date on the calendar for the sector anywhere in the world, as well as the chief launching pad for the planetwide success of *made in Italy* design was held in Milan in 1961.

It was exactly ten years earlier that the parades of Italian fashion had begun in Florence,

another case history of success, another pillar of *made in Italy*.

Thus Italian design and fashion are respectively celebrating, in this year of 2001, their fortieth and fiftieth birthdays. Consequently, we decided to commemorate the anniversary of fashion along with that of design, by trying – I believe for the first time – to bring together, in a cultural operation that is also intended to be "systematic", these two fundamental aspects of our country's international image as well as items in its balance of trade.

Anniversaries run the risk of turning into pompous occasions and often have a somewhat morbid atmosphere. In an age like ours, the more time presses, the more we are afraid of forgetting and being forgotten. But this is not the case with Italian design and fashion.

Yet there is a double motivation for celebrating design and fashion together: two reasons that can help to cancel out the rhetoric of commemoration and make this co-anniversary an opportunity to blow a breath of fresh air through received ideas about design and fashion rather than just blowing their trumpet.

The first reason is that over the last half-century design and fashion have represented not just the main export of our economy, but also the highest product of our culture, even if official channels do not seem to have ever taken much notice of the fact. So following their development in parallel allows us to examine the whole recent history of our country, in its richness as well as its contradictions, from a privileged, modern, dynamic and cosmopolitan point of view.

The second reason is that fashion design and industrial design are two phenomena that are closely related in many ways, but which have always kept a distance from one another and have always been studied separately: so to look at them together may turn out to help us understand something more about both and to present us with a picture of the state of the contemporary culture of design.

It is to the first motive that the exhibition *Made in Italy?* is dedicated, with the question mark placed there deliberately to raise questions about what is a usually triumphal expression. For the things that are made in Italy and have become familiar everywhere in the world over these last fifty years are not just fashion and design, or *La dolce vita,* Parmesan cheese, Solaia wine and those bright red cars from Maranello, but also the perennially stalled politics and perpetually chaotic traffic (or the other way round), the Assyro-Babylonian bureaucracy, the civic morality as unstable as the sides of our mountains, as murky as our rivers and as unalluring as our concrete-covered coasts, three kinds of terrorism, four kinds of mafia and six almost identical television channels. You will say: "These things happen in the best of families." Perhaps, but not with the same effrontery, tenacity, theatricality, spontaneity, collusion, frequency, complacency and resignation as here. Presenting this fifty-year-long and fascinating tangle has been the objective of the exhibition. Which, with its blend of commentary, custom and history, of gravity and irony, of tragedy (i.e. representation of myths) and comedy (i.e. representation of real types), needs to be visited with an open mind, equally ready for wonder and indignation, for amusement and embarrassment: for that daily gymnastics of the emotions in which Italy has always coached us.

Made in Italy? is an exhibition divided into five different scenes.
The first scene – *Belvedere,* mounted by Achille Bonito Oliva with the coordination of Manuela Gandini and the staging of Pierluigi Cerri – looks at the intense poetic relationship that six great foreign artists have had and continue to have with Italy and with some of the ideas that are traditionally associated with it. Joseph Kosuth presents a work dedicated to Music, Hidetoshi Nagasawa turns his attention to Nature and Nam June Paik to Image, while Panamarenko is interested in Genius, Julian Schnabel in Memory and Chen Zhen in Spirit. This "belvedere" of ideas and emotions is introduced by an important and emblematic work by Michelangelo Pistoletto, the *Venus in Rags,* which can almost be seen as a symbol of the deprivations and nobility of the "land of fashion", and extends into the exhibition's other sections with works by Lucio Fontana, Mario Schifano, Pino Pascali, Mimmo Paladino, Francesco Clemente, Vanessa Beecroft, Vladimir Dubossarsky and Alexander Vinogradov. The final image is entrusted to Luigi Ontani.

The second scene, entitled *Memory,* has been organized by two figures who are landmarks in Italy's culture and its good image in the world: Gae Aulenti and Luca Ronconi. *Memory* is a view of forty years in the life of our country, from 1951 to 1991, and examines

the close dialogue that fashion and design have held with its controversial vicissitudes: events and historical developments illustrated through performances, news reports and headlines carried by major newspapers, film clips and television images that, for good or ill, reflect the evolution that has taken place in the mentality and in the patterns of behaviour and consumption of Italians. This space will also house three provocative and destabilizing installations by the avant-garde theatre group Fura dels Baus, examining the reality of those "years of lead" that interrupted the course of the seventies. Several prominent experts have collaborated on *Memory*: Vanni Pasca and Laura Lazzaroni for design; Paola Acquati, Cristina Brigidini and Aurora Fiorentini for fashion; Paolo Mereghetti for the cinema and Paolo Murialdi for journalism and the news reports.

Brockenhaus – which is meant to be the opposite of *Bauhaus* – is the third scene of the exhibition, with Oliviero Toscani as its curator. In an abandoned industrial space set in a sort of pre-historic future we find, covered by the dust of time, an extraordinary collection of garments and objects that have been in vogue over the years from 1951 to 2001: heaps of television sets, mountains of typewriters, piles of designer lamps, tables and chairs and of designer clothes covered with cobwebs. There will be lights, sounds and video images that come and go as if there was a defective electric contact. Everything passes, Toscani is warning us, but not completely.

The fourth scene, *Flavours*, is a project by Gaetano Pesce and Andrea Pezzi. Within a metaphorical and extraordinary landscape of Italian gastronomy created by one of the most

21

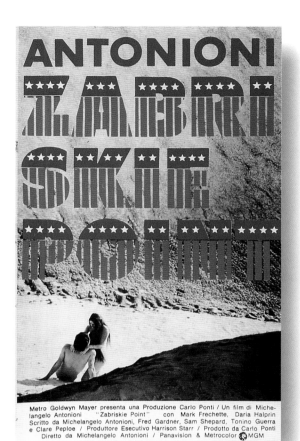

ANTONIONI ZABRISKIE POINT

Metro Goldwyn Mayer presenta una Produzione Carlo Ponti / Un film di Michelangelo Antonioni "Zabriskie Point" con Mark Frechette, Daria Halprin
Scritto da Michelangelo Antonioni, Fred Gardner, Sam Shepard, Tonino Guerra
e Clare Peploe / Produttore Esecutivo Harrison Starr / Prodotto da Carlo Ponti
Diretto da Michelangelo Antonioni / Panavision & Metrocolor ⊕ MGM

*La dolce vita, by Federico
Fellini, 1960
(G.B. B/Neri Archives)*

*Play bill for Zabriskie Point, by
Michelangelo Antonioni, 1970
(Team/Grazia Neri)*

visionary designers in the world, Pezzi has orchestrated a series of pithy statements on the subject of food made by around thirty prominent Italians from the worlds of culture, politics, sport and entertainment. In modes that range from reminiscence to quasi-Pavlovian reaction, these celebrities comment on some of the topoi of Italian cuisine: spaghetti, tortellini, risotto, pizza, oil, wine, basil, baba…

The fifth and last scene is entitled *Allegory* and has been organized by Pier Luigi Pizzi, with video installations by Enrico Ghezzi. It is a sort of new, technological and ironic *Excelsior Ball* dedicated to the leading lights in design and fashion of the last decade, that is from 1991 up to the present day, and to their most recent objects and garments, which are presented by Pizzi in a setting of great effect, tinged in a lovely Ferrari red, in which Ghezzi has framed an impressive and amusing video montage on their work.

This is the exhibition *Made in Italy?* – but you will learn more by visiting it or reading the words of its curators in the following pages – and the first of the reasons for celebrating design and fashion together. On the second reason, i.e. the question of the kinship between design and fashion, the various authoritative and thoughtful essays published in this catalogue will pass judgment.
But on design and fashion – or rather: on Design & Fashion – I too have something to say, however confused and immodest my contribution may be. With the aim, moreover, of pointing out how this motive is at bottom connected with the first, which has served as the ideal and the concrete starting point for the exhibition.

***

Fashion and design are close relatives but, as has already been said, separate. With its customary pragmatism, the English language even recognises that they inhabit the same semantic realm by making use of the same word in both applications, as in fashion design and industrial design. Hence they are "separated under the same roof". It could be said that that common roof is the act of design and the culture that is associated with it. In reality, however, such a claim would be true and false at one and the same time.
Truer of industrial design and falser of fashion design, if by the *act of design* and the *culture of design* we mean something still tied to a modern view of society in the classical sense: an optimistic society that places its trust in rationality and in technological and scientific progress and that is still Fordist in its management of production and consumption. A society that functions in a predictable and patronising, reassuring and authoritarian manner; that directs and defines the identity and roles of each one of us from above, in a rigid and fixed way, relying on the passive qualities of those who carry out these orders; which thinks in the long term and the large number, whether it is a question of standardised products, jobs in big factories or programs of social security.
If, however, we shift our gaze further forward and acknowledge the fact that we are heading toward a model of society and economy that we are not for the moment able to define in any other way than as "post-", then it is fashion rather than industrial design that displays some novel (and revealing) features on the terrain of the project and its related culture. In fact fashion seems to be better suited to a reformulated culture of design, capable of adjusting to a pluralistic and ever changing society that is uncertain and unpredictable, flexible and unstructured, fragmented and incoherent and less and less national and more and more multiethnic. A society that thinks and acts in the short term and produces and consumes in short cycles; that dispenses with any common criterion of normality and focuses instead on the individual and on his or her free and responsible choices; that makes personal identity a multiform dimension, a discontinuous palimpsest, not binding on everyone but, if anything, more like a game of relationships and aesthetics in which the body, the senses and the pursuit of pleasure and global prosperity take on a new centrality and where the main preoccupation is staying open to the new.

Yet design thinks fashion "is superficial and thinks only of glamour". Fashion, on the other hand, tends to think that design "is too serious and sees itself as highly intellectual".
Even the idea and image that design and fashion have of one another are false and true

at the same time. Design was born and has always been aware of working in a modern industrial society on the point of turning into a mass society. For its part fashion works in the most post-modernly and post-industrially evolved market and for the most capricious, personalised and streetwise customer that can be found today. Indeed it has helped to invent both of them, proposing them as obligatory models of reference for other industrial sectors as well and giving concrete expression on the plane of the organization of production to things like the industrial region, networking, just-in-time and total quality.

In spite of all this, many stylists still tend to present a pre-modern hieratic image of what they do, rooted in the craft tradition of the past: an image that is very distant from the modern culture of design. Industrial designers, on the other hand, have always flirted with the cultural awareness that has grown up around their work. They have done so from the height of their professional status and cloaking themselves in a halo of social commitment that derived from their being, as they have been ever since the time of William Morris, representatives of the enlightened ideology of progress and of that generous and paternalistic utopia summed up in the thought that "even the poor should be able to enjoy something beautiful as well as useful every now and then". A utopia that is resoundingly contradicted today by the fact that the products of design are not really within many people's reach. Fashion and stylists, on the contrary, are universally popular precisely because they are always making a come-on to a few of the rich, beautiful and powerful. The old *haute couture* has become *prêt-à-porter* without losing its high connections: once they were aristocrats and the wealthy bourgeoisie, now they are mostly movie and rock stars. Fashion is in every sense part of the society of mass culture and mass communications, but is a little ashamed of it and has always strived to obtain the same cultural and intellectual status as design.

It seems, in other words, that fashion, founded in social snobbery, envies cultured and democratic design, while the latter snubs fashion but is secretly envious of the money that its stylists make, of its pervasiveness and effectiveness of communication and of the vast amount of interest and praise it receives from the masses.

So the reality and image of the relations between design and fashion are intricate and intriguing. Yet this is further confirmation that design and fashion express, together and separately, ambiguities and problems which, observed comparatively and disentangled without tricks and illusions, are also invaluable to a better understanding of the world in which we live.

Fashion as design of the body in movement and industrial design as design of objects in everyday use and the domestic environment have many more elements in common today than they did in the past.

It is already the case, unlike in the days of the Great Couturiers and the Great Masters of Design, that young stylists and designers are related figures, often interchangeable in their training, milieu and culture of reference, in their tastes and work experience. And this cre-

26

ative mishmash embraces many others as well. It is important to understand what new possibilities may arise from this fluidity of ideas, things and roles.

Today people's bodies and the world of objects are much more decisive components in the construction of personal identity than they could have been just half a century ago, when work, family, religion, class and political ideology defined social roles and the individual modes of conduct more extensively and rigidly. Today fashion and design find motives for convergence in a complex world that now acknowledges its complete artificiality, even retrospectively. For some time now we have dispensed with a simplistic use of the concepts *useful, form/function* and *beautiful* in evaluating their products: we know that clothes are no longer used just to cover people's nakedness or chairs simply to sit on (if there ever was any time when these were their sole functions) and that beauty is not just a quest for and contemplation of the harmonious, the sublime, the absolute, the true. Nowadays we include new and more sophisticated dimensions in these concepts. And even if we were to argue that, through clothing and objects, all that fashion and design do is to devise technological prostheses for our body, we would then be forced to admit that our very ideas of body and of technology are no longer the same as they used to be and have now assumed new forms, functions and uses.

The body is the great discovery of our age. Superficial fashion has made a profound contribution to this discovery: we may be irritated by the caprices and the unbearable self-absorption and silliness of many of its "authors", by the mass narcissism, hedonism and individualism that went hand in hand with its triumph in the eighties, but it is also through these attitudes that we have moved on to a less restrictive and more positive view of the body and, in parallel, a less frigid and idealistic one of the mind. This has opened the door to a new and deeper sensuality and sensitivity in the relations between people, especially between men and women, but also between people and things: a tactile dimension has emerged in articles of everyday use that was hitherto unknown or denied.

Advances in technology can frighten us when they seem to be out of control and to threaten our environment and our integrity independently of our own actions. But the other side of the coin is that technology is becoming interwoven with our lives, lighter, invisible and flexible: it multiplies not just our physical strength but also and above all our mental and sensorial capacities. If advances in technology have made it possible for design to pay more attention to the aesthetics of objects and less to their functions, these new technologies are now allowing it to interface directly with the human body, with its sensitivity, its tactility. The horizons of the traditional idea of ergonomics are broadening: with the radical changes that are taking place in work, the design of the tools that we use to do this work also has to change. The adoption of these new techniques by industry permits design to free itself from the obligation to mass produce articles in large batches and from the idea of a "beauty for all" imposed from above. It will still make use of mass production, but in small and customised batches (just as craftsmen have always done), giving the idea of "beauty for few" a significance that is not antidemocratic but simply (or perhaps it would be better to say *complexly*) pluralist.

In short, the culture of design has to adapt to this new era which is taking shape. And industrial and fashion design, which represent the most creative side of this culture and the

one most concerned with aesthetics, can help in this as long as they are capable of learning from one another and of mending their respective ways.

***

Here we come back to the first motive for our commemoration, i.e. the parallel history of design and fashion and of Italy from the fifties to the present day that is presented in the exhibition. A motive that is particularly important to me as I am not a sociologist investigating communication but quite the opposite, and communication and the cultural projects connected with it are my real interest and my bread and butter. And it is as a communicator that I ask myself: why did fashion and design (which from the fifties onward, even though living separately under the same roof and independently of one another, conducted a formidable and spontaneous publicity campaign on behalf of Italy that amply made up for the country's many shortcomings), why, as I was saying, did the two liveliest, most dynamic and most important sectors of contemporary industry and culture in Italy and abroad not enjoy an institutional status in this country commensurate with the role that they played and continue to play?

I believe that the reason is because in Italian officialdom what has prevailed up to now is an outmoded and clumsy conception of industry and culture, wholly taken up with pursuing and achieving modernity for the society and the economy in the classic sense, when what was actually needed was to be able to look beyond this modernity and to grasp the material – and therefore social and economic – importance of two aspects of production entailing such a high degree of immateriality – i.e. aesthetics and communication – as do design and fashion. Measured by this old and clumsy yardstick, design and fashion have been viewed up to now as sectors of marginal economic importance and cultural significance in the modern development of the country, rather than as crucial factors and advanced and strategic models of postmodern industry and culture: in other words as cultural industries and cultures of design suited to the contemporary world.

You want proof of this? It was only after enormous effort that the exhibition *Made in Italy?* was able to find a suitable venue, which only by chance was a place as important as the Palazzo della Triennale (which was luckily made available by the cancellation of a previously scheduled event). This happened in Milan, the Italian and international capital of fashion and design, but a city that has still not set up a museum of either fashion or design (and by "museum" I mean a cultural centre that conserves without mummifying, that builds up a collection but also educates and carries out research, that celebrates the past and at the same time promotes the future, that knows how to speak to professionals as well as interest the general public). And it follows an event like the Salone del Mobile, which is one of the most important in the world in this sector and which has demonstrated with this exhibition, among other things, that it is able to adopt that overall, systematic vision which is by now common talk even at the barber's.

Mere lack of understanding (as I tried to explain above) or the simple banality of evil?

The fundamental and original contribution that Italy can make to the future development of a world that is turning more and more into a global village, its unique selling proposition as an adman would put it, lies precisely in the working-through of the model of planning and research proposed by fashion and design, given that the aesthetic and cultural dimension is going to become more and more decisive as a means of directing and possibly reorganizing technological society.

Dostoevsky said that beauty would save the world. A major designer and theorist of design (as well as a close friend), Andrea Branzi, has recently qualified this by saying that we must at least try to save beauty from attack by the world. Design and fashion can help us to do so. At least if we want to be helped.

I. Belvedere

by Achille Bonito Oliva
exhibition design by Pierluigi Cerri

Belvedere

Achille Bonito Oliva

Captions edited by Manuela Gandini

Michelangelo Pistoletto

Venus of the Rags
1967
white Carrara marble
200 × 250 × 100 cm
Courtesy Fondazione Pistoletto, Biella

Venus of the Rags (Venere degli stracci),
a work in many versions, was created
in the period of protest and opens the
gate to the *Belvedere*.
The contradiction of beauty
and misery, art and the everyday,
the classical and life, is manifest
in the accumulation of multicoloured
rags held by a Venus whose shoulders
are turned and who does not offer
herself completely.
This perfect model of femininity is the
incarnation of the beauty of an Italy in
rags deeply poor and infinitely rich.

"The problem arises: are places above all and solely the result of the consequence of their disposition? Or on the contrary does the disposition derive its nature from the predominance of the place it encompasses. If the latter is the case, then we should examine what needs to be done and use space in the creation of localities, we should design localities as the result of the interaction of places".

Heidegger's proposition (*Art and Space*, 1969) forms the epigraph of the *Belvedere* which takes its name from the tradition of the Italian garden in which Nature is trained and enclosed in accordance with stylistic canons that transform natural growth into a formal effect. In this case, it is the nature of art that is developed from the start to the end of the exhibition route.

As is well known, the nature of art corresponds to the twofold principle of the organic development of the imagination and its confinement within an enclosure in objectively perceptible language. Its perceptibility is the result of an image passing through a painting, a sculpture or an installation, i.e. formal modularities that bring into existence the results of an individual's imagination under the eyes of the observer.

Belvedere presents a rolling and varied countryside produced by Italian and foreign artists who, during the second half of the twentieth century, interpreted themes representative of Italy and formalised them in their art.

From the vantage point of contemporary art, which includes underground passages hidden to the eye, it is possible to direct the astonished gaze of the public over a vast panorama of iconographic elements whether figurative, abstract, pictorial, sculptural or simply pervasive of space.

Like any observation terrace, both ends are guarded by statues and grotesques, stylemes in keeping with the artistic countryside.

The *Venere degli stracci* (Rag Venus) by Michelangelo Pistoletto is a worthy opening piece that can be viewed either as an example of sculptural harmony or as a multicoloured mass of clothes in a short-circuit between a memorial to timeless plasticity and an accumulation of the vitality of everyday experience.

This commendable *incipit* forms the start to a sequence of spaces in which the exotic plants of foreign imaginations have been planted. Artists from the East and West sow their seeds in the convoluted enclosure of the *Belvedere*.

Once again, the *Grand Tour* has produced its effects, and wondrous exotic forms take root in the fertile soil of the Italian garden producing visual interpretations on themes of memory, spirituality, intelligence, nature, image, music and irony.

This section reflects and confirms the appeal of Italian art and the history of foreign artists who have made the pilgrimage to our culture and land.

The importance of memory permeates the vast output of the American artist Julian Schnabel who makes wide use of stimuli taken from an iconographic history filled with visual catalysts. The harmony of the image is an inevitable consequence of the typically American gestural vitalism and the typically Italian sense of measure in which it is swathed.

The Chinese Chen Zhen provides the remains of a temple as an architectural legacy that forms a dialogue with the conception of the surrounding countryside. The interior and exterior of the temple become the dimensions of a contemplative movement that includes an outward and inward gaze. It signals the syntax of a mental construction that finds a welcome in the traditional hospitality of Italian art.

Panamarenko, the Belgian artist, seems to endorse the Tuscan quality of our observation terrace with his two Leonardo-like designs for a possible flight. He has produced soft sculptures in the form of wings that lie on the ground and which suggest to the observer that they might be used to liberate oneself from our slavery to the gravitational pull.

The nature of the Japanese Hidetoshi Nagasawa's sculpture is so internalised that sculptural form disappears in a mix of shapes made from non-invasive material that leaves them in a state of suspension and imbued with the sense of a finite infinity.

Traditionally, Italian art is for the most part figurative as a result of its Catholic and Counter-Reformationist history. This has been the starting point for the computerised works of the Korean artist Nam June Paik who creates his perpetually moving televisual images in codified containers in the form of a colossus and of a boot. The circular eternity of the Colosseum in Rome and the geographical shape of the Italian peninsula become inevitable forms for installations.

The beautiful music of Rossini has fascinated the American Joseph Kosuth who has arranged neon versions of the Italian's musical scores along a space made musical by the light. The light thus interprets the full score in a conceptual shift that implicates the observer's space in an inescapable rhythm. Technology acts as the counterpoint to the melodious anthropology of Italian tradition.

The *Belvedere* is completed by a pictorial section for which works have been commissioned. The Russian artists Vladimir Dubossarsky and Alexander Vinogradov present a fresco of icons that represent the world of fashion. It is a landscape of humans that touches on the triumph of kitsch which seems to refer to the *Triumph of Death* by Orcagna in Pisa cemetery. It is a combination of Slav irony and Italian stylism that succeeds in being both cutting and humorous.

Following the successful grafting of foreign plants, the *Belvedere* welcomes the fruits of the fantasy of Italian artists who, since 1950, have produced magnificent works of great expressiveness in a variety of forms.

First comes Lucio Fontana with the surgical precision of his cut linked to the erotic deftness of gesture and the constant standard of repetition. An airy opening in space and a surmounting of the wall of painting. Then there is Mario Schifano who brought depth to surfaces during the 1960s and has depicted, like a tattoo on the skin of the painting, symbols of a daily existence that mark Italy's transition to an era of advanced technology.

The deep wound caused by World War II has now healed and the unpredictable eroticism of modern Italian civilisation prevails.

Since the end of the 1960s, Pino Pascali has been firing symbolic shots at the 1970s, shifting art from pure association with natural materials to well-depicted representation. The theatre of the image takes the upper hand over the expressive force released by the use of simple materials, preparing the way for the developments of the Transavanguardia artistic movement with decorations in the form of silkworms on the floor.

During the 1980s, Francesco Clemente brought cultural nomadism and stylistic eclecticism to painting, incorporating oriental emptiness and its western opposite in the space on the canvas. He was the first to return to the beauty of this contrast which delicately invades the canvas.

Mimmo Paladino entwines the abstract and the figurative, decoration and figuration into an iconography that includes the perennial signs of the archaic and the vibrations of a present in order to seek depth and a fertile and continuous space.

During the 1990s, the Transavanguardia returned artistic value to photography, video and installations, in a constant attempt to represent the subjectivity that now tends to be seen in cloning.

Thus, at the end of the last century, Vanessa Beecroft presented photographic images of performances in which the standard of female bodies was multiplied in space. The scene was literally filled with versions of the same body model but belonging to disparate civilisations, both western and eastern.

The *Belvedere* closes with figurative emblems of one of its typical ornamental representations, the grotesque. Luigi Ontani's ceramic work is another example of the Italian garden and its history of art. Its presence has created controversy being a sculpture munificently offered by a private individual to Milan City Council to adorn a public space but not accepted. The work has now come out from the intimacy of the private collection and has temporarily taken its rightful place in the public gaze.

Belvedere offers a series of creative works produced by Italian and foreign artists that bear witness to the fertility of a historically cosmopolitan land on which every kind of iconographic crop can be raised. The spiritual nourishment provided by the art of *Belvedere* does not require genetic engineering, and the biotechnology of the works is always the fruit of individual imagination using creative and disparate materials and processes that fertilise the public thinking.

Belvedere is therefore Heidegger's space-maker and art is still able to provide the observer with a view. Not of places to be owned but most certainly fertile for both mind and body.

Julian Schnabel

Pino Pascali
1985
oil on wooden panels
277 × 370 cm (work in five parts)
photo by Mimmo Capone
Courtesy Gian Enzo Sperone, Rome

Pino Pascali is a tribute by Schnabel to the Italian artist. Evocative, emotional, driven, his work is influenced by immaterial fragments of existence, places, phrases, graffiti or by the memory of great historic works.

In 1985, when the capital was violently covered in graffiti by fans of the Rome club, who won the championship, the American artist began to use yellows, reds, and ochres in his paintings: the colours he saw everywhere on the surface of the city.

The adventure of Schnabel, an artist understood everywhere, moves from the street to the *Divine Comedy*, from the initials of a name on a wall to the Renaissance, with the cancellation of values.

Joseph Kosuth

Fragments of Rossini (Guests and Strangers)
1999
white neon lights
various dimensions
photo by Studio Argento, Pesaro
Courtesy Galleria Franca Mancini,
Pesaro, and Lia Rumma, Naples

Omaggio a Rossini visualises the concept of music with ethereal lightness. The notes in the spaces, via lights and scores, materialise Italian culture in this work.
It is a subtle, ambient homage, which allows one subject to slide into another, in a moment of recollection.
In his semantic experimentation the American artist, who lives between Rome and New York, combines past and present, art and music, in a harmonious mix that becomes elusive.

Chen Zhen

Zen Garden
2000
alabaster, metal, wood, plastic
plant, light
320 × 300 × 175 cm
photo by Attilio Maranzano
Courtesy Galleria Continua,
San Gimignano

Zen Garden is the maquette of an octagonal temple without a roof that forms a celestial centre, an infinite passage. Designed for the hill at Volterra and constructed using local materials by Tuscan artisans, the temple, multi-religious and secular, contains a Zen garden in which large alabaster human organs are placed, illuminated on the inside and pierced by enormous surgical irons.
Chen Zhen superimposed East and West in his work, confronting the theme of medicine, illness and the body. He celebrated the sanctity of life and the body, drawing on the experience of his long haematic illness.

Panamarenko

The Great Fritz
2001
mannequin, pedestal, propeller, rocker, belts and reels
200 × 280 × 45 cm
Courtesy Galleria Continua, San Gimignano

The Great Fritz is a helicopter to wear and to activate, run by human energy. A rotary system, operated by the force of arms only, accumulates energy in a rotating mass formed by a steel disc. The mechanism is a large propeller made of reinforced wood in a live corner, balanced by a counter-weight (the kinetic accumulator disc). When activated you can fly for a few seconds. Utopia and Leonardo da Vinci style imagination in Panamarenko are part of that *Italian life* which the Belgian artist has transformed by inverting the letters of the two words in *nailati efil* for the very logo.

Hidetoshi Nagasawa

The Hill of Ipomoea
2001
project
marble
450 × 100 × 350 cm
Courtesy Studio Casoli, Milan

"The purpose of sculpture is not to imitate nature. Rather, it is to create another nature." This phrase by Hidetoshi Nagasawa, who in 1967 arrived in Italy by bicycle from Japan, is a clear interpretative key to his work, which can be placed in numerous urban contexts to create other natures in the unnatural contemporary landscape.

La collina di Ipomea, visually light as a cloud, is in reality extremely heavy. Made of marble, it reflects the temporality of passing and at the same time it affirms itself as a testimony to it. The light and the smell of the Mediterranean are connected to energy lines that link, like as star, one point to another.

Nam June Paik

Colosseum
1990
installation composed of monitors, old empty television sets, neon lights and fragments of reproductions of classical statues
400 × 600 × 300 cm
photo by Fabrizio Garghetti
Courtesy Fondazione Mudima, Milan

Colosseo is a meeting between history and electronics. Nam June Paik achieves an impossible imperial temporal and spatial shift relating to the horizontal situation of information on microchips.
The stones of the Colosseum are full and empty monitors. The monument is the representation of hyper-contemporaneous ruins, full of carcasses and plaster fragments.
The material ("dirty energy") alternates with the immaterial ("pure energy") where Joseph Beuys, in the Paik videos, continues to speak with the coyote and the images become electrified hysterically.

Vladimir Dubossarsky
and Alexander Vinogradov

How are You, Ladies and Gentlemen?
2000
oil on canvas
295 × 585 cm
Courtesy Claudio Poleschi Arte
Contemporanea, Lucca

How are you Ladies and Gentlemen? is
an allegoric painting, ironic and
symbolic, on Western leadership as
seen from the East. It is the
relationship between nature and
fashion, in which designers, models
and actresses with well-known faces
are laid bare by the two Russian
artists, who find a primordial trace of
life in the jungle and transfer it to the
era of globalisation.
Lacking their designer names and
social wear, the characters (among
them are Prada, Missoni, Valentino,
Armani, Ferré, Cerrutti) are immersed
in the kitsch of a very highly probable
televised Garden of Eden.

Luigi Ontani

Mediolanum Cricket
1995
polychrome ceramics
95 × 47 × 46 cm
Rosa Sandretto collection, Milan

With the *Grillo Mediolanum, Belvedere* closes. It ends with the sculpture by Luigi Ontani that the Milan municipality, during the Formentini council of 1996-97, firmly refused because it was considered irreverent. The bearded dwarf like Leonardo, with a *panettone* on his head on which is placed the *Merda* *d'artista* by Piero Manzoni, with the *mo* scale tiers on a waistcoat and holding Fontana's egg in his hands, is a metaphor, an allegory of "made in Milan", with the tail and hoof of a lamb. In this exhibition the sculpture that today is held in the private house of the collector is made public in *Made in Italy?*.

II. Memory

by Gae Aulenti and Luca Ronconi
with an installation
by La Fura dels Baus

Luca Ronconi

In the tormented market of cultural values, amongst speculations about ethics and large-scale political wastelands, gnosiological enthusiasms and metaphysical depreciation, aesthetic euphoria and spiritual collapses, the already tendentiously inconstant evaluations of human events in the "souvenir sector", come up against a veritable earthquake: it is a truth that needs to be restored to the list of the most common commonplaces that memory – as capricious as the famous blindfolded goddess and with a similar frequent difficulty in focusing upon events – is able to give and remove value to things with an inconstancy and fickleness which is, to say the least, disconcerting. The more memory tries to return to the past and restore it to the intact freshness of its essence, the more it tumbles into oblivion: memory is not only that which is preserved, but also, and perhaps above all, that which is irredeemably lost or which is at least restored but accompanies us in a transformed, unrecognisable manner, the final metamorphosis of an entity that has by now vanished.

Having to recount the story of four decades of Italian fashion and design between the fifties and the nineties in an exhibition, giving a summary view of the tortuous, not to mention contradictory unravelling of our recent history, we thought it necessary – as well as entertaining – to focus upon this shift, an endemic irony that corrodes doctrines and traditions, philological enquiries and incursions into revivals, multiplying the levels upon which the relics that the past consigns to us may be read. Through the labyrinthine tunnel of time, we have tried to ensure that the images projected by the designers be refracted in the partial, deforming mirrors of memory, and it was in this changing kaleidoscope of reflections that memory revealed to us its most genuine and authentic nature as judge of what "has been". With the severe filter of the proverbial – although no less objective – advantage of "hindsight", garments and accessories remembered ambiguously reveal their entire ambiguous relationship with the period from which they spring. Thanks to a ruthless, although playful, "chronological" retaliation, at the moment when they are consigned to the perpetual pantheon of memory, the icons of fashion and design, apparently planned for a present that looks to the future, reveal themselves actually to be the subjective and just as arbitrary correlatives of the present that has generated them and destined for a precarious tomorrow in which they waste away.

Gae Aulenti

Made in Italy? in our section is called *Memory*, and considers the period between the fifties and the eighties.

Memory is not only history, is thus not scientific or systematic material, but is material of memory, and hence tendentious. We try to remember, but we do not want to put in order.

To do this, we have had to enter other disciplines: not only the design and fashion that are part of this exhibition in general, but also history and news, cinema, literature, art. These constitute flashes of multiple relationships.

It is suggested that these years from the past be reviewed through the variations that time has wrought by opposition or by coincidence: it is a "second-hand exhibition", so it is possible to test new cognitive processes.

With Luca Ronconi, the work for the general layout of the exhibition has been extremely profitable, both from a critical point of view, and from the point of view of space, and in particular as regards the preparation of the sound-track which will be broadcast from the wall opposite the accumulation of objects.

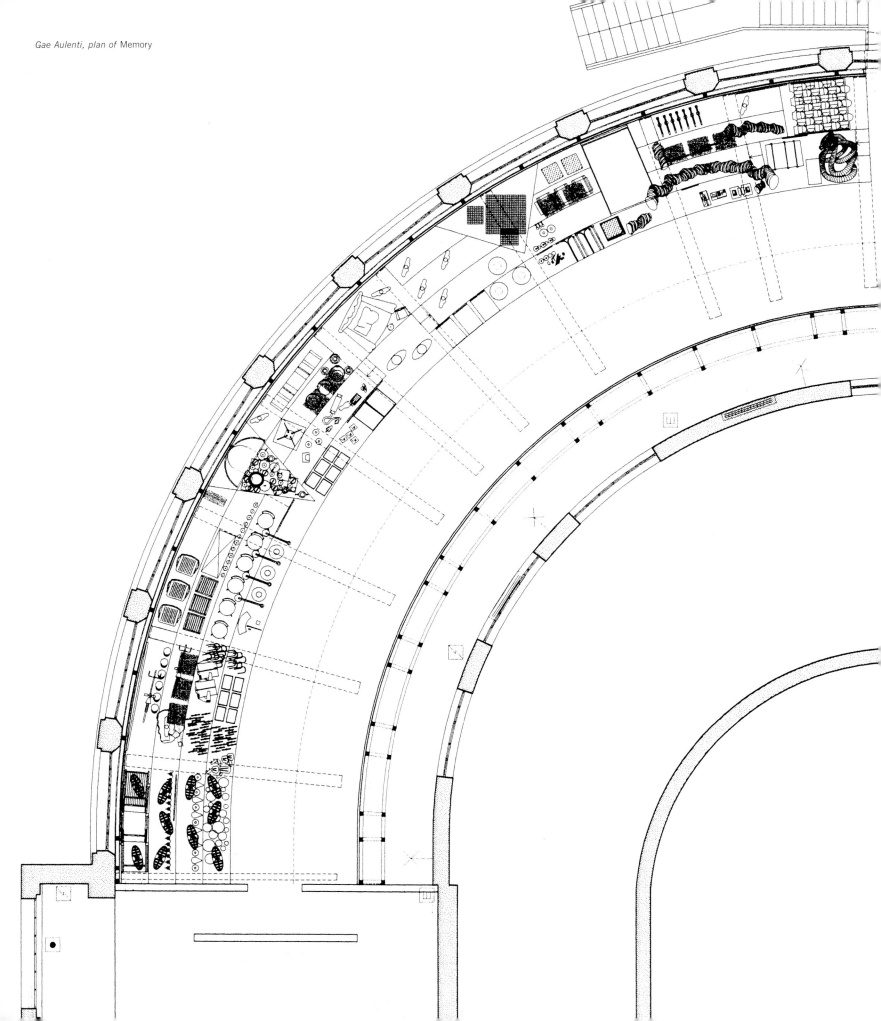

Gae Aulenti, plan of Memory

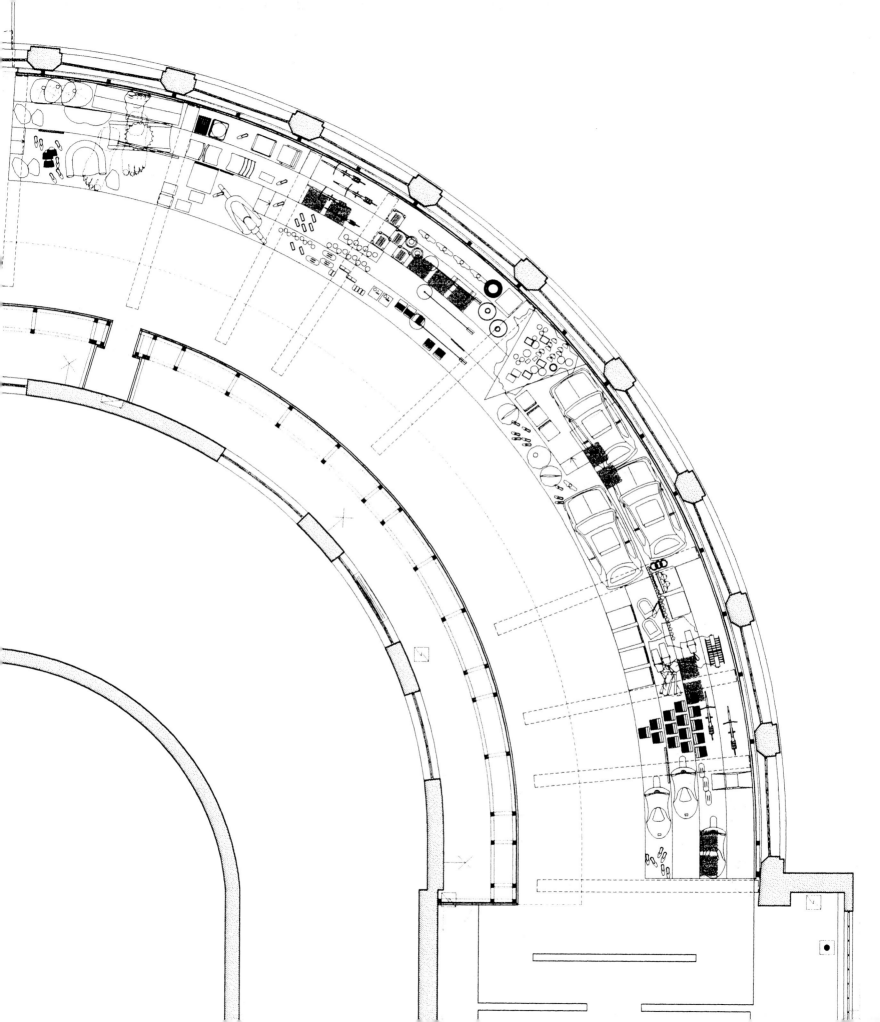

"PRATONE"

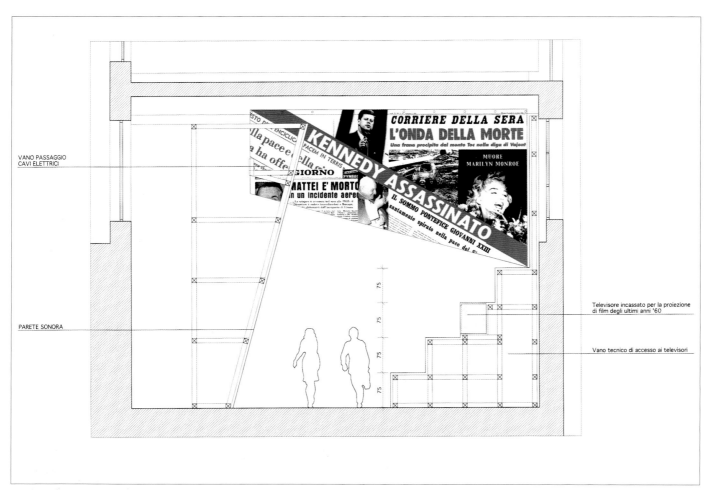

VANO PASSAGGIO
CAVI ELETTRICI

PARETE SONORA

Televisore incassato per la proiezione
di film degli ultimi anni '60

Vano tecnico di accesso ai televisori

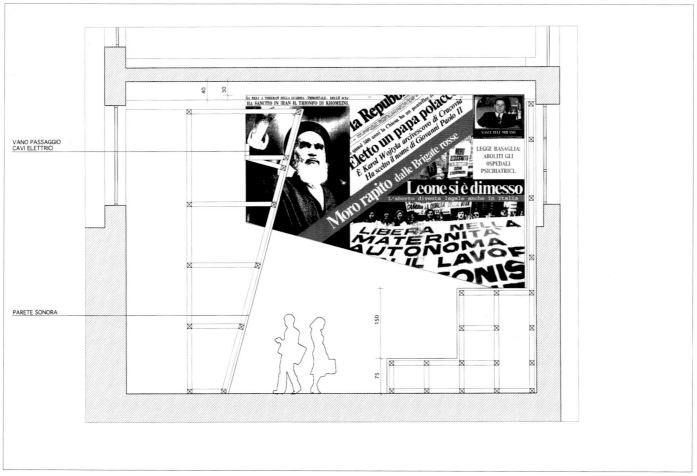

VANO PASSAGGIO
CAVI ELETTRICI

PARETE SONORA

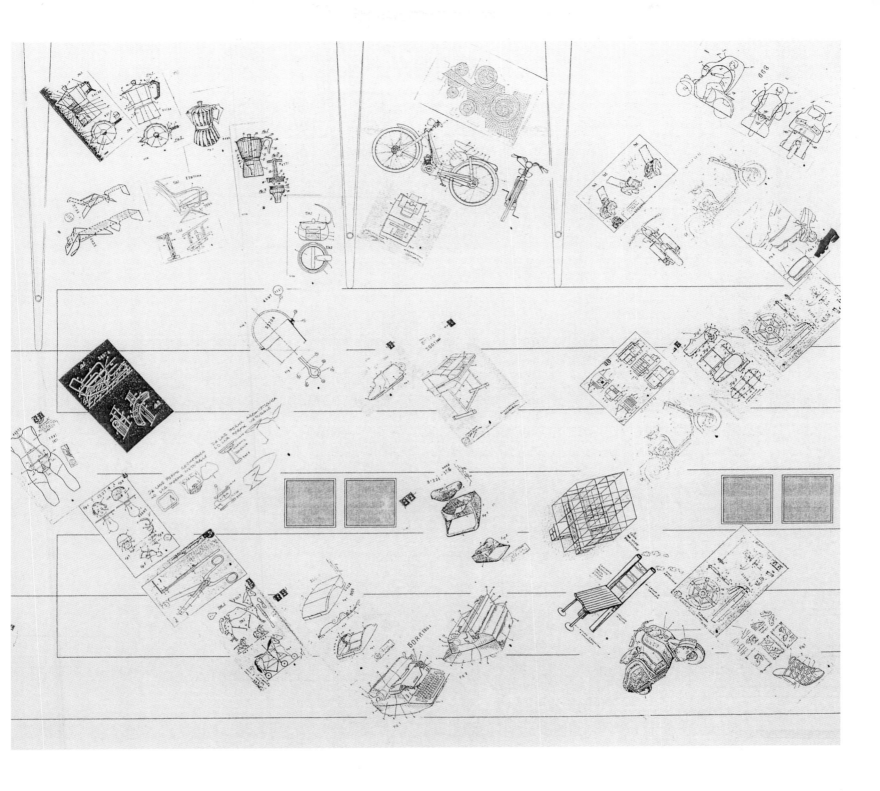

*Gae Aulenti, project
of Vele for* Memory

*Gae Aulenti, collage
of blue-prints for* Memory

In the exhibition

Ferragamo
Suede shoe with wood and calf insert with treads, 1938

Ferragamo
Sandal with multicolor sea leopard upper and cork insert covered with the same material, 1940

Ferragamo
Sandal with multicolor "cellophane" crocheted upper and cork insert covered in kid leather, 1941-42

Ferragamo
Sandal with raffia upper, painted wood and Cuoital insert, 1942-44

Alfonso and Renato Bialetti
Moka Express espresso coffeepot
Bialetti, 1945

Bruno Munari
Singer chair
1945 (Zanotta 1991)

Corradino D'Ascanio
Vespa 98 scooter
Piaggio, 1946-47

Ferragamo
"Invisible" sandal with nylon thread and kid toecap, wood insert covered with F-shaped kid leather, 1947

Gucci
Bamboo bag, article 0633, 1947-67

Bianchi Corsa bicycle
Edoardo Bianchi, 1950

Giulio Minoletti
ETR 300/Settebello train, *Belvedere* car (photograph)
Breda for Ente Ferrovie dello Stato, 1950

Marcello Nizzoli
Lettera 22 typewriter
Olivetti, 1950

Franco Albini
Luisa chair
Poggi, 1951

Ferragamo
Sandal with braided kid leather upper and "Kimo" satin stocking, 1951

Marco Zanuso
Lady chair (photograph)
Arflex, 1951

Pierluigi Torre
Lambretta LD 125 scooter
Innocenti, 1952-56

Gio Ponti
Zeta sanitaryware
Ideal Standard, 1954

Marco Zanuso
Refrigerator
Homelight, 1954

Gino Colombini
Polyethylene objects
Kartell, 1954-57

Lorry tyre *Artiglio*
Pirelli, 1955

Emilio Pucci
Siciliana collection, print silk blouse and "cigarette" pants (photograph)
1955

Capucci
Dieci gonne dress, red silk taffeta
1956 Spring/Summer Haute Couture collection

Achille and Pier Giacomo Castiglioni
Spalter vacuum cleaner
REM, 1956

Dante Giacosa
Nuova 500 car
FIAT, 1957

Gio Ponti
Superleggera chair
Cassina, 1957

Emilio Pucci
Cotton print outfit (photograph)
1957

Capucci
Scatola line, white silk shantung and black silk crepe dress
1958-59 Fall/Winter Haute Couture collection

Emilio Pucci
Capsules made of white/black "Emilioform" and embroidered for evening (photograph)
1959

Lucio Fontana
Concetto spaziale, Natura, 1959-60
(bronze, cm 41 x 49 x 46)

Lucio Fontana
Concetto spaziale, natura, 1959-60
(bronze, cm 42 x 58)

Lucio Fontana
Concetto spaziale, natura, 1959-60
(bronze, cm 40 x 48)

Emilio Pucci
Calcio in costume collection (photograph)
Late fifties

Emilio Pucci
Oyana print cotton shantung
Early sixties

Vico Magistretti
Carimate chair
Cassina, 1960

Flexible embossed flooring
Pirelli, 1960

Emilio Pucci
Ski capsule made of "Emilioform" (photograph), 1960

Gucci
Jackie O handbag.
1960-69

Achille and Pier Giacomo Castiglioni
Arco lamp
Flos, 1962

Achille and Pier Giacomo Castiglioni
Taccia lamp
Flos, 1962

Emilio Pucci
Marilyn wearing a silk blouse with a "Mirrors" print
Photograph by George Barris
1962

Mario Schifano
Coca-Cola, 1962
(paper on canvas, cm 140 x 160)

Marco Zanuso and Richard Sapper
Doney 14 television
Brionvega, 1962

Rinaldo Donzelli
Graziella bicycle
Carnielli, 1964

Bruno Munari
Falkland lamp
Danese, 1964

Marco Zanuso and Richard Sapper
4999 children's chair
Kartell, 1964

Marco Zanuso and Richard Sapper
Algol 11 television
Brionvega, 1964

Marco Zanuso and Richard Sapper
TS 502 portable radio
Brionvega, 1964

Valentino
Red silk crepe dress with tulle cape decorated with ostrich plumes and red stones
1965-1966 Fall/Winter Haute Couture collection

Achille and Pier Giacomo Castiglioni
RR 126 radio
Brionvega, 1966

Vico Magistretti
Eclisse lamp
Artemide, 1966

Emilio Pucci
Cotton shantung, "Checker" pattern
1966

Afra and Tobia Scarpa
Coronado sofa (photograph)
C&C Italia (now B&B Italia), 1966

Marco Zanuso and Richard Sapper
Grillo telephone
Siemens Italia, 1966

MV Agusta 500 3-cylinder motorcycle
Agusta, 1966

Archizoom Associati
Superonda chair
Poltronova, 1967

Anna Castelli Ferrieri
4970-84 square modular units
Kartell, 1967

Joe Colombo
4867 chair
Kartell, 1967

Jonathan De Pas, Donato D'Urbino, Paolo Lomazzi, Carla Scolari
Blow inflatable chair
Zanotta, 1967

Valentino
Red silk crepe dress with shoulder straps embroidered with sequins, gold and silver rhinestones
1967-1968 Fall/Winter Haute Couture collection

Ken Scott
Framed pillow from the *Il circo di Ken* collection offered to guests at his fashion show for sitting on the steps of the circus set up in Rome on the Appia Antica road
1968

Ken Scott
Photograph of the *Il circo di Ken* collection, with "Etiopia", "Somalia" and "Sumatra" prints
1968

Ken Scott
Piece of ban-lon fabric with the words *Il circo di Ken*, 1968

Ken Scott
Presentation of the *Il circo di Ken* collection
Photograph by Ugo Mulas, 1968

Ken Scott
Boots from the *Il circo di Ken* collection, with shoe and leg in ban-lon fabric, printed with "A sangue freddo", "Beku Wak-Wak", "Ghepardo" and "Canard" designs, 1968

Pino Pascali
Bachi da setola (five elements made in acrylic sponges, various sizes), 1968

Rodolfo Bonetto
Magic Drum portable radio
Autovox, 1969

Joe Colombo
Cabriolet Bed (photograph)
Sormani, 1969

Piero Gatti, Cesare Paolini, Francesco Teodoro
Sacco chair
Zanotta, 1969

Vico Magistretti
Selene chair
Artemide, 1969

Gaetano Pesce
Up 7/Piede chair
C&B Italia (now B&B Italia), 1969

Giancarlo Piretti
Plia chair
Anonima Castelli, 1969

Emilio Pucci
Silk jersey mini-dress, "Tulip" print, 1969

Ettore Sottsass jr., Perry A. King
Valentine typewriter
Olivetti, 1969

Emilio Pucci
Long print jersey dress, "Pheasant" design
Early seventies

Emilio Pucci
Cotton shantung, "Siva" print
Early seventies

Missoni
Tai Missoni work notes for studying new
textures and color combinations
Seventies

Giorgio Ceretti, Pietro Derossi, Riccardo Rosso
Pratone chair
Gufram, 1970

Joe Colombo
Tube Chair
Flexform, 1970

Gianfranco Frattini, Livio Castiglioni
Boalum lamp
Artemide, 1970

Elio Fiorucci
Accessories
Fiorucci Archives, 1970-75

Missoni
Brunetta's design for the *Put together* collection
1970-71 Fall/Winter collection

Piero Gilardi
Sassi chair
Gufram, 1971

Emilio Pucci
Apollo 15 space mission emblem
(photograph), 1971

Studio 65
Bocca sofa
Gufram, 1971

Superstudio
Quaderna table and stool
Zanotta, 1971

Gruppo 9999
Italy: The New Domestic Landscape exhibit
poster, 1972

Enzo Mari
Sof-Sof chair
Driade, 1972

Richard Sapper
Tizio lamp
Artemide, 1972

Studio 65
Capitello chair
Gufram, 1972

Mario Bellini
Divisumma 28 calculator
Olivetti, 1973

Mario Bellini
Logos 50-60 calculator
Olivetti, 1973

Vico Magistretti
Maralunga sofa (photograph)
Cassina, 1973

Valentino
Red silk chiffon and crêpe dress
Spring/Summer 1973 Haute Couture
collection

Fiorucci
Image for the Fiorucci boutique shopping bag
Fiorucci Archives, 1974

Enzo Mari
Proposta per un'autoprogettazione (book)
1974

Walter Albini
Blue plaster bust made for the collection
presentation at the old Fiorucci
"multispazio"Via Torino
1976 Spring/Summer Collection

Walter Albini
Guerriglia urbana
Photograph by Alfa Castaldi
1976 Men's Collection

Mario Bellini
Logos 42 calculator
Olivetti, 1976

Enzo Mari
Aggregato modular lighting system
Artemide, 1976

Enzo Mari
Box chair
Anonima Castelli, 1976

Walter Albini
Portrait
Photograph by Carlo Orsi
Fall/Winter men's collection, 1976-77

Giorgio Armani
Advertising campaigns, 1976/91

Giorgio Armani
Creations, 1976/91

Vico Magistretti
Atollo lamp
O-Luce, 1977

Enzo Mari
Capitello modular table system
Driade, 1977

Vico Magistretti
Nathalie bed (photograph)
Flou, 1978

Alessandro Mendini
Poltrona di Proust
Studio Alchymia, 1978

Gianfranco Ferrè
Designs, 1978/90

Michele De Lucchi
Small household appliances (prototypes)
Girmi, 1979

Michele De Lucchi
Sinerpica lamp
Studio Alchymia, 1979

Luca Meda
Caffè Concerto coffee-maker
Girmi, 1979

Ettore Sottsass jr.
Le strutture tremano table
Studio Alchymia, 1979

Michele De Lucchi, Ettore Sottsass
Rolls of silk-screened laminate
Abet Laminati, 1981

Household objects
Alessi, 1980-95

Biker clothing and accessories
Dainese, 1980-91

Ettore Sottsass jr.
Carlton cabinet
Memphis, 1981

Daniel Weil
Radio Bag, 1981

Luxottica eyewear
1981-91

Giorgio Armani
Time magazine cover (photograph)
1982

Ufficio Tecnico Cinelli, Antonio Colombo,
Paolo Erzegovesi, Gianni Gabella
Laser racing bike
Cinelli, 1983

Cinzia Ruggeri
Ziggurat dress, 1982

Michele De Lucchi
First chair
Memphis, 1983

Cinzia Ruggeri
Picture with Lévi-Strauss dress
Fall/Winter collection1983-84

Prada
Black canvas backpack, 1984

Versace
Oroton black and silver dress
1984-85 Fall/Winter Collection

Enzo Mari
Tonietta chair
Zanotta, 1985

Alberto Meda, Paolo Rizzatto
Berenice lamp
Luceplan, 1985

P Zero tyre for powerful cars
Pirelli, 1985

Cinzia Ruggeri
Cristalli liquidi dress, 1985

Aldo Rossi
Teatro Domestico
Designs from 1985 for the *Il Progetto
Domestico* exhibit 17th Triennale of Milan,
1986

Valentino
Red silk crêpe dress with black satin bows
1985 Spring/Summer Haute Couture
Collection

Versace
Oroton black dress with hand-made gold
designs
1985-1986 Fall/Winter Collection

Antonio Citterio
Sity sofa (photograph)
B&B Italia, 1986

Michele De Lucchi, Giancarlo Fassina
Tolomeo lamp
Artemide, 1986

Giandomenico Modolo
Kronotech racing bike
Modolo, 1986

Paolo Rizzatto
Costanza lamp
Luceplan, 1986

Dolce e Gabbana
Photographs by Fabrizio Ferri
1987 Spring/Summer Collection

Gianfranco Ferré
White silk gazaar blouse, black silk cady skirt,
satin ribbon belt
1987 Spring/Summer Collection

Gaetano Pesce
I Feltri chair
Cassina, 1987

Aldo Rossi
Milano chair
Molteni & C., 1987

Jasper Morrison
Thinkingman's Chair
Cappellini, 1988

Aldo Rossi
La Cupola coffee-maker
Alessi, 1988-89

Dolce e Gabbana
Dress
1989 Spring/Summer Collection

Vico Magistretti
Silver chair
De Padova, 1989

Alberto Meda, Paolo Rizzatto
Titania lamp
Luceplan, 1989

Alessandro Mendini
Wristwatches
Swatch, 1989/94

Borek Sipek
Glass
Driade Follies, 1989/91

Moschino
No Comment press campaign, 1989
Photograph by Stefano Pandini

Philippe Starck
Luci Fair lamp
Flos, 1989

Philippe Starck
Juicy Salif juicer
Alessi, 1990

Alessandro Mendini
clay miniature *Poltrona di Proust*, 1991

Francesco Clemente
Facciamo a camiciate, 1991
(Paper on canvas, cm 130 x 316)

Philippe Starck
Miss Sissy lamp
Flos, 1991

Valentino
Photograph by Giampaolo Barbieri, 1991

Mimmo Paladino
Testimone (Witness), 1993
(bronze, h. cm 150)

Mimmo Paladino
Testimone (Witness), 1993
(bronze, h. cm 150)

Vanessa Beecroft
VB 37.040, 2000
(vibracolor, cm 127 x 177)

Centro Stile Dainese and Aldo Drudi
Safety jacket 20,
Dainese, 2000

Centro Stile Dainese and Aldo Drudi
G. Flash 20, cowhide jacket
Dainese, 2000

Alessandro Mendini
Oggetto banale, wood and painted
aluminium-coffee maker, 2000

Tyre
Pirelli, 2000

Centro Stile Dainese and Aldo Drudi
D-Jet city helmet
Dainese, 2001

Romeo Gigli
Romeo Gigli video tape by Ilvio Gallo

Giuseppe Leone
news photograph for report on Sicily

Design and memory

Vanni Pasca

Memory is the title of the section organised by Gae Aulenti and Luca Ronconi. Working hypothesis: "… an interpretation of forty years of our country's existence, from 1951 to 1991… fashion and design's continuous relationship with the country's much-discussed events: chronicles and history illustrated through performances, articles and headlines from major newspapers, film clips, television pictures..", writes Luigi Settembrini general curator of the exhibition. Therefore this is not a design exhibition in the classic sense of the term: it is not an orderly sequence of industrial products arranged in accordance with a precise yardstick bearing witness to research on technical or typological innovations and formal elaborations.

"Memory" is anyway a complex term. It has been given a myriad of philosophic and scientific definitions over the course of time and in various ways we preserve a memory of this legacy, a memory which intersects with the empirical memory of a given period and the events that defined it.

So, if we refer to design, selective (Bergson would say "empirical") memory immediately brings to mind an object that is an icon of an era. This is immediately followed by something like a flow of conscience that brings a whole universe of objects to the surface. The first, selected object evokes others through "contiguity" or contrasts with others through "similarity" (R. Jakobson).

Let's think back to Italy of the fifties: a few icons come to mind, one of which will surely be the Fiat 500, the car that put the Italian masses on the road (appearing a long time after America's Model T Ford in the first decades of the last century, or the Volkswagen Beetle, the Citroen 2CV and Issigonis' legendary Morris Mini). Other icons immediately follow through "similarity": the souped-up Lancia Aurelia convertible driven by Vittorio Gassman in *Il Sorpasso* (*The Easy Life*). Then the Golf designed by Giorgio Giugiaro in the seventies that was behind Volkswagen's recovery. Or the flame-red Ferraris, the symbols of eighties' ostentation.

A virtual mnemonic sequence which if interrupted is replaced by other chains formed according to "contiguity". In this case next to the 500 appear the Autostrada del Sole – the motorway running through Italy – and the Pirelli building, two symbols of Italy's economic boom. Pirelli's experiments with foam rubber for car seats and Marco Zanuso who, through foam rubber, launched the industrialisation of sofas and armchairs, "padded seating elements", that later continued with a harder-wearing soft plastic, polyurethane.

And so the associations continue: at the end of the sixties the pop designers used polyurethane to create soft sculptures in the shape of a vast pasture or a woman's red mouth (and Mae West's mouth comes to mind, interpreted as a red velvet sofa when Salvador Dali painted a whole room of her face in the thirties).

Therefore associations and contiguities, which maintain a certain order based on ordered or orderable sequences, are thrown into disorder by other memories. Memory is often subject to these short circuits which suddenly connect two events from two different periods. So if Pirelli produced, in the fifties, new tyre treads, in the eighties it continued this research in collaboration with MIT's legendary Media Lab and its director Nicholas Negroponte: from the Italy of post-war recovery to the Italy of electronics and digitalisation in a global world.

Of course, you could carry on playing this game ad infinitum, but at this point memory appears exactly like a huge "storehouse of ideas" (J. Locke) that seem unordered and unorderable.

In the opinion of the writer the exhibition presents memory in ways reflecting the above explanation. It has selected the symbolic icons of each decade and has surrounded them with chains of contiguous objects within a flow of information which places them within the reality of the collective experience, referring back to them in successive settings with new configurations of objects, news or events that trace threads through time, provoking visual and conceptual short circuits at intervals until this multi-linear path sediments into a kind of "belly of the soul", as St Augustine described memory.

A production, or *mise en scène*, with an immediate, enthralling allure. But, at the same time, a possible point of departure for a future venture: not a return to an ordered, coherent arrangement, but a window onto new ways of interpreting memory, history, Italian design. Firstly, by abandoning the self-referentiality of past interpretations which seemed to evolve purely within a self-sufficient concept of "project culture". Secondly, by building associative and contiguous chains that forge a link with international design and with the experience of other countries that have played a leading role in it (e.g. the United States). This does not mean doing away with the originality of the Italian experience but rather reinterpreting it within the broader scenario, from which it drew crucial indications and to which, over the years, it has made significant contributions.

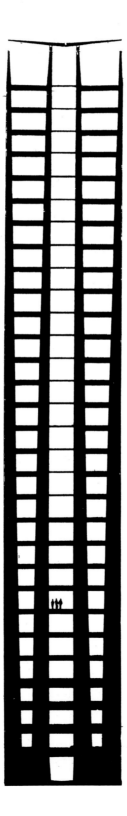

Fashion and Memory
Luigi Settembrini

A philosopher once said that, if we were to suddenly awake from a secular sleep, the thing that would immediately reveal to us the world we had happened into would be the fashion. Fashion as a system of signs, fashion that, more than any other language, has a privileged relationship with the most important discovery of the twentieth century, the body; fashion, finally, that precisely because of this, its nature, though perpetually rushing headlong forwards, is always terribly and automatically dated. Fashion is in itself both future and memory: the memories of those who wander *à la recherche du temps perdu* capture, even before the common meaning of things, the style of a hat, a suit, a haircut. Fashion and memory, therefore. But which memory? Memory is an ambiguous and multipurpose definition. Memory as representation? As a show? As a tale? Historical memory? Collective? Personal? Memory as a study? Memory that simply has something to do with recollections?

In order to celebrate fifty years of Italian fashion in an exhibition (a minefield if ever there was one), being foolishly lovers of risk, we have given priority to the most dangerous path, that is, that of personal memories as such. It would have been more correct to represent historical memory. But also a great deal more obvious, easier, less tendentious, less "layman-like" and therefore (even if this may seem a contradiction) less critical. Let us explain. The historian and the critic do not have critical (in the sense of selective) memory precisely because he *must* remember everything and those who must remember everything cannot afford to remember only what they would remember for they were not historians. The memory of the historian is professional, comprehensive, and therefore without possible selective judgement; in contrast, that of the layman is critical (selective) precisely because it is full of holes. The memory of the historian is not made of recollections: that of the layman is.

For this section of fashion *Made in Italy*, we could propose a serious, unexceptionable selection, with all the fashion designers and all the firms in their rightful place. This, however, has already been done and – you can be sure – will be done again a thousand times in the future. It seemed more interesting, more debatable, to us to mention only those people we remembered. The public will not find the presence of many stylists who have contributed, with their great and deserved success, to the success of Italian style. They will find those that the curators' memory, for once not that of specialists, has recollected. And remembered not so much because they were successful but because they profoundly marked the ages of Italian Style, they had the stature to interweave themselves with the history of this country; they contributed, even if humbly, to the great epochal changes.

You will find Ferragamo's sandals in the exhibition not only because they were greatly liked and widely sold but because the clever shoemaker from the South invented a new way of walking.

You will find Emilio Pucci not because he was divine and a marquis but because he was the unrivalled master of public relations who more than any other contributed to the happy metamorphosis of the Italian image of the post-war period.

You will find Valentino not because his models today descend the steps of Piazza di Spagna in the great *ennui* that is TV but because, for forty years, he has been synonymous with timeless femininity and absolute international elegance.

Roberto Capucci with Ester Williams, 1956 (Historical Archives Capucci)

Salvatore Ferragamo and his models wth "Kimo" satin stocking (photo: Locchi, Florence)

Marilyn Monroe with blouse and slacks by Pucci (photo: George Barris)

You will find Ken Scott because he was an extraordinary interpreter of the provocations, the fun, the colour of '68.

You will find Giorgio Armani not for his gigantic glacial real estate, but because he is the father of fashion "Made in Italy" on a planetary level, the inventor of modern, democratic, politically correct fashion, the man who alone knew how, with his unstoppable international success, to counterbalance the image of the Red Brigades and the years of bullets and bombs.

You will find Versace, the sophisticated, intelligent interpreter of the "vulgarity" of the years of the restoration, and of that woman that a rival recently defined a "zoccola" [whore]. The last and great homage to the memory of the stylist.

You will find others too. Walter Albini, the statuesque Capucci, Gucci, Dolce e Gabbana and their Sicily, the sempiternal Missonis, Moschino the *enfant terrible*, Cinzia Ruggeri, Elio Fiorucci, the playmaker of a magic moment for innovation and change, ethnic Romeo Gigli, sumptuous Gianfranco Ferré, minimalist Prada, whose black backpack is (perhaps a little sadly for the period in question) the strongest image of a decade.

It is here that the choices of the exhibition dwell and it is certainly no fault of those who are not there, nor is it the fault of their value, their quality, their advertising budgets, their current accounts, but simply of our secular memory (therefore, as you already know, full of holes).

Veruschka wears a dress by Valentino, Fall/Winter 1965-66 Haute Couture collection (photo: Henry Clarke)

Dolce e Gabbana, Spring/Summer 1987 Haute Couture collection (photo: Fabrizio Ferri)

Fiorucci, Image for the Fiorucci boutique shopping bag, 1974 (Archivio Fiorucci)

Ken Scott, Il circo di Ken/Ken's Circus collection, Rome, 1968

Bellissima, *by Luchino*
Visconti, 1951
(G.B. B/Neri Archives)

Cinema and memory

Paolo Mereghetti

Reviewing the history of Italy through films might seem a bit of a risk, especially when, in our case, we are only indicating films that were contemporary to the narrated facts. Yet it may also afford pleasant surprises: while we might not discover something new about our country's history, we may at least be able to understand a bit more about Italian cinema. By reviewing Italian films (especially from the fifties and sixties) with a bit of retrospection, we can understand how important cinema was in the Italian culture, and how it influenced the national thinking. Though it was not a sort of animated version of Beltrame's magazine covers, cinema frequently borrowed from the legends – and facts – of Italy.

One only has to take a look at the films by the great Totò to realize how most plots basically derived from a chronicle of Italian society. Over the years and in various films, Totò participated in the Tour of Italy and was a contestant on the *Lascia o Raddoppia?* quiz show; he appeared in lavish vaudeville shows or took part in the "dolce vita" in Rome, exploiting their popularity or copying it, according to a concept of entertainment that starts out from real life and returns to reality after being transfigured on the screen. This subject can be repeated in many other films, where the picnic in Fregene or the dream of a first car, a Sunday at the stadium or the generation war between rock singers and crooners become the idea (at times just a hint, and more concrete other times) for two hours of cinematic mirth.

But this is not only valid for highly popular but mediocre films. Although they pursued a very personal, rigorous directing style, Visconti and De Sica, Fellini, Antonioni and Rossellini embraced the concrete reality of Italy as the vibrant setting for their films. As a matter of fact, it almost seemed as if they needed it. This is also the lesson of neo-realism, which shaped the Italian film industry in the fifties: the need to anchor one's expressive universe within a concrete, accurate story that is immediately recognized as Italian. The inhumanity of the affluent and the humanity of the poor that emerge in films such as *Europa 51* or *Miracolo a Milano* are not only ideological slogans or moralistic sermons: they are also the result of a precise ability to insert everyday details, "anthropological" notions and factual elements in film.

Cinema was a window on the real world, which nourished it and gave it life.

That is why the concrete story of a country could become a film plot (and transfiguration). The audience expected to recognize the world in which it lived and the society in which it struggled on the screen, regardless of whether that screen showed the tears of Yvonne Sanson or the smirks of Alberto Sordi, the one-liners of Totò or the curves of Sophia Loren, the suffering of Eduardo De Filippo or the rage of Cervi and Fernandel. Hunger, fatigue, love, dreams, hate, and hopes took shape and strength on the screen only as long as they were concrete, recognizable and identifiable forms and forces.

Cinema in the sixties continued to follow this lesson and use this artifice, turning films into the perfect instrument that revealed the progress of innovation - even before many people realized it. Certain films (for example, *Una vita difficile* by Dino Risi, the long-ignored *La vita agra* by Lizzani, *Io la conoscevo bene* by Pietrangeli, and naturally *La dolce vita* by Fellini) interpreted the contradictions of Italian society with extraordinary foresight. They are authentic two-bit sociological treatises that perfectly identified the raw nerve, the guilty conscience, and the living nightmare. And, of course, the names do not stop here: Bellocchio and Samperi, Germi and Ferreri, Zampa and Rosi, Monicelli and Pasolini, Lattuada and Scola, Petri and Brass, all – in one way or another – chose to describe through their films a country changing its skin, some accentuating the grotesque side and others the rage, some underlining the contradictions and still others the frustrated dreams, some inspired by cowardice and others by courage…

The problem is that harmony and insight did not last. Intensified social strife made it more difficult to understand our society, and cinema was affected by this confusion. The profound analysis of the fifties and sixties was replaced by the schematism of the seventies. In-depth analysis turned into facile and rigid reflection.

Those were the years of police action films and comedies that confused sexual liberation with dirty jokes: they were dark years for society, so it was inevitable that the same was true for the cinema, which at best was only able to protest with shock and alarm, expressing its own confused anguish. This is quite apparent in the lack of films on terrorism and, above all, the longer interval of time between the occurrence of real events and their appearance on film. It was hard to figure out what was happening in Italy and find a point of reference, so imagine how difficult it was to use this situation as the background for a film plot.

Thus, in these years (for reasons that naturally are not only sociological but also economic: take, for example, the crisis in the Italian film industry, starting with lower production and fewer movie-goers) there was a break between the real world and mythopoetic capacity. Cinema "lost" its ability to absorb the moods of society and transfer them in its own works. The rules of the genre (or even sub-genre) eventually prevailed over the osmosis between art and reality, between creation and observation. And how difficult it is to find films that portray the eighties! There were a few guffaws, a few timid tears, and a few scathing commentaries, but the ability to observe and portray Italy basically took place through other channels and spectators. And we are still paying the consequences of this loss today.

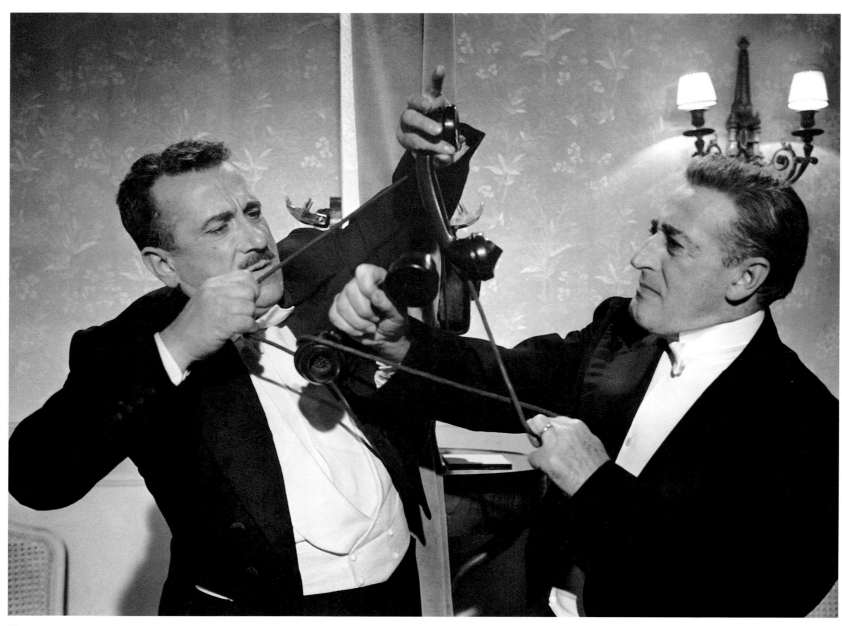

I soliti ignoti, *by Mario Monicelli, 1958* (G.B. B/Neri Archives)

Il sorpasso, *by Dino Risi, 1962* (G.B. B/Neri Archives)

List of films in the anthology

The forties and fifties

Abbasso la miseria!, 1946, by Gennaro Righelli (the "bourgeois" temptations of a fruit vendor who became rich with the black market)
Fuga in Francia, 1948, by Mario Soldati (lingering fascism and immigration abroad)
Totò al giro d'Italia, 1948, by Mario Mattoli (the legend of bicycle racing)
I pompieri di Viggiù, 1949, by Mario Mattoli (the triumph of vaudeville)
Domenica d'agosto, 1950, by Luciano Emmer (fun in the old days: picnics)
Bellissima, 1951, by Luchino Visconti (cinema as a shortcut to success)
Miracolo a Milano, 1951, by Vittorio De Sica (the humanity of the poor)
Europa 51, 1952, by Roberto Rossellini (the inhumanity of the rich)
La tratta delle bianche, 1952, by Luigi Comencini (illusions of success)
Don Camillo, 1952, by Julien Duvivier (the national path to the bipolar system)
Cinque poveri in automobile, 1952, by Mario Mattoli (the legend of the car)
Ti ho sempre amato!, 1953, by Mario Costa (the problem of unwed mothers and the city/country dichotomy)
Napoletani a Milano, 1953, by Eduardo De Filippo (immigration to northern Italy and the myth of Milan)
Un americano a Roma, 1954, by Steno (the myth of the Stars and Stripes)
Totò, lascia o raddoppia, 1956, by Camillo Mastrocinque (the triumph of television)
Il grido, 1957, by Michelangelo Antonioni (the proletariat not only has class problems)
I ragazzi del juke box, 1959, by Lucio Fulci (rock-and-rollers versus crooners)
L'Italia non è un paese povero, 1960, by Ioris Jvens (produced by Mattei, the need for national modernization)
Una vita difficile, 1961, by Dino Risi (from Resistance fighters to the economic boom, a parable of a country and its compromises)

The sixties

I soliti ignoti, 1958, by Mario Monicelli (why we needed the economic boom)
La dolce vita, 1960, by Federico Fellini (the legend of Rome)
Il sorpasso, 1962, by Dino Risi (the euphoria of the economic boom)
I mostri, 1963, by Dino Risi (the contradictions of society)
Le mani sulla città, 1963, by Francesco Rosi (the contradictions of politics)
Chi lavora è perduto, 1963, by Tinto Brass (rejection of integration)
La vita agra, 1964, by Carlo Lizzani (intolerant of affluence)
Io la conoscevo bene, 1965, by Antonio Pietrangeli (the illusions of the sixties)
I pugni in tasca, 1965, by Marco Bellocchio (anti-bourgeois rebellion)
Signore & Signori, 1966, by Pietro Germi (provincial hypocrisy)
Grazie zia, 1968, by Salvatore Samperi (politics through sex)
Teorema, 1968, by Pier Paolo Pasolini (sex as politics)
Dillinger è morto, 1968, by Marco Ferreri (the bourgeois rebellion)
Il medico della mutua, 1968, by Luigi Zampa (social climbing and the national health system)
Io, Emmanuelle, 1969, by Cesare Canevari (changes in sexual customs)
Indagine su un cittadino al di sopra di ogni sospetto, 1970, by Elio Petri (police power)
Venga a prendere il caffè da noi, 1970, by Alberto Lattuada (the hypocritical and sexually repressed middle-class)
C'eravamo tanto amati, 1974, by Ettore Scola (a parable of the leftist movement and its ideals in the fifties and sixties)

*La terrazza, by Ettore Scola, 1980
(© E. George - Sygma/Neri)*

*Ginger e Fred, by Federico Fellini, 1986
(© Fabian - Sygma/Neri)*

Locandina per Speriamo
che sia femmina, by Mario
Monicelli, 1986
(G.B. B/Neri Archives)

Back-stage del film Impiegati,
by Pupi Avati, 1984
(© Andrea Marcaccioli/Neri)

Compagni di scuola,
by Carlo Verdone, 1988
(Team/Neri)

The seventies

In nome del popolo italiano, 1971, by Dino Risi (the contradictions of the justice system)
La classe operaia va in paradiso, 1971, by Elio Petri (the birth and death of the workers' consciousness)
Il sindacalista, 1972, by Luciano Salce (spontaneity and class struggles)
Milano calibro 9, 1972, by Fernando di Leo (the city becomes a jungle)
Vogliamo i colonnelli, 1973, by Mario Monicelli (coup d'etat temptations)
Milano odia: la polizia non può sparare, 1974, by Umberto Lenzi (anguish in the face of spreading urban violence)
Il cittadino si ribella, 1974, by Enzo G. Castellari (the myth of private justice)
Roma violenta, 1975, by Franco Martinelli (rebellion against "tied hands")
Atti impuri all'italiana, 1976, by Oscar Brazzi (early signs of the sexual revolution)
Un borghese piccolo piccolo, 1977, by Mario Monicelli (the silent majority)
Io sono mia, 1977, by Sofia Scandurra (a woman's view of feminism)
Prova d'orchestra, 1979, by Federico Fellini (Italy on the verge of an abyss)
La terrazza, 1980, by Ettore Scola (intellectuals and politics)
La tragedia di un uomo ridicolo, 1981, by Bernardo Bertolucci (the middle class facing terrorism)
Colpire al cuore, 1983, by Gianni Amelio (terrorism as a generation gap)

The eighties

Eccezzziunale... veramente, 1982, by Carlo Vanzina (soccer and the many faces of Italy)
Impiegati, 1984, by Pupi Avati (the doldrums of a white-collar job)
Speriamo che sia femmina, 1986, by Mario Monicelli (post-feminism)
Ginger e Fred, 1986, by Federico Fellini (the triumph of private TV networks)
Yuppies - I giovani di successo, 1986, by Carlo Vanzina (Milan's club set)
Compagni di scuola, 1988, by Carlo Verdone (revival in private life)
Palombella rossa, 1989, by Nanni Moretti (resurgence of politics)
L'aria serena dell'Ovest, 1990, by Silvio Soldini (the generation gap and dashed dreams)
Ultrà, 1991, by Ricky Tognazzi (violence in the stadiums)

Belvedere.
Art and memory
Achille Bonito Oliva

Captions edited by Manuela Gandini

Lucio Fontana

Spatial Concept, Nature
1959-60
bronze
diameter 55 cm/60 cm/75 cm
Courtesy Fondazione Lucio Fontana,
Milan

In an inexhaustible experimentation
with materials, spaces and dimensions,
Lucio Fontana, founder of
"*spazialismo*" (1948), explores – via
abstractionism and the "informal"
movement – the road that leads him to
attempt to go beyond the material.
Cuts, tears, holes in the canvases;
round terracottas and bronzes
lacerated as though struck by meteors:
testimony to an era that prepares itself
for the conquest of space, in which
boundless hopes coexist with the great
tragedy of war. The *Spatial Concept
Nature* are disturbing and primordial
sculptures that appear to contain the
energy of the cosmos.

Mario Schifano

Coca-Cola
1962
paper on canvas
140 × 160 cm
Private collection, Milan

In the first part of the 1960s, Schifano
let out the magic word Coca-Cola.
Contemporaneously, on the other side
of the planet, Warhol was lining up,
one after another, bottles of this
legendary American drink. Each artist
worked without knowledge of the
other as communication then was not
as it is today. The light of the boom, in
the middle of *bicycle thieves,* began to
project itself on the Rome that each
day met for an aperitif at Rosati. The
product, the logo, the advertising sign
quickly entered the collective
imagination and captivated the artistic
generation that followed the
"informal" movement. The evocative
Coca-Cola label, alive and almost
liquid, became the emblem of those
years.

Pino Pascali

Bachi da setola
1968
cinque elementi realizzati in scovoli
di materiale acrilico
dimensioni varie
Collezione privata, Asiago

Pino Pascali lavora nella pubblicità per
il *Carosello*. Si mantiene creando
personaggi e storielle, con ironia sottile
e trasversale si diverte come un
bambino a fare oggetti d'arte che
ricordano grandi giocattoli. Il cannone,
il ponte militare o i *bachi da setola*, fatti
con setole di scope multicolori, sono
installazioni che occupano lo spazio di
un immaginario sempre più leggero e
pop, ma nello stesso tempo che guarda
avanti e precede gli eventi.
Nel gioco c'è anche la violenza e uno
sguardo critico e ironico, innovativo,
troncato all'improvviso dalla morte
precoce dell'artista.

Francesco Clemente

Facciamo a camiciate
1991
carta su tela
130 × 316 cm
Collezione privata, Milano

Esponente della transavanguardia,
Clemente mette in scena lo scherzo,
l'autobiografia, il segno leggero di un
gioco buffo come *Facciamo a camiciate*.
Il sé è al centro di una mitologia
personale, evanescente, erotica.
Pulsioni e desideri si disvelano perché,
spiega Achille Bonito Oliva nel suo
testo teorico sul movimento, "gli artisti
della fine degli anni Settanta, quelli
che io chiamo della *trans-avanguardia*,
riscoprono la possibilità di rendere
lampante l'opera mediante la
presentazione di un'immagine
che contemporaneamente è enigma
e soluzione". In quest'opera tutto è
sottosopra, compaiono frammenti
anatomici in un campo d'azione
non decodificabile.

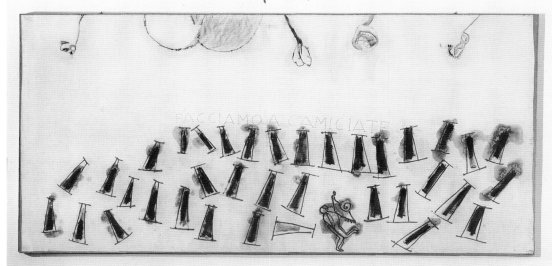

Mimmo Paladino

Witness
1993
bronze
h. 150 cm
Courtesy Galleria Cardi, Milan

Emerging from the moralism of the 1970s, artists began to reflect once again on their own and others' existential condition. Mimmo Paladino explores the infinite range of possibilities in art, experimenting with the idea of the continuous centrality of man. The typical silhouette of the artist returns in many forms and, in this sculpture entitled *Witness,* confirms all the profundity of existence. The many faces of man, the worlds which overlap and alternate in a single instant, birth and pain, appear to be expressed contemporaneously in the witness. "Does not the garden hide more mysteries than the forest? – Paladino wrote – "Art does not coincide with life, ever! Because as is noted it's often good to use the knife for your future image".

Vanessa Beecroft

VB 37,040
2000
Vibracolour of the performance in Tokyo
127 × 177 cm
Courtesy Galleria Paolo Curti, Milan

Her work, a symbol of end-of-the-century trends, is on the borderline between existence and fashion, flesh and appearance, cloning and globalisation. Women in series wear the same panties, the same red and orange coloured wigs and have the same metaphysical plaits. They are the contemporary myth: they provoke and remove seduction.
The empty, indifferent or resigned expressions of the models, contrasting with the embarrassed and voyeuristic gazes of the public, provoke a visual, lively and indigestible short circuit.
The countless young women exhibited are living sculptures: the clones of living sculptures that Piero Manzoni, with a different aim, began to endorse forty years ago.

La Fura dels Baus

The seventies. Years of disillusionment, years of terrorism. The utopia of the sixties with its hopes of improving the world through goodwill breathed its last.

"Flower power is over"; it was time to pass to direct action. The energy crisis threatened to paralyse industrial growth and destroyed the dream of unlimited progress. Student and trade union protests became more radical. The world militarised once more and social and political expression were no longer limited to peaceful demonstrations. Terrorist organisations sprang up throughout the world and the horror of dictatorships spread across South America.

Italy saw the birth of the Red Brigades, which seemed to owe their name more to the blood they spilled than to their political colour. Their *modus operandi* became emblematic, transforming itself into the other face of "Made in Italy", which established itself as a world-wide phenomenon in this decade. The Fura dels Baus, born in 1979, probably was in part the heir of this climate of profound social and political revolt, and it translated all this latent violence into an artistic movement that expressed itself in multidisciplinary actions. On this occasion, they try to reflect the atmosphere of instability and disorder, marked by the presence of arms on the street, that Italy lived through in its years of terrorism.

The Theatre group La Fura dels Baus is supported by Ministerio de Educación y Cultura, Generalitat de Catalunya/Departament de Cultura and in collaboration with Iberia, Copec and Ayuntamento de Gavá.

III. Brockenhaus

by Oliviero Toscani

Conversation between Oliviero Toscani and Isabella Mazzitelli

edited by Isabella Mazzitelli

Oliviero Toscani was ten years old when the war ended and Italy was rapidly and chaotically rebuilding. In the euphoria of this rebirth, the first tiny seeds of *made in Italy* products were sown and quickly began to sprout. A forest would later grow. A jungle of objects, a tangle of lamps, a plethora of chairs, tables, easy chairs, radios and televisions, beds and kitchens would arrive in waves and deposit in layers like geological eras, occupying the homes of Italians who used to be farmers, then factory workers and later white-collar workers. From one day to the next, these people longed to be, imagined themselves to be and behaved like solid middle-class folk.

Oliviero Toscani, who was born in a old Milanese apartment building and, even as a child, had an eye for the contradictions of society and the weaknesses of the human spirit, observed and recorded everything. Today that intense and incisive effort, which took place over fifty years, has been transformed into a moody, expressionistic installation, In what only appears to be a chaotic bric à brac, the main theme is once again – in typical Toscani style –a revealing exposé of the dark and hypocritical side of the world that announces with a smirk that "the Emperor has no clothes". Here, *made in Italy* is nude. Although powerful, respected, and revered, it has been unveiled by its own vanity.

The installation is called "Brockenhaus". Toscani explains, "It's like those stores in Switzerland and Germany where people who are short of cash and want to decorate their home go to search for furniture and objects. And people who want to empty their apartment full of stuff that usually can't be sold go there, too: they don't make a profit, but their only expense is a phone call to have the thrift shop truck come." It's a place for students where you can find all sorts of objects, like things washed up on shore, that have escaped the paradise of indispensable items or the inferno of destruction."

That is how Oliviero Toscani sees *made in Italy* products: "I've always been fascinated by its genesis and mentality. After the war, there were still people in Italy who were homeless, who lived in grottos with no electricity or water. And hundreds of thousands emigrated to work as bricklayers in Switzerland or factory workers in Turin and Milan. Yet Assyrian-Milanese design already existed back then: a taste for luxurious, opulent and basically useless things that made women feel affluent or socially prominent as they copied the lifestyles of the rich and famous, an idea that was mainly based upon imagination and hearsay because millionaires would have never dreamed of decorating their homes that way. On the other hand, Italians have these weaknesses: they're Ferrari fans, they identify with and dream of a car that they will probably never see up close in their lifetime."

This is the "absurdity", the contradiction that keenly interests Toscani. He says: "In a climate of *Rocco and His Brothers,* I studied art in Zurich and taught arithmetic to illiterate Italians who spent time in the 'Free Colonies', centers which were founded in Switzerland by the anti-fascists during the racial persecutions. I was twenty years old back then, in 1960; on one hand, I saw these poor, courageous people who had left Italy to work 12-hour days and were living all alone, without their families, in Swiss containers. On the other hand, when I went back to Milan and visited my sister Marirosa who with her husband Aldo Ballo photographed design, I came into contact with this other aspect of Italian society. Each time, in their studio full of Golden Compass awards, there were brand new lamps and sofas, which they honestly portrayed in what seemed to be perfect incongruity."

"This style was created for the rich and affluent, for people and tastes that completely contrasted with what I, a student of the Bauhaus school, loved: simplicity and an aesthetic and ethical rigor. That school produced concepts and objects which are still extremely modern, even today. Modernity has nothing to do with a certain point in time: everything that is modern, is timeless. A Bauhaus chair is modern. *Made in Italy* products aren't modern. Why? Because it's the line full of wishes and whims, useless and superfluous things, indecent and asocial objects. It was not made for everyone, but for a powerful few. Fashion is the same. What do you think will go down in history? A gorgeous evening gown that is basically useless, or T-shirts and jeans? We Italians were even capable of selling and wearing ironed jeans, jeans with a crease! That's Italy, and that's our strength: being obscene and beautiful at the same time. Perhaps our life is not based upon rigor and simplicity, but on the opposite, and is therefore full of errors."

Oliviero Toscani accepts these contradictions with sarcastic benevolence, but he rejects them when they are too strident and annoying. And since he feels that times are ripe today, he has decided to display that very recent yet extremely remote past. "Now that we've all grown up a bit, I hope there is a better society out there that is richer, not in terms of material wealth but in decency. That is why those objects and the way people use them are a thing of the past, stored up in the attic along with crinolines, corsets and rouge. Since *made in Italy* products are like rouge, creating

Photo by Oliviero Toscani

'Brockenhaus' was like opening Grandma's trunk, and when you enter the exhibit, you should feel as if you're going back in time."

Toscani says there is no criticism on his part, but only acknowledgment and even recognition. "You just have to have the courage to challenge yourself. I don't want this to be a commemoration – Italian style is rhetorical, but has never particularly moved me – but my eyes are like a child's: I'm a newborn who scrutinizes everything carefully, but with innocence." What Oliviero Toscani saw rummaging through Grandma's trunk, and what visitors will see, is a hodgepodge of objects. "There are dozens of chairs, lamps, sofas created by designers who filled homes with pointed, rigid, angular things – perfect for injuring children who fell against them – and then there are satellite TVs designed back when satellites didn't exist, which were created as science fiction gizmos when Italy didn't even have highways, and televisions that didn't work but were gorgeous when switched off – what a genius, the guy who designed a television that was only beautiful when switched off!"

Oliviero Toscani's keen gaze causes him abhor what he calls "conventional design", "educated, polite, for hoity-toity ladies", but it also makes him admit that it was a great opportunity. "All this has created jobs for many people and it encouraged considerable entrepreneurial courage – there has never been stupidity in *made in Italy* production. We also realized there was lots of energy around, a chance to become more open-minded, and to do something beyond the ordinary.

"Unfortunately, it was a wasted occasion. Few people understood what was going on in the world. I'm thinking of Ettore Sottsass and the *Valentine* typewriter back in the sixties: but Sottsass had lived in America and was a rich Milanese flower child."

Oliviero Toscani's imaginary trunk in his fabulous thrift shop full of objects seeking re-qualification – "Objects aren't bad: just don't use them" – contains things found at junk dealers, lent by producers, and provided by Toscani himself: "There's a truckload of my stuff, and I'm happy to have brought it." What? A contradiction? Not at all! In his home in the Tuscan countryside of Casale Marittimo, everything is in its place. You just have know where: Made in Italy objects melancholically keep each other company in a shed, which contains everything except *Le bambole* by B&B Italia, the chairs shaped like a model's body that Toscani photographed for Busnelli in 1972. "They're in the Horse Office: you can prop your boots up on them." He laughs.

IV. Flavours

by Gaetano Pesce and Andrea P

Immaginary Dialogues on the Birth of "Flavours"

Luigi Settembrini

A mid-September afternoon, in Cosmit's offices at Foro Buonaparte in Milan. Titti Santini and Luigi Settembrini are sitting at a desk. The conversation hinges on the Made in Italy? *exhibition.*

Settembrini – Apart from fashion, design, cinema and chronicles, I'd like to present Italian gastronomy in a different way, without the same old cooks and the same old experts, without the same old special evenings dedicated to the same old regional specialities …

Santini – Why don't you ask Andrea Pezzi? Pezzi's a kind of pop youth culture icon and he was the mind behind *Kitchen* which is the only truly original television cookery programme. And Pezzi's young and it seems to me you need young people.

* * *

A morning at the end of September 2000, in a hotel in Montecatini where Andrea Pezzi had presented a show the evening before. Settembrini waits for Pezzi in the foyer. Pezzi appears looking like death warmed up, not having slept much.

Settembrini – Dear Andrea, how are you?

Pezzi – Hum mmm mmm.

Settembrini (deliberately unfeeling) – If you'll allow me, I'll tell you what it's about.

Pezzi – Be my guest.

Settembrini – We'd like you to take part in an exhibition.

Pezzi – As a painter I'm nothing to write home about.

Settembrini – It's got nothing to do with painting. It's got to do with Italian style. Or, in your case, Italian cookery. The idea's this: you, in the exhibition, do a kind of *Kitchen*. In other words you, together with leading figures in culture, entertainment, politics and sport, talk about Italian food.

Pezzi – Copy *Kitchen*? No, self-plagiary is a criminal offence. Perhaps something different. I'd have to think about it. What do you mean exactly by exhibition? Would I have to cook for the inaugural evening?

Settembrini – I rather had the idea of something that would last for the whole forty days. You wouldn't have to cook but talk about gastronomy.

Pezzi – For forty days? Perhaps with videos… and who'd be doing the layout?

Settembrini – Gaetano Pesce would be perfect. [*In Italian* pesce *means fish*].

Pezzi – As it's about cooking I'd say he's ideal. Who's Pesce anyway?

Settembrini – Good grief, young people! Get informed! Pesce's a designer, perhaps the most visionary designer in the world.

Pezzi – Why is it you project gurus can never avoid using the word "visionary"?

* * *

Beginning of October 2000 at the Oyster Bar in New York. Settembrini and Pesce are sitting at the bar.

Settembrini – As I told you on the phone …

Pesce – Tell me again because I didn't understand a thing.

Settembrini - Splendid. Well, I was thinking of you designing a setting for Italian gastronomy in an exhibition on Italian style. I envisaged a strongly imaginative kitchen, something that's a metaphor for Italian cuisine.

Pesce – Why is it you project gurus can never avoid using the term "strongly imaginative"? And that you seem to revel in the word "metaphor"?

Settembrini – If you prefer, I could say a vision …

Pesce – Look, this isn't Lourdes. Anyway I know what you mean. You want a imaginative, strong, perfect image, something never seen before, remarkable, even extraordinary. Well, you've come to the right person. Anyway who's Pezzi, the one you said was going to present the whole thing?

Settembrini – Good grief, you old folks! Get a life! Andrea Pezzi is a kind of pop youth culture icon…

Pesce – Why is it you project gurus can never avoid using the word icon? But does Pezzi know who I am at least?

Settembrini – Are you kidding? Pezzi is a great fan of yours. In fact he told me either you did the setting or he wouldn't be in it.

Pesce – He's not dumb, is he!

* * *

The next day Settembrini phones Pezzi from New York.

Settembrini – Andrea, Pesce has accepted. He's crazy about the idea.

Pezzi – But does Pesce know who I am at least?

Settembrini – Are you kidding? He's a great fan of yours. In fact he told me if you didn't present it he wouldn't be in it.

Pezzi – He's not dumb, is he!

* * *

One evening at the beginning of January 2001, in Pezzi's house in Milan.

Settembrini – Dear Gaetano this is Andrea. Dear Andrea, this is Gaetano.

Pezzi – I've heard so much about you, it's great to know you at last!

Pesce – Likewise. Pezzi's all they talk about in New York.

Pezzi – They're not dumb, are they these Americans!

* * *

Pezzi shows Pesce around the house, a very attractive loft overlooking one of Milan's canals.

Pesce – Lovely place.

Pezzi – What do you think, should I hang a curtain between the bedroom and the living room?

Settembrini – What if we talk a bit about the exhibition?

Pezzi – Just a minute, I want to show Gaetano the downstairs pool.

Pesce – An underground swimming pool? You're a well-paid icon!

Pezzi – I can't complain. But I've made an exception for this exhibition, I'm practically working for nothing.

Pesce (to himself) – That's worrying.

Settembrini – Now what if we talk a bit about the exhibition?

Pezzi – Let me cook first.

* * *

The three men move into Pezzi's kitchen which takes up a huge central area in the house. Above the kitchen is a glass roof that can be opened and closed via a mechanism. At the touch of a button the roof slides back on itself. A metaphoric kitchen, to say the least (but Settembrini's careful not to say so).

Pesce – Wow, now this really is a metaphor of a kitchen!

Pezzi smiles, Settembrini scowls. Pezzi cooks, Pesce and Settembrini drink some fine wine.

Pesce – Tell me about your family.

Pezzi - Sure.

Settembrini – And what if we talked a bit about the exhibition?

* * *

Great dinner. Obviously the conversation dwells on everything but the exhibition. Settembrini is visibly nervous.

Pesce – Do you mind if I smoke?

Pezzi – You'd be the first to smoke in here. I hate smoking. But if you'll let me open the roof, you can smoke. There's always a first time for everything.

* * *

Pezzi activates the electric mechanism to open the roof. Pesce smokes. Settembrini freezes.

Settembrini – Before they whisk me off to the emergency room, could we talk a bit about the exhibition?

Pezzi (closing the roof) – Oh, alright, if you have to go on about it… I've got an idea I thought would be fun. In the space we have, I'd like to put a whole load of monitors, of televisions, in a circle, with just one isolated television in the middle. There'd be a close-up of me on the isolated television. Without speaking, I'd turn my head left and right, looking at the important personalities we'd roped in. These people would look at me from their screens. My image, this time looking at the audience, would say a single word, like "spaghetti", or "risotto", or "pizza" and so on. No recipes, just individualising the stereotype Italian dishes and their ingredients. As soon as I say "spaghetti" all the personalities would start to talk about spaghetti. In unison, so that the visitor in the centre of the room will hear a kind of jumbled babble, a very Italian hubbub with everybody chatting about spaghetti. But if the visitor approaches a screen they'll be able to hear clearly how one particularly personality prefers to cook spaghetti. After spaghetti we can do risotto, tomato and basil, parmesan, oil, wine, pizza, rum baba… What do you think?

Pesce – Fantastic. I can just picture the audience's reaction.

Settembrini – Will they be violent? Will they want their money back?

Pesce – No. They'll open their mouths in wonder. They'll go "ohhh!"

Pezzi – I like it when the audience goes "ohhh!"

Pesce – Now I'll tell you my idea. I don't want a kitchen. Too old hat. I want Andrea to put his screens amidst a landscape made of the ingredients and dishes he said before. Parmesan mountains and valleys, basil pastures, oil lakes, wine rivers, spumante-spouting fountains, trees made of trenette with pesto and in the middle of this landscape an armchair made of spaghetti… What do you think?

Pezzi – Fantastic. I know just how the audience will react.

Settembrini – They'll have us certified?

Pezzi – No. They'll open their mouths in wonder. They'll go "ohhh!"

Pesce – I like it when the audience goes "ohhh!"

Settembrini – Let's hope it's all right on the night.

Flavours according to Andrea Pezzi

I love to cook.
I love to enhance each flavor in the things I make.
I love the mouth.
I love to think of it as a huge grindstone that makes everything the same.
I love the way the tongue picks out flavors.
It seeks them, one by one. It recognizes them, then it blends them all together again.

To become a tongue. To taste the choral flavor of words, but knowing how to move and recognize the poetry of some and the thrill of others.

FLAVOURS is the way I wanted to chew the words of some of the people responsible for great Italian products.
Monitors that speak of food, mulling over it as if it were a part of their memory.

Flavours according to Gaetano Pesce

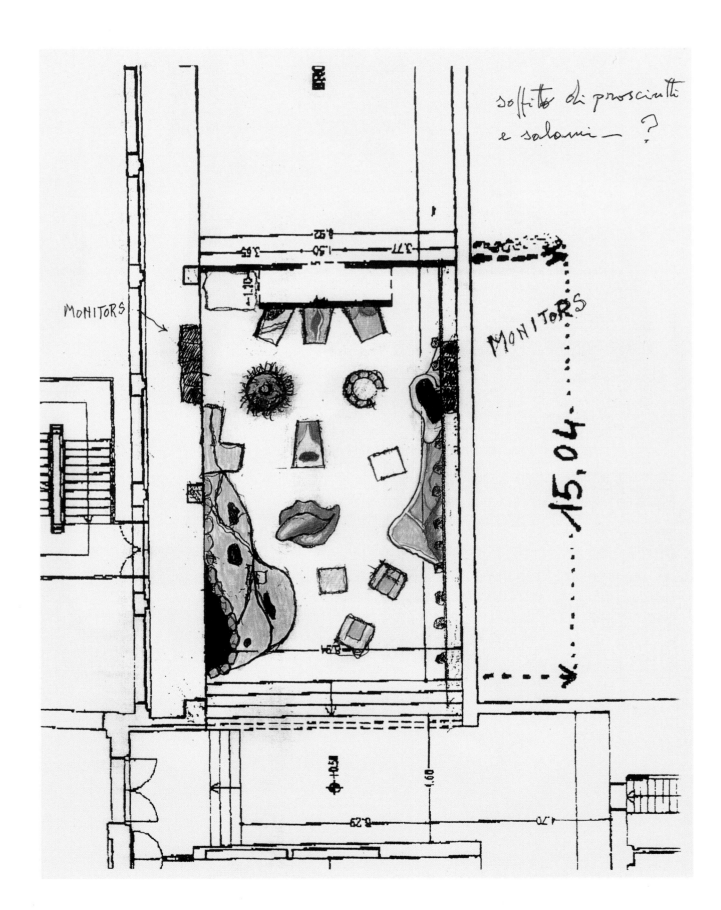

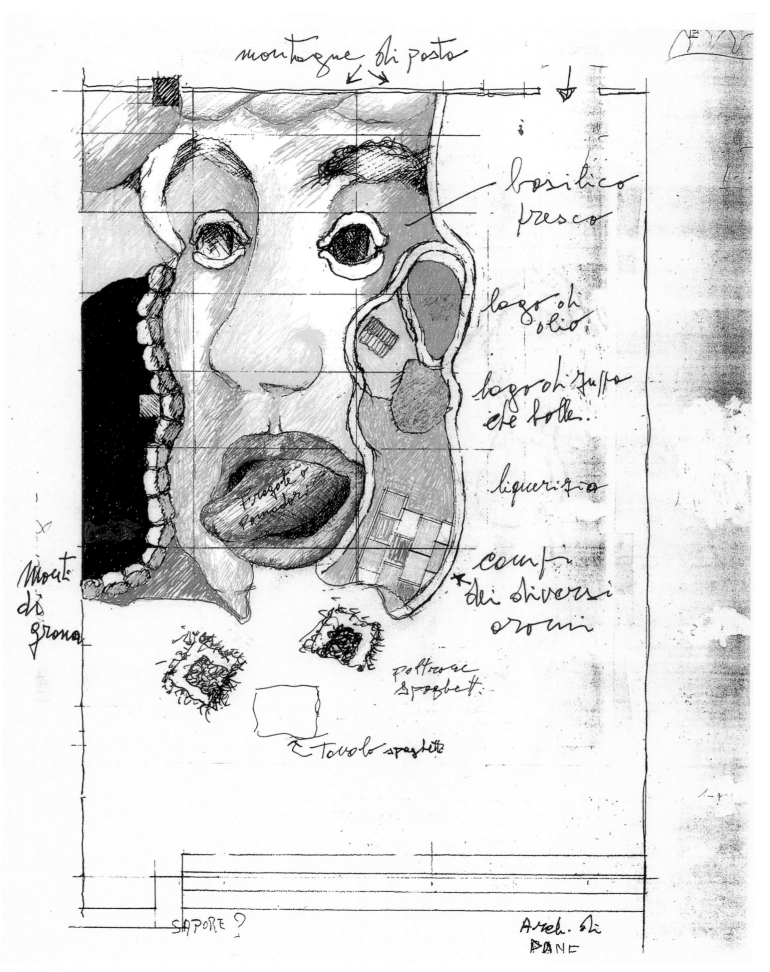

montagne di pasta

basilico fresco

lago di olio

lago di sugo che bolle...

liquerizia

campi di diversi ortaggi

Monte di grana

Fragole o pomodori

poltrone spaghetti

tavolo spaghetti

SAPORE ?

Arch. di PANE

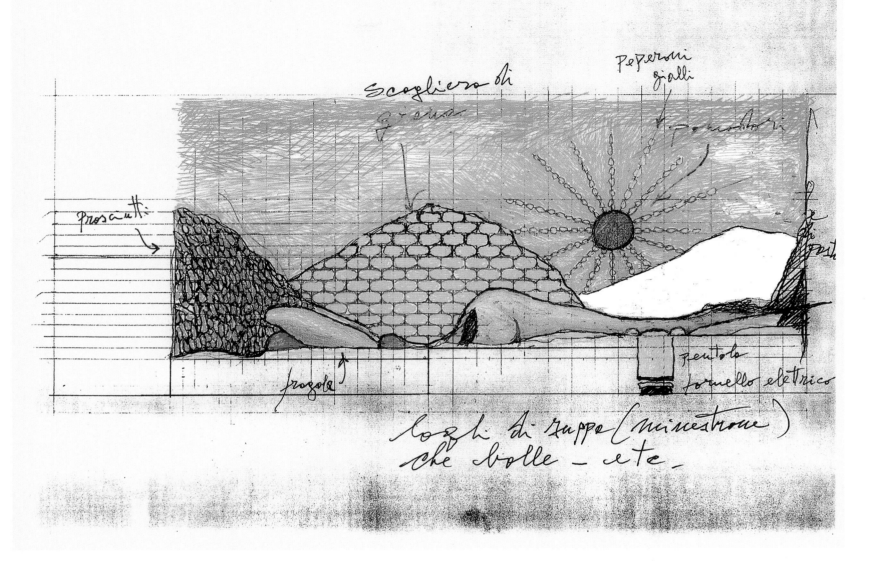

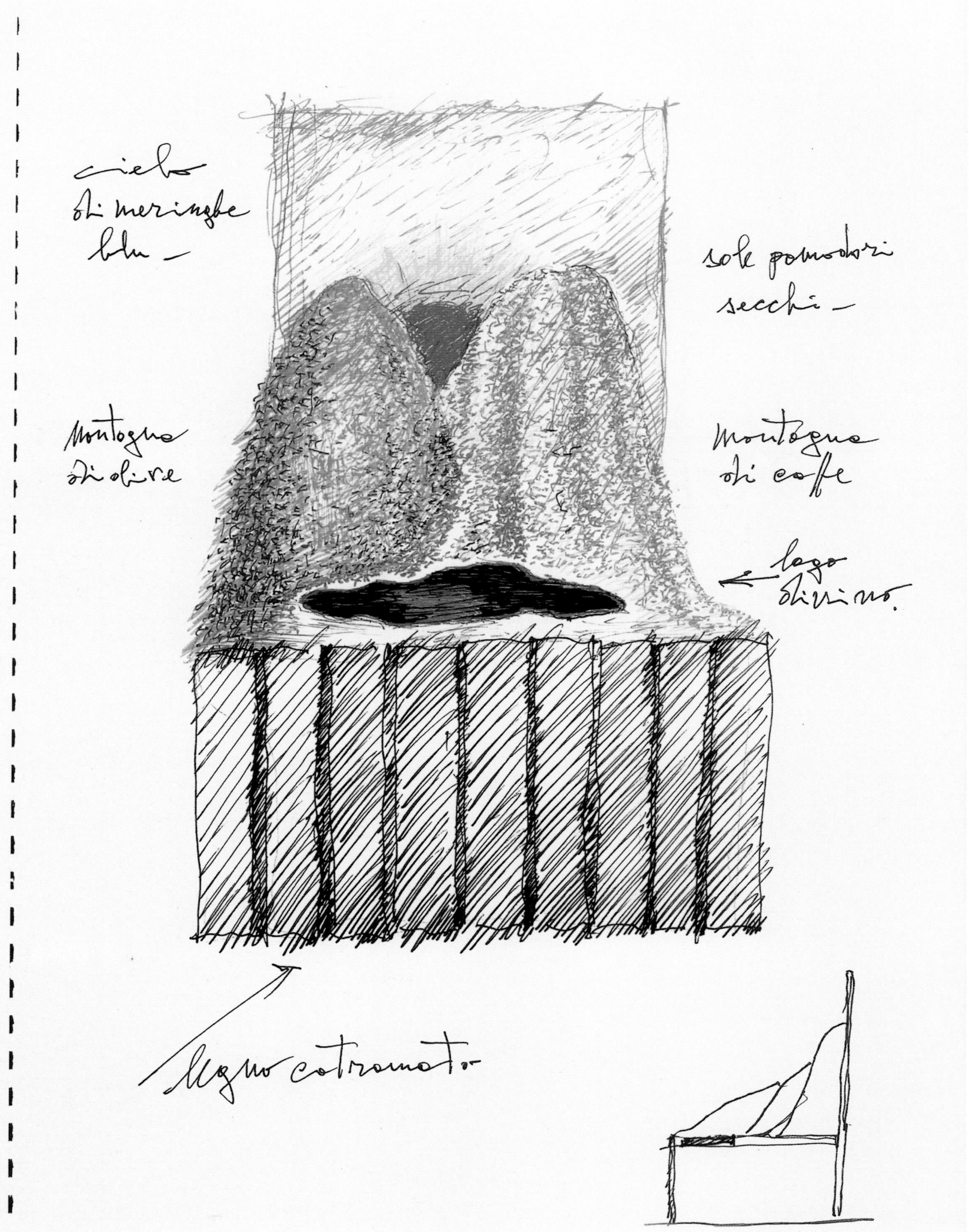

cielo
di meringhe
blu —

sole pomodori
secchi —

Montagne
di olive

Montagne
di caffè

← lago
divino.

legno cotramoto

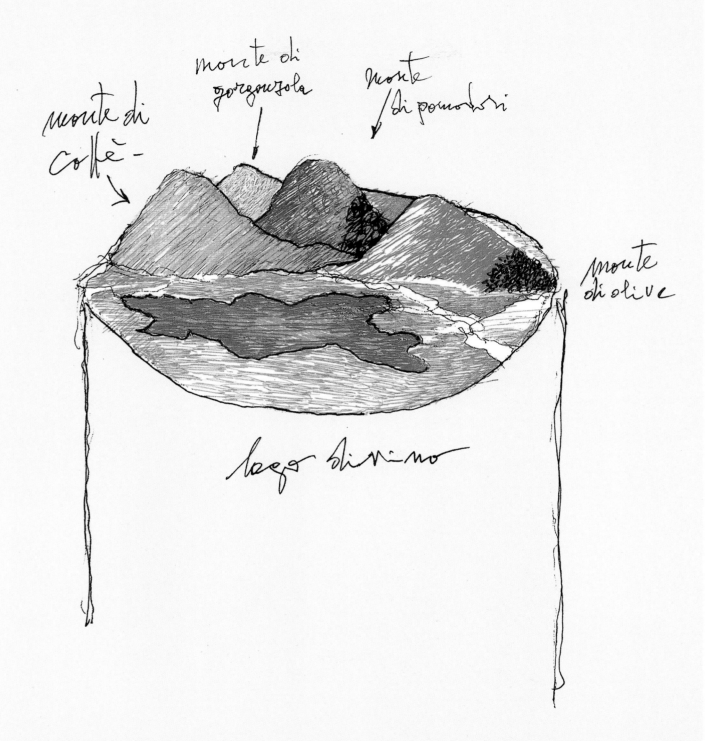

monte di
gorgonzola

monte
di pomodori

monte di
caffè-

monte
di olive

lago di vino

il soffitto dello spazio ?

grande
vestito di spaghetti
alla salsa di
pomodoro —

Poltrona di spaghetti
secchi—

Alberi?

la Torre del profumo delicato della caciotta "fresca"

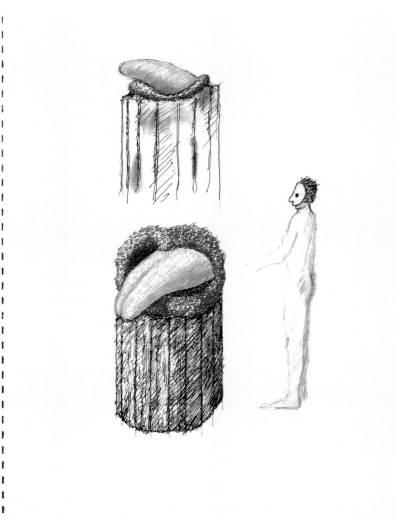

V. Allegory

by Pier Luigi Pizzi
video-installations
by Enrico Ghezzi

Exchange of letters between Pier Luigi Pizzi and Luigi Settembrini

Concerning the fifth nucleus of *Made in Italy?*, which the curator wanted to represent as a triumphal allegory of design and fashion of the decade between 1991 and 2001.

Translator's note: Blob *is a nightly TV programme which takes an ironic view of itself, politicians and society in general as presented on TV in the previous 24 hours.*

Valencia, 5th October 2000

Dear Pigi,

Congratulations as ever. The show was at once moving and entertaining, a great pleasure. I'm very happy I came to see you in Madrid!

Yesterday evening, when I asked whether you would be willing to collaborate with our exhibition, producing the finale (and I confirm that it should be a sort of triumph of the last ten years of *made in Italy*), I had the sensation that the theme, although it might interest you in a general way, worried you because of the lack of humour that afflicts not so much design as fashion. I think, however, that an interpretation of that world, provided by your intelligent and elegant hand (and a rightful, indeed perhaps even required, dose of irony) would provide just the non-stately and non-self-referential celebration which we need and are seeking.

All the best
Luigi

Venice, 15th October 2000

Dear Luigi,

You asked me for an ALLEGORY that depicts design and fashion design with reference to the last decade of the 20th century in Italy. I have first of all to overcome the natural ALLERGY that I get every time I think in terms of commemorative enumerations.

I try to restore an *ALLEGRO* mood by finding a symbol that is simple, direct, fast, the fastest, one that draws in, is full of emotion, stimulating, triumphal on the stage of the WORLD. I think I've found it: it is called FERRARI F1. The only other thing that springs to mind is *BLOB*. Therefore, I ask you to obtain the assistance of ENRICO GHEZZI for me. You wanted a galop for the end-of-millennium EXCELSIOR BALL: is this it?

My warmest regards
Pier Luigi

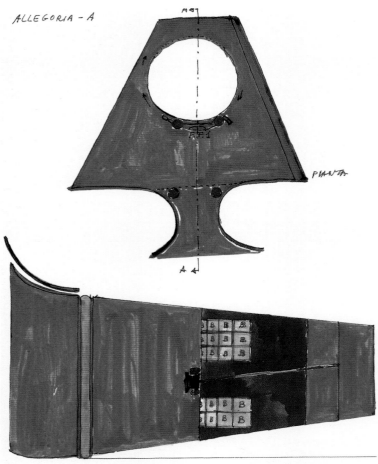

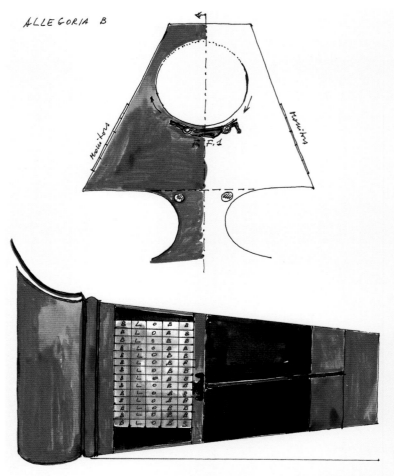

Luigi Settembrini e Franco Laera
skira @ skira.it
da Pier Luigi Pizzi

Venezia 2.2001

Cari amici,
tra i tanti progetti di Allegoria – Made – in – Italy elaborati,
ne ho scelti due, che vi mando. Vogliamo parlarne
insieme? Da domani sono reperibile a Londra per i
prossimi dieci giorni. Aspetto di sentirvi.
Grazie. Cari saluti da fra luigi ———

Progetto ALLEGORIA . Ingresso all' Implurium della Triennale

The History   *edited by Guido Vergani*

Design and fashion: driving forces of Italy

Rinaldo Gianola

*The work of small and mid-sized industry
(photo: Aldo Ballo)*

Made in Italy is not a mental category, but blood, sweat and tears. It is the woman in Carpi who has set up a knitwear factory in the space under the staircase; it is the furniture maker from the Brianza who goes round the world selling his sofas, perhaps without even being able to speak a foreign language; it is the firm in the Veneto that "subcontracts" for one of the big names. I still seem to hear ringing in my ears the words of the Minister of Industry, a capable man with a caustic tongue who, a few years ago, perhaps fed up with a sleepy discussion, electrified his audience of manufacturers with the real, concrete and palpable image of the locomotive of the national economy. There can be no doubt: if Italy did not have its furniture and fashion industries it would not be one of the leading economic powers in the world. Instead of participating in the G8 summits, our country would be limping along behind, in a reserve position.

The figures, seemingly so dry and cold, are in this case highly significant, explaining the rapid growth of what has probably been the most dynamic part of the Italian economy since the war. At the end of the nineties the turnover in the textile and clothing sector was around 90 trillion lire ($ 46 billion), and that of the wood and furnishing sector around 64 trillion ($ 33 billion). The trade balance is substantially in surplus for both sectors: 24,300 billion lire for textiles and clothing, 10,220 billion lire for furniture. Fabrics, clothes and furniture make an overall contribution to Italy's balance of trade of over 34 trillion lire (1999). These sectors, in fact, are redoubtable exporters: in 1999 we sold fabrics and garments to the rest of the world to a value exceeding 44 trillion lire, and furniture worth 17 trillion.

Historically, the boom in production and exports dates back to the eighties, a phenomenon that was probably favoured by a combination of factors, including the low level of the exchange rate for the lira, the proliferation of new entrepreneurs, the development of innovative products and a greater readiness on the part of industry to seek markets abroad. Of course, even before this Italian products had found a market in the world, but it was in the eighties that the country's approach to exportation became systematic and started to constitute an articulate and solid creative and industrial complex. In the space of just ten years, from 1981 to 1991, *made in Italy* changed its aspect and dimensions completely: the turnover in the textile and clothing sector tripled over the decade from 24,527 billion to 74,000 billion, while that of wood and furniture leaped from 6780 to over 45,000 billion. A true revolution that overtook companies, stylists, designers, markets and employees alike. At the end of the nineties these sectors employed over a million people (about 700,000 in the textile and clothing sector, 400,000 in that of wood and furniture), i.e. a quarter of the total number of people working in the entire manufacturing sector in Italy.

So the size of the economic and industrial contribution made by fashion and furnishing to the balance of Italy Inc. is decisive: the generation of resources, profits, ideas and jobs by these sectors probably has no parallel in other areas of production. The success of the enterprise, products and industrial organisation of these activities, synonymous with *made in Italy*, has set its mark on the postwar period, fueled the economic miracle and changed, in a continuous and unpredictable metamorphosis, the taste, style and social behaviour of Italians and of consumers all over the world. To be sure, fashion and furniture, with their families of entrepreneurs, with their inventories of products and trends, with their stylists and architects, with their design and magazines, with the Triennale and the RIMA (acronym of the Riunione Italiana Mostre for l'Arredamento, or Italian Union of Furnishing Shows, which operated from the end of the war up until 1953), with their extremely active trade associations, with the Chamber of Fashion and the COSMIT, were the very essence, the constituent and irreplaceable element of that "Italian road to capitalism" described years ago in a famous report by the British journal *The Economist*. Today we can say that this entrepreneurial philosophy, this original marriage between the individuality of the craftsman and mass production on an industrial scale, has permitted the economic emancipation of the country through the formation of an entrepreneurial class conscious of its responsibilities and the diffusion of a network of enterprises throughout the territory, from the areas specialising in a single product, masters of flexibility and innovation that have been studied for years by the Americans and Japanese, to the creation of true economic groupings with an international reputation and dimension.

Back in the fifties and to an even greater extent in the following decade, the Italy Inc. of small and medium-sized enterprises had realised the need for decentralisation of production and put it into effect, in broad outlines anticipating the so-called "de-localisation" of the global economy. The nature of the economic miracle, of Italy's transformation from a predominantly agricultural country into an industrial power, should not be identified solely with the Fiat of Mirafiori or the Pirelli of the Bicocca, with the factories of the great concentrations of workers, but also, and perhaps above all, with the towns of the dynamic Italian provinces, from Prato to Castel Goffredo, from Montebelluna to Agordo, from Biella to Carpi, from Brianza to Sassuolo, training grounds of an authentic spirit of enterprise, of an artisan and industrial creativity, champions of the "just-in-time" approach years ahead of the various Japanese or European versions of the "integrated factory" and, to put it more simply, expressions of the intuition and determination of *made in Italy*".

Few economic phenomena are as typically Italian as the furniture and fashion industries. These two sectors have many points in common: they are frequently similar in their origins, in their control and management by families, in their dimensions, in their capacity for innovation and in their aggressive attitude toward markets. But, as often happens to brothers who at one and the same time resemble each other greatly and not at all, even these bastions of the Italian economy diverge in other important aspects. According to a certain received wisdom in journalistic and academic circles that has become widely accepted with the passing of the years, fashion is individualistic and imaginative, while the furniture industry is well planned and organised. The former fosters the ephemeral, the dream, the illusion, in step with the very short time span of a show, the rapid succession of the seasons or a bombastic advertising campaign. Furniture, on the other hand, partly because of its intrinsically material character, represents solidity of enterprise; it is the expression of an established culture that evolves through the efforts of architects and designers, and of specialised magazines.

Fashion, according to some commentators, is "chaotic" and "anarchic," relying more on self-government than on organisation and driven by an *élan vital* of Bergsonian memory that infects stylists and manufacturers alike. Fashion, again, flouts the traditional model of enterprise based on the centrality of material aspects and of the factory, replacing it by the direct and preferred management of such immaterial functions as design, image, brand and marketing. In the wood-furniture-furnishing sector, on the contrary, it is not possible to do without direct control of the production process and the factory maintains its predominant role. At the most, the functions of communication and advertising can be delegated to outside agencies.

Distinctions, differences and similarities are important to understanding the origins, evolution and operation of this fundamental part of the economy and society. But, in any case, there is nothing new under the sun: we Italians are all children of the crafts. We were artisans before we became industrialists and we are following a track that was beaten long ago. We have a long history and a rich culture. Were not the Futurists the first to idealise and manipulate objects in common use and consumer goods, cars and clothes, furniture and real estate? It is highly likely, as sociologists and economists have pointed

out in the past, that fashion and furniture found themselves on the same tracks, after the war, and that their explosive growth was fueled by the progressive refinement, and expansion, of consumption. In other words, as often happens in these cases, distinctions are fine for discussions, as a basis for theory, whereas everyday practice and reality are more simple: they are rooted in work and commitment, in ideas and people. Just as they always have been over half a century of *made in Italy*.

Ever since that summer of 1947, when an Italy still bleeding from the wounds of the war saw the inauguration of the Triennale, indeed of the "proletarian Triennale" as it was called at the time because, in keeping with the dramatic character of the times, the only question tackled was that of housing, the "most real, most deeply felt, most dramatic problem, the object of anxiety, of desire and of hope for millions of Europeans", as the presentation of the exhibition put it. Certainly, in those years of hardship and American aid, between Popular Fronts and Civic Committees, the question of furnishing was reduced to a minimum, given that there were not enough houses and those that there were showed no obvious signs of modernity and comfort. At the beginning of the fifties only 10 percent of Italian dwellings had a bathroom. Yet it was in those very days that the foundations were laid for the country's rebirth.

A few figures will help us to grasp the nature and dimensions of the growth in the furniture industry. In the 1951 census the total number of households in Italy was 11,411,000; by 1991 they had become 25,029,000; the number of rooms, over the same period, had increased from 37,342,000 to 104,152,000 and the percentage of people who owned their own homes had risen from 40 to 69 percent. The growth in domestic consumption, therefore, became a driving and decisive factor in the success of the furniture-furnishing sector, which was coupled, later, with the boom in exports first to the European Community and then to the whole of the world. Here is a significant figure: in 1951 the amount of money spent on furniture in Italy was 120 billion; in current lire, this had risen to 2278 billion by 1976, a growth of 1892 percent.

As soon as the world war was over, the country's entrepreneurial and creative fabric was laboriously brought back into operation, proposing initiatives and devising innovations that were to translate into lasting successes over the course of the years. An example: the Kartell company was created as far back as 1949; the idea for it came from Giulio Castelli – a student under Giulio Natta, later to win the Nobel Prize, at the Milan Polytechnic – who saw the new materials and new technologies as an ideal territory to be explored by the Italian school of design. In this setting, at that extraordinary laboratory which was the Olivetti company in Ivrea, products were developed like the Lexicon 80 (1948) and then the Lettera 22 (1950), typewriters that earned themselves a place in New York's Museum of Modern Art of New York as expressions of Italian industrial culture. And then, in a historic sequence, Italians were to use and love such popular symbols of the country's rebirth as the Lambretta, the Vespa, the Cinquecento, the Giulietta and the rounded refrigerators of the Fumagalli brothers.

Similar innovations were taking place on the fashion front. In the February of 1951 Marchese Giovanni Battista Giorgini, armed with nothing more than his determination and experience, organised a show of garments by a small group of couturiers at his own home, Villa Torrigiani in Florence, in front of an audience of a few foreign journalists and buyers from a number of American department stores. These were the first cries of a newborn baby that was to grow up quickly. So many people wanted to attend the next parade, staged in July, that it was moved to the city's Gran Hotel and, in July 1952, to Palazzo Pitti, one of the emblems of the fashion world. It was the beginning of the great awakening. Mussolini had tried to break the monopoly of French fashion with the Fascist concept of autarky, ordering the couturiers not to copy Parisian models. In the postwar years Italian women, in spite of the scarcities with which they were faced, revived their taste for dressing up and tried to make do with whatever they could lay their hands on. As they did so, however, they discovered Italian fashion growing up around them, with limited economic means and extraordinary talent.

It is in Florence that we can find the exemplary metaphor of Italian fashion: that of Guccio Gucci, the leather craftsman who founded the most fractious dynasty in the sector and initiated one of the most resounding successes in the story of *made in Italy*. Starting life as a craft workshop and ending up a synonym for luxury and elegance, Gucci has survived decades of quarrels, diasporas and family tragedies. Over the last twenty years it has faced the risk of bankruptcy and then the piecemeal sale of its stock by the heirs. At a certain point it came under the control of Arab capital in the form of Investcorp, which made a killing by floating the company on the Amsterdam and New York stock exchanges. Today Gucci is a Dutch-owned company, run by a lawyer of Calabrian origin, Domenico De Sole, and a Texan stylist with a name that could have come right out of a Western, Tom Ford. The venture has become one of the richest and most prestigious labels on the international fashion market, to the extent that – so the story goes – two such champions of French capitalism as Francois Pinault and Bernard Arnault declared war on each other in an attempt to take it over.

In the fifties, Italian furniture commenced the transition from a craft to an industry. This was in part due to the revival of the great shipping companies. Italians recalled that they were a people of navigators and the ship-owning families found themselves at the heart of economic power. Angelo Costa was elected president of the Confindustria, the Italian Manufacturers' Association. The age of the transatlantic liner and the cruise ship transformed the suppliers of one-off pieces into manufacturers on an industrial scale who were able to combine mass production with high-quality materials, tight delivery schedules and the prestige of the designer and the label. And so figures like Cesare Cassina, Osvaldo and Fulgenzio Borsani, Sergio Cammilli, Dino Gavina, Roberto Poggi and Carlo Molteni arrived on the scene. Arflex was formed, the product of an extraordinary pairing between a traditional manufacturer like Pirelli, which made foam rubber and elastic belts, and the architect Marco Zanuso. These were the years in which the areas specialising in the production of furniture took shape. In the Northeast, for example, there were Maurizio Tosi and Fantoni, the Snaidero of kitchens that took on Salvarani of Parma and Aurelio Boffi of the Brianza.

Furniture, furnishing and fashion were part of the history, the social and economic changes, the shifting patterns of behaviour of the sixties, those fabulous and terrific years of the boom. In Italian politics, it was the decade of the centre-left, while economically the period was marked by the nationalisation of electric power. The world experienced the Cold War and Vietnam, the emergence of the Beatles and the miniskirt and the beginning of the conquest of space. We Italians did some great things. At Aswan in Egypt, we built the most modern dam in the world. Milan and Naples were finally linked by the expressway known as the Autostrada del Sole. Milan saw the inauguration of its subway, the first modern work of urban infrastructure in Italy. There was even a pope, John XXIII, of great humanity and boundless popularity. Fashion and furnishing followed the exhilarating course of this river in full flood. In 1961 the Salone del Mobile, or Furniture Show, made its debut, going on to become a true international showcase for *made in Italy*, as well as a means of creating a synthesis between the industrial, organisational and cultural requirements of the sector.

The Salone del Mobile set out to represent the creative vivacity of design and industry at a moment when they were able to exploit new ways of thinking, such as the overcoming of the sharp distinction between the "plain" and the "luxurious", employing new materials and making use of efficient production processes. Among others, there had been the groundbreaking work of Gio Ponti for Cassina and Marco Zanuso for Borletti and Brionvega. These were followed by the lines designed by Magistretti for Artemide and by Zanotta's Sacco, symbols of the evolution, especially in the industrious Brianza region, of a craft, or perhaps we should say an art, that would lead to an industrialisation combining advanced technical solutions with companies of modest size. The sixties saw the foundation of C&B, i.e. Cassina and Busnelli, later to become B&B, i.e. Busnelli and Banche, the emergence of Driade and the shift of a manufacturer like Acerbis from the production of period furniture to experimenting with modern designs. Masters of lighting appeared, such as Gino and then Riccardo Sarfatti, and Sergio Gandini with Flos. So this was the period in which Italian companies, especially those in the sectors of textiles and clothing and of furniture, set out to show that they were capable of "opening up to the world" as Raffaele Mattioli, legendary head of the Banca Commerciale, put it. Mattioli viewed this infectious explosion of ideas and initiatives as the international affirmation "of the natural talent and genius of our people". The story goes that a congenial private club for millionaires passing through the quiet British colony of Hong Kong was furnished exclusively with Italian furniture of the highest quality and that, almost by accident, its lounges turned into a grand showroom for our furniture industry.

If the sixties saw the definitive revival of the economy and a rapid industrial development that created jobs and revenue, but also immigration, social tensions and discrimination, the following decade coincided with the first major restructuring of Italy Inc. The double whammy of the oil shock, first following the Arab-Israeli Yom Kippur war and then as a consequence of the Islamic revolution in Iran, forced the industrialised economies of the West to rationalise their manufacturing processes, to cut costs and diversify their sources of energy, which had hitherto appeared almost free, and to increase their competitiveness. Italy smarted as inflation grew, along with the public debt, and industry cut jobs. The "years of the bullets", as that period of conflict and terrorism came to be known, were truly difficult, especially in comparison with the happy-go-lucky sixties, but it was during this time of crisis that the traditional strong points of the furniture and furnishing industry were reinforced through opportune reorganisation.

In spite of the overall difficulties faced by the economy, the sector maintained and strengthened its fundamental characteristics: small companies, flexibility of production, an emphasis on design. Concentrated in three main areas, the Brianza, the Triveneto and the province of Pesaro, the furniture industry found the magic formula of its growth in the direct relationship between the designer and the entrepreneur and between the factory that produced the goods and the diffuse network of workshops and craftsmen that provided designs, materials and ideas. In these years an ever more important role was played by the Salone del Mobile, which made up for one of the system's shortcomings, i.e. the low level of investment in promotion and advertising, by providing an international showcase for this Italian product. The other main shortcoming was the limited commercial capacity.

This was not a glorious time for our industry. And yet these years saw the germination of ventures that were to achieve success and popularity on the mass market for clothing and furniture and the emergence of the very fashion designers who, in the eighties, would become the champions of *made in Italy*, representatives not just of a highly profitable business but also of a typically Italian creativity that was to take foreign markets by storm. They saw the birth of the phenomenon of Benetton, a truly international Italian name, and, on the other front, the emergence of Natuzzi who, starting out from the sofa-making region of Bari and Matera, ended up on Wall Street. Rosario Messina's Flou struck root, inventing the "textile-bed" to overcome the opposition of furniture

stores that did not want to sell duvets. And then came the opulent eighties. Everything was fashion, everything had a designer label. Things went to such an extreme that designers had to be called in even to sell spaghetti. It seemed like something straight out of Thorstein Veblen's illuminating, and venomous, *Theory of the Leisure Class*, in which he talks about extreme wealth and "conspicuous consumption". But the excesses, probably an inevitable part of any new wave of creativity and enterprise, were not sufficient to break the toy.

Stylists and clothes, designers and furniture, all fostered myths and models, but beyond the image, the ephemeral, the publicity, there was also the concrete reality of a formidable economic undertaking. *Made in Italy* became a collective industry and its mission was expansion throughout the world, not just into the traditional markets of Europe and America, but also in Japan and the Far East. And it was in the eighties, at a time when the triumph of Italian fashion was making headlines and the former employee of La Rinascente, Giorgio Armani, ended up on the cover of *Time*, the national furniture industry rose to the top of the list of world exporters, overtaking Germany, thanks to a model of creativity and production that was by now well established and highly efficient, and to the appearance of new and highly active economic groups. The sector's propensity for experimentation found expression in research into innovative materials – glass, aluminum, plastics – and their application, and in the generation of new projects like Memphis, the invention of Ernesto Gismondi and Ettore Sottsass.

In the world of fashion, behind the figures of Armani, Ferré, Valentino, Versace, Krizia and Missoni, acknowledged as the masters of this late twentieth-century "Renaissance", lay not just ideas and sketches, but also factories and workers. The stylist went hand in hand with industry. The creator sought reliable partners who would impart value and industrial substance to his or her inventions. The parade, the publicity campaign, the top model, the glossy magazine covers were useful, and how! But more was needed.

Armani bought the traditional manufacturer SIMINT and worked with GFT. Ferré linked up with Marzotto and then ended up being taken over by a dynamic neophyte of the industry, It Holding, which had already produced the youth lines of Versace and others. Valentino was taken over by HDP, a large holding company with diversified interests (from the *Corriere della Sera* to Fila). Evidence for the continuing vitality of the sector has been provided by the emergence, even in very recent years, of previously unknown names and the success of groups like Dolce & Gabbana and Prada.

Made in Italy, at the turn of the millennium, is changing its dimensions and updating its strategies. Small is still beautiful, to be sure. But bigger is better. At the end of the nineties the process of concentration of fashion houses and businesses accelerated, with mergers and takeovers at astronomical prices the order of the day. In the era of globalisation, labels have a worldwide reach or nothing. To finance the huge investments required, companies are turning to the stock market, even at the risk of shattering the original, sound even if not always pacific, family dimension. Italian fashion accounts for a fifth of the entire world market. Milan stands out not just as the capital of design, but also of industrial innovation. The city attracts stylists and designers from all over the world, and in the process has been transformed into a multicultural "school". And the contribution of the wood and furnishing sector is still fundamental, not just for the balance of trade: the constant interest in experimentation with advanced materials, the use of sophisticated technologies and the development of new manufacturing processes all confirm the vitality of a solid entrepreneurial structure that is able to find in the past and in tradition the resources and ideas it needs for the future. But those who stand still are lost, and modernization continues. *Made in Italy* is already on the Internet, the new frontier.

Italian design: elements of history

Vanni Pasca

The 1950s: in Milan the Pirelli skyscraper was built (1955-56), a symbol of the post-war reconstruction of Italy and of the new role of the city in a country that was on the way to becoming industrialised and modern. The architect was Gio Ponti, a professor in the Architecture faculty at Milan University. Cassina, a company with an artisan tradition that was beginning to produce furniture industrially, asked Gio Ponti to design a chair (1957). The *Superleggera* was born, quickly becoming famous as a symbol for Italian design and the country's new modernity.

The 1990s: Milan has become the base for great, world-renowned designers such as Achille Castiglioni, Vico Magistretti and Ettore Sottsass, for trade fairs such as the *Salone del Mobile* and *Smau*, for universities and design schools, and for specialist magazines. It has become the city for design, the point of reference for design-oriented companies and for designers all over the world who come here to exhibit and become known to the media but above all to Italian industries.

Italian design between these two periods is complex due to the multiplicity of paths it took and the variety of styles and proposals that make up the story: these notes do not claim to be a history but will focus on some issues considered essential by the writer.

From reconstruction to the economic boom

In 1946, less than two years after the end of the war, two magazines, *Lo Stile nella casa e nell'arredamento*, which Gio Ponti founded in 1940, and *Domus*, managed at that time by Ernesto Nathan Rogers, were committed to mobilising the architecture culture to focus on the country's reconstruction.

Both magazines launched a debate against "reproduction furniture", a term used to refer to the continuation of the eclecticism of 19th-century historical styles that dominated production and the market at the time. The debate was continued with vigour by the design culture over the years that followed. *Lo Stile*, on a page of large typeface, ironically wrote, "too many producers and consumers exist, incredibly, for the most incredible style (such as that of *Chippendale...* or *Cantù*)".

It was in this atmosphere that a number of important exhibitions were held. In 1946 *Rima* (Italian Conference for Furniture Exhibitions) organised a show on the theme of low-cost furniture at the Triennial building, where the architecture culture had conducted many experiments in the 1930s. In 1948 many of the best Italian architects who were either young or already famous, such as Albini, Castiglioni, Gardella, Magistretti, Zanuso and others, took part in an exhibition in Milan organised by Fede Cheti, creator of furniture fabrics. The furniture presented in the show can be linked to the support for rationalism and an attempt to translate it into an artisan production situation. As a whole, it was a declaration of almost ostentatious modesty, a distinct preference for simplicity and sobriety; this was a reference not only to the rejection of "reproduction" furniture, but also of the laboured refinement of "20th-century style".

In the second half of the 1940s, the most significant changes and the most interesting designs addressed the problem of transport. The reconstruction of the railway network gave rise to the legendary *Settebello* (1949), where Minoletti, inspired by the great American trains of the 1930s, moved the driver's car above the carriages, allowing the end carriages to become observation cars. He furnished these with swivel armchairs according to a design, later abandoned, which raised the theme of relations between passengers during travel.

In the same period, with the reconversion of companies from war production to civil production, Piaggio and Innocenti respectively introduced, with the *Vespa* and the *Lambretta*, a new typology – the scooter – which became an icon of Italian design throughout the world. It passed many generations, transforming from an economic vehicle for transport to work to a vehicle for women and the young. It was reborn in the 1980s, created in versions that were also stylistically reinvented in other countries.

La first modernity

In Italy in the 1950s certain events can be identified which, acting on each other, defined the development of design in the following decades. Three factors in particular require brief analysis.

1. Firstly, certain developments in progress were profoundly transforming and modernising the socio-economic orientation of the country. Industrialisation was progressing; emigration from south to north, and from the countryside to the city, was taking place; with the increase in the average wage, purchasing power increased, the standard of living rose and consumption grew. The picture of daily life changed with the motorization of the masses, electrical appliances and television. The Italians, following the *Vespa* and the *Lambretta*, began purchasing the *600* and then the *500*, both designed by Dante Giacosa (who had earlier designed the *Topolino* for Fiat in the 1930s). The sleek, aerodynamic coffee machine *Pavoni*, designed by Gio Ponti, appeared in bars, substituting earlier coffee machines with vertical boilers. In the home, old pedal sewing machines, often made of cast iron with floral motifs, were replaced by small electric sewing machines resembling abstract sculptures. An example was the *Mirella* designed by Marcello Nizzoli, who also designed the *Lettera 22*, the portable typewriter that later became an icon in the era of journalism. Castiglioni transformed the image of the vacuum cleaner, creating a small, light object, polished and coloured, that was made of nylon. Gino Colombini designed a series of objects in plastic, which were also light and coloured, and which substituted galvanised sheet-metal buckets and tubs in the home. There was an increase in the demand for technical goods, from the refrigerator and the washing machine to the television. And in relation to "whitegoods", Italy became the leading producer in Europe in a short time, mainly by forming small businesses that aggressively appeared on the market and collaborated with designers. As a consequence the home and the way it was organised changed, starting with the bathroom and the kitchen. Ponti and Zanuso designed sanitary objects having rounded and continuous contours (the internal bathroom gradually became the standard). The same Zanuso designed refrigerators and "American-style" modular kitchens (as they were called at that time as American films strongly influenced lifestyles), but also armchairs in which foam-rubber substituted the springs of the upholsterer, paving the way for research into new materials for the industrialisation of furniture.

2. The demand for modern furnishings also began to emerge, in opposition to the traditional home. At the time in certain areas of Italy there were a number of small artisan businesses, such as carpenter's workshops with few employees, that were beginning to mechanise production. In a short period of time they transformed into small-to-medium small, family-run, industrial companies in a sector that would continue to maintain a highly fragmentary nature. A number of these entrepreneurial carpenters, in the Brianza area in particular, sensed the growing demand for furniture by Italians who aspired to a home that expressed their adherence to modernity, intended as civil progress or, if nothing else, as a status symbol. These were the same Italians who were purchasing a car, electrical appliances and the television, and who desired a home that represented their having forgotten a largely agricultural country with its static life patterns. They were resourceful entrepreneurs who wanted their companies to propose goods able to respond to the demands of an evolving market. As a group they wanted to successfully participate in the new modernity that was already present in America and Europe and developing in Italy. They

gambled on the fact that a real market would open up for the modern piece of furniture, machine produced in relatively large series; the gamble paid off because in the following years the Italian home changed enormously with respect to traditional models. Having a modern house, with a bathroom, electrical appliances, television and modern furniture, became a symbol for supporting a new attitude typical of an industrial and urban society, especially in northern Italy. The spread of modern furniture increased gradually but constantly, modifying the preceding situation that was characterised by the strong consumption of "reproduction" furniture.

3. These entrepreneurs were innovative and risk-taking people; they invested in new markets but they lacked the necessary know-how to confront such a process of change: they required knowledge of which people could help them understand which products to offer this new desire for modernity. For this reason, as they travelled throughout Europe purchasing machinery to work wood or acquiring knowledge of new plastic materials, they sought out designers capable of designing the objects of the new modernity. These entrepreneurs, especially those in areas such as the Brianza district, gravitated to the Milan of the Triennial, the Pirelli skyscraper and the faculty of Architecture. In Milan there was a generation of architects that during the Fascist era had looked to European countries for avant-garde art, modern architecture and that professional practice baptised design, which had had as its epicentre a German school of the 1920s, the legendary Bauhaus. These architects, as far back as the 1930s, had tackled the subject of the form of technical objects, such as the radio, and of decor and metal furniture. Their roots lay in Italian rationalism, their point of reference was the Bauhaus experience, the work of Le Corbusier and also of the Viennese tradition, from Loos to Hoffmann. Following the war they carefully observed the work of the great American designers, from Charles Eames to Florence Knoll, from Eero Saarinen to George Nelson, but also the simple and light-coloured wooden furniture from the Scandinavian countries, such as the work of Alvar Aalto or Kaare Klint. The theme of the house, of furniture and of modern decor was strongly felt, due to the fact that the reconstruction of the country was in progress, and also because the theme of lifestyle was given specific theoretical and moral importance in the context of a

tradition that saw architects of differing tendencies come together. As Rogers wrote, furniture and town planning "are the extreme polarities of the activity of a modern architect". Moreover, in the 1930s some of the best known architects had a means of experimenting with the modern idea of the home, sometimes in designs of houses for the *haute bourgeoisie*, but above all in designing experimental homes for exhibitions at the Milan Triennial.

At the 10th Triennial of 1954 Caccia Dominioni, Gardella, Magistretti and others curated the *Mostra dello "standard"*, aimed at demonstrating the "possibilities that open up to those who use range furniture in the home ". These were the same people, Italian and foreign, who presented work in the earlier section *Mostra del mobile singolo*, curated by Albini, the Valles and others. In 1960 in the 12th Triennial a range of objects appeared designed by Castiglioni, Zanuso, Tobia Scarpa and Magistretti that reflected mature professional skills that could form a rapport with the nascent furniture industry.

In this situation, entrepreneurs and architect-designers met and in some cases formed partnerships that lasted in time. The designer often took on the role of consultant; he or she would also have some expertise in marketing and be an art director to some extent, in addition to the obvious role of designer. The designer generally collaborated with companies that on the whole were too small to have staff in any real sense. The company owner was often a strongly dynamic person, so much so that often he became a designer. However, he was often too much of a centralist to establish a focussed relationship other than with a person he felt possessed the charisma of an exponent of a culture recognised by modernity, such as that of architecture and design. A special relationship between designer and technical staff within the factory also ensued from this; these technical people were often from a modern technical culture that had not lost contact with a sophisticated artisan tradition, typical of pre-war joinery and structural carpenters' workshops. Moreover, Italian design culture perceived that interior design was breaking away from both the art deco tradition and the historicism of 19th-century eclecticism. At the same time, though, it rejected, in large measure, the break with the history of 20th century avant-garde culture; on the contrary, it committed itself to a re-reading and re-interpretation of the typologies and the tradition of lifestyle.

The convergence of these elements – the modernisation of the country, the development of the production of technical goods, the transformation in an industrial sense of furniture production, the architect-designer – led to the development of Italian design. It was a dynamic design culture founded on modernising technology and production, typological experimentation and the reproduction, at times almost excessive, of models and images.

4. There is a further important aspect to this issue: together with the development of design culture, the extraordinary skills of Italian industry, in particular that of the furniture industry, unfolded. These skills included self-promotion, and together championing design as symbol of the new modernity via the creation of a series of initiatives that gradually formed into a solid and well-defined communications industry.

In Milan ADI was born (Association for Industrial Design, 1956), which represented a key moment in the battle for the success of industrial design and modern furniture over reproduction furniture. *La Rinascente* instituted a prize, the *Compasso d'Oro* (1954), which was later managed by ADI and which continues to this day. The Milan *Salone del Mobile* opened (1961). An overwhelming number of magazines were born, more or less directly financed by the furniture industry: a particularly interesting example is *Ottagono*, founded in 1967 by eight companies which were the most progressive at the time. In the first part it published modern architecture and design projects not attributed to the eight companies, and in the second part it published furniture designed for these projects, often by the same architects whose work appeared in the first part. The final part of the magazine indicated a select network of shops all over Italy that sold the pieces. Indeed, the role of the shop needs to be taken into consideration. Shops that sold the "modern" asserted their identity with shop-fittings often created by the very

same company designers, for whom they organised shows and conferences, resulting in the creation of a publicity network for the new aesthetic of modernity. This is how the relationship between company, designer, communications industry, distribution and market was forged, in a synergetic circuit that grew gradually over the years.

5. At the beginning of the 1960s Italian design was booming. It is important to highlight that the industrialisation of furniture was made possible chiefly through the introduction of new materials. For example, polyurethane allowed for the development of the stuffed furnishings sector, and with this some of the most successful designs of the time were born, such as the *Coronado* divan by Tobia Scarpa (1966) and the *Maralunga* divan by Vico Magistretti (1973). Plastic made a new generation of domestic objects possible, from the polythene baby's chair by Zanuso and Sapper (1964) to the *Selene* by Magistretti (1969). However, in 1973 the increase in petroleum prices, due to the Yom Kippur War, strongly limited the market potential for objects in plastic. Finally, in the 1970s, the use of chipboard to produce sectional modular furniture became more widespread. This grew from the desire to create true dividing walls (like the *Oikos* by Antonia Astori, 1973), but spread to furniture for all rooms of the house, from the wardrobe to the bookcase, resulting in the creation of a further large industrial sector. The 1960s also brought a strong development in the lighting industry, with some lamps becoming icons of the period, such as the *Arco* by the Castiglioni (1962), the *Eclisse* by Magistretti (1966) or *Tizio* (1972) by Richard Sapper. Design also reinvented gift goods with the objects of Enzo Mari.

Italian design however, was not only furniture and a few examples may be cited to demonstrate this. At the Centro Stile Fiat, Dante Giacosa worked and Giorgio Giugiaro began his career. Giacosa was the designer of

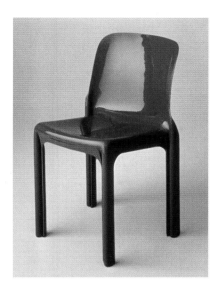

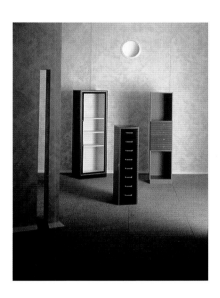

the *600* and the *500*; Giugiaro was the man who would design, among other things, the *Golf* (1974), which strongly contributed to the revival of the Volkswagen, and the *Fiat Panda* (1980). There was the Olivetti-Ettore Sottsass and Mario Bellini collaboration. There were the Brionvega radios and televisions of Marco Zanuso working for the Castiglionis. Notably, Zanuso in collaboration with Richard Sapper designed a telephone, the *Grillo* (1966), which did not achieve great success but which anticipated by decades the typology of the mobile telephone. Italian architect-designers created technical goods (automobiles, radios, televisions, typing machines, calculators, refrigerators etc.), and not only furniture. However, the 1970s introduced a series of problems in international competition for Italian companies producing technical goods. For example, Olivetti experienced continuing problems in shifting from mechanics to electronics. Brionvega, aiming at the aesthetic "plus" of design, became unaffordable because large international companies dominated the competition for electrical products. As a consequence, Italian designers became increasingly connected with the furniture, lighting and home goods sectors, and Italian design gradually came to signify a relationship between the designer, in the majority of cases an independent architect, and small-to-medium small companies producing furniture. The image of Italian design that prevailed in the mass media and in the collective imagination was increasingly tied to goods for the home. Moreover, as Vittorio Gregotti wrote, "Magistretti, Aulenti, Joe Colombo, Tobia Scarpa…and others, provide, with a brilliant quality for inventing, the elegance of plastic solutions, an authentic new culture of design for the home".

Of course the transformation of the home of Italians, from "reproduction" furniture to modern furniture, was considerable. In 1968 in Italy about 70 percent of consumption in the sector continued to be of furniture in the classical-traditional style; ten years later more than 60 percent of demand was directed to furniture in the modern style, that is, influenced by design. The early 1970s saw the gradual beginnings of an export industry accompanied by intense marketing activities aimed at achieving international success, which was surpassed only by that of fashion in the 1980s. And between 1973 and 1978, Italian exports of furniture increased strongly: the share of national production exported passed from 10 to 27 percent.

The explosion of complexity

Mention has already been made of the complexity of Italian design and of the multiplicity of paths it took. Stephen Leet in the *Harvard Design Magazine* (Summer 1998) wrote: "there are many icons which are symbolic of Italian design: the names Armani, Cinelli, Castiglioni, Ponti, Ferrari, Maserati, to name a few; the international status of Milan as the centre for fashion and design … In the 1960s it was the *Sacco* armchair, the red plastic Olivetti typewriter, inflatable furniture, and Dustin Hoffman's red Alfa Romeo spider in *The Graduate*".

This is an analysis coming from a particular monitor, in this case American. Nevertheless it is true that the image of Italian design outlined in this essay, and which continued in the 1980s with a clear market leadership, had found an alternative in the 1960s, above all in terms of the impact of its image. At the 1964 Venice Biennale pop art was introduced. It was born in England in the 1950s; there, for example, the sculptures of Paolozzi (totems with thick tiers, vivid colours, diverse materials) were created. These sculptures seem to anticipate, with their deliberately antithetical stylistic elements of thin walls, neutral tones and rationalist object compositions, the bookcases Sottsass produced in the early 1980s. In the 1960s, and still in England, these ideas continued with the Archigram group, that introduced into architecture the themes and strategies of the visual arts, proposing the acceptance of chaos and

the obsolescence of metropolitan culture. Pop art was developing in the USA, taking as its subject the everyday object, discarded and misshapen, and making reference to technological culture and popular new urban culture, comprising pinball machines, jukeboxes, comics and science fiction. The new perspective of the object asserted by Pop Art took shape in Italy in two ways. The first was that of radical design, or anti-design, which generated opposition to consumer society and the role orthodox design played within it. Improbable objects were designed that had aesthetic shock value and a political message; examples include the famous *Superonda* (1967) and *Safari* (1968) couches by Archizoom or the range of *Quaderna* tables (1971) by Superstudio. The other path was baptised pop design, and favoured irony, crowding-out, and play, and it produced some well-known objects: the *Blow* inflatable armchair and the *Joe* armchair shaped like a large baseball glove, both designed by De Pas, D'Urbino, Lomazzi (1967 and 1970); the *Sacco* armchair, filled with small polystyrene balls so that it took the shape of the person sitting in it (Gatti, Paolini, Teodoro 1969); the *Pratone* by Ceretti, Derossi, Rosso, members of the Strum Group (1970) where, as in many objects of the period, polyurethane was no longer used as upholstery but as a material able to take an independent shape (adopting the idea of the Castiglioni brothers for an armchair designed for an exhibition at Villa Olmo at Como in1957).

In 1972 a large exhibition was held at Moma in New York that had an important title: *Italy: The New Domestic Landscape*. In this show Italian design appeared in all its forms: rationalist design, pop design, anti-design, furniture, technical objects, technological utopias, automobiles, even leaflets that were a political protest regarding the housing shortage problem. It was the first clear appearance on the international stage of the unique phenomenon of Italian design, and it had an affect on many people both for its vitality and peculiar versatility.

The second modernity

The end of the 1970s saw the emergence of criticism of the "*grand récit*" (to use a then famous expression by Lyotard) of rationalist design.

In substance, the 1980s began in Italy under the mark of postmodernism, with two processes involved.

The first began with the foundation of the Alchimia office by Adriana and Alessandro Guerriero (1976), "the first example of designer producers … orientated towards the environmental and psychological study of objects (universal "kaleidoscope"), designing opportunities for the definition of a new theory of romantic design". 'Kaleidoscope' was a term traditionally used (for example by Gillo Dorfles) as a derogatory critique of departure from "good design", such as the American streamline style of the1930s. Here it was deliberately adopted as a program to follow and, in the same way, "romantic" really meant "anti-rationalist". This was supported by Ettore Sottsass and Alessandro Mendini; they designed an icon of this transition phase, the *Proust Armchair*. They projected colours onto an old reproduction armchair using the "*pointillistes*" technique (à la Signac).

A short time later Sottsass broke away from Alchimia and founded another group, Memphis (1981). With this group he designed furniture, objects, lamps, plates, glasses, but also radios, ties and so on, in a lucid and eclectic style, taking pleasure in the play of colours and the magical-ritual presence of the objects. It was an attempt to proclaim a new international style, a new "total work of art" in which art and life intertwine. The illusion was alive that "there can be, through drive and language, a happy and problem-free continuity" as Filiberto Menna wrote at the time.

On the other hand, Mendini believed that it was necessary to continue formulating, with conscious resolve to remain on the fringes, the relationship be-

*Achille and Pier Giacomo
Castiglioni*, Arco, Flos 1962
(photo: Aldo Ballo)

Richard Sapper, Tizio,
*Artemide, 1972
(photo: Aldo Ballo)*

Vico Magistretti, Eclisse,
Artemide, 1966

Archizoom, Superonda,
Poltronova, 1967

108

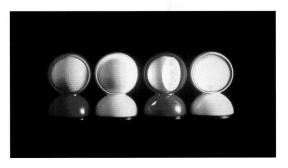

tween art and design. He continued with Alchimia, presenting objects nourished by linguistic contamination, in a type of "neo-futurism" which played on mixing quotes from real life, reviewing the historical avant-garde and images gathered from the mass media. And Mendini theorised the "pictorial design", a new "creative circle" of art and design, of designer-artist and artist-designer.

There was an attempt, therefore, to substitute the rationalist paradigm, accused of functionalist and scientist rigidity, with an opposing one, founded on art as a model, on artisan craft relating to the anti-industrial debate, and the resurfacing of important themes in 19th -century romantic culture. A number of principles were considered: the re-evaluation of emotions and feeling; irony as a response to the fall of the great *récits*; the elevation of the mystic and magical aspects of life; an idea of creativity as self-expression free of any restraints (from which the de-standardisation and de-functionalisation of the object derives); the reappraisal of the folk spirit of low-level language, with the revival of banal, kitsch, and urban language; the use of the open form, fragments, lyric poetry and a continuous working on language, cleansed though, of the pedagogic and political intentions present in the themes of the "linguistic break" and in the aesthetic shock of the century's avant-garde cultures.

In the background French hermeneutics theory was operating. It was influencing Italian philosophers such as Gianni Vattimo in relation to the decline of art in the general aestheticisation of existence authorised by the advent of electronic technology, the medium of that aesthetic experience as abstracted perception commented on by the German theorist of the 1930s Walter Benjamin.

In reality, next to these phenomena, which were all widely covered by the "mass media", the opposition to rationalism paved the way throughout the decade for a lively pluralism of language. The tendency, above all by young designers, was to look to art as a reference. But in fact it was not so much art, with its trends, its experimentation and its culture, that was made reference to. It was more the artist, interpreted as free translator of individual drives and unfettered by practical and communicative needs, artifice and subject of world aestheticisation as an extension of the dominion of the mass media discussed by so many philosophers.

With the coming of the 1980s, Italian fashion finally burst onto the scene. It was characterised by a unique designer-industry relationship, in which the designer was the major figure. A range of designers, in particular furniture designers, looked to fashion designers with the idea that even in design it was possible to put forward, for business, a new type of creative designer distinguished not so much by experimental quality or method as by a strong and media-recognisable presence.

It is important to keep in mind that a light company financed Memphis while a furniture company entrusted a collection to Mendini. In general, Italian industries were open to experimenting, both in the hope of renewing the victory Italy had had with rationalist design, and also in order to achieve image success on the international stage.

In reality, a second type of phenomenon that distinguished the decade was tied to the fact that globalisation began to be felt. Italian industries, already widespread on the national market, sought to secure overseas markets. In this context the formulation of new strategic lines emerged, which made reference to postmodernism chiefly in the sense of a new image and communication culture.

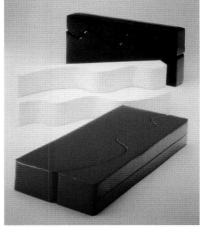

Alessi is a company that has existed for decades and produces normal tableware. At Alessi, as in many Italian companies, a new generation was taking over management. Under the guidance of Alessandro Mendini the *Tea and Coffee Piazza* collection was born: a range of silver objects in a very limited series, shown in galleries and museums all over the world. It comprised eleven dinner services conceived as buildings around a square, designed by architects (not only Italian), such as Charles Jencks, Michael Graves, Hans Hollein, Paolo Portoghesi, Robert Venturi and so on, and relating to a richly eclectic discourse of relations with history. In the meanwhile (1980) at the Venice Biennale Paolo Portoghesi presented, to great media publicity, the *Strada novissima*, a series of symbolic façades designed by postmodern architects. Alessi achieved enormous success with its publicity strategy, and became internationally synonymous with postmodern design in a period in which postmodern architects, with their "scandalous" anti-rationalist buildings, were creating a stir in non-specialist press throughout the world. This was followed by the production, throughout a decade, of a range of objects at a much more moderate price, from the coffee-pot by the Italian architect Aldo Rossi to the juicer by the French designer Philippe Starck. Rather more than daily use objects, they were conceived as gift goods, a new generation of knick-knacks, and were strong and immediately recognisable symbols.

As art director of Swatch from 1993, Mendini gave life to another winning strategy by designing an object at a deliberately low price. The new watch created by Swiss engineers to halt Japanese supremacy had styles gathered from the world of art. Gradually however, inspiration came from the imaginary worlds of the young generation, transforming an economic object into a cult object and reinventing a mass market, with the brand shops becoming places for the celebration of the ritual, for a product whose market was already fully saturated.

In this way many Italian companies in the 1980s launched themselves in overseas markets and developed strategies that became invaluable experiences. They called the most famous architects at an international level to collaborate with them, those who were receiving great attention by the world media at the time, who were returning to a neo-classical language or throwing themselves into whimsicality. This signified associating the name of the company with a person made famous by the media, and also entering an overseas market with a product designed by a locally well known architect. In addition, it meant the adoption of a new role for Italian companies, that of a business which became a production workshop for projects by designers from all over the world, with the result that as a group the companies became a type of seismograph for international trends.

In the mid-1980s Memphis and then Alchimia closed. With regard to the language of objects, what emerged was a tendency to reflect on the poverty caused by the simplification of the "aesthetic" to frivolity, according to a definition by the Italian philosopher Gianni Vattimo, and by the proliferation of forms, the cause of an excess of "noise", of "semiotic pollution". Memphis and Alchimia, which triumphed on the pages of magazines but remained limited to the field of luxury artisan goods, had limited market success and this erased interest in the industries of postmodern design. On the wave of current thinking, the tradition of Italian design became visible again, a tradition of design constituted by rationalist architects working since the 1950s and younger architects working in the evolution of that tradition. It must be added that this tradition, in terms of production, market and design itself, had continued with quiet success. To cite a few examples of this: Mari (*Tonietta* chair, 1985), Magistretti (*Silver* chair, 1989) and new designers such as Antonio Citterio (the enormouly successful of the *Sity* couch, 1986). The rationalist and neo-rationalist current reaffirmed itself within the emergence of a general trend toward a "new simplicity". New companies and new designers also emerged: and so Paolo Rizzatto and Alberto Meda designed a superb range of lamps that successfully defined the elements of Italian design of this phase.

110

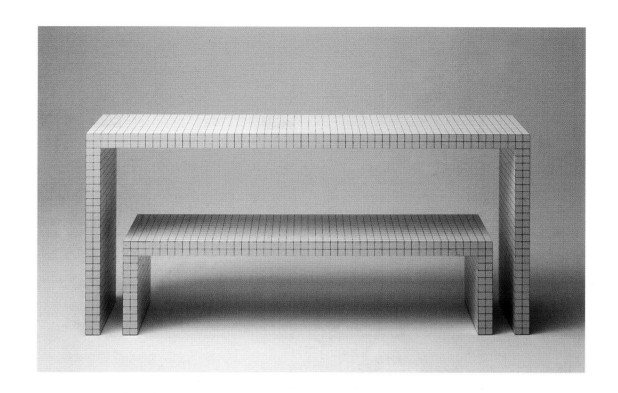

111

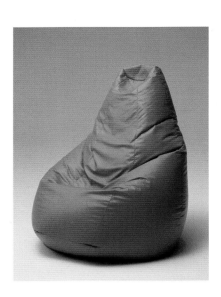

Piero Gatti, Cesare Paolini,
Francesco Teodoro, Sacco,
Zanotta, 1969

Jonathan De Pas, Donato
D'Urbino, Paolo Lomazzi, Joe,
Poltronova, 1970

Giorgio Ceretti, Pietro Derossi,
Riccardo Rosso, Pratone,
Gufram, 1970
(photo: Paolo Mussat Sartor)

Straddling two centuries

The pluralism of the 1980s has already been discussed and, as mentioned, within it there were trends that diverged both from the general dominant "baroque" and the return to history observed for some years at the end of the decade. In fact there were shared experiments from the opposition to the exaltation of form with a desired essentiality. Gradually they converged toward a paradigm of "new simplicity" which caused the end of the postmodern image. It had been excessive and aggressive at a formal level and typical of groups such as Memphis, of designers such as Sottsass or Mendini. The mass media had given it great space and it had strongly affected the international imagination.

Apart from the Italian rationalist tradition mentioned above, the Japanese and their "new wave" comes to mind. In the 1970s it had been intent on architectonic rationalism and American minimal art, yet maintaining the tradition of Heian period architecture and furniture and of zen "contemplation without object". The names range from Shiro Kuramata to a number of architects such as Toyo Ito, Kazuo Shinoara and Hiromi Fujii who in the 1980s designed pieces of furniture for Italian companies also. At the same time designers of rarefied elegance exerted their influence, such as Issey Miyake, whose fashions displayed the interweaving of essential geometric forms, moving in space, utilising cloths and pleating of quality.

Another current of experimentation involved the many English designers such as Jasper Morrison who from the end of the 1980s opened the way to a real minimalist trend distinguished by restraint and linguistic rarefaction. Jasper Morrison made express recognition of his esteem for master designers such as Magistretti, who had taught for many years at the London Royal College of Arts, and Castiglioni.

In 1993, these words appeared on the wall of a gallery in Milan: "This is the time of composed design, of a serene soul, of more authentic feelings". The phrase was by Rei Kawakubo, the Japanese designer who created Comme des Garçons: it was a declaration of poetics but it also expressed a sensibility that was then spreading among young designers. Ten years earlier, in 1983, Kawakubo had presented her collection at the Paris shows (together with another Japanese designer, Yohii Yamamoto) where it had attracted a great deal of attention for its radical simplicity. In Milan Kawakubo presented small tables and chairs in light-coloured wood, having a basic geometric style, softened slightly by defined contours, and held together by pins made of the same wood. By a calculated choice, in the adjoining room of the same gallery there was a small show dedicated to the Italian architect Franco Albini, with some of his furniture pieces from the 1950s having a sober and spare elegance.

In the summer of the same year, at the Venice Biennale, one of the most interesting experiences was the opportunity to visit two neighbouring installations, one of the film director Pedro Almodovar and the other of the theatre director Bob Wilson.

Hypertrophied, turgid, coloured, Almodovar's space was filled with pieces of furniture, lamps and sculptures, pop art and neo-symbolism, Andy Warhol paintings and Ettore Sottsass objects, heterosexual and homosexual eroticism, vitalism and sense of death.

Memory, the other installation, was profoundly captivating: the large rectangular hall of the old salt warehouses, the *Magazzine del Sale,* left intact with brick walls and wooden roof beams, was articulated into three spaces with simple interventions of subtle symbolic density. Light, reverberating musical echoes defined the real dimensions of the space; the visitor advanced on a floor treated like Burri's "cretto" toward the end wall where there was a blind window.

Putting to one side the distinguishing features of Almodovar and Wilson's work, there were two formal and clearly opposing situations. It seemed legitimate to read the first installation as a metaphor for the apparent agitation typical of the 1980s, and the second as an expression of that minimalism, or that simplicity, that began to denote the 1990s. Reflecting then, on design, reference was made to the 1970s and an analogous opposition, that of pop art and minimal art (both of which influenced developments in design). What come to mind are the anthropomorphic and technological totems of the English sculptor Paolozzi (1965) mentioned earlier. These were certainly known to Sottsass when fifteen years later for Memphis he was designing polychrome bookcases with thick panels and disturbing robot-like shapes. Or, in a contrary way, certain *Untitled* (1968) pieces by the American minimalist artist Robert Morris also come to mind, types of essential, rarefied *dormeuse* in wire meshing, the same material which was much used later by Japanese minimalist designers. Or the *Judd bar*, dedicated to Donald Judd, designed in 1980 by Shiro Kuramata in Tokyo.

The same year, 1993, represented the year in which the new phenomenon of minimalism, or the new simplicity, completely emerged. In a warehouse of an abandoned factory an Italian company exhibited the objects designed by a range of young designers, exponents of the "Brit new wave", the chief among them being the London minimalist Jasper Morrison.

The 1990s were thus largely characterised by the spread of the minimalist viewpoint which, after a certain period, appeared to spread more as fashion than as experimentation. Contributing to this was the fact that companies were working increasingly towards establishing complex strategies ranging from defining the identity of the company to communication. In the context of globalisation, Italian industries understood that the problem was no longer one relating simply to exports. Rather, it related more and more to a skill in acquiring an identity that would be recognised and would act as a point of reference on the international stage. Publicity, catalogues and advertising, which were often curated by fashion photographers, demonstrate a focus by companies on defining a new, all-encompassing lifestyle, so much so that in some cases they attempted to transform themselves into magazines, on the model of "Colors" by Benetton. In relation to products, certain companies aimed at designing collections characterised by reference to a formally homogenous domestic panorama, in which every piece of furniture existed because it was part of the definition of a unitary style line, rather than for its own intrinsic characteristics. Or, contrary to this, there were companies that aimed at producing single pieces, independent of each other, distinguished by a limited set of formal constants, of materials or technology, which together defined the company image. In this context the choice for many companies was minimalism, with its elegant and recognisable simplicity, as it was parallel to analogous tendencies in fashion, also in relation to adaptability for industrial production. Visiting the Milan *Salone del mobile* in the last few years, clearly there is a growing number of companies emerging, flanking the historic ones, with well-designed stands and products, and with a significant improvement in average quality of products. Here there is a tempered minimalism, or a gentle simplicity. It appears to be a language that allows access by many companies to the "good salon" of Italian design, in addition to the acquiring of modern taste by a band of the public once anchored in eclectic design. (Here one thinks of the Giorgio Armani boutiques in Paris, Naples, and Milan, currently being designed by Claudio Silvestrin, the "Mister Minimum" of London design.)

Of course there is more also. One thinks of designers like Stefano Giovannoni, who introduced, and not only in objects, a type of "young" language, from gadgets to round and "playful" forms, distinguished by pastel colours. At an international level, intersecting with Starckian citations and allusions to the graphics of Japanese video games, this young language created a kind of new mannerism in the "kids forever" range.

Yet again, in a contrary way, one thinks of the range of experimentation common to young people all over Europe that relates to the relationship between design and ecology. This trend, inaugurated by the Dutch Droog Design "network", works almost for a parallel unofficial market, a market for those who are not interested in the market, as Renny Ramakers said. It is a kind of "non design" for young consumers who are interested in moderately priced creative objects that are based on reuse, and *bricolage*. The objects give new meaning to what already existed and what is being produced (it must be remembered that for a time much reference was made to the work of Castiglioni by the young, international *bricolage* trend). They are objects born as designs for oneself, for one's own home, for one's own desires. They are often self produced with basic materials, with technology that is sophisticated yet easily accessible, with a cleverness that involves being able to transform processes, optimising already existing equipment, and often reusing industrial components that are simply reassembled. They are then offered to a shop to be sold; or presented to a company in the hope that they produce it. This is sometimes successful. For example, *Erbale*, designed by three young designers (Becchelli, Bortolani, Maffei, 1996), is a sheet of plastic that can be suspended from a wall or a window, with plastic containers for holding flowers or plants that are connected by small narrow tubes that bring water. It became a hit. In general, however, it cannot be said that this period saw the firm emergence of a new set of young Italian designers.

There is yet another issue regarding Italian design culture. Recently the French theorist Paul Virilio drew attention to the risks resulting from new technology, such as virtualisation, that "derealises the presence of the other, the presence of things " and asked, referring to designers: "what is the future of the manual object, of the tactile object?" According to Virilio, the compression of time created by telecommunications, of transmissions in real time, leads to the reduction of the world to outlines, summaries and key words, diminishing the sense of objects to a pure sign. This is all to the detriment of the development of narrative, "with the disappearance of the richness of events". Virilio calls on architects and designers to oppose this reduction.

In this sphere Italian design has, both in terms of its tradition and current developments, a very interesting role to play. Take, for instance, a lamp designed by Paolo Rizzatto and Alberto Meda (Fortebraccio, 1998): it has two robust articulated arms; the one which holds the light bulb has a joint which allows it to rotate in two directions, horizontally and vertically. The arms have an organic and anthropomorphic form, and hold a head that can have different sizes, according to the different sources of light, but which always terminate in kind of handle or large thumb that also carries the switch and makes it easy to use. It is an object defined by a complexity of elements, technological, linguistic, of materials, of memory, that the design translates into formal simplicity. A simplicity that does not deny, therefore, but highlights the quality of narrative, of the "richness of event" as Virilio says, in antithesis to the reduction of objects to pure signs with media effectiveness. This love for what is simple, intended not as reduction but as "resolved complexity", to use the sculptor Costantin Brancusi's definition, is in the tradition of Italian design, continues to distinguish it, and is what makes it interesting at the present time.

There is a further element that must be highlighted. From the 1980s Italian companies have become the preferred point of reference not only for Italian designers but also European designers. In this way objects produced today by Italian companies but created by designers such as the French Jean Nouvel or Philippe Starck, the English Jasper Morrison, Tom Dixon or Ron Arad, the Spanish Oscar Tusquet, the Czech-Dutch Borek Sipek, the Japanese Kazuo Shinohara and Toshiyuki Kita and so on, go by the name of Italian design. To cite one example, a designer like Starck owes his international fame in large measure to the Italian companies he began to collaborate with from the beginning of the 1980s and for whom he continues to work.

However, since the 1990s we are experiencing the formation of a wide and interesting network of young and very young designers, and no longer only European. Globalisation, with the entry of entire geographical areas into the international market, has created a strongly competitive situation, in which design has become increasingly more competitive for companies. The number of countries which are investing in design schools and supporting design-oriented companies (from Taiwan to Korea, from Singapore to Brazil) is increasing; the number and typology of industries that work with designers is also increasing. It is becoming gradually clearer how the role of design is growing and expanding in this era of globalisation, of the information society, of post-Fordism, in other words of this third phase of the industrial revolution. And the companies that are operating on the world market are in fact finding themselves at the centre of a network of designers that obviously no longer comprises only Italian designers but also young new generations from many countries. In this way growing relationships are being established between Italian companies and young designers who are not only European, but Brazilian, American, from the Far East and so on. If in the 1980s Italian companies had directed themselves to the great postmodern architects in order to strengthen the appeal of their image on the international market, today they have become very quick at identifying and putting into production the work of young quality designers. These same designers, on the contrary, do not find, for one reason or another, companies with the same openness and orientation toward design in their country of origin. This is certainly one of the most interesting aspects of Italian design today: a range of Italian companies operate as workshops of that new European and world design that has distinguished the end of the last century and is distinguishing the beginning of the new century.

There is a corollary: Milan has in the meanwhile become the preferred place for the exhibition of these phenomena. Architects, designers, graphic artists, photographers, journalists, critics, publishing companies, magazines, universities, design schools, exhibition and trade shows, consulting and advertising agencies and highly specialised printing houses constitute a very complex working network. It is a network that sustains design and publicity activity of a series of small and medium-sized companies that, well represented in a district near Milan, Brianza, are today established in areas of many other Italian regions. But Milan operates as the centre for a broad communication network that today comes from everywhere. It is a city with a high density of young designers from many countries who, after having attended their school, remain to work. On the other hand, young designers come from all over the world to show their work during the *Salone del mobile*, in the hope of being noted by both the media and above all Italian companies. As such Milan has become the preferred exhibition place, the magnet and also the showcase, of new trends. The city's role is growing as a place of international publicity that revolves around design, and also as an exhibition place for young design from all countries and the stage for its showing.

There is a great deal of synergy between Milan, Italian companies and the world network of young designers. The new century therefore opens with a clear phenomenon: the area of design-oriented Italian industries, a typically Italian phenomenon, is gradually becoming a workshop for international young design. This distinguished the end of last century and will presumably long distinguish the next century also, in that tension which today appears to be expressed between globalisation and local identity. And in this picture Milan's very role as a city placed at the crossroads between local and global will be redefined.

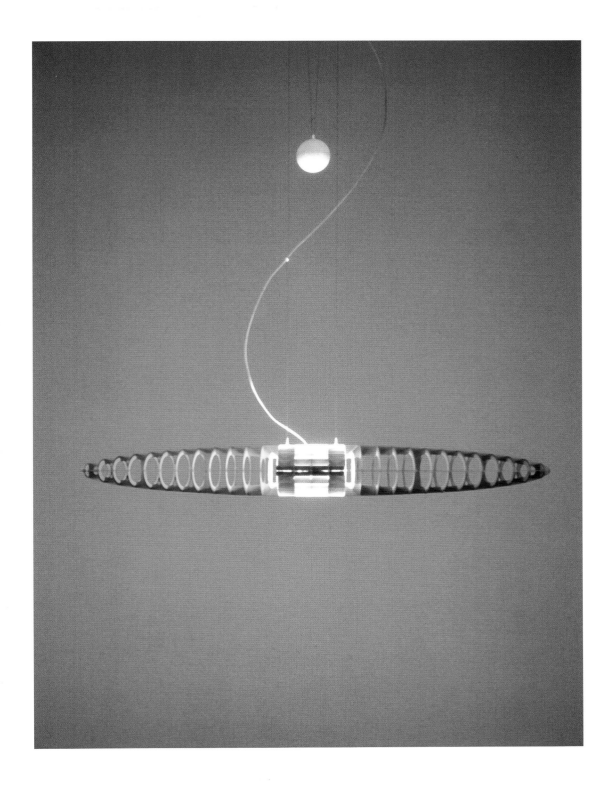

From exhibit to event: the Salone del Mobile "case"

Laura Lazzaroni

Furniture Show poster, 1961, 1962, 1963, 1964, 1965

The *Salone del Mobile* will celebrate its fortieth birthday in 2001, most years of which have been spent in notoriety and under scrutiny.

The following newspapers and magazines wrote about the 2000 version of the *Salone* and its secondary show *Rooms and Secrets* held at the Rotonda della Besana: *Le Soir* and *De Standaard* in Belgium; *La Tribune, Le Figaro, Le Monde* and *Libération* in France; *Financial Times Deutschland* and *Süddeutsche Zeitung* in Germany; *Financial Times* and *Wall Paper* in Great Britain; *Estado de Minas* and *Garzeta Mercantil* in Brazil; *International Business Daily* and *Xin Ming Evening Daily* in China; and *Chicago Tribune, Financial Times Usa, International Herald Tribune, Los Angeles Times, New York Today, Star Tribune, The New York Times, The State, Union Tribune* and *Washington Post* in the United States to mention only some.

It seems straightforward and almost obvious but it was not always like that.

Gio Ponti wrote in *Il mobile italiano* in 1958, "In the world of furniture, Scandinavia is gaining that predominant and exclusive renown that Switzerland has achieved for watches. Let merit be given where it is due, but if that is painful for Italians, it is also due to the failings that exist in our industry because there is a fondness, an expectation, for Italian furniture design in all importing countries, including Scandinavia itself"[1]. An important demonstration of this particular interest was the invitation to participate in the *Furniture Exhibition* in London in 1958, a roundup of the best of British design. For the first time, the organisers decided to exhibit examples of foreign furniture and invited Italy[2], Sweden and Finland to contribute, a telling indication of the importance of Nordic design at the time.

Although Scandinavian furniture only represented 3 percent of the Italian market[3], the Italian companies whose products were contemporary in design – with very rare exceptions – copied the Scandinavian style thus creating the Italian version known as "teak style"; this trend was also influenced by the great attention paid to the style by fashionable magazines of the period.

The rest of the industry continued to produce the "traditional", monumental style of furniture little suited to export that stemmed from the traditions of the last twenty years of the 19th century in Brianza and Cascina. It went by this vacuous label simply because it had no specific style that suggested any other name. The production of faithful copies of period styles (French, English, German and even Italian from the Renaissance to maggiolino style) was enormous thanks to the undeniable skills of Italian craftsmen.

Ponti continued, "If the crisis is to be overcome, original *modern* designs must be produced in conjunction with architects because it is with modern furniture that the Scandinavians are justifiably beating us, and this needs to focus our attention on that segment of the market based on reproduction antique or reproduction modern designs. These fraudulent and uncontrolled items satisfy a certain sector of the market but they are not enough to tackle a crisis; this can only be overcome with modern 'Italian' products"[4].

This was not a new argument in *Il mobile italiano*, a magazine established in December 1957 with the purpose of resolving the question of the relationship between designers and manufacturers by putting businessmen and designers together[5]. The editor at the time was Carlo De Carli and the publisher the Centro Pubbliche Relazioni behind which was hidden Tito Armellini, the Director of the Italian Federation of Wood and Cork Industries, the manager and publisher also of *L'Industria del legno*[6] and future Secretary-General and principal promoter of Cosmit, the organising committee for the *Salone del Mobile Italiano*. Right from the start, therefore, the awareness existed of the need to follow a very precise path to bring about the rebirth of the Italian furniture industry, and the name of the path to tread was "design". It was a hard task but

one to which De Carli and Armellini committed themselves utterly.

Tommaso Ferrari, the Secretary-General of the Milan Triennale, wrote as follows on the subject of De Carli's suggestion for greater collaboration between artists, engineers and companies: "If I did not know of your and Armellini's steadfastness, I would doubt the possibility of seeing the Italian furniture industry brought to a satisfactory point and set on a new road, let alone that the problem might be solved. […] Too many producers are deluding themselves that they can continue to sell the same old designs, happy with the small local market, while we are all watching, for the moment impotently, as the international and even the Italian market is being won over by foreign companies, in particular from northern Europe. […] It is time to admit, De Carli, that the title of your magazine, *Il mobile italiano* ["Italian furniture"], no longer corresponds to reality; can anyone tell me what the distinguishing features of Italian furniture are? The effort that you and our common friends have put in will most surely be crowned with success when we are able to recognise Italian furniture with ease – in a shop, house or exhibition – as occurs today with the furniture of the countries mentioned above"[7].

If, on the one hand, much was written in the pages of *Il mobile italiano* of the indispensable need to introduce design into the furniture industry, on the other, exports were identified as the way to continue once the already glimpsed saturation of the home market was reached following the end of the period of reconstruction. In addition to the possibility of crisis in the domestic market (which seemed too limited for the production requirements of the time and which actually occurred in 1964-65), the import/export ratio was producing major worries because, although exports increased from 1957 on and the balance of trade was healthy, the import figures were continuing to rise much more strongly than exports[8].

The best solution to the exports problem seemed to be the creation of consortia among producers, a strategy that was recognised as one of the winning cards played by Scandinavian design (without taking anything away from "Nordic style").

On 17 March 1958, the National Institute of Furniture Makers was founded within the Italian Federation of Wood and Cork Industries but it was to be better known as IFI (Italian Furniture Impex). It was a consortium formed by twenty-two companies whose aim was to encourage the exportation of Italian furniture through collective participation at fairs and exhibitions in Italy and abroad. The President was Mario Dosi and the Secretary-General Tito Armellini. In November 1959, IFI opened the *Permanent Exhibition of Italian Furniture* in Via Varese in Milan which was only open to foreign businessmen. In 1960, it was present with a large stand designed by Enzo Strada at *Möbelmesse* in Cologne, the most famous exhibition of European furniture and the promoter some years earlier of Nordic style.

Once back from Cologne, renewing his invitation to Italian furniture producers to unite in a single consortium and admitting the indisputable supremacy of Denmark, Sweden, Finland and Norway who had presented their products in a single, enormous stand, Armellini wrote, "Competing with the Scandinavians is […] a pointless exercise because of their creative abilities, product quality and commercial organisation made possible by a natural willingness to work as a group"[9]. And he continued, "If it was possible for the Scandinavians to establish 'their style', why can't we counter it with 'our style'? […] The task that we have set ourselves is a gruelling one but where there is the enthusiasm and commitment of architects and the sense of responsibility of the producers in an atmosphere of reciprocal esteem and collaboration, this ambitious goal should be attainable"[10].

Again in the pages of *Il mobile italiano*, Dino Brivio

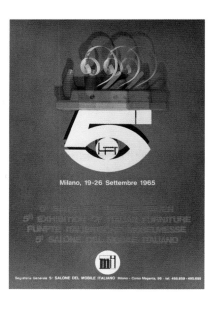

anticipated the announcement of what was to be the *Salone del Mobile Italiano*, "One could not honestly say that the many furniture exhibitions being organised around Italy will have any specific effect on consumption; the limited nature of the individual initiatives, whether provincial or local, ensures that the many millions of lire spent, undoubtedly with the very best of intentions but also with a touch of jealous or envious parochialism, are simply being thrown to the wind to judge by the scarcity of results. [...] If these small and restricted exhibitions are useless, and perhaps even damaging, it would not be a bad idea to take the International Fair in Cologne, which produces excellent results for German and Nordic producers, as our example. Why not organise a large exhibition that specialises in furniture on an annual or biennial basis? This idea has already been put forward by a noted industrialist in Cantù, Angelo De Baggis, with a letter written to the Secretary-General of the Milan Fair, Guido Michele Franci"[11].

De Baggis' idea was realised by Armellini who held talks with the Fair's management and succeeded in getting the space required for a wide-ranging "vertical" exhibition.

The press conference for the official presentation of the *Salone del Mobile Italiano* was held on 25 February 1961. The *Salone* was organised by a committee made up of Alessandro Colli (President), former President of the Italian Federation of Wood and Cork Industries, Angelo De Baggis (Vice President) and Tito Armellini (Secretary-General), with Mario Dosi as honorary president. The other founders were Michele Barovero from Turin, Franco Cassina from Meda, Cesare Castelli from Bologna, Davide Colombo from Milan, Antonio Dal Vera from Conegliano Veneto, Vittorio Dassi from Lissone, Angelo Marelli from Carugo, Angelo Molteni from Giussano, Silvano Montina from San Giovanni al Natisone, Mario Roncoroni from Cantù, Attilio Santambrogio from Cabiate, Maurizio Tosi from Rovigo and Vittorio Villa from Concorrezzo – all owners of large Italian furniture-producing companies – with Manlio Germozzi, the President of the General Confederation of Craftsmen[12].

The composition of the committee fully reflected the ratio of companies whose production was based on "design" to those who were "traditional" in style but, of all the members, only Cassina had ever asked for the collaboration of architects and designers, and he had started at the end of the 1920s!

One of the great merits of the *Salone* was its success in bringing together, from the fifth edition on, more than 70 percent of the entire potential furniture industry in the country thanks to its non-selective and nationwide nature. And that figure was to rise to 80 percent in 1969, and 90 percent in the modern era.

It was in the prestigious location of the Fiera Campionaria (Exhibition Centre) that Milan challenged the trade fairs of Cologne and Paris. The idea of holding the show every year, soon matched by Cologne and Paris, was held right from the beginning by Armellini, and that rhythm produced positive results in competition between companies, the movement of technological skills and abilities, and the creation of an Italian style[13].

The first show (24-30 September 1961) was attended by 328 exhibitors and covered three floors of Pavilion 34 and one in Pavilion 28 for a total surface area of 11,860 square metres. It attracted the presence of 11,300 Italian members of the trade and 800 from abroad. The fourth edition drew 818 exhibitors, covered the above pavilions plus nos. 29 and 29B for a total area of 32,000 square metres, and attracted 20,739 Italian members of trade and 2,237 from abroad. This comparison gives an idea of the commercial importance of the *Salone* which was underlined by its export figures: a rise from 5,837 million lire in 1960 to 15,906 million in 1964.

The commercial importance of the *Salone* right from its earliest years was undeniable[14] and this has been confirmed by the figures relating to industrial production of furniture (which increased constantly between 1960 and 1970) and by the transformation of production from typically manual craftsmanship to predominantly industrial[15] or pseudo-industrial.

Most of the furniture exhibited during the first four years of the show was "traditional" Italian, faithful copies and interpretations of period furniture, Chippendale and Provençal-style reproductions, English colonial style, items based on 14th-and 15th-century models, and a minimal presence of contemporary furniture, mainly in "teak style"[16].

The first four years were marked by a strong turnover of exhibitors until the *Salone* settled down, and by the increasing interest of companies including those who had already set out on the path of design and formal renewal. The example of Poggi was symbolic: Poggi exhibited at the first edition of the *Salone* but did not return, probably as a result of the few companies offering similar products. In fact, of the large companies that we are used to including among the convinced supporters of Italian design in the years prior to the creation of the *Salone*, only Boffi, Cassina ed Elam, Pierantonio Bonacina and Vittorio Bonacina (who, however, are part of the very specific sector that produces wicker furniture), Giuseppe Rossi (now Rossi di Albizzate), Saporiti, Sormani and Stildomus (who began its collaboration with architects at the end of the 1950s) have exhibited at the *Salone* uninterruptedly from the first year[17].

The other big names waited to see which direction the *Salone* would take. In 1964 the distance between the furnishings exhibited in the sector dedicated to production at the *XIII Triennale* – though few in number[18] – and what was presented at the *Salone* seemed unbridgeable. At the *Triennale*, Arflex (which still did not appear at the *Salone*) presented two new armchairs, the *Fourline* and the *Woodline*, designed by Marco Zanuso; Cassina presented the *905* by Vico Magistretti; Poggi exhibited some items designed by Franco Albini and Franca Helg; and Bernini (which also did not attend the *Salone*) showed its *Combi-Center* by Joe Colombo. Even Kartell preferred the *Triennale* to present its seat *4999* by Marco Zanuso and Richard Sapper.

But the *Triennale*'s policy towards designer products, for which it usually reserved an area that was small in comparison to the importance of the output at the time, began to arouse a certain amount of dissatisfaction in producers and in the pages of magazines. On the occasion of the 1964 *Triennale*, *Domus*, for example, wrote, "If the space dedicated to products had been greater, it would naturally have been possible to display more items (which were perhaps relegated to the show's storerooms) and which will therefore have to wait for the next *Triennale* or be known of through other channels. But their absence means that we cannot know what of point development, or regression, modern design has reached"[19].

This dissatisfaction became more acute at the following *Triennale* in 1968 and Pier Carlo Santini wrote in *Ottagono*, "Now it is time to make a choice: either interior and industrial design (and perhaps craft products) should be a central theme of the show or they should back out and more suitable shows be found for them"[20]. The section dedicated that year to "Italian expression and production", "which was unable to say no to Italian furniture producers"[21], will be "relegated to the gardens which can be reached via an umbilical cord that underlines the diversity of quality between 'culture' and practical activities"[22] and "its extraneousness and relative unimportance compared to the central theme of the show"[23]. And nor can one ignore the fact that between 1965 and 1972, a period of creative verve which saw an acceleration in the application of new technological discoveries in the world of furniture[24], only one edition of the *Triennale* was held (the

*Furniture Show poster, 1966,
1967, 1968, 1969, 1970,
1980*

14th in 1968: the *Triennial of challenge*) as opposed to the eight editions of the *Salone del Mobile*.

It was just chance therefore that the 1965 *Salone* saw the appearance of several important companies which had been encouraged by a decision made by Cosmit (proposed by Manlio Armellini and supported by Franco Cassina, Dino Boffi, Alberto Burzio of Arflex, Osvaldo Borsani of Tecno, Giulio Castelli of Kartell and others) that was important for the development of Italian design in general and for the success of the *Salone del Mobile* in particular. The decision was to create a sector specially reserved for designer furniture on the third floor of Pavilion 30 – a "selection in non-selection" – a step that had not been taken by other European fairs.

Thus Arflex, Bernini, Kartell (which had made a fleeting appearance at the 1963 *Salone*), Martinelli Luce, MIM and Tecno[25] were able to exhibit their products alongside Boffi, Pierantonio Bonacina, Cassina, Cinova, Saporiti, Sormani and Stildomus in the large commercial fair that had become the most important in the industry in Italy in just a few years[26] and which attracted a growing number of visitors and journalists.

The important German newspaper *Handelsblatt* wrote that the companies on the third floor of Pavilion 30 had given life "to a small Triennale with their many creations"[27], while a comment in Paris recognised in Pavilion 30 "the accomplishment on an industrial level of what architects had proposed in various furniture competitions, [...] a premise to a real rebirth"[28] and admiring in the items on display "that meticulous care and permanent refinement that had made Italian handcrafts a kingdom of quality"[29]. Whereas some recognised "the presence of good modern designs"[30], others had already noticed the desire to amaze which was to play a large role in Italian furniture design in the years that immediately followed.

Identifying a genuinely Italian design line, the publication *Meubles et décors* remarked on the presence of furniture designed in accordance with the criterion that it referred to as "science fiction": "perfectly suited to modern requirements, they are examples of an unchanging way of being, of conceiving and of creating. The careful observer will note the combination of logic with gratuitous whims. Dear to the Italians, this last element is a real challenge, a continual need to surprise, almost to irritate"[31].

Also convinced that some items might seem extravagant to visitors, *Home Furnishing Daily* placed great importance on the fact that Italian designers were not happy simply to disengage themselves from the past but that they actually looked to the future in their search for completely new forms[32].

This concept was heard again in the *Echo du Meuble*: "there is electricity in the air in the modern furniture industry in Italy. [...] Italian furniture is unquestionably original and cannot be compared to that of others: it always gives the impression it is experimental though without ever abandoning its character; it is constantly in search of renewal and of a perfection that is not of this world. Contemporary Italian furniture does not accept the function of table, seat, bed, wardrobe etc., but penetrates ever deeper into forms that suit new ways of living and new requirements"[33].

"Furnished blocks" were particularly admired: the *Combi-Center* (Bernini), *Personal Container* (Arflex) and *Mini-Kitchen* (Boffi) by Joe Colombo, and the *Mobile Totale* by Titina Ammannati and Giampiero Vitelli for Giuseppe Rossi (now Rossi di Albizzate).

1965 was also the year in which the first secondary exhibition organised by Cosmit was held; it was entitled *Retrospective to document the design of furniture in Italy from 1945 to the present day* and was an unusual example of a "vertical" fair within a cultural domain. The show was divided into three parts corresponding to chronological periods: the years around 1950, the period from then till 1960, and the subsequent period

till 1965. The sections included the most important episodes to have taken place in design from a cultural point of view in which design was understood to refer to any object on any scale, including architecture and landscape design, though without neglecting the support of the technical press.

The aims were explicitly stated in the pages of *L'Industria del legno* with the statement, "The show is undoubtedly lacking in many respects but wanted to be a symbol of the attempt to open a debate on the past twenty years in order to map out the continuous development that has marked them and, above all, to point out how they may evolve in the future"[34] as, "if, on the one hand, the strong development of the furniture industry in Italy is worthy of a mention following improvements made in quality and technology, on the other hand it is opportune to consider that several deficiencies still scar the sector, for example, the very limited number of cases where design is integrated in the production cycle as an essential and irreversible phase, the almost total absence of opportunities for budding designers to train, the lack of exchange of information and experience, and the slide into a neo-stylistic phase by the products of modern formalism"[35].

1965 can therefore be viewed as the turnabout of the *Salone*[36], an opinion borne out by the appearance of the first article on the exhibition in the pages of *Domus*.

That year, the third floor of Pavilion 30 hosted 30 exhibitors out of a total of 1073[37], still a derisory proportion that would remain as such in the years to come despite a gradual increase in surface area and in the number of exhibitors[38]: the market share of "modern furniture" rose from 4 percent in 1960 to 30 percent by the end of the decade[39] compared to the 45 percent of "traditional" furniture and the 25 percent of reproduction furniture.

In the 1966 show, it seemed as though the creative vein of Italian design was running dry; there was nothing any more to suggest an "aesthetic hypertrophy"[40] might follow, resulting from, above all, the frequent referrals to forms and motifs used by the neo-avant garde in the visual arts.

The general impression was however very positive with the shock value less strong than the previous year and the confirmation of the overtaking of Nordic design by its Italian rival. "Scandinavian out, Italian in" was the title of an article on the *Salone* in *Furnishing World*[41] which stressed "how modern Italian furniture has succeeded in overtaking and distinguishing itself from the Scandinavian style that dominates furniture design in other countries"[42]. The number of exhibitors rose to 1,160 to cover a surface area of 48,000 square metres. The number of Italian visitors reached 27,272 and 2,826 came from abroad, while the sales turnover during the show represented 70 percent of the annual overall value of furniture sales in Italy, a percentage that was to rise yet further in the years to come.

"That [...] self-possessed imaginativeness and [...] creative daring that are inconceivable in other fields"[43] – were already looming in the 1965 and 1966 shows and were to "explode" the following year when Italian designers translated into objects the new modes of living that characterised the period up until the start of the 1970s.

In 1967[44], design succeeded in winning itself more exhibition space and a greater slice of the market[45] although it was still less than that represented by "traditional" and reproduction furniture (the companies with the greatest turnover in these years were those whose products were mainly aimed at the Arab markets).

When the Paris Salon was held in January, *Le Figaro* ran an article titled "The Italians throw furniture into confusion"[46] in reference to the worldwide dominance that Italian designers achieved by "inventing" new items of furniture that matched new modes of living. The theme was taken up again in September by the

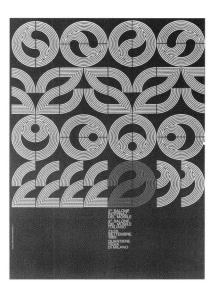

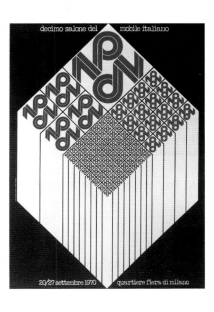

Italian and foreign press when the Milan *Salone* was held, with the difference that this was the first international event, meaning that Italian furniture was now in competition with products from other countries.

The publication *L'officiel de l'ameublement* did not hesitate to emphasise the strongly alternative character of modern Italian furniture compared to that of the rest of Europe. "The daring, the originality and the open-mindedness of certain pieces can at times actually create feelings of annoyance but that does not get in the way of the most important fact which is that of showing the desire to radically change the conceptions and commonplaces of today and to place furniture on the same level of irreversible development as the styles of contemporary life and requirements of our age, reaching for horizon that we will see in 1970 or at least in 2000. The forms, aesthetics, colours, materials, the purpose of the object and its functionality are all undergoing profound transformation and excite interesting and incessant study"[47].

The Italian press, too, generally more cautious, recognised this moment as a turning point in the field of design. *Abitare* wrote, "The foreign presence at the *Salone* has highlighted a fact that seems to be of the greatest importance: for many years, world furniture production was dominated by Denmark but today it is Italy that offers the most interesting ideas and leads a radical turnaround in the design trends of domestic furniture. Nor does it seem that these are simply new formal expressions of a successful vein, or just experiments with new technologies, but the prospect of an approach to living that is increasingly suited to modern existence, that is to say, furniture matched to models of behaviour that are undergoing continual and rapid transformation"[48]. And *Domus* stressed the extraordinary variety of the phenomenon due to the presence of "interesting novelties: for the brilliance of their conception, the quality of their design, and the use of new techniques and materials"[49]. Both Vienna[50] and London[51] praised the incredible quantity of formal and technological innovations, and, in a veiled manner, *Mobel Kultur* recognised that one of the reasons for the success of Italian design was the lack of marketing, with its philosophy of "'not leaving anything untried' in order to understand if the market was prepared to praise the risk and effort involved"[52].

Examples were: Zanotta with *Blow* by De Pas, D'Urbino, Lomazzi e Scolari and the *Throw Away* by Willie Landels, Poltronova with *Superonda* by Archizoom and *Kubirolo* by Ettore Sottsass jr., Kartell with the *4867* seat by Joe Colombo and the modular paintings by Anna Castelli Ferrieri, and C&B Italia (who in their founding year, 1966, had presented *Coronado* by Afra and Tobia Scarpa and *Amanta* by Mario Bellini which were practically ignored by the Italian and foreign press) with *Lombrico* by Marco Zanuso.

From this year on, modern design furniture began to occupy most of the pages of magazines dedicated to the *Salone* as well as those of the furniture industry press (with the result that developments in production in general were more difficult to follow) reflecting the extraordinary interest the phenomenon raised.

In 1968, only Cologne exceeded the Milan show in surface area though not in the number of exhibitors. The *Salone* of that year had 1,431 exhibitors (109 more than the previous year) covering an area of 63,456 square metres and requiring two new pavilions, nos. 33 and 35. And the number of visitors rose to 32,886 Italians and 5,052 foreigners.

L'officiel de l'ameublement commented on the daring of the designers at the 1968 *Salone* but even more so on the Italian manufacturers, "It is pleasing to report the opinions of a number of foreign manufacturers who are very attentive to what is happening in Italy [...]. They think their Italian colleagues are very courageous … and that, for their own part, they would do well to follow in their footsteps!"[53]. The article continued, "the daring of some of the creators [...] evi-

dently causes a sort of fear in dealers who find it difficult to imagine that consumers could be enticed by such originality that is, sometimes, it must be said, really rather peculiar"[54].

In 1969, the year that Cosmit decided to hold a new fair called Sasmil for furniture accessories and components[55], the *Salone* took in ten pavilions compared to the two in 1961, and drew 1,514 exhibitors, 38,435 Italian visitors and 6,174 people from abroad in confirmation of its commercial value.

The 1969 show was entitled *Up! Up!! Up!!! in Milan*[56] in a clear reference to the *Up* series by Gaetano Pesce sold "vacuum-packed" by C&B Italia but not only that. The show had a strong impact and boasted great technological innovations.

However, this is not a suitable forum to catalogue the *Salone* year by year[57]. The purpose here is to identify the origins of the *Salone* as a commercial exhibition and the driving force of the industry and to describe how it developed into the setting where changes in taste and the state of design are displayed.

An authoritative recognition of the success of Italian design in the world came in 1972 with the show *Italy: The New Domestic Landscape* at the Museum of Modern Art in New York under the guidance of Emilio Ambasz. In the wake of this exhibition, the *Salone del Mobile* in Milan confirmed itself more and more strongly as "the most sensitive indicator of the variations in the economic and formal trends in the furniture industry"[58].

In acknowledgement of the role it had played in the history of design, Cosmit was awarded the Gold Compass award twice: in 1987 "for having wished, right from the first edition of the *Salone del Mobile*, to highlight with extreme clarity the products of the sector that is most aware of design, thus contributing to the increase in breadth of the application and cultural value of design, including by means of the constant attention paid to international communication". Then, in 1998, for the *Salone*'s image co-ordinated and designed by Massimo Vignelli/Vignelli Associates New York, which, being "extremely dynamic and distinguished by an excellent use of colour, avoids the repetition frequent in the graphics sector without abandoning its seriousness, and unifies different elements in a lively and non-conventional manner". Also in 1998, the AISM (Italian Association for Marketing Studies) awarded Cosmit its Tagliacarne Prize for the ability of its marketing policy to spread culture.

In addition to the fair, Cosmit has for some time put on important cultural events by means of which it promotes the culture of furnishings and design throughout the world.

Giuseppe Maggiolini, cabinet-maker (1987) brought together a selection of items of furniture produced by those unrivalled masters of marquetry, Maggiolini, his son Carlo Francesco and their workshop.

Furniture as asphorisms. Thirty-five pieces from Italian rationalism (1988): this was a selection of pieces of furniture made in Milan, Como and Turin between 1927 and World War II by the most famous Italian designers of the period. The exhibition toured the world in just a few years: New York and Chicago in 1989, Helsinki in 1990, Rome in 1991, and Stockholm, Ljubljana (for the world congress of the International Council of Societies of Industrial Design) and Naples in 1992.

Neoliberty and its environs (1989) presented a selection of furniture that had in common their adherence to the Neoliberty movement which in 1960 attempted to set up an "Italian style" to counter the dominant Nordic style of the period, though without immediate success.

Italian furniture 1961-1991. The various ages of language, organised by Pierluigi Cerri and Claudia Donà. The exhibition was held at the Palazzo della Triennale in Milan to coincide with the 30th *Salone* and with its shift from the month of September to April. The dis-

play was a celebration of the thirty-year relationship between Italian furniture and the culture of design.

More recently, Cosmit has organised large retrospective shows dedicated to great designers: Achille Castiglioni and Joe Colombo (1996), Vico Magistretti and Gio Ponti (1997), Alvar Aalto (1998), and Bruno Munari and Ettore Sottsass jr. (1999). The exhibition dedicated to Castiglioni was also put on in Barcelona as part of the "Disseny Spring" in 1995, at the Carrara Academy of Modern and Contemporary Art in Bergamo (1996), at the Vitra Design Museum in Weil am Rhein and at the Museum of Modern Art in New York (1997), at the Living Design Center Ozone in Tokyo, at the Museum of Art in Niitzu and at the De Beyerd Municipal Centre of Contemporary Art in Breda in 1998.

In 2000 Cosmit organised the show *Rooms and Secrets* planned by Luigi Settembrini at the Rotonda della Besana. Managed by Achille Bonito Oliva and under the artistic direction of Franco Laera, the show brought together works by some of the most important individuals in the cultural and artistic fields around the world: Marina Abramovic, Ghada Amer, Massimo Bartolini, Dumb Type, Peter Greenaway, Maria Teresa Hincapié, Eriko Horiki, Ben Jakober and Yannick Vu, Ilya and Emilia Kabakov, Emir Kusturica, Mladen Materic, Yoko Ono, Michelangelo Pistoletto, Peter Sarkisian, Daniel Spoerri and Robert Wilson. The show was a great critical and public success drawing 33,000 visitors.

With the exhibition *1951-2001 Made in Italy?*, Cosmit wishes once more to enhance the cultural aspect of its fair events and to help hold high the name of the *Salone*, of Milan, and of the design creativity that has always been one of Italy's strongest points.

[1] G. Ponti, "Crisi del mobile, produttori, architetti", *Il mobile italiano*, Milan, no. 5, April 1958, p. 3.

[2] The Italian section was organised by Lodovico Belgiojoso, Enrico Peressutti and Ernesto Nathan Rogers with the collaboration of ADI (Association for Industrial Design); it presented a collection of the best products resulting from the collaboration of the most famous Italian designers (Franco Albini, Luigi Caccia Dominioni, Vittorio Gregotti, Vico Magistretti, Angelo Mangiarotti, Gio Ponti etc.) with the best known Italian furniture companies (Poggi, Tecno, Arflex, Cassina, Pierantonio Bonacina, Azucena etc.).

[3] The statistical data – when not referring to the *Salone* – are taken from market research carried out by ICE (National Institute for Foreign Trade) or from books on the economy of the furniture industry. Cf. S. Leonardi, *Produzione e consumo dei mobili per l'abitazione in Italia*, Feltrinelli, Milan 1959; S. Silvestrelli, *Lo sviluppo industriale delle imprese produttrici di mobili in Italia*, Franco Angeli, Milan 1980; C. Dematté, *L'evoluzione dell'economia italiana dopo gli anni Cinquanta*, in C. Donà (ed.), *Mobili Italiani 1961-1991. Le Varie Età dei linguaggi*, Cosmit, Milan 1992, pp. 15-19; V. Castronovo, *Società e stili di vita, ibid.*, pp. 21-27; M. Florio, *Perché l'industria italiana del mobile ha avuto successo, ibid.*, pp. 29-33.

[4] G. Ponti, "Crisi del mobile" cit., p. 3.

[5] Each edition contained an article entitled "An example of collaboration" that illustrated the successful results of the co-operation of a company with an architect.

[6] The rather particular monthly magazine *L'Industria del legno* (The wood industry) was founded in 1949 by Tito Armellini with the aim of resolving various problems in the furniture industry (topics during the first year, for example, were *The manufacture of planks from compacted wood chips* and *The loosening of trade restrictions*); however, it did not turn up its nose at printing a roundup of furniture products, announcements, exhibition reviews and any topic related to furniture production. The first edition in 1949 quoted, "This publication [...] will be a forum to work out the problems that beset the industry, to provide a rich source of information and the means to achieve that fusion of initiatives that today, even more than the past, represents the necessary premise for development". Both technical and demonstrative, with emphasis on text rather than pictures, and originally little known as it was "progressive", it was to become in a certain way the house organ of Cosmit in which announcements of the various Fairs were given and where reviews of the best products were published. The editor was Manlio Armellini, son of Tito Armellini, who was to become Secretary-General of Cosmit in 1974 and who is currently managing director of Cosmit spa, the company that manages the yearly *Salone del Mobile Italiano* and which is responsible for Federlegno-Arredo, the largest Italian body in the wood and furniture industries, with its associations broken down by product type and representative bodies of craftsmen and dealers in the sector. Technical support was the responsibility of the Editing Committee, composed of a group of experts in various fields able to write on a broad range of subjects or to select figures whose opinions on specific topics were authoritative (for example, Bruno Munari and Tomás Maldonado on design).

[7] T. Ferraris, "Lettera del Segretario Generale della Triennale sui problemi del mobile italiano", *Il mobile italiano*, Milan, no. 2, January 1958, p. 3.

[8] For example, compared to 1958, exports in 1960 had increased by 74.7 percent in absolute value but imports had risen by 113.4 percent.

[9] T. Armellini, "Insufficienze della partecipazione italiana alla Fiera del Mobile di Colonia - necessità della fusione dei Consorzi", *Il mobile italiano*, Milan, no. 3, 8 March 1960, p. 1.

[10] *Ibidem*, p. 2.

[11] D. Brivio, "Una rassegna specializzata del mobile potrebbe essere ospitata alla Fiera di Milano", *Il mobile italiano*, Milan, no. 6, 23 April 1960, p. 10.

[12] The signers of the memorandum of association each paid 100,000 lire to cover the early costs of administration.

[13] There was another decision, this one opposed by Armellini, that was to end by being of great importance to the *Salone*: despite article no.9 stipulating "The *Salone* and its display areas shall be fitted out in accordance in a uniform style and with elegant dignity by the Technical Committee" (as occurred in all other European fairs, including Cologne and Paris), in 1963 Maurizio Tosi fitted out his stand disregarding the rules. Immediately, Article no.9 was forgotten and at the 1964 edition competition between companies was based not just on product quality, but also on the style and design of the stand.

[14] In the first three months of 1962, for instance, the value of exports rose 13.6 percent compared to the same period in 1961 and the overall value of exports for the year rose by 8.1 percent.

[15] Cf. S. Silvestrelli, "Innovazioni organizzative e ristrutturazioni aziendali", in *id.*, *Lo sviluppo industriale* cit., pp. 97-131.

[16] Although workers in the industry complained, as borne out at the *V Congresso del Mobile* in Trieste in 1962, the excessive copying of Nordic furniture underlined the needs to move to mass production and to encourage the collaboration of architects with manufacturers; the preference of the public, too, was slowly moving towards "modern" furniture. This is shown by the results of the survey carried out by *Abitare* in 1962 which, though they should be treated with caution as they represented a group of highly educated users, indicated a clear preference for modern furniture. Cf. *Referendum*, *Abitare*, Milano, no. 10, November 1962 and "I risultati del nostro referendum", *Abitare*, Milan, no. 14, March 1963, p. 45.

[17] Actually, the *Salone* from 1961 on was attended by several companies that, in a certain sense, were to "grow" with the fair during the 1960's, caught up by the growing success of Italian design: for example, Molteni, Flexform and Busnelli.

[18] Cf. A. Pansera, *Storia e cronaca della Triennale*, Longanesi & C., Milan 1978, pp. 493-529.

[19] C. C., "Alla XIII Triennale di Milano", *Domus*, Milan, no. 418, September 1964, p. 18.

[20] Pier Carlo Santini, "XIV Triennale", *Ottagono*, Milan, no. 10, July 1968, p. 32. Cf. also Eugenio Gentili, "Ma a che serve questa Triennale?", *Abitare*, Milan, no. 69, October 1968, pp. 45-46.

[21] Virgilio Vercelloni, "In morte della Triennale", *Il Confronto*, Peschiera Borromeo, June 1968.

[22] *Ibidem*.

[23] A. Pansera, *Storia e cronaca* cit., p. 560. For an analysis of the entire show cf. *ibid.*, pp. 531-571.

[24] The Eurodomus shows, organised by *Domus* every two years from 1966 onwards, were unable to compete with the *Salone*, at least in terms of influence, perhaps because of their formula – which did not attempt to "make a selection but *promote a selection*, or rather an 'auto-selection'" – and for their less frequent occurrence.

[25] Acerbis also made its debut at the 1965 *Salone* but only exhibiting period furniture. It was only in 1968 that it decided to begin working with architects and designers with its *Programma Compass* by Giorgio Decursu, Jonathan De Pas, Donato D'Urbino and Paolo Lomazzi.

[26] The *Salone* had quickly demonstrated its superiority to other furniture shows in Italy, including the *Mostra selettiva del mobile* in Cantù (1955) with its many competitions, jury and prizes, Mario Comense's 1958 *Biennale dello standard nell'arredamento*, and the *Salone del Mobile* in Pesaro (1956) for which the organising committee was more or less the same as the Milanese show. The success of the *Salone*, at that time only commercial, was due to two clearly defined factors: the decision not to be selective (the policy of "selecting while not selecting" was to be essential to its success as the preferred exhibition of Italian design), and its location in the pavilions of Milan Fair which, with the Campionaria (1920), had become the emblem of the city considered the moral and economic capital of the country.

[27] W. Scott Deiter, article on the 1965 *Salone del Mobile*, *Handelsblatt*, Düsseldorf, no. 199, 14 October 1965 (cited in "Commenti della stampa estera sul 5° Salone del Mobile Italiano", *L'Industria del legno*, Milan, no. 10, October 1965, p. 727).

[28] J. Dantel, article on the 1965 *Salone del Mobile*, *L'officiel de l'ameublement*, Paris, no. 180, November 1965 (cited in *Commenti della stampa* cit., p. 724).

[29] *Ibid.*

[30] D. Williams, article on the 1965 *Salone del Mobile*, *Furnishing World*, London, 7 October 1965 (cited in *Commenti della stampa* cit., p. 725).

[31] B. Bouffanet, article on the 1965 *Salone del Mobile*, *Meubles et décors*, Paris, n. 808, November 1965 (cited in "Altri commenti della stampa estera sul 5° Salone del Mobile Italiano", *L'Industria del legno*, Milan, no. 11, November 1965, p. 789).

[32] Cf. E. V. Massai, article on the 1965 *Salone del Mobile*, *Home Furnishing Daily*, New York (cited in "Altri commenti della stampa estera sul 5° Salone del Mobile Italiano", *L'Industria del legno*, Milan, no. 12, December 1965, p. 820).

[33] F. Defour, article on the 1965 *Salone del Mobile*, *Echo du Meuble*, Brussels, no. 10, October 1965 (cited in "Altri commenti della stampa"

Poster for the first Furniture
Show, 1961-1991

Poster for the 10th Lighting
Show, 1985

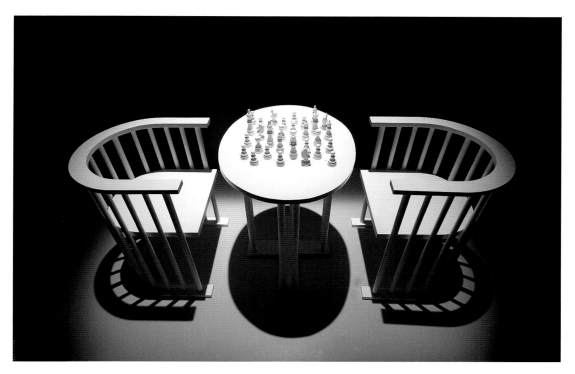

cit., December 1965, pp. 821-822).

[34]Il Comitato Organizzatore della mostra, "Mostra retrospettiva per una documentazione sul design del mobile in Italia dal 1945 a oggi", *L'Industria del legno*, Milan, no. 9, September 1965, p. 690.

[35]*Ibid.*, p. 689.

[36]Since then, in fact, only Gavina, Azucena and Danese have not exhibited at the *Salone*. But Dino Gavina, after selling his company to Knoll International, presented the furniture of the company Simon International at the *Salone* from 1971 onwards.

[37]The exhibition area measured 38,000 square metres in Pavilions 28, 29, 29B, 34 and the three floors of the new Pavilion 30 (notwithstanding the umpteenth increase in surface area, in 1965 more than 100 applications to exhibit had to be turned down) and there were 24,666 Italian visitors and 2,465 from abroad. The value of exports was 21,932 million lire.

[38]A number of new companies were founded during the second half of the 1960s – the best known being C&B Italia (now B&B Italia) in 1966, Driade and Gufram in 1968 – and the transformation of some others into the leading lights of the industry behind which the rest followed unseen for a number of years (e.g. Acerbis and Flexform in 1968, and Tisettanta the following year).

[39]The share was not entirely attributable to designer furniture but, more generically, to "modern" designs.

[40]R. De Fusco, *Storia del design*, Laterza, Bari 1988, p. 268.

[41]"Scandinavian out, Italian in", *Furnishing World*, London, 29 September 1966 (cited in "Commenti della stampa estera sul 6° Salone del Mobile Italiano", *L'Industria del legno*, Milan, no. 10, October 1966, p. 1230).

[42]*Cabinet Maker and Retail Furnisher* was of the same opinion: "One of the most significant aspects of the Italian collection was that the furniture was typically Italian and outstandingly individualistic; one did not have that mortifying experience that so often is felt in England and Scandinavia, that the designs are the same as you move from stand to stand. The teak shone in Milan by its absence". Article on the 1966 *Salone del Mobile*, *Cabinet Maker and Retail Furnisher*, London, 6 October 1966 (cited in "Commenti della stampa" cit., p. 1231).

[43]B. Bouffanet, article on the 1966 *Salone del Mobile*, "Meubles et décors", Paris, n. 820, November 1966 (cited in "Commenti della stampa" cit., p. 1232).

[44]The 1967 show welcomed 1,382 exhibitors of which 60 were foreign; the surface area measured 60,805 square metres and there were 28,984 Italian and 4,621 foreign visitors.

[45]The Japanese had always ignored Italian furniture but that year in particular they began choose Italian design.

[46]"Gli italiani scompigliano i mobili", *Le Figaro*, Paris, January 1966 (cited in "Salone Internazionale del Mobile - Parigi 1967", *L'Industria del legno*, Milan, no. 1, January 1967, p. 1346).

[47]J. Dantel, article on the 1967 *Salone del Mobile*, *L'officiel de l'ameublement*, Paris, n. 204, November 1967 (cited in "Echi sulla stampa estera", *L'Industria del legno*, Milan, no. 11, November 1967, p. 1750).

[48]"Il Salone del Mobile", *Abitare*, Milan, no. 62, January-February 1968, pp. 30-31.

[49]C. M. C., "A Milano, il Salone del Mobile", *Domus*, Milan, no. 456, November 1967, p. 20.

[50]"The 7th *Salone del Mobile* [...] provided [...] an exceptional offering of new creations like nothing ever seen in Europe". Cf. the article on the 1967 *Salone del Mobile*, *Die Presse*, Vienna, 4 October 1967 (cited in "Altri commenti", *L'Industria del legno*, Milan, no. 10, October 1967, p. 1718).

[51]Cf. "An infinite number of ideas from the Italians", *Furnishing World*, London, 12 October 1967 (cited in "Altri commenti" cit., p. 1719).

[52]Article on the 1967 *Salone del Mobile*, *Möbel Kultur*, Hamburg, n. 11, November 1967 (cited in "Echi sulla stampa estera" cit., p. 1760).

[53]J. Dantel, "La défi italien: devenir d'ici à cinq années le premier exportateur de mobiliers européen", *L'officiel de l'ameublement*, Paris, n. 216, November 1968, p. 106 [*T.d.A.*].

[54]*Ibid.*

[55]After *Sasmil* (international show of accessories and semi-finished products for the manufacture and finishing of furniture), in 1974 it was the turn of *Eurocucina* (international biennial show of kitchen furniture), the first show in the world dedicated exclusively to this sector. In 1976 there was *Euroluce* (international lighting show); in 1982 the producers of Cosmit and GemUfficio decided to bring together in a single fair the entire office furniture sector, thus creating *Eimu* (international biennial show of office furniture), which was at first associated with *SMAU* (international show of office furniture and equipment) and today with the SIM (international furniture show); and in 1987 there was the *Salone del Complemento d'Arredo* (furniture accessory show). Since 1998 there has been the *SaloneSatellite*, a showcase for young designers from all over the world.

[56]Henry Owen, "Up! Up!! Up!!! in Milan", *Cabinet Maker and Retail Furnisher*, London, 10 October 1969, p. 57.

[57]On this subject, cf. L. Lazzaroni, *35 anni di design al Salone del Mobile*, Cosmit, Milan 1996.

[58]A. Pansera, *Il design del mobile italiano dal 1946 a oggi*, Laterza, Bari 1990, p. 37.

"Stanze e Segreti", Milano,
Rotonda della Besana, 2000
Mladen Materic, La Cuisine
(photo: Attilio Maranzano)

"Stanze e Segreti", Milano,
Rotonda della Besana, 2000
Emir Kusturica, Basement
(photo: Attilio Maranzano)

February 1951. Italian fashion is born. Not even Mussolini succeeded in accomplishing as much.

Guido Vergani

There was no catwalk in the Neoclassical salon in Villa Torrigiani in Via dei Serragli, Florence where Italian fashion was about to be born "at floor level" using a short path between the seats and armchairs. It was a fashion show put on at home, carefully planned and very precise but of necessity "amateur". The library was transformed into a workroom for the last touches to the clothes and the guest bedroom into a storeroom for the accessories, hats, shoes and costume jewellery. There was a piano and there was a "tapeur". The library was also used as a dressing room and make-up room for the models. Unusually, the buyers arrived together, and there was no scrum of fashion journalists at the door as Giovani Battista Giorgini ("Bista") had deliberately limited the number of invitations. The occasion was a test and if it was going to go badly, it would be better to avoid the lights and attention of the media. It already seemed risky enough that *Women's Wear Daily*, *Daily News Record* and *Retailing Daily*, the publications belonging to the Fairchild Group, had already briefly announced the event as it would no longer have been possible to disguise any failure as a private consultation. Giorgini had already spoken of a session on the possibilities of creating an "Italian look" and inviting buyers from the large American stores, almost imploring them so as to break down their scepticism.

Anyway, Giorgini had kept quiet as he had been asked to do by the fashion houses involved in the show. Only six journalists had been invited to this debut: Elisa Massai, the correspondent of *Women's Wear Daily*, Elsa Robiola, editor of *Bellezza* and sent by the weekly magazine *Tempo*, Gemma Vitti of the *Corriere Lombardo*, Vera Rossi of *Novità*, Misia Armani of *I Tessili Nuovi* and *Omnibus*, and Sandra Bartolomei Corsi of *Secolo XIX*.

The sequence and the activities of the three days had been planned to produce the greatest return. Everything was designed around a programme that shrewdly placed the high society work to be done in a setting that would arouse the snobbish weaknesses of the American guests: on 12 February 1951 there was to be the presentation of day clothes, sportswear, boutique fashions and the accessories; the next day was a rest day; 14 February was reserved for the parade of the evening dresses and the grand finale, a ball to which Giorgini had invited all of Florence's aristocracy in addition to everyone involved with the show. The invitation read: "The aim of the evening is to show off Italian fashion. Ladies are therefore asked to wear dresses of pure Italian inspiration".

"The stakes were immediately high on the first day", wrote Roberta Orsi Landini, an expert on Italian fashion. "The buyers' interest was aroused straightaway […]. What they were supposed to notice directly was the dissimilarity with Parisian fashions, in particular the difficult evening dress category. On the 12th, the clothes for the boutiques, sports and free time were paraded before the day clothes. This was a type of collection that Paris did not present and that bore no comparison with the sophisticated images of French fashion. The clothes were surprising, young and fresh, the colours an unexpected triumph, the quality remarkable, the prices extraordinarily good. The buyers soon understood that a market sector of enormous prospects was opening. They were immediately able to recognise a business opportunity but also had sharp eyes for the haute couture in which the alternative nature and rebellion against the old domination by Paris were perhaps less evident".

The "coup de thèatre" was the result of Giorgini's deep understanding of the American market. Twenty-five years as a purchasing agent for the US, as the "eye" that monitored the best of Italian products for the large stores in New York, San Francisco, Dallas and Chicago, and as the ambassador for beauty, refinement and handcrafted products, had provided him with a highly sensitive understanding of the needs of the American public, consumer trends, the fickleness of taste, and which Italian products might just catch on.

Consequently, wrote Roberta Orsi Landini, "he had sensed what would be the winning characteristics of an

Italian fashion: clothes, lines, trends suited to the changes of a world in fast progress. […] The American market was the mirror of the Italian future: women that worked and who were obliged to use public transport, to spend all day out of the house but without in any way wishing to relinquish personal style and elegance. They – and soon also we – needed a fashion product that was less sophisticated and complicated than what Paris was offering. Time was moving ever faster towards mass production and a more practical, youthful fashion".

"Today it might seem no more than a gimmick", said Elisa Massai who was present at that first show, "but, at that time, the idea of opening a fashion show with what was apparently less important, informal fashion for a small seaside shop was courageous and intelligent. To bring on the knitwear, clothes for the beach, and clothes for the boutiques was like overthrowing tradition, the ritual of haute couture. But Giorgini did it and it was a sign of talent, of intuition. He knew that those designs were in line with the taste, the customs and the way of American living. He was no fool, he was attentive and he understood. The big names were Franco Bertoli, Clarette Gallotti, Avolio, and Emilio Pucci. If the programme of the show had been a menu, that unsophisticated fashion was much more than an aperitif, it roused the buyers' hunger".

A hunger also for Sorelle Fontana, Jole Veneziani, Simonetta, Fabiani, Marucelli, Noberasco, Carosa, Schuberth and Vanna whom the fashion columnists referred to as "creative dressmakers" and who were participants in the first collective design show in the somewhat capricious world of fashion. Each fashion "house", each individual had his own history and own glory, and even if they were flaunting their reputations a little, they were also putting them on the line.

The dressmakers were behind the scenes in the library or in the guest room with the models. Germana Marucelli, the great talent and pioneer of Italian style since the period of autarchy, worked with pins attached to her own dress, muttering hoarsely in Tuscan dialect. Emilio Schuberth recited into his jewellery and bracelets as he made the final adjustments with the understanding of his twelve years experience as an atelier and of top Rorna clients. Schuberth belonged to the group of designers of extravagant clothes, in contrast to those of Simonetta whose avant-garde, anti-conformist black *mises* for the beach were splashed across the pages of the English and American versions of "Vogue" in 1948. She was not risking much due to her relative inexperience, and much less than the traditionalist Alberto Fabiani who had inherited an atelier that had always had strong contacts with Paris and clients who were interested in dressing uniquely in French style.

Zoe, Micol and Giovanna Fontana were risking everything; they were born into the fashion world of their dress-making mother, Amabile, at Traversetolo near Parma, then went to Florence already much talked of following the attention they received from the picture press when then created a Hollywood dream of a wedding dress with a five metre train for Linda Christian, who married Tyrone Power in January 1949 in the Basilica of Santa Francesca Romana.

It was not the American stars, however, who shot the Carosa label of Giovanna Caracciolo to fame. She had no background in fashion but entered it from professional passion, "worrying behind a godet, in anguish over every little imperfection and raving over a particular black spot", as described by Quinto Conti who worked with her.

"On the morning of 12 February 1951", Matilde Giorgini, the daughter of "Bista" recounted, "the parades went ahead. There was absolute, inscrutable silence. Was it from fixed attention or embarrassment? Not a word, no applause, not a nod of approval or sign of boredom. Nothing was given away by a gesture or an expression on the faces of the few, impassive guests. My father was standing next to the door of the library-cum-changing room and my mother was in another strategic

*Emilio Pucci outfit, Florence,
1956
(G.B. Giorgini Archives-photo:
G.M. Fadigati)*

*Emilio Pucci in Capri in the
fifties.*

*Carosa outfit, Florence, 1955
(G.B. Giorgini Archives)*

position. They were bewildered. No-one understood how things were going. When the last model filed off, the applause began but it was no proof of commitment, it could just have been politeness. My father went up to the buyers and asked, 'Was it successful? What do you think?' Stella Hanania, the buyer for I. Magnin, replied, 'Paris was not nearly so exciting', and Gertrude Ziminsky of B. Altman said, 'It was well worth the trip'. The whole Giorgini family felt elated. It had worked. Stylists, seamstresses, premières, ironers and dressers beamed into the salon. Italian fashion had been born!".

Another and more probing sign that an Italian look might have caught on, or, rather, was about to catch on, was the account of the "two days" of fashion shows published on 15 February on the front page of *Women's Wear Daily*. It talked of the "real success" decreed by the buyers, particularly for the innovative sports clothes with their inventive details such as Bertoli's straw and pearl applications, Noberasco's lace, the needlework on the evening dresses, the handcrafted wools and silks of Tessitrice dell'Isola, and the resort-wear of Simonetta Visconti. The accessories too merited a section of their own. The prices were also given: 195 dollars for a tweed capecoat by Vanna, 9-12 dollars for the cotton summer clothes by Tessitrice, and 25-40 dollars for Marucelli's creations.

Giovan Battista Giorgini succeeded in something that not even Benito Mussolini had, smashing the French monopoly in fashion and sales. Paris represented fashion and was apparently invulnerable. While Giorgini was dreaming of an Italian style, Italian dressmakers were spending thousands of the old-fashioned, heavy French francs to buy fabrics and patterns that were exclusive to Dior, Balenciaga, Fath, Patou etc. to appease the hunger of their clients who, after the long fast enforced by the war, were voracious for French fashions, "fashion-fashion" as they used to say to distinguish it from surrogates.

It had seemed an overambitious project destined to end up like so many other attempts during the first fifty years of the 20th century. To those members of the industry that Giorgini had attempted to involve, nearly all of whom in vain, it seemed that old and disastrous paths were being followed once again: the path of Rosa Genoni, a socialist and the precursor of feminism, who exhibited clothes inspired by the Italian Renaissance at

the Milan Expo of 1906 and, later, found an ally in the actress Lyda Borelli who wore designs on stage that clearly reflected great Italian periods of history. The path too of Giuseppe Visconti, the father of the film director Luchino, who said in 1910, "Italy has all the technical and artistic possibilities to launch its own fashions on the world". And the path followed by Fascism when it encouraged stylists to put an Italian slant on their designs.

Mussolini had urged the matter even before sanctions obliged Italy to look after itself. Standing on a platform against the background of Castello Sforzesco in Milan in May 1930, he proclaimed, "Italian fashions in furniture, in decorations and in clothing do not yet exist; it is possible to create them, we must create them". The order gave rise to a great number of "fashion rallies" with the aim of banning all French fashion papers and magazines. In April 1933, the elected Italian fashion capital, Turin, organised shows and parades in the name of "national elegance" and Mussolini telegraphed, "If the start is good, what follows will be even better; it's a question of faith". The faith was also supported by decrees from on high. At the end of October 1935, the Fascist regime launched the National Fashion Authority which had the task of matching clothing to the needs of the period of autarchy. Italians were to "use only Italian products" and happily wear "lanital" i.e. caseine wool.

Fashion was also supposed to make itself independent of its subjection to Paris but tailors and seamstresses demurred because their clients preferred Parisian fashion or at least something that approached it. At that point, the Fashion Authority invented a badge of guarantee to be assigned to clothes "of Italian design and production". In any collection, at least 50 percent of the clothes had to exhibit the guarantee or there would be a fine of between 500 and 2000 lire. The fashion houses would often obtain the badge but hide it from their clients because otherwise the clothes would remain unsold. The belief that chic could only come from Paris was consequently as invulnerable to Mussolini's legal decrees and orders as it ever had been. Some kernel though had been sown and on the catwalks of Villa d'Este, Campione, Mirafiorì hippodrome, and in the ateliers of Milan, Turin and Rome, the fashion houses of Ventura, Palmer, Battilocchi, Ferrario, Cori, Gandini, Zecca, Fercioni, Bigi, Biki, Vanna and Tizzoni displayed their talent in obedience to the order to "create and dress *all'italiano*".

Yet, once peace returned, it was realised that the "psychological subjection" to Paris had never gone away and it quickly resurfaced. But those decrees and orders had perhaps prepared the soil and educated the public to the idea that an Italian fashion could be created just as, many years later, the Italian Communist Party argued in vain of the possibility of an Italian road to Socialism.

"The autarchy had obliged the fashion houses to abandon at least a little the convenient habit of buying in Paris, copying in Italy and selling", said Elisa Massai in an interview for the book *La Sala Bianca. Nascita della moda italiana* edited by Pitti Immagine and Electa. "The 'nationalist' idea of an Italian fashion was not, however, forgotten. Our craftsmen were of the first order and the fashion houses too. Our men's tailors were some of the best in the world. Often the materials that passed through the hands of the British had only the label in English and were in fact Italian products. The plan for an Italian fashion that was not beholden to France was not at all far-fetched. There was a suitable breeding ground and enough experience. During the period of autarchy and the war, something changed: the designs were plagiarized yet they contained a degree of novelty but then, it's true, the dressmakers returned to Paris to pay tribute".

Mussolini had failed so how did Giorgini succeed in turning round a century old habit at the start of the 1950s with the country still reeling from five years of war? Perhaps because the soil had been fertilised by those first attempts, but certainly because the idea of inciting the fashion houses to creative autonomy, of organising them, and of giving them a common strategy was not based on the elitist, snobbish domestic market conditioned by French traditions but focused on America, which, though also in thrall to the haute couture of Paris, was capable of commercial pragmatism. There was a chance that the American market would open up to a fashion (and prices) that could act as an alternative to the French "dictatorship".

Among Giorgini's most important clients were I. Magnin of San Francisco, Bergdorf Goodman and B. Altman of New York; these were the best American department stores, which, to remain the best in haute couture, were obliged to look to Paris and buy from Patou, Dior, Balenciaga and the many other master designers. Inevitably, America had a close business relationship with Paris but Giorgini's professional and Florentine sense of awareness had been aroused by the "Pucci case" which had shown how much the American market needed unpretentious designs for a more relaxed, colourful and informal style. After the war, in which he had fought with honour, Emilio Pucci had found himself wracked with "shocking debts" so, to try to get some money coming in, he set to designing and producing sandals and simple clothes in alliance with the craftsmen of Capri. With friends around the world and successful at arousing the enthusiasm of women and the well-to-do, Pucci is an extraordinary and intelligent self-propagandist. In 1947 he appeared in the pages of *Harper's Bazaar* which recounted how he had created, in almost just one day at St. Moritz, a complete ski outfit for a friend who had lost her baggage. The story not only explained the event but showed a photograph of the outfit and it was this that set off the commercial instinct of Lord and Taylor, a department store on Fifth Avenue. Their request to him to produce a series of the outfit was the first of a long and highly successful career.

At the end of the 1940s, Giorgini put the finishing touches to his idea of an Italian look for the USA, the "Pucci case" was just lifting off in the States. It was the signal that a market opportunity existed that could be acted on, but it was not the only sign: supplied by the first wool and cotton yarn that the Unrra and Erp plans of American help shipped to Italy, the Italian knitwear industry began to sell to Britain and the United States in 1949-50. These were the first bridgeheads of a programme that Giorgini's brilliant plan was to turn into a triumph. Dorville House in London was discovering

Laura Aponte, Marisa Arditi and Lea Galleani but already in October 1949, American buyers had visited Milan to buy fashion designs from Noberasco, Vanna, Fercioni and Tizzoni. During the same period, buyers from Bergdorf Goodman were in Rome where they had paid a visit to Simonetta and placed an order for some of their clothes. In June 1950, Odette Tedesco, the buyer for I. Magnin, opened the American door to Olga di Grésy and her Mirsa label. It was a limited top of the range order but an example of the way things were moving. Almost at the same time, Bettina Ballard, the editor of *Vogue* and her rival Carmel Snow, the editor of *Harper's Bazaar*, were enthusing over the bold turquoise and shocking pink "rags" produced by Pucci and, on Capri, discovered Simonetta Visconti Colonna of Cesarò (Simonetta) and Clarette Gallotti (Tessitrice dell'Isola).

An opening existed but it needed to be widened, perhaps by force, in order to create an authentically Italian look that did not imitate the French one. The establishment of such a look, Giorgini was certain, would put into place an engine that would power not just the clothes and accessories sectors but also the leather and straw industry in Florence, the lacemakers in Burano, the glass industry in Murano and the pottery firms of Bassano. The problem was that Italy had lost its image. The war, the infamy of the Fascist regime and the desolation of the country had stained the country, leaving the high quality Italian-made products struggling to regain their lost positions. It was necessary to find something that could boost them all, perhaps the fashion industry but that would need to be reinvented almost from scratch. Just thinking about it made it seem like madness when Italy itself was metaphorically still in patched clothes itself although industrial production in 1947 had risen from 70 percent of the 1938 level to 89 percent in 1948 and 104 percent in 1950.

Giorgini obstinately concentrated on this particular form of madness even at the cost of bluffing, telling white lies and playing cards he still did not have in his hand. Never was there a more Italian story as far as the need to invent, pretend, improvise, risk and dream was concerned.

That kernel of interest in Italian style existed but to enlarge it, it was necessary to convince the stylists to take the great leap of independence and to say goodbye to the comfortable life of reproducing others' ideas. But having got a yes out of them, the problem was still a difficult one: how to put the fashion houses in contact with the purchasing strategists of the large American and Canadian stores. It was necessary to persuade the buyers that there really was an Italian style, that it was worth seeing and that it was worth making the trip to Florence to see, given that the plan to present the show at the Brooklyn Museum in New York had fallen through. Charles Nagel, the director of the museum, had been enthusiastic but it required a sponsor willing to pay out between 25 and 33 thousand dollars and the proposal to top management at Altman's had fallen on deaf ears, partly because of the cost but mostly and justifiably because of their lack of belief in its success as an investment. Their friend Giorgini had promised a new, original and Italian look but the costs were too high to permit a "yes" with no guarantees. They wrote to Giorgini on 20 October 1950, "It would be fatal for us to present designs that were simply imitations of Parisian fashions" wishing that the show could be put on in Italy so that their buyer, Miss Meison, could be there in person. Their suspicion was valid. Giorgini was only holding a pair of jacks but his determination and almost patriotic conviction were such that he was playing as though he had a royal flush. In the end, however, his tenacity and strength of mind ended up by actually producing a royal flush.

The American "thumbs down" was given on 20 October but just a month and a few days later, on 27 November, Giorgini fearlessly replied to Altman's that he had arranged an exhibition in Florence on the days that immediately followed the Paris shows. The invitations (really more of an announcement of intention) were also

G.B. Giorgini with his wife and guest, Florence, Boboli, 1952
(G.B. Giorgini Archives)

Carosa outfit, Florence, 1955
(G.B. Giorgini Archives-photo:
G.M. Fadigati)

Sala Bianca, Antonelli
fashions, Florence, 1955
(G.B. Giorgini Archives-photo:
G.M. Fadigati)

Schuberth outfit, Florence,
1955
(G.B. Giorgini Archives-photo:
G.M. Fadigati)

sent out on 27 November to Bergdorf Goodman, Escobosa of I. Magnin in San Francisco, and Henry Morgan in Montreal. Giorgini was deeply convinced of his beliefs though they had no basis in fact, strongly enough to take a leap in the dark. The survey he had made of the traditional fashion houses before the 27th had been catastrophic. There were two problems to be overcome: the Italian stylists' fear of being cut off from the circuit of the French ateliers, of no longer being able to drink at the well of ideas, designs, fabrics, and exclusive sales rights, and the stylists' belief that their clients were almost completely conditioned by the equation "Paris = elegance". That psychosis was often insuperable.

"My father did not know the world of the fashion houses", recalled Matilde Giorgini. "Of course he contacted the houses that were referred to in the magazines that specialised in female fashion. He toured the famous names and was met by a series of refusals of the type, 'You're crazy. Don't even think about it. Paris would shut the door in our faces'. But my father was obdurate. He had faith in what he was doing and a massive serenity in the face of the tempests of life and work. The rejections by the most famous names might have caused a storm though, actually, it was already a flood. What was he to show the buyers who had in principle already accepted to make an extra trip to Florence out of friendship and support for the industry? Papa never wavered. He simply took his offer to those houses who today would be known as the 'up and coming names' and he hit the bullseye".

On 28 December 1951 – just over a month before the possible days of the show – Giorgini wrote to those up and coming names, "Since 1923 I have been in contact with the North American market and I represent many of the best companies that import our arts and crafts products. The world of fashion was never referred to in any practical sense as Paris is their lifeblood. However our fashion accessories have always been very much appreciated: bags, scarves, gloves, umbrellas, shoes, jewellery etc. As the USA is now warm in its attitude towards Italy, it seems to me that this is the moment to attempt to establish our fashions in that market. For that reason, seeing as the Paris collections are being shown to American buyers during the first week of February and August, we must get organised to be able to show our own collections during the same period. As I have already had agreement from several of the best fashion houses, this is my proposal.

"Date: second week of February and August each year. Place: Florence. Formalities: each haute couture house should bring a minimum of 20 designs (morning, afternoon, cocktail, evening) and one (or better two) house models; each house pays its own costs and contributes 25 thousand lire to the Giorgini office for the costs of organisation and reception of the guests. Sales: to be dealt with directly between the houses and the foreign buyers. In the interests of the houses, it is an explicit condition that the designs exhibited are purely and exclusively Italian in inspiration. It will not be easy in this first show in February to have a buyers' auction as they are convinced that Italian style is derived from Paris and therefore their interest is limited. On the other hand, we have all seen Italian designs published in *Vogue* and *Harper's Bazaar* under American and French by-lines. It is therefore in our interest to show that throughout history Italy has always been a *maestra* in the field of fashion, that she has maintained her genius and is still able to produce with a spirit of originality. The first show will be held in the Giorgini home on 12 and 14 February 1951 as indicated in the enclosed invitation. Please be kind enough to answer as quickly as possible if your house would like to participate".

Everything stemmed from this letter of exhortation which played on Italian pride and included a white lie. This was the beginning of the Italian domination of ready-to-wear fashions, the massive expansion of the knitwear and clothing industries, the Sala Bianca, Pitti Immagine, Modit, Milano Collezioni, Moda In and the

innumerable shows of Italian fashion, and the sensational phenomenon of stylism that exploded in the mid-1970s bringing in its wake valuable contributions to the country's balance of trade.

The white lie: it was not actually true what Giorgini had written about "agreement from several of the best fashion houses".

Around the end of December 1950, just two months from the deadline, Giorgioni had attracted two major names to the project at most and a few maybes. It was the letter that made the difference, bringing thirteen fashion stylists into Giorgini's fold. Nine were from the top echelons: Simonetta, Fabiani, Fontana, Schuberth and Carosa from Rome, and Marucelli, Veneziani, Noberasco and Vanna from Milan. Then there were four names that would present boutique fashions: Emilio Pucci, Avolio, Bertoli and Tessitrice dell'Isola.

The letter was sent on 28 December 1950. On 13 January, the Fontana sisters wrote, "Your invitation has attracted much attention from our house and those of Schuberth and Carosa", but they were not prepared to give a final yes and, "in the name of the above mentioned houses", they ask that "there should be at least seven or eight buyers present from the large American stores who are willing to purchase".

It was a guarantee that Giorgini could not give. He had only managed to extract vague promises from the buyers preparing for their trip to France to be present at the Paris shows. They did not want to be discourteous but the heralded Italian style did not raise their curiosity, in short, they were sceptical. Perhaps, in the end, they wouldn't come. No-one confirmed their participation. "I made them come fraudulently", recounted Giorgini to Oriana Fallaci in 1959. "I told each of them that their direct competitor would be there. It was, of course, a risky business". In the end, on 11 February, they arrived, "almost making fun of me and stressing the favour they had done me by coming to Florence". Those that arrived were Gertrude Ziminsky of B. Altman & Co in New York; John Nixon of Henry Morgan in Montreal; Ethel Francau, Jessica Daves and Julia Trissel of the New York Bergdorf Goodman, Stella Hanania for I. Magnin in San Francisco, Hannah Troy and Martin Cole of Leto Cohn Lo Balbo, large manufacturers on Seventh Avenue in New York, and the importer Ann Roberts. These were the leading figures in the American and Canadian clothes markets. If that group had as much as muttered a single criticism, it would have been the end of the dream for Italian fashion.

The country had by now left behind the tragic legacy of the war. Industrial production in 1951 had risen to 27 percent more than the pre-war level of 1938. The national income had also reached the pre-war level but it was not yet the end of the tunnel and nor was it nearing the boom period. It was not just chance that Giovanni Battista Giorgini had thought of sowing the seeds of an Italian style at that period of the country's history and economy, nor was it simply luck that the seeds found fertile soil. Unique among the industrial sectors, the cotton and wool industries had already returned to their 1938 levels in 1947.

After the closing show on the evening of 14 February – that of the evening dresses – Giorgini and his thirteen apostles made their calculations: it was a victory for Italian fashion. Two or three days later, the extent of the victory became apparent in a letter to Giorgini from Bettina Ballard, fashion editor of *Vogue*, the sacred cow of fashion journalism, who complained she was upset that she had not been present at the Florence show. "In sincerity, your show was too close on the heels of the French collections for me to leave Paris. But I was given reports by Jessica and Franco of Bergdorf Goodman and from Cole of Leto Cohn Lo Balbo. Everyone was very interested in Italy and so is *Vogue*. I am sure that we will do something together very soon". That "will do something together" sanctioned, with the official blessings of a recognised authority, the right of the fledgling and eventful scheme to get off the ground and also added to the grapevine gossip

that the July show was "not to be missed". The grapevine was so effective that there was a rush of buyers and journalists for the collections: the three hundred requests which obliged the shows to move from the Giorgini house to the larger rooms of the Grand Hotel.

The humidity and the heat on 19 July made Florence very sticky. A trainload of buyers and journalists had arrived from Rome the evening before where they had arrived from the USA. They assembled around the empty space where the catwalk was to be erected attempting to glean a little physical comfort from the breeze but even this was a wall of heat. The buyers represented the entire American clothing network while the twenty seven journalists were headed by the representatives of the foreign press: the two eternal rivals *Vogue* and *Harper's Bazaar* in the respective persons of Bettina Ballard and Carmel Snow, then Sally Kirkland of *Life*, Fay Hammond of the *Los Angeles Times* and Matilde Taylor with Elisa Massai for *Women's Wear Daily*.

There were ten haute couture stylists presenting collections, and Carmel Snow was so moved by the creations of Jole Veneziani that she presented her with a rose saying, "You deserve a gold medal but unfortunately I haven't got one; take this rose instead as a sign of my appreciation". The group that had been present in February (Carosa, Fabiani, Fontana, Simonetta, Marucelli, Veneziani, Noberasco and Vanna) had been joined by Fabri of Turin and Maria Antonelli of Rome; Maria Antonelli had cut her teeth as an assistant at Battilocchi, then gradually established herself with her talent, creativity and openness of character.

The whole of 20 July was dedicated to boutique and sports fashions with the collections of Emilio Pucci, Avolio, Mirsa, Clarette Gallotti and, as would be said today, with the second lines of Jole Veneziani and Simonetta. These simple, functional and youthful fashions, wrote Misia Armani, reflected "the practical, essential and modern style of Americans". A twenty-year old boy without either a boutique or sportswear collection was seen crying "disconsolately in a corner" by a journalist while the protagonists, extras and spectators of the three day event in Florence enjoyed the traditional closing ball. "He was the unknown figure in this story", wrote Nietta Veronese in *Illustrazione Italiana*. "He had created a wonderful collection but the others would not let him show it. It was, however, sold just the same". Today, Roberto Capucci, the unknown boy, does not remember crying. "Certainly, I was very upset. I had only just opened my own dressmaking shop in the Via Sistina in Rome. I had been encouraged to do so by a woman of great passion, Maria Foschini, who acted as my protectress. I had dressed Isa Miranda, Clara Calamai and Elisa Cegani but I still remained unknown generally. I had not yet come to the forefront but it was Maria who made it possible. When Giorgini's first show emerged almost from secrecy and word began to go around of a second show, Maria hurried to Florence with a bundle of my designs. Giorgini received them, saw my work and was surprised but there was no room left to enter me in the list of shows and, in addition, it would have required the agreement of the others, the 'founding' group. That smiling, good-hearted man – who had no hint of desire for personal gain from this project – thought the problem could be overcome by offering me five 'tableaux' – five sets of clothes to be shown – during the final ball in Via Serragli but the others came to know of it and vetoed the idea. Perhaps they were not completely wrong. I was coming from nowhere without even having worked my way up in a house so I could hardly expect to be welcomed with open arms, but this set the precedent that every new name who wished to show a collection had to obtain the consent of the founding group and, gradually, from those who had been co-opted. That evening I was unable to show my clothes but word was passed around and there was a deal of curiosity. The next day, Giorgini invited the buyers to visit his house to see my collection and they took the lot."

Those few July days were also profitable for the other ten haute couture houses and the five "boutique" style houses. "It seems that the store buyers made many purchases with the emphasis on simple, sporty designs", wrote Oriana Fallaci. Sales were solid and strongly on the up compared to the first show. But success was threatened by small-minded conflicts, parochial envy and individualism and the first split occurred when Simonetta and Fabiani decided to show their collections in Rome. Giorgini's group signed up new recruits and on 18-22 January 1952, the third Italian fashion show was held with Marucelli, Vanna, Noberasco, Veneziani, Favro (from Turin), Antonelli, Carosa, Sorelle Fontana, the now accepted Roberto Capucci, Gabriellasport, Schuberth and a handful of boutique firms: Tessitrice dell'Isola, Veneziani-Sport, Giorgio Avolio, Valstar, Luisa Spagnoli, Emilia Bellini, Giuliana Camerino, Mirsa, Franco Bertoli, Luciana, Coppola e Toppo, and Glans-Magnani. The buyers represented companies like I. Magnin of San Francisco, Henry Morgan of Montreal, Carson Pirie Scott of Chicago, Ben Zuckermann and Gimbel Brothers of New York, Gordon Marsh of Boston, Racliff Chapman of London, Wettergreen of Stockholm, Lebof, Berlowitz and Braunscheweing of Zurich, Ancon Exchange System of Nuremberg, and Koebl of Munich. And for the third time, the sales, reproduction agreements and orders were extraordinary: seven billion lire overall, a huge figure considering that the average monthly wage for a clerk was only fifty thousand lire. The Florence shows were bursting with success. The *New York Times* wrote on 29 January 1952, "The Italian design clothes, superlative materials and prices that are the half of the French ones seem destined to attract buyers. There is no doubt that Florence is about to take the place of Paris". But did Italian fashion really have a solid base on the eve of its debut in the Sala Bianca in the Pitti Palace? Many articles and a private letter from Elsa Robiola – editor of *Bellezza* and correspondent of the weekly magazine *Tempo* paint an accurate portrait of the growth of the Italian fashion houses and the problems the fashion industry was undergoing.

The letter was written in Paris on 17 February 1952 and sent to Giorgini. "Unfortunately, the Paris collections overall are everything that the Paris name represents. Unfortunately, the effort that the French stylists distressingly put into their work (because business is bad and the mood of the nation is very poor) is still disciplined and harmonious; unfortunately, the organisation of French fashion is perfect. We must admit it objectively if we are to act seriously. The prestige of the Italian names is not yet strong enough; it will take years and years of hard work to get to the point that the French have reached". It was possible, we are to suppose, "to get to the point that the French have reached" but only by gritting teeth; fortunately, tenacity was one of Giorgini's strong points.

The third "Italian High Fashion Show" had only shortly been over when Giorgini started looking for a more suitable site than the now rather restricted Grand Hotel. It needed not just to be large but also meaningful, partly a "mirror" of the historical and artistic traditions that he always stressed to legitimise a claim to Italian style and elegance when dealing with foreigners. In his search for such a place, is was almost automatic for Giorgini to think of the ballroom in the Pitti Palace, the Sala Bianca, with its rows of mirrors, immense chandeliers from Murano, Neoclassical stuccowork, and vast, harmonious proportions. To use such a location, all kinds of authorisations were required yet Giorgini managed to get them.

The seating capacity of the Sala Bianca was not perfect but it allowed Giorgini to hold firm to a fundamental principle of his strategy, that of having a shared catwalk. At the debut show of February 1951, the "all together" concept turned out to be a winning formula, offering savings in time and effort for the buyers and journalists who, in Paris, were obliged to rush from one atelier to another. It was also ideal for the small houses whose number of designs was limited and functioned as

a sort of sieve that allowed selection of those who would display. In addition, it presented an image of Italian fashion as an overall fact rather than as a series of single, perhaps short-lived, houses in competition with one another, yet it was probably the shared catwalk and single site that fuelled the breakaway of some houses to Rome. It happened in summer 1952, when Italian style once again took over the Pitti Palace, that Schuberth and Sorelle Fontana preferred to show their collections in Rome. The Milanese newspaper, *Corriere della Sera* had sent one of its top journalists, Raffaele Calzini, to Florence and gave him pieces high billing by printing them on page three. There were 350 buyers from the United States, Britain, Sweden, Germany, Holland and Norway. The event lasted five days with haute couture collections from Antonelli, Capucci, Carosa, Ferdinandi, Giovannelli Sciarra, Polinober, Marucelli, Vanna and Veneziani and sixteen sportswear and boutique fashion labels. This fourth "Italian High Fashion Show" was the first time the show was put on with an alliance between the fashion houses and the textiles industry. Right from the start in February 1951, the quality of Italian fabrics had been one of the winning cards in the overall success of the clothes.

Those days in Florence were full of joy for the Italians as a result of the success of the location, the pact between the stylists and the fabric manufacturers, and the critical and commercial success of the designs ("Emilio Pucci's collection of sportswear had already been sold twice before the catwalk session, and I. Magnin had authorised its buyer to purchase 65 haute couture models at 150 thousand lire each rather than the 45 of the year before", wrote Elisa Massai in *24 Ore* on 29 July 1952). However there was a feeling of bitterness in the increase of the split with Rome which threatened not only the show in Florence but the future of the recently recreated Italian fashion industry.

Two powerful names in fashion journalism came to the defence of Giorgini: Elsa Robiola appealed for help for the man "who has earned himself the general's stripes" in *Tempo*, and Irene Brin wrote in the weekly magazine *La Settimana Incom*, "War has now been declared between Rome and Florence with small, minor wars that involve Turin, Milan and even Naples. […] If Italian fashion wants to survive – and it must – it has to come together on times, place and organisation. A city must be chosen in which, for three days, buyers will be shown ten designs (no more!) from each company, pre-

sented one after the other with the maximum of decorum and simplicity in a collective, orderly and relaxed manner. Italian fashions are excellent on the whole but we do not have a Balenciaga: only by rotating and contrasting our various talents can we produce the best effects. The ten designs for each stylist are of fundamental importance: buyers want ideas, not the repetition of ideas. […] The essential thing is to offer a varied, appealing and concentrated sample: buyers […] want only to use their highly limited time in the most efficient way possible".

This sharp criticism had some effect. The programme of the fifth "Italian High Fashion Show" held in January 1953 bore the logo of the Ente Italiano Moda (Italian Fashion Authority), a public body that had bowed to the patronage of the Florentine organisation. This represented the almost governmental recognition of Florence as the single vital and functional centre for the presentation and sales of Italian fashions.

Behind his professional smile, Giorgini knew how to bite: those involved in the Roman split (except for Schuberth) did not give in but founded the Sindacato Italiano Alta Moda (Italian High Fashion Syndicate) with a statute that forbade participation in the show in the Sala Bianca. This was an outright declaration of war. Rome had stated its right to control the affairs for as many houses as wished to join it because the journey to Florence incurred such expenses. In fact, the split had also been caused by the "promiscuity" of the show represented by "everybody together" for the two or three days of the parades. The instigators of the split, Simonetta and Alberto Fabiani, had thought better of the situation and returned to the Florentine ranks where they were welcomed with open arms by the *pater familias*, but the rest of the Romans held fast. Giorgini, referred to as "the Christopher Columbus of Italian fashion" by the American press, did not give in passively. "The march of Italian fashions is being slowed and obstructed by all those shows that, unsupported by any degree of expertise, try to imitate and exist on the edges of the Florence show." Fay Hammond wrote in the *Los Angeles Time*, "Giorgini is the only one in Italy who knows what he is doing".

Nor did he give in. Smilingly, he counterattacked. That same year he persuaded Florence City Council, the Chamber of Commerce, the Association of Industrialists, and two boards related to the city's tourist industry to band together to form the Florence Italian Fashion Centre, an authority that would be responsible for the

Fabiani outfit, Florence, 1960 (G.B. Giorgini Archives)

Galitzine outfit, 1960 (G.B. Giorgini Archives)

Sala Bianca, Krizia's first fashion show, Florence, 1964

The designers participating in the Sala Bianca, Florence, 1957

show and act as a sort of public bulwark against the moves made by the Roman breakaway companies that were taking advantage of the silence on the matter of the government authorities. Unfortunately, the bulwark had difficulty in functioning. In 1955 there were thirteen organisations that concerned themselves with Italian fashion "in different cities, with different intentions and with different members". But at the time of the January show, Irene Brin spoke of the "long-lasting success" of Florence where Antonelli, Capucci, Carosa, Fabiani, the Florentine Guidi, Marucelli, Schuberth (another prodigal son), Simonetta and Veneziani displayed.

The "long-lasting success" and the certainty that much of that success depended on personal respect and friendship were not enough to comfort Giorgini who was worn down by "betrayal", travel, incomprehension, and the need to row against the currents of confusion and petty jealousies.

The ninth Italian High Fashion Show in January 1955 was attended by 500 buyers and 200 accredited journalists; it was also the occasion of Giorgini's letter of farewell and thanks to all those involved with its organisation: buyers, journalists, stylists and backroom staff. They were all mentioned by name. He explained in the letter that, now that the teething problems of Italian fashion were over, he could move aside without compromising what had been created. Also that the houses could now show their collections where, how and when best suited themselves. The reaction was immediate and affectionate and, after the last parade on the evening of 27 January, Giorgini was pushed onto the catwalk of the Sala Bianca where he was presented with an album bound in green leather filled with the signatures of all those who had been part of the Florence adventure since February 1951 in a friendly plea not to give up. Certain of the friendship and affection that surrounded him, Giorgini decided to remain in command but his threatened resignation – which may simply have been tactical – had not done away with the disputes and petty vendettas. Nothing changed in the politics of the fashion industry. The threat was a sudden decline in an industry that the figures indicate was in full expansion. In 1955, Italian haute couture had exported clothes worth 1,280 million lire compared with the 454 millions in 1952. The trend was up, as was clear from the crowd of buyers that attended the eleventh show at the end of January 1956. There were more than 300 representing 109 shops and department stores but another shadow now hung over

the event: Simonetta and Fabiani had once again left the Florence contingent to show their collections in their ateliers in Via Gregoriana and Via Frattina in Rome. This second departure refocused the controversy and accusations of egoism flew. "Italian stylists", wrote Maria Pezzi in *Corriere d'Informazione*, "have become more capricious and inconstant than prima donnas. They are making life for the organisers more and more difficult and a constant source of surprises".

The quarrel between Rome and Florence continued. In June 1957, Eugenia Sheppard, fashion journalist for the *New York Herald Tribune* dedicated an article to the "Italian pandemonium". Running up to the July show in the Sala Bianca, Giorgini had to produce miracles to prevent the walkout of Carosa and Capucci in addition to that of Simonetta and Fabiani. To keep all four in the fold, he had to accept that they gave a preview of their collections in Rome as had already been announced. The pandemonium became more complicated. The textile producers had withdrawn from their alliance with Giorgini two years earlier and put on their own show in Milan. In this chaos, for the first time Giorgini took a public position with an article and not just a report to those involved: "The great success of Florence has unfortunately been counterproductive to Italy in that numerous schemes have spawned from it, all without the necessary expertise for success, thereby muddying the water and destroying the unity that had made it possible to win such a hard battle".

When, at the start of 1958, the accounts were totted up, it was realised just how much gain had resulted from his long, intelligent dedication to the industry marked by his obstinate tenacity and an infinite patience that helped to absorb the vexations and attacks. "The export data for the clothing and fashion industries are eloquent", wrote Luciana Olivetti in *La Nazione*. "From 80 billion lire in 1950, the figures rose to 171 billion in 1956 and 208 billion in 1957 despite fallbacks everywhere else in the world. This represents an increase of 150 percent in six years." For two years, Italy had been the largest European exporter to North America of materials and articles of clothing having overtaken England and France. The export of wool and silk had quintupled in six years whereas the export of outer knitwear had risen sixteen fold. Women's clothing had passed from the low 45 million lire of 1950 to 1,800 million in 1957 and leather footwear from 208 million in 1950 to almost 1,900 millions in 1957.

Florence was able to resist the siege of alternative shows only as a result of these economic results. The number of buyers in Florence in January 1959 was 600, and the number of department stores, shops and manufacturing companies in January 1961 was 219 (double those of 1956) represented by 83 British, 46 German, 35 American, 4 French, 4 Canadian, 3 Austrian and 2 Dutch buyers. The pressure of numbers in Florence did not weaken as a result of the Rome schism because the companies that broke away from Florence (sometimes with an immediate re-entry) were more than made up for by the increasing numbers of companies specialising in knitwear, sportswear and casual clothes that wished to display their wares in the Sala Bianca. In summer 1960, eighteen companies were allowed to present collections (Laura Aponte, Avolio, Baldini, Bertoli, Camisene, Celi, De Simone, Falconetto, Glans, Mirsa, Myricae, Naka, Paola Nucci, Scarabocchio, Toninelli, Valditevere and Vito). In January 1961, there were nineteen plus seven companies offering millinery, six secondary lines, top name boutique designers, and forty-six accessory producers.

The "Giorgini system" had entered the 1960s with its sails filled despite the Roman offensive, the switching back and forth of certain names, the bungles created by the various organisational authorities in competition with one another, and the slowness shown by the Italian government in understanding the importance to the national economy of the "Made in Italy" label. During the first decade of activity, the increase in purchases made by foreign buyers was around 9000 percent. Giorgini had certainly not just rested on his laurels: he had recreated the fashion industry in the role of an "ice-breaker" to be followed by a fleet of accessories companies. He had brought knitwear and children's wear to the catwalk in 1954, leatherware in 1955, teenager fashions in 1962 (Wanda Roveda) and lingerie in 1964 (Irene Galitzine). Men's fashions debuted in their own right in 1963 with a collective presentation from men's stylists but they had been a complementary parade to the women's fashions since 1952 and had launched the career of the Roman stylist Brioni.

Giorgini had always believed in – much earlier than anyone else – the future of boutique fashions and then ready-to-wear which first appeared in the Pitti Palace in 1956; they were then shown in Milan in 1957 and 1958 in the conviction, later corroborated, that they represented the future of clothing. And Giorgini prepared the ground for that future by increasingly allowing young designers specialising in ready-to-wear designs to show their collections in the Sala Bianca.

"It was Giorgini's exclusive and extraordinary intuition that fashion buying was changing", said Mariuccia Mandella of Krizia. "The increasing wealth of nearly all the population shifted the emphasis from haute couture to mass produced clothes that were not really based on fashion." But it was just this foresight that was to boomerang on Giorgini when Florence was accused of mixing the sacred (haute couture) with the profane (boutique fashions and ready-to-wear) and of thinking of money rather than art.

"The invasion had begun", remembered Roberto Capucci who went to Paris in 1962. "We, the pioneers, were a united group despite the moves to Rome. Some of us felt a little besieged and thought perhaps it was a quirk of Giorgini's or maybe another example of Italian individualism". Giorgini suffered for it but he was deeply convinced – and he showed it straightaway in the July show of that year – that Italian fashion should be made up of the many, not just a few famous names. He was able to declare to the American press with pride and determination that the foundations of Italian fashion were "sturdy and untouched" by the Roman venture because sometimes famous names like Biki came back to Florence, and because there were so many flourishing young companies that were later to achieve fame, like Sarli, Mila Schon, Giuliano, Centinaro, Enzo, Baratta, Galitzine, Lancetti, Balestra, Forquet, Krizia, De Barentzen, Ken Scott, Palloni, De Luca, Mingolini-Guggenheim, Valentino.

The foundations had been so well built that they remained sturdy even when Giorgini was obliged to bring his successful lead to an end in spring 1965 as a result of the undermining of his position. In fourteen years he had produced twenty-nine shows (as the spring-summer show of January 1965 was also his), first presenting the fledgling industry to the world, then protecting it as it grew in strength, and finally trying to tame its teenage rebelliousness. The roots remained sturdy even when the Milanese – Albini, Krizia and Missoni – abandoned the Sala Bianca in 1972 and decided to present their collections in their own city, opening the way to the luxury ready-to-wear clothes that the Milano Collezioni have successfully and prosperously presented for almost 30 years. Those were the roots of the giant the Italian fashion industry is today.

Milan, the laboratory of Italian Style

Maria Vittoria Carloni

The great success of the Italian ready-to-wear fashions that send foreigners into raptures is, in a certain sense, the result of a conceptual notion in which comfortable, casual fashions made using the highest quality materials, traditional methods and skilful workmanship are simply mass produced. Pioneers like Krizia and Missoni became famous for their luxury knitwear, items that Americans want regardless of price. Falling between haute couture – which has dropped in popularity – and industrial clothes production – which has risen – Italian ready-to-wear fashions are not just a style of dressing but a new attitude that mirrors social change.

Milan, a hotbed of design during the 1990s, became the centre of Italian Style during the 1970s. "It was the right moment in a city where many avant-garde fashion houses and ateliers decided to focus on ready-to-wear designs", as Lucia Sollazzo, a fashion and customs journalist for the newspaper *La Stampa* for twenty years as well as a writer of elegant prose and poetry, wrote in her book *Tutti in vetrina - Il romanzo della moda italiana* on Italian fashions, published in 1996 by Longanesi. "And dynamic, witty personalities like Cinzia Ruggeri tempted the public to try alternative styles of dress. The new stylists sparked off a new atmosphere and stimulated the interest of the press and foreign buyers. They produced, in short, something different, better than the simple 'off-cut from the atelier to be industrially produced'; they understood the processes and rhythms in detail, and supplied the manufacturers with designs that could be reproduced over and over without being unfaithful to themselves or to the expectations of the public; the public that they watched to gain an understanding of how society was developing and being transformed. Armani still claims that he walks the streets to get ideas that might be useful for creating variations on his favourite themes."

It was a revolution that arrived unannounced, almost on the quiet. "I would be lying if I claimed I understood immediately how important Milan was to be as the motor and capital of ready-to-wear", recounts Maria Pezzi in her book *Una vita dentro la moda* (Skira, 1998). "I was aware of [Italy's] strengths: the beauty of the materials, the quality of the manufacturing, with Maramotti and Rivetti at the head. But I had no idea of the extent of phenomenon it was to become. The 'Ken Scott case' gave me an inkling. Scott is an American from Fort Wayne in Indiana who had been a successful artist in Paris and the States before he took a house and workshop in Milan. This was an unusual choice but he explained, 'Here there is everything: long established companies that produce textiles and accessories, large clothing manufacturers and the best silk producers in the world. Here there is a tradition of almost craftsmanlike dedication to perfection'. I received another sign in 1997 from the presentation of five ready-to-wear collections, Basile, Misterfox, Sportfox, Callaghan and Escargot, all designed by Walter Albini, a genius who is incapable of practical administration. It was organised at the Circolo del Giardino by Aldo Ferrante, a former sales rep who became a manager with a sixth sense for the potential of ready-to-wear. Three hundred models were used and the rewards were the plaudits of the exhausted press and an immediate burst of sales."

That overpowering fashion show is a good marker to represent the start of Milan's and Italian fashion's irresistible rise and an illustration of the route taken by so many of the top ready-to-wear designers (Ferré, Versace, Armani, Moschino etc.) who had spent years designing for other labels before going solo (Albini only presented his first men's and women's collection in London for spring-summer 1973). "Albini invented a new image for women with jackets, trousers and chemises; he reintroduced the revival in an intelligent, elegant and inventive form making critical use of irony and contrast", wrote Isa Tutino Vercelloni in the *Dizionario della Moda* (Baldini & Castoldi) who was

Albini's friend and admirer. "He created a total look characterised by detachment and unaffectedness, endowing details and accessories with a maniacal perfectionism which, to him, are more important than the outfit itself. The stylist gave a crucial boost to Italian ready-to-wear fashion by applying design to fashion in an innovative way."

The pioneers of the export capital of Italian style, Milan, shared an original vision. In 1974, Krizia and Missoni moved to the city from Florence where they had enjoyed many seasons of success. The change signified the move from handstitched clothing to mass production, though retaining the same quality of article, elegance and innovation in the materials used, and precision and fluency in the forms, and not forgetting the lessons taught by the two great French designers of the 20th century, Paul Poiret – who freed women from the corset – and Coco Chanel, who made refined use of the jersey. Design talents of different ages and backgrounds gathered in Milan where they were organised by the intuitive Beppe Modenese to present their designs on the catwalks rebuilt in the pavilions of the Fiera (Milan Exhibition Centre) and to deal with textile manufacturers, also important players in the fashion surge, in the Ideacomo fair at Cernobbio.

These developments were recounted for the first time in the 1984 book *L'Italia della moda* written by Alfa Castaldi and Silvia Giacomoni and published by Gabriele Mazzotta; Mazzotta is a militant Milanese publisher fascinated by artistic movements. In the same road is also published an important avant-garde magazine, *Data*, edited by Tommaso Trini.

Castaldi had produced the portraits over a decade and Giacomoni examined the lives and works of the stylists to understand the reasons for their success and their links with society, entrepreneurial activity and visual culture like architecture and design. "The Italian look came into being when this traditionally poor country finally felt it had been freed from having to dedicate itself to satisfying only basic needs", wrote Giacomoni. "After buying refrigerators, washing machines, televisions, and a house at the seaside, the Italians of the emerging classes who wished to forget regional and rustic clothing styles had no desire to identify themselves with the better-off classes of other countries, so they joyfully turned to what seemed to offer a new style of dress that dispensed with the traditions in which elegance equalled sophistication".

As interpreters of the changing times, and the evolution in customs and tastes, the Milan stylists were seen as modern demiurges. "I do not believe such a large group of creative personalities – despite their individual leanings, motivations and aspirations – had ever been gathered together in one sphere", observed Gillo Dorfles in his catalogue of the October 1991 exhibition in memory of Enrico Coveri at Museo Pecci in Prato, Tuscany (Coveri's birthplace). "And above all, I do not believe that the phenomenon is only to be considered the result of economic and commercial factors, nor of skilful promotion. I would almost say that many of those wishing to follow an artistic vocation in Italy were able to enter this field of self-expression and that they have found a means of exercising an influence that they would not have been able to in other spheres".

During the tumultuous 1970s, social observers had to understand the sweeping away (which occurred rather late in Italy) of the leftist student politics of the late 1960s and of the American pacifist and hippie movements. The task of deciphering the new social trends – in particular the crisis of male and female roles and identities provoked by the women's movement – fell to cultural anthropologists, semiologists and the new post-Jung and post-Reich psychoanalysts. It was the task of the stylists to interpret the new signs and needs and to invent a new image and, in 1975, in Giorgio Armani's first collection, presented at Carminati restaurant in Piazza Duomo in Milan, the destructured jacket was introduced. Lauded by the press and

Ken Scott (second from right),
Gianni Versace, Jean-Baptiste
Caumont and Muriel Grateau,
mid-seventies

chased by buyers, it was to become the fashion item of the moment.

"They were looking for a style for the new career woman that would support her in her confrontation with men", explained the stylist in an interview with *Panorama* in February 1997. "It was the right answer for that moment; it cleared away traditional elegance and suggested a new way to dress, in a looser and more dynamic style. The logical answer at the time was men's jackets made softer for women so that they did not lose their femininity." It brought instant success after years of working his way up, and, in 1976, he founded his own company, "Giorgio Armani", with his partner Sergio Galeotti. The company had no intention of producing clothes, just ideas. "We started from there, financing ourselves. The move from the offices in Corso Venezia and Via Santa Cecilia to Palazzo Durini was very important; it cost a fortune in rent but was an investment in image."

Planning image and fashion as anthropological design form the style of Gianfranco Ferré who made his debut in 1978. Born in Legnano near Milan where he still lives in his family home, Ferré is nicknamed the "Gran Lombardo" for his bulk but it is a definition that he likes as it expresses a constancy and capacity for work, as well as the pleasure he takes in daily routine and material things which he transfers into his fashion work.

"I am very proud of my training as an architect, and of the analytical and logical method I use that draws out my creativity", Ferré loves to say, "but I also try not to fall into the traps of being too rational or of abstract simplification".

Another of the new boys of 1978, the thirty-two-year old Gianni Versace from Reggio Calabria, brought his unmistakable method of combining references to his Milan debut. Utterly open-minded in his citations, in his mixing of styles and in his use of history – even personal – Versace succeeded in becoming unique and recognisable in his exaltation of femininity and seductiveness, using a rare skill for synthesis and a delicacy in his use of excess. His choice of the head of Medusa as his trademark harked back to Magna Grecia and a world of extreme colours and sensations that perfectly suited the return to hedonism and egoism of the 80s after the years of terrorism and energy crisis in the 70s. It was the period of flaunting one's wealth and one's athletic, perhaps aesthetically engineered, body but it was also a time in which the new look was inspired by the Rococo and Baroque styles of the 18th century.

In a 1998 interview with the weekly magazine *Specchio* on Versace, Richard Martin, who was curator of the Costume Institute of the Metropolitan Museum in New York at the time, observed, "The 18th century is always present in fashion. It is an option for us, an outlet that leads to the extravagance, spectacle and ostentation that we search for in our lives".

However there was also a search for roots and a sense of self-indulgence that brought a young pair of stylists into the limelight during the 1980s, the Sicilian Domenico Dolce and the Venetian Stefano Gabbana, whose label Dolce & Gabbana seems embarked on an unstoppable ascent. Their styles are based on a return to the knitwear, needlework and handstitching of Domenico's Sicily, a strong interpretation of Mediterranean beauty and femininity, sartorial skill, a dose of Anglo-Saxon traditions and a passion for cinema and rock music.

This explosion of creativity attracted new talents, like the Fendi sisters who found the Milanese catwalks the right stage for their luxury handstitched products, and Karl Lagerfeld (a French-German designer who had gone to work for Krizia in the 1970s) who reworked furs with eccentric and sublime designs. The wave of energy also stimulated originality in ready-to-wear collections that were to take the Fendi name into the world top ten of luxury brands. Then there was Laura Biagiotti from Rome and Genny from the Marches, the men's collections that all the big names contributed to, including Valentino with his Oliver line, and Nicola Trussardi from Bergamo, who had moved on from the family business of glove-making to offer a traditional yet aggressive ready-to-wear line. In using La Scala theatre to present his clothes, he scandalised the well-to-do of Milan who felt the temple of opera had been violated by this upstart from the "rag trade".

Marching to a different tune to the conformism to wealth and conspicuous consumption was the mocking spirit of Moschino, whose approach was to fire upon the enemy using their own weapons: he used classic, well-constructed forms and the finest cuts high quality tailoring could supply but distorted and disarranged in a surreal fashion. "There is no creativity without chaos", he liked to say. Moschino wished to leave as much choice as possible in the way his customers might dress. "Impositions are prohibited: if you liked what you were wearing last year, then wear it this year and maybe next year too." In short, he was a revolutionary, a prophet and herald of the "conceptual" fashion that characterised the 1990s.

Another radical was the thirty-four year old Romeo Gigli from Castel Bolognese near Ravenna, who made his debut in 1983, with his elegiac skinny young girls draped in opulent, refined and colourful materials of an insubstantial transparency.

The Milanese designer Miuccia Prada was the grandchild of Mario Prada and ran a shop of luxury items such as bags, shoes and cases in the Galleria Vittorio Emanuele; in 1989 she sold the family business and presented her first collection of women's wear. Although consumerism and hedonism were still riding high in western life, the conceptual fashions of young Miuccia took a different angle; almost immediately described as minimalist, Prada fashion is in fact the cultured reworking of the aesthetic disorder of our age but without any degree of abstraction. Prada *is* Miuccia, the shy, middle-class girl who has been turned into a public figure, a girl who happily goes bare-legged when the temperature is below zero, who wears woollen socks with sandals, who will wear a long chiffon skirt over a rough tweed one, the girl who has invented windcheaters for evening wear. Today, however, Prada is also a group and one of the most successful in Italian fashion. It is run by Miuccia's husband, Patrizio Bertelli, and has its production and research workshops into new materials, styles and public customs in Tuscany.

Almost thirty years have passed since the debut of Walter Albini in Milan and fashion has become a phenomenon that has a massive impact on society, culture and the economy; it is a global and virtual phenomenon in which articles and consumption have to respond not just to the laws of production but, more importantly, to the constantly changing values of society.

The phrase "Made in Italy" has now become a conventional definition for products that have that unique style created by Italian designers. Even the word style has become itself a rather skimpy garment in its power to describe the designs produced by certain eccentric and imaginative minds. For a decade, Cinzia Ruggeri has made use of the vocabularies of the different languages of fashion, design, anthropology, ecology, sculpture and painting in her behavioural and kinetic clothes that feature light and liquid crystals, and which refer to buried emotions and memories. The eclecticism of her works is much more suited to schools, gardens or art galleries for their presentation than the catwalks and fashion shows of Milan.

Meanwhile fresh analyses and more appropriate slogans are produced in the attempt to describe accurately the new Italian miracle at the start of the new millennium, for example, the exhibition *Volare, l'icona italiana nella cultura globale* ("Flying, the Italian icon in global culture") organised by Pitti Immagine in the Stazione Leopolda in Florence at the start of 1999, and

*Left to right: Luciano Soprani,
Aldo Ferrante, Gianfranco
Ferré, Walter Albini, Giorgio
Armani, mid-seventies
(photo: Carlo Orsi)*

the book edited by Giannino Malossi that was published for the occasion by Bolis Editore. What is it that still makes Italy so attractive? What is it about the country that makes people willing to pay so much money?

A co-ordinated plan to create an image of Italy does not, and could never, exist, partly because the country has never been considered as a "power", even during the attempts by the Fascists in the 1920s. Italian products – clothes, furniture, cars, motor-cycles and cooking – and even non-products like art, the countryside and opera have been successful because they have been made desirable by the image of Italy that everyone shares.

This image is the basis of the new success of the Florentine company Gucci which has unquestionably been one of the stars of the last few seasons at Milano Collezioni despite being designed by a Texan, Tom Ford, and owned by a public company quoted on the Amsterdam and New York stock markets. The public desire for this image brings added value and provides a source of income to the country in an example of how an immaterial, cultural phenomenon affects the purely impersonal nature of financial balances and industrial activity. It took the Italian fashion industry back into

growth in 2000 after two years of crisis with a 5 percent increase in production of clothing, knitwear and footwear worth 48,160 billion lire, while the domestic market rose by 54 billion lire.

These are encouraging signs but they are only a partial description: according to the architect-art director-stylist Quirino Conti, fashion will be saved by its virtuality by which he means not just the use of e-commerce which is revolutionising distribution and relations between producers and consumers, creators and clients. "Empty clothes shops do not mean the death of fashion just as empty stadiums are not representative of the death of football. There will be other places for doing business, created by the collective imagination and public desire", he prophesies. Perhaps places like Armani Store in Via Manzoni in Milan which was opened at the end of 2000, twenty five years after the first Armani show in Ristorante Carminati. The store is almost a portrait of the world of the stylist who is once again one of the forces that power Italian fashion.

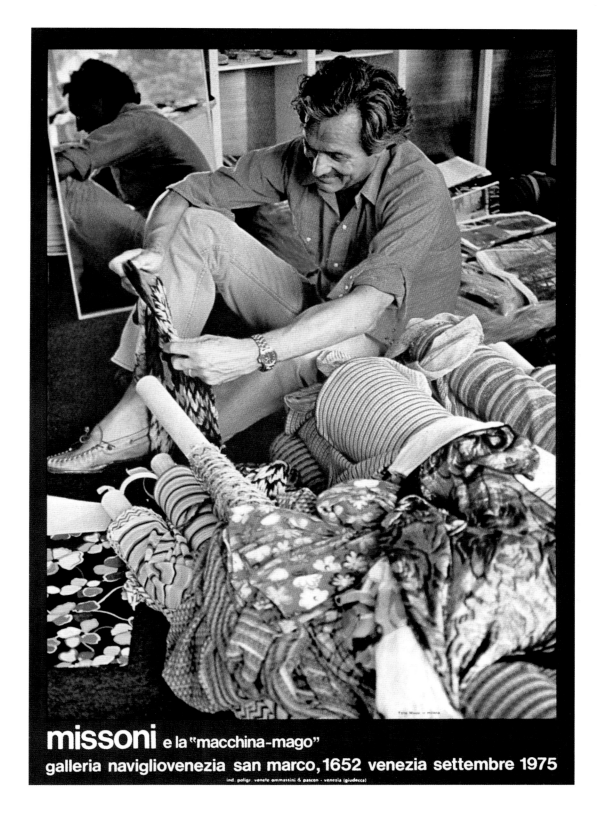

missoni e la "macchina-mago"
galleria navigliovenezia san marco, 1652 venezia settembre 1975

*Giorgio Armani and Naomi
Campbell
(photo: Angela Quattrone)*

*Gianni Versace
(photo: Richard Avedon)*

*Gianfranco Ferré
and Nicola Trussardi
(photo: Roby Schirer)*

Domenico Dolce and Stefano
Gabbana
(© Gian Paolo Barbieri)

Moschino's "Stop the fashion
system" poster

Tom Ford

Prada outfit from the 1988
Fall/Winter collection

Stephan Janson's 1999-2000
Fall/Winter show in Milan,
Porta Venezia train bypass
(photo: Roberto Gamba)

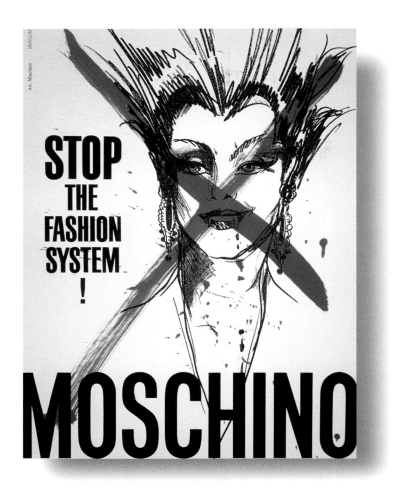

1951-2000 Facts, protagonists, stories

January

Ezio Vanoni's tax reform becomes law.

Milan. Out of 1,275,000 inhabitants, almost 366,000 are employed in industry.

5. General Ike Eisenhower, victor of the war in Europe on the Western Front, is appointed supreme commander of the Atlantic forces.

18. Eisenhower's visit to Italy triggers anti-NATO demonstrations and incidents: four deaths.

27. Aldo Cucchi and Valdo Magnani resign from the PCI (Italian Communist Party) in protest against the party's excessively pro-Soviet and Moscow-oriented policy.

29. First Festival of Sanremo. Nilla Pizzi wins with *Vola colomba*.

February

Milan. First coin-operated telephone booth on piazza San Babila.

The average monthly wage of a worker is 26,790 lire, while the cost of living for a typical family of four people is around 50,000.

12. **First Italian fashion show organized by Giovanni Battista Giorgini at Villa Torrigiani on via dei Serragli in Florence. It marks the entry of "made in Italy" into the world of fashion.**

12. The shah of Iran marries Soraya Esfandiari.

26. Palmiro Togliatti turns down the post of director of the Cominform in Prague and, after two months in the Soviet Union, resumes the leadership of the Italian Communist Party.

March

7. The law on rearmament is passed.

30. The Communist member of parliament Laura Diaz is sentenced to eight months of imprisonment for insulting the pope.

April

Franco Albini designs the *Margherita* armchair for Vittorio Bonacina and the *Luisa* armchair for Poggi, Marco Zanuso the *Lady* armchair for Arflex.

United States. The Senate committee investigating the Mafia, headed by Estes Kefauver, outlines the map of "Cosa Nostra's" power: Frank Costello in New York; the Fischetti, Accardo and Guzick "trio" in Chicago; Albert and Antonio Anastasia, with a monopoly of illegal betting; Lucky Luciano, from exile in Italy, organizer of the alliance between the Sicilian and American Mafia.

6. At the Fiera Campionaria in Milan, directed by Michele Guido Franci, the Soviet Union presents an official stand for the first time at a Western trade fair.

9. General Douglas MacArthur, hero of the war in the Pacific and commander of the UN troops in the Korean War, is relieved by the American president Truman for his attempts to widen the conflict to China.

18. The European Coal and Steel Community (ECSC) is born. The treaty abolishes Customs tariffs on the most important raw materials between the member nations.

May

25. The British diplomats Donald Maclean and Guy Burgess flee to the Soviet Union after years of espionage.

27. Partial local-government elections. Around 18 million Italians vote. The DC (Christian Democrats) lose about ten percentage points, the left (PCI and PSI, the Italian Socialist Party) gets 37 per cent of the vote. In Milan the Socialist mayor installed after the liberation, Antonio Greppi, is defeated. His place at Palazzo Marino is taken by the Social Democrat Virgilio Ferrari.?

June

The Milan soccer team wins the championship with the Swedish trio Gren, Nordhal and Liedholm.

10. Fiorenzo Magni wins his second Tour of Italy.

At the end of the Tour of Piedmont, Serse Coppi, brother of Fausto Coppi, skids on the ruts of a road in Turin and dies from a brain hemorrhage.

July

Corrado Alvaro wins the Strega literary prize with *Quasi una vita*.

Hugo Koblet triumphs at the Tour de France.

16. Resignation of the sixth De Gasperi government. Ten days later, the leader of the DC forms a new administration in alliance with Ugo La Malfa's Republicans. Liberals and Social Democrats abstain.

20. Abdullah, king of Jordan, is assassinated at Jerusalem, in the Omar Mosque.

August

23. Breakdown of the Anglo-Iranian talks on petroleum. In Teheran, the prime minister Muhammad Mosaddeq nationalizes the British oil holdings and their exploitation.

31. The Marshall Plan of aid to a Europe brought to its knees by the war comes to an end.

September

6. Italy has the right to join the UN. This is announced by the United States, Great Britain and France, which declare themselves ready to revise the peace treaty.

8. The peace treaty between the United States and Japan is signed in San Francisco.

October

16. Egypt abrogates the treaty that had devolved the control and management of the Suez Canal to Great Britain since 1936.

17. British troops occupy the canal zone.

27. The Conservatives win the elections in Great Britain. The old lion Churchill returns to power.

31. SS major Walter Reder is given a life sentence for the massacre carried out in reprisal at Marzabotto: 1830 victims.

November

1. The Minister of foreign trade, Ugo La Malfa, liberalizes trade. The decision will turn out to be a mainspring of the economic boom.

7. Frank Sinatra and Ava Gardner get married.

14. Floods in Polesine: around a hundred deaths, 18 thousand people evacuated.

December

Industrial production, which in 1947 had only been 70 per cent of what it had been in 1938, had risen to 89 per cent in 1948 and to 104 in 1950. It reaches a level of 127 per cent in 1951. The national product is already at prewar levels. Exports have almost tripled in the space of four years: 26 billion in 1947; 71 in 1950. The gross national product has grown by 5.3 per cent and will continue to rise, with peaks of 6.6 in 1959 and 8.3 in 1961.

21. The victors of the Second World War, with the exception of the Soviet Union, soften the terms of the peace treaty with Italy. The restrictions on rearmament are abolished.

24. Libya becomes an independent state: a monarchy, ruled by King Idris.

For the first time, the 9th Triennale dedicates a section to the theme of industrial design with the exhibition *La forma dell'utile* ("The Form of the Useful"), organized by Ludovico Belgioioso, Francesco Buzzi Ceriani, Max Huber and Enrico Peressutti.

The Teatro dei Gobbi is founded: Franca Valeri, Alberto Bonucci and Vittorio Caprioli. It makes its debut in Rome with *Carnet de notes*.

On the movie screens, Luchino Visconti's *Bellissima* (*The Most Beautiful*) and Vittorio De Sica's *Miracolo a Milano* (*Miracle in Milan*), Elia Kazan's *A Streetcar Called Desire*, Kurosawa Akira's *Rashomon*, Carlo Lizzani's *Achtung, banditi* and *Guardie e Ladri* (*Cops and Robbers*).

In the bookstores, Alberto Moravia's *Il conformista* (*The Conformist*), Goffredo Parise's *Il ragazzo morto e le comete*, J.D. Salinger's *The Catcher in the Rye*, Marguerite Yourcenar's *Mémoires d'Hadrien* (*Memoirs of Hadrian*), Samuel Beckett's *Molloy*, Andrea Zanzotto's *Dietro il paesaggio* and Giovanni Comisso's *Le mie stagioni*.

Lucio Fontana publishes the *Manifesto del Spazialismo* (*Manifesto of Spatialism*).

At the 9th Triennale Lucio Fontana, in collaboration with the architect Luciano Baldessari, decorates the main entrance to the building with 300 meters of neon strip lighting.

In Milan the Museo Poldi Pezzoli reopens following repair of the damage it suffered during the war.

Peter van Wood leaves Renato Carosone's group and, singing *Tre numeri al Lotto*, *Butta la chiave* and *Via Montenapoleone*, becomes a star of Milanese nightlife and the record industry.

Walter Chiari triumphs in the review *Sogno di un Walter*.

Deaths of André Gide (Nobel 1947), the actress Dina Galli, star of *Scampolo* and *Felicita Colombo*, the architect and city planner Giuseppe De Finetti and the politician Ivanoe Bonomi.

1952

January

United States. The Communist "witch hunts," launched and stoked by Senator Joseph McCarthy, focus chiefly on Hollywood and on New York intellectuals.

3. Founding congress of the Social Democrat Party, born out of the split in the Socialist Party engineered by Giuseppe Saragat. Giuseppe Romita is elected Secretary.

February

1. The Scelba law designed to curb the reemergence and activity of Neo-Fascist movements is passed.

6. King George VI of England dies. He is succeeded on the throne by his daughter Elizabeth.

9. Nomadelfia, the "city of children" founded and run by Don Zeno Saltini, is closed down and cleared at the request of the Holy Office of the Vatican. Dissenting Catholics protest.

16. Zeno Colò wins a gold medal in the downhill race at the Winter Olympics in Oslo.

26. With his film *Umberto D*, Vittorio De Sica "is fostering the disruptive roads of skepticism and despair" and doing "Italy a very poor service." The accusation comes from Giulio Andreotti.

March

4. Pia Bellentani is tried for the murder at Villa d'Este. She will receive a ten-year sentence.

20. The people of Trieste demonstrate in the streets to lay claim to their right to be part of Italy.

29. The Soviets explode their first atomic bomb.

April

5. Severe penalties for an occupation of lands in the Foggia region that occurred in 1950. The laborers are sentenced to up to three years of imprisonment.

16. Turin. The president of Fiat Erio Codecà is shot and killed. There is talk of a politically-motivated crime, but it will never be proved.

May

3. Gaspare Pisciotta and Vincenzo Badalamenti, lieutenants of the bandit Salvatore Giuliano, are given life for the mass murder at Portella delle Ginestre, where they had ambushed and shot workers celebrating Mayday in 1947.

17. On the occasion of a television broadcast whose set was designed by Lucio Fontana, the *Manifesto of the Spatial Movement for Television* is distributed.

20. Tensions rise between Italy and Yugoslavia over the Trieste question.

25. The Monarchist shipowner Achille Lauro is elected mayor of Naples. The methods used in his election campaign are highly controversial: a *quid pro quo* of land for land.

27. The European Defense Community is formed. Under its terms France, West Germany, Italy, the Netherlands, Belgium and Luxembourg are to set up a supranational armed force. The pact will fail because of reluctance on the part of France.

June

Fausto Coppi wins the Tour of Italy. He will go on to dominate the Tour de France.

24. Moscow throws its weight heavily behind Tito in the tussle with Italy over Trieste.

July

Egypt. *Coup d'état* by the army officers Naguib and Nasser. King Farouk is forced into exile.

8. Alcide De Gasperi, in an interview with *Il Messaggero*, calls for a strengthening of the executive branch and laws to "regulate" the press and the trade unions. The Cold War makes him feel the need for a "protected democracy."

19. Helsinki Olympics. Italy brings home eight gold medals: those, among others, of Pino Dordoni (50 kilometers' walk), Edoardo Mangiarotti (fencing), Irene Camper (fencing) and Agostino Straulino and Nicolò Rode (sailing, star class).

22. **Italian fashion "occupies" the Sala Bianca at Palazzo Pitti. Three hundred and fifty buyers and journalists attend the parade of clothes by Antonelli, Capucci, Carosa, Ferdinandi, Giovanelli Sciarra, Polinober, Marucelli, Vanna, Veniceni and sixteen designers of boutique fashion and sportswear.**

August

10. The first supranational European body, the High Authority for Coal and Steel, is set up in Luxembourg.

September

Arturo Toscanini's last concert at La Scala.

17. President of the Republic Luigi Einaudi makes Don Luigi Sturzo, founder of the People's Party and pioneer of Catholic involvement in politics, a senator for life.

23. Rocky Marciano wins the world heavyweight boxing title, after a long period of domination by Black fighters.

October

At Malpensa airport, two "bands," the Original Lambro Jazz Band and the Milan College Jazz Band welcome Louis Armstrong, a.k.a. "Satchmo," by playing *Muskrat Ramble* from a flatbed truck.

18. The Council of Ministers approves the draft electoral law providing for a majority premium. The opposition see the law as a "fraud."

November

In Kenya, white colonists are slaughtered in the revolt of the Kikuyu warriors known as the Mau Mau.

1. The USA tests the first H bomb, or thermonuclear hydrogen bomb, in the Marshall Islands.

4. General Eisenhower wins the presidential elections by a landslide and brings the Republicans back into the White House after an absence of twenty years.

December

Industrial production exceeds 50 per cent of prewar levels. Exports represent only 6.1 per cent of the gross national product, as compared with 21.3 per cent in France.

4. Uproar at Palazzo di Montecitorio, seat of the Chamber of Deputies, during the debate over the new electoral law.

Franco Albini designs the *Cicognino* table for Poggi and the *Fiorenza* armchair for Arflex.

Milan acquires Michelangelo's *Rondanini Pietà*, placing it in the museum of the Castello Sforzesco.

On the big screen, Charlie Chaplin's *Limelight*, Federico Fellini's *Lo sceicco Bianco* (*The White Sheik*), De Sica's *Umberto D*, Roberto Rossellini's *Europa 51* (*The Greatest Love*), Luigi Comencini's *La tratta delle bianche* and Julien Duvivier's *Le Petit Monde de Don Camillo* (*The Little World of Don Camillo*).

In the bookstores, Vasco Pratolini's *Le ragazze di San Frediano*, Cesare Pavese's *Il mestiere di vivere*, Italo Calvino's *Il visconte dimezzato* (*The Cloven Viscount*), John Steinbeck's *East of Eden*, Giuseppe Marotta's *Gli alunni del sole* and Francesco Serrantini's *L'osteria del gatto parlante* (Bagutta Prize). Foundation of the magazine *Realismo*, edited by Raffaele De Grada.

Le Corbusier builds the Unité d'habitation at Marseilles.

General Fulgencio Batista stages a *coup d'état* in Cuba.

A new 100 lire banknote in brownish red on a yellow ground comes into circulation. It will buy four newspapers or a liter of Chianti or four eggs.

At La Scala, Maria Callas triumphs in the *Vespri Siciliani*.

Deaths of Benedetto Croce, Maria Montessori, Evita Peron, the tenor Aureliano Pertile and the former queen of Italy Elena of Savoy in exile at Montpellier.

1953

January

On the catwalk of the Sala Bianca the fashion designer Ferdinandi makes a splash with an idea that has since been imitated hundreds of times: using a black model, Dolores Francine Rheney, to show his white suits.

8. At its thirtieth conference, the PSI underlines its separation from the PCI.

14. Alcide De Gasperi tables a question of confidence on the proposal of a majority electoral law, described by the opposition as a "fraudulent law."

20. General strike declared by the CGIL (General Federation of Italian Trade Unions) against the "fraudulent law," which is approved by the Chamber the following day after seventy hours of battle. It will receive its final hearing in the Senate, after further fierce clashes, on March 29.

February

10. The ENI (National Hydrocarbon Corporation) is established.

March

The new Fiat 1100 makes its debut at the Geneva Motor Show.

4. Death of Joseph Stalin: he has been leader of the USSR and the party since 1924.

9. Pietro Nenni and Palmiro Togliatti attend Stalin's funeral.

April

4. The president of the Republic, Luigi Einaudi, dissolves Parliament.

22. The new ambassador of the United States in Italy, Claire Boothe Luce, lands at Naples.

May

Inter soccer team wins the soccer championship.

1. Opening of borders and free trade in coal and steel between the six member countries of the ECSC.

23. A cyclone brings down the spire of the Mole Antonelliana in Turin. Six dead.

29. Mt. Everest is conquered by Edmund Hillary and Sherpa Tenzing.

June

Italian knitwear enters the Metropolitan Museum in New York with twelve "pieces" by Albertina (Giubbolini).

7. General election. The "fraudulent law" fails to be put into effect by just a few votes and so the parties in alliance, from the DC to the PRI (Italian Republican Party) and from the PSDI (Italian Social-Democratic Party) to the Sardinian Action Party, do not obtain the majority premium. The DC still gets the highest percentage of the vote: 40.1. The PCI gets 22.6.

17. The workers of East Berlin demand shorter working hours. Tanks are called in. Violent clashes. The city is in a state of siege.

20. Demonstrations protesting the execution of Ethel and Julius Rosenberg, charged in the United States with spying for URSS.

July

3. De Gasperi is given a mandate to form the new government, but his attempt fails in the Chamber on the 28th of the same month.

27. The armistice signed at Panmunjon puts an end to the war in Korea. The country is divided in two at the 38th parallel.

August

2. Cabinet crisis. The Christian Democrat Attilio Piccioni attempts to form a government, but also fails. Giuseppe Pella tries and succeeds, winning a vote of confidence.

30. Fausto Coppi wins the world cycling championship on the Lugano circuit. The movie cameras catch a fleeting glimpse of a beautiful woman among the people celebrating on the podium. No one is yet aware that this is the "lady in white."

September

The glossy magazines are more and more full of gossip about a love affair between Princess Margaret of England and Peter Townsend, hero of the Battle of Britain.

The Agnona Wool Mill is founded.

11. The Carabinieri in Milan arrest the journalist Guido Aristarco, editor of Cinema Nuovo, on a charge of defamation of the armed forces, for a screenplay published by the magazine that mocked the conduct of Italian soldiers in Greece. It is entitled the Armata s'agapò (The Army of Love).

15. Winston Churchill wins the Nobel Prize for Literature. General Marshall, deviser of the plan of aid to postwar Europe named after him, is awarded the Nobel Prize for Peace.

24. General strike proclaimed by the CGIL, CISL (Italian Federation of Trade Unions) and UIL (Italian Labor Union) to obtain a minimum wage.

October

8. The United States and Great Britain withdraw their troops from zone A of the Free Territory of Trieste and hand over power to the Italian government, but the latter lays claim to the whole of the Territory. On October 12 the Soviet Union sends a note of protest to the USA and Great Britain.

22. In an interview with the Agence France-Presse, Tito threatens invasion of zone A if it were really to be placed under Italian administration.

22. Fifty-five people are killed by floods in Calabria.

November

5. Demonstrations in Italy on behalf of Trieste: the police open fire on the crowd: six dead and a hundred wounded.

15. Tito softens his stand on Trieste, proposing that the city go to Italy and that zone A be divided on the basis of ethnic criteria.

December

5. An agreement is reached for the simultaneous and immediate withdrawal of troops from the border between Italy and Yugoslavia.

A group of Roman couturiers sets up the Sindacato Italiano Alta Moda ("Italian High Fashion Association"), whose statute forbids members from taking part in the shows held in the Sala Bianca at Palazzo Pitti in Florence.

Milan. First municipal bylaw aimed at controlling air pollution.

Milan. Il dito nell'occhio by the trio Dario Fo, Franco Parenti and Giustino Durano opens at the Piccolo Teatro.

Milan. The State University is installed in the reconstructed Ca' Granda.

Milan. Exhibition by Picasso at Palazzo Reale.

Mario Valentino, who will become famous as a shoe stylist, leaves his father's store in Naples and starts his own business.

Launch of Renzo Rivolta's Isetta: three wheels, egg-shaped body, central door, 198 cubic centimeter engine. It costs 335 thousand lire.

Florence. Gucci leaves the old head office on Lungarno Guicciardini and moves to Palazzo Settimanni.

Milan. Maria Callas sings Medea at La Scala. It is her consecration and the audience goes into delirium. This marks the beginning of her legend and of her rivalry with Renata Tebaldi, who had been chosen by Arturo Toscanini for the concert celebrating the reopening of La Scala on May 11, 1946, and had hogged the limelight ever since.

The monthly Civiltà delle macchine, edited by Leonardo Sinisgalli, comes out. It will remain in publication until 1961.

In the movie theaters, Fred Zinnemann's From Here to Eternity with Frank Sinatra and Montgomery Clift, Federico Fellini's I vitelloni, Jacques Tati's Les Vacances de Monsieur Hulot (Mr. Hulot's Holiday) and Eduardo de Filippo's Napoletani a Milano.

Rima produces the DU30 chair designed by Gastone Rinaldi.

In the bookstores, Carlo Cassola's Il taglio del bosco, Ray Bradbury's Fahrenheit 451, Mario Tobino's Le libere donne di Magliano, Alain Robbe-Grillet's Les Gommes (The Erasers) and Leonardo Borgese's Primo Amore (Bagutta Prize).

At the theater, Samuel Beckett's Waiting for Godot.

The monthly Playboy comes out in America.

Third class is abolished on the Italian railroads.

Deaths of the actor Ruggero Ruggeri, the journalist and writer Raffaele Calzini and the painter Raoul Dufy.

1954

January

Four hundred kilometers of methane pipeline are brought into function.

A vacation on Capri finally makes the affair between Fausto Coppi and Giulia Occhini public.

3. At 11 a.m. the presenter Fulvia Colombo announces the start of regular television broadcasts from Milan.

5. The government of Giuseppe Pella resigns and the period of political instability commences.

6. The American ambassador Claire Boothe Luce asks Washington for new economic aid to Italy and orders from its industries, but suggests excluding those companies where the majority of workers belong to the Communist-dominated CGIL.

30. Amintore Fanfani's attempt to form a government fails: 303 deputies vote against it.

February

Coco Chanel reopens her fashion house on rue Cambon, which had closed down in 1939.

Duilio Loi beats the Dane Johansen on points and becomes European lightweight champion. The Milanese boxer will retire in 1962 after a career spanning fourteen years and 126 matches, with 115 victories, eight ties and only three defeats.

5. The centrist parties create an alliance in support of Mario Scelba, called on to form the new government. The process will not be completed until the government receives a vote of confidence in the Senate on March 10.

9. Gaspare Pisciotta, the Mafia lieutenant who sold out Salvatore Giuliano, is poisoned by a cup of coffee in the Ucciardone prison at Palermo.

10. Marilyn Monroe performs for the American troops stationed in Korea.

13. The last groups of Italian prisoners of war return from the Soviet Union.

March

A pilot in the RAF and father of two girls changes sex: a surgical operation turns him into a woman.

The Florence Center for Italian fashion is set up.

18. The Scelba government proposes measures against "political forces whose dependence on foreign countries is proven" and checks on the commitment to democracy of government officials.

April

At La Scala, Ingrid Bergman recites the lines of Claudel in Arthur Honegger's *Jeanne d'Arc au bûcher*.

Carlo De Carli's chair *683* is brought into production by Cassina and Osvaldo Borsani's *D70* sofa by Tecno.

3. The writer Giovanni Guareschi, who has published two fake letters from Alcide De Gasperi to the Allies asking them to intensify the bombing of Italian cities in the weekly *Candido*, is sentenced to one year's imprisonment.

May

Pius XII canonizes Giuseppe Sarto, pope under the name of Pius X.

4. Tragedy in a lignite mine at Ribolla (Grosseto): 42 dead.

7. The French, under siege for weeks at Dien Bien Phu, surrender to the Vietnamese troops of General Giap.

June

Franco, Silvio and Piergiorgio Rivetti take over the GFT and relaunch Facis.

At the world soccer championships in Switzerland, Germany beats Hungary and wins the title. The stadium rings proudly to the anthem *Deutschland über alles*.

29. Amintore Fanfani is elected Secretary of the DC.

July

31. Ardito Desio, Milanese by adoption, leads a mountain-climbing expedition to conquer K2. Achille Compagnoni and Lino Lacedelli reach the peak.

August

19. Death of Alcide De Gasperi, father of the Republic and Prime Minister from December 1945 to May 1953.

30. Death of Cardinal Schuster, bishop of Milan. He is succeeded by Giovanni Battista Montini, later to become Paul VI.

September

Mariuccia Mandelli, a.k.a. Krizia, starts to design and sell clothes. She goes round the boutiques with a heavy suitcase, acting as her own representative.

4. The French army begins to withdraw from Indochina.

9. Short period of arrest and enforced residence for Giulia Occhini, "guilty" of adultery.

18. The Foreign Minister, Attilio Piccioni, resigns over rumors about his son Piero's involvement in the Montesi scandal. The son will be arrested three days later. The whole affair will turn out to have been blown up out of proportion for political reasons.

30. On death row at San Quentin prison in California, Caryl Chessman begins the long legal battle that will keep him alive until 1960.

October

5. Trieste is returned to Italy, following the memorandum of understanding between Great Britain, the United States, Italy and Yugoslavia.

26. Flooding in the Salerno region kills 300 people.

26. Italian troops enter Trieste after ten years of Allied military rule.

30. *Milano Sera*, edited by Mario Bonfantini and Elio Vittorini, ceases publication. It had been founded on August 7, 1945, and had achieved a circulation of 200,000 in the years immediately after the war.

November

Cairo. Gamal Abdel Nasser assumes the presidency of Egyptian Republic.

12. **Death of the fashion designer Jacques Fath.**

December

23. Christian Democrat deputies Mario Melloni and Ugo Bartesaghi quit the party in protest against the Paris accords that allow the countries of the Western European Union to make independent use of their armed forces and approve the immediate admission of West Germany to NATO. Melloni joins the PCI and will become famous for his Fortebraccio column in *L'Unità*.

At the suggestion of Cesare Brustio and Augusto Morello, La Rinascente funds the Compasso d'Oro award for industrialists, craftsmen and designers whose products are a synthesis of technical, functional and aesthetic characteristics.

The municipal government of Milan returns to Palazzo Marino, rebuilt after the bombing.

Launch of *Stile industria* (published until 1963), edited by Alberto Rosselli, and *La rivista dell'arredamento* (now *Interni*), founded by Giovanni Gualtiero Görlich.

At the movies, Elia Kazan's *On the Waterfront* with Marlon Brando, Kurosawa Akira's *Shichi-nin No Samurai* (*Seven Samurai*), Vittorio De Sica's *L'oro di Napoli* (*The Gold of Naples*) with Sophia Loren, Luchino Visconti's *Senso* (*Wanton Contessa*) with Alida Valli and Federico Fellini's *La Strada* with Giulietta Masina.

Emilio Pucci wins the Neiman Marcus Award, the American Oscar of fashion.

Milan. The Padiglione d'arte contemporanea, or PAC, is inaugurated. It has been designed by the architect Ignazio Gardella.

Milan. Baj and Dangelo exhibit at the Galleria Schwarz, along with the former members of the Cobra group Karel Appel, Guillaume Corneille and Asgar Jorn.

The *movimento nucleare* joins the *Mouvement international pour une Bauhaus imaginiste*.

Dante Isella publishes the first critical edition of Carlo Porta's poems, Alberto Moravia his *Racconti romani* (*Roman Tales*), Goffredo Parise *Il prete bello* (*The Priest Among the Pigeons*), Simone de Beauvoir *Les Mandarins* (*The Mandarins*) and Françoise Sagan *Bonjour tristesse*.

Design takes its rightful place at the 10th Triennale with the *International Exhibition of Industrial Design*, organized by Achille and Pier Giacomo Castiglioni, Roberto Menghi, Augusto Morello, Marcello Nizzoli, Michele Provinciali and Alberto Rosselli. The first International Convention of Industrial Design is held to coincide with the exhibition.

Deaths of the painters Henri Matisse and André Derain, the conductor Wilhelm Furtwängler, the writer Vitaliano Brancati and Bruno Angoletta, inventor of "Marmittone," a character in the *Corriere dei Piccoli*.

1955

January

Works start on the petrochemical complex at Ravenna.

Five hundred buyers and two hundred journalists attend the ninth parade of Italian High Fashion on the catwalk of the Sala Bianca in Florence.

18. Pietro Secchia, one of the leaders of the PCI, is pushed onto the sidelines of the party.

February

11. American loan of almost 16 million dollars to finance imports from the United States.

March

Anna Magnani wins the Oscar for the Best Performance by an Actress in the film *The Rose Tattoo*.

3. After disappearing for four years, Bruno Pontecorvo, a scientist at the Atomic Energy Authority research station at Harwell in England, holds a press conference in Moscow to launch an appeal for a ban on nuclear weapons.

10. At the Geneva Motor Show, Fiat presents the 600. It costs 590 thousand lire.

14. Fausto Coppi and Giulia Occhini, the "lady in white," are sentenced to two and three months of imprisonment for adultery respectively. The legal code still considers the woman to be more responsible than the man.

29. Shift in the balance of power in the union elections held at Fiat: the FIOM-CGIL drops from 63.2 per cent to 36.7. The CISL, allied to the Union of Independents, gains a plurality with 40.4 per cent.

April

Bialetti puts the "Moka Express" coffeemaker on sale.

At La Scala, Maria Callas and Luchino Visconti startle conservatives with a realistic *Traviata*.

5. Reaching the age of eighty, Winston Churchill retires from politics: he is succeeded as Prime Minister by Anthony Eden.

28. Elections at Montecitorio for the president of the Republic. At the fourth count, the following day, the Christian Democrat Giovanni Gronchi is elected.

May

The phenomenon of Pierre Poujade emerges in France: a politician who sets out to fight heavy taxation.

14. The Warsaw Pact is established. It is the response of the countries of the Eastern Europe to NATO.

21. The government launches a ten-year plan for the construction of expressways.

June

1. First meeting of the ministers of the European Coal and Steel Community.

12. Le Mans. During the "24 Hours," the Mercedes driven by Pierre Levegh plunges into the crowd. The fuel tanks explode: eighty dead.

22. The Scelba government resigns. It is replaced by the first government led by Antonio Segni, which will win votes of confidence in the Senate and the Chamber between July 18 and 22.

July

19. Geneva. Meeting of the leaders of the four big powers, Bulganin, Eisenhower, Edgar Faure and Anthony Eden. It represents the first sign of a thaw.

31. Last death sentence passed in Great Britain.

August

8. Vallauris, the village on the Côte d'Azur where Pablo Picasso lives, celebrates the artist by organizing a corrida in his honor.

September

2. Antonio Maspes becomes world cycling champion in the professional speed trials.

21. Dream wedding: in Venice, the fifteen-year-old Ira Fürstenberg marries Prince Alphonse von Hohenlohe.

October

The first issue of the weekly *L'Espresso* comes out. Its editor is Arrigo Benedetti.

November

11. Wanda Osiris triumphs in the review *La granduchessa e i camerieri*.

19. *Lascia o raddoppia?*– the Italian version of the quiz show *Double Your Money* – makes its first appearance on television, conducted by Mike Bongiorno. It will glue Italians to the little screen.

December

Milan. At the Piccolo Teatro Giorgio Strehler stages Bertolazzi's *El Nost Milan*.

Lascia o raddoppia?, the quiz show conducted by Mike Bongiorno, reaches the peak of its ratings after the elimination of the contestant Lando Degoli by a question on the contrabassoon.

Prima ballerina Violette Verdy renounces the repeat performances of Prokofiev's *Cinderella* at La Scala and leaves the role to the unknown Carla Fracci: she is an immediate hit.

8. A split in the Liberal Party leads to the creation of the Radical Party. Thirty-two Liberal councilors turn their backs on Malagodi. They constitute almost the entire left wing of the party.

14. Italy is admitted to the UN by unanimous vote. Previously the Soviet Union had used its veto.

The fashion designer Ken Scott, with his partner Vittorio Fiorazzo, opens a studio-cum-store on via Sant'Andrea in Milan. The "Falconetto" label is born.

At the theater, Arthur Miller's *A View from the Bridge* and Tennessee Williams's *Cat on a Hot Tin Roof*.

Dante Giocosa designs the 600 car for Fiat, Gino Valle the *Cifra5* clock for Solari, Achille and Pier Giacomo Castiglioni the *Luminator* lamp for Arform, Colombini a pail for Kartell and Osvaldo Borsani the *P40* armchair for Tecno.

Milan. Out of every 1000 inhabitants, 556 possess a car, motorcycle or moped.

Milan. The first Alfa Romeo *Giulietta* emerges from the gates of the Portello factory.

The high fashion industry exports clothes to a value of 1,280 million lire.

La Piccola Scala opens.

Ugo Mursia founds his publishing house.

Lucia Bosé marries the bullfighter Dominguin. The year after, her former fiancé Walter Chiari will get back into the headlines again for a flirt with Ava Gardner.

In the bookstores, Pier Paolo Pasolini's *Ragazzi di vita* (*The Ragazzi*), John Ronald Tolkien's *Lord of the Rings* and Vasco Pratolini's *Metello*.

At the movies, *Aparajito* (*The Unvanquished*) by the Indian director Satyajit Ray. It wins the Golden Lion at the Venice Festival in 1956.

Deaths of Albert Einstein, the discoverer of penicillin Alexander Fleming, the writer Thomas Mann, the Spanish philosopher José Ortega y Gasset, the actor James Dean, the racing-car driver Alberto Ascari, the painter Anselmo Bucci, the poet Paul Claudel and the socialist Rodolfo Morandi.

January

26. The Winter Olympics open at Cortina d'Ampezzo. The Austrian Tony Sailer wins three gold medals (downhill race, slalom and giant slalom) and becomes the idol of the games.

February

Milan. At the Piccolo Teatro, Strehler stages Brecht's *Die Dreigroschenoper* (*The Threepenny Opera*).

2. Partinico. Arrest of the writer Danilo Dolci for heading the opposite of a strike, the plowing of an uncultivated piece of land. He is sentenced to one month and twenty days in prison. Solidarity from the left and from intellectuals.

2. Snow in Rome, Naples and Liguria. It is one of the harshest winters of the century.

14. Moscow. Twentieth Congress of the CPSU (Communist Party of the Soviet Union). Nikita Khrushchev denounces Stalin's crimes and personality cult.

28. Death of Don Carlo Gnocchi, "father" of children disabled in the war.

March

14. At Barletta, the police open fire on the crowd that has gathered in front of the food stores of the Papal Welfare Office: two dead.

21. The electoral law is passed: adjusted proportional representation, with allocation of seats at a local level and utilization of the "remainder" at the national level.

24. Amerigo Dumini, one of the killers of Giacomo Matteotti, is released from prison. Given a life sentence, he has served eight years.

April

3. National conference of the PCI. Palmiro Togliatti is circumspect on the anti-Stalinist shift in the Soviet Union.

17. Moscow. The Cominform, an information bureau founded in 1947 as an alliance between the Communist parties of several different countries, is abolished.

10. Montecarlo. Grace Kelly marries Prince Ranieri of Monaco.

21. The first issue of the newspaper *Il Giorno* comes out. It is edited by Gaetano Baldacci.

23. The Constitutional Court is set up.

May

4. Mysterious death of Lionel Crabb, marine scientist and commander in the British Navy, while operating as a "frogman" in Portsmouth harbor, where a Soviet cruiser with President Bulganin and CPSU Secretary Khrushchev on board is at anchor.

28. In the local government elections, the PSI and PSDI increase their share of the vote in the large municipalities and there is talk of reunification. The DC holds its own. In Bologna, the Communist Giuseppe Dozza defeats Giuseppe Dossetti, ideologue of the Christian Democrat left.

June

Milan. A long strike by stockbrokers commences: it will last for three months.

13. *Nuovi argomenti* publishes an interview with Togliatti on the 20th Congress of the CPSU. The Communist leader asserts that the process of building a socialist society is still on track, while admitting that Stalin's errors "cannot but have seriously limited the successes of its application."

22. Fierce debate over the de-Stalinization of the Central Committee of the Communist Party. Fabrizio Onofri accuses the party leaders of abandoning the line of an "Italian road to socialism."

28. Three hundred dead and thousands of wounded among Polish workers demanding wage rises who are attacked by tanks. The grave crisis will be resolved by Wladyslaw Gomulka.

July

At Palazzo Pitti in Florence, Roberto Capucci is acclaimed by the international press as the best Italian fashion designer. Christian Dior declares: "In Italy you have a boy wonder. If he is ever in Paris, I hope he comes to see me."

1. Di Vittorio, secretary of the CGIL, publicly declares his solidarity with the Polish workers. He will be reprimanded in an editorial by Togliatti published in *l'Unità*.

26. The passenger liner SS *Andrea Doria*, flagship of the Italian merchant navy, goes down in the Atlantic, 45 miles off the Nantucket lighthouse, after a collision with the SS *Stockholm*: 55 dead.

August

8. Belgium. At Marcinelle, 237 miners (139 of them Italian), die trapped underground in a coal mine.

20. The National Liberation Front in Algeria draws up its "revolutionary manifesto."

25. A meeting is held between Nenni and Saragat, leaders of the PSI and the PSDI. They discuss the reunification of their parties.

September

8. In Milan the Socialists support the centrist administration of Mayor Virgilio Ferrari from the outside. It is the first step toward the center-left coalition of 1960.

October

23. Revolt in Hungary: students, intellectuals and workers rise against the Communist dictatorship. Imre Nagy, a liberal Communist, forms a coalition government and announces Hungary's exit from the Warsaw Pact. On November 3 Soviet tanks intervene and Imre Nagy is replaced by the pro-Soviet János Kádár.

27. The CGIL condemns the Soviet intervention in Hungary. Two days later, 101 Communist intellectuals demand profound reform and dispute the line put forward in *l'Unità*, where the Hungarian uprising has been labeled a "counterrevolutionary putsch."

29. Israel attacks Egypt with the support of Great Britain and France, which have not got over President Nasser's decision to nationalize the Suez Canal.

November

16. Guido Cantelli is appointed permanent conductor at La Scala. Eight days later, the young maestro dies in a fire aboard a DC 6 taking off from Paris.

19. The American ambassador to Italy Claire Boothe Luce resigns.

22. Melbourne Olympics. Italy wins eight gold medals, along with eight silver and twenty bronze.

26. Agreement between Italy and the USA for a "post-occupation clandestine network" called Stay Behind. This is the *operazione Gladio* whose existence will be revealed in 1990, causing great controversy.

December

8. Congress of the PCI. Togliatti revives the strategy of the "Italian road to socialism."

31. The White House announces the "Eisenhower Doctrine": all countries menaced by communism will receive aid, in money and arms, from the United States.

Achille and Pier Giacomo Castiglioni's *Spalter* vacuum cleaner is brought into production by Rem and Marcello Nizzoli's *Divisumma* calculator by Olivetti.

Milan. The Feltrinelli publishing house is born.

Milan. The San Siro stadium is inaugurated after a doubling of its capacity: it can now house up to 100 thousand spectators.

Work begins on construction of the expressway from Milan to the south of Italy, the Autostrada del Sole.

Designers, entrepreneurs and critics set up the ADI, Association for industrial design.

Milan. The Casa della Cultura opens. Its sponsors include Antonio Banfi. Ferruccio Parri is the first president.

Return of the undefeated Ribot to the San Siro racetrack: it has won the Arc de Triomphe twice, the Jockey Club at Milan of 1955 and the King George VI and Queen Elizabeth Stakes at Ascot in 1956.

In the bookstores, Allen Ginsberg's *Howl*, Tanizaki Jun'ichiro's *Kagi* (*The Key*) and Eugenio Montale's *La bufera e altro* (*The Storm, and Other Poems*).

The brothers Domenico, Gaetano and Orazio Rossi found Comber, a pioneering company in the ready-to-wear sector, and call in the young Pierre Cardin to design its collections.

At the theater, John Osborne's *Look Back in Anger*.

It is the year of the first rock 'n' roll, launched by Elvis Presley.

At the movies, Ichikawa Kon's *Biruma no tategoto* (*The Burmese Harp*), Pietro Germi's *Il ferroviere* (*Man of Iron*), Ingmar Bergman's *Det sjunde inseglet* (*The Seventh Seal*) and Camillo Mastrocinque's *Totò lascia o raddoppia*.

Deaths of Filippo de Pisis, Bertolt Brecht, Piero Calamandrei and Ezio Vanoni, the architect of Italian tax reform.

1957

January

The battle of Algiers commences. It will last until October. The French troops, with the paratroopers of General Massu at their head, are essentially defeated.

9. In Great Britain, change of the guard at Downing Street. Anthony Eden resigns and is replaced by Harold McMillan.

11. A law gives the ENI a monopoly over prospecting for oil in Italy.

16. Death of the ninety-year-old Arturo Toscanini. He is buried in Milan.

19. Venice. The Montesi trial opens. The principal defendants will be acquitted.

February

1. The editor of the newspaper *Dolomiten*, organ of the Südtiroler Volkspartei, is arrested and charged with instigating and organizing the bomb attacks in Upper Adige.

6. Cooperation between the PCI and PSI ends. The decision is taken at the Socialist congress in Venice, following a speech by Secretary Pietro Nenni. To everyone's great surprise, the party sends its greetings to the patriarch of Venice, Angelo Roncalli.

March

5. Pius XII accuses the Italian government of failing to defend the sacred character of Rome. The problem arises over bills advertising the films *Poveri ma belli* (*Poor but Beautiful*) and *Miss spogliarello* (*Miss Striptease*).

19. *L'Osservatore Romano* attacks the suggestion of an opening of the Christian Democrats to the Socialists.

25. Rome. On the Campidoglio the foreign ministers of Italy, France, West Germany, Belgium, the Netherlands and Luxembourg sign treaties establishing the European Economic Community.

April

Federico Fellini wins an Oscar for *La strada*.

Cassina produces Gio Ponti's *Superleggera* chair. It becomes an icon of design.

2. Dissension between the Italian president and the Ministry of Foreign Affairs. The government does not endorse a letter from president Gronchi to the American president Eisenhower on the subject of foreign policy as it considers it too soft toward the Arab countries.

17. The Social Democrats lay down conditions for unification with the PSI which the latter regards as unacceptable: support for the Atlantic Alliance, the quitting of left-wing administrations and a break with the PCI even in the General Federation of Trade Unions.

May

6. The Social Democrats leave the Segni government, which resigns.

13. The driver Alfonso De Portago, while competing in the Mille Miglia, comes off the road on the stretch between Mantua and Brescia and mows down nine spectators. He too is killed instantly.

18. First spotlights on Adriano Celentano at the rock 'n' roll festival in the Palazzo del Ghiaccio at Milan. The singer makes his debut there with a band he calls the *Rock Boys*: Enzo Iannacci is on piano, Giorgio Gaber on guitar.

June

Milan. Digging in via Giotto and piazza Conciliazione: work starts on the city's subway.

10. The new government led by the Christian Democrat Adone Zoli resigns: it is not willing to accept the deciding votes of the far-right MSI (Italian Social Movement).

July

2. Turin. The Fiat *500* makes its debut. The design is by Dante Giocosa. With a top speed of 85 kilometers per hour, it costs half a million lire.

8. Temperatures soar to record heights and kill seventeen elderly inmates of a nursing home in Venice.

14. At a National Council of the party held in Vallombrosa, the Christian Democrat Secretary Amintore Fanfani makes a cautious opening to the PSI. The voices of dissent are loud.

23. Antonio Giolitti quits the PCI. He is followed by many intellectuals. The exodus is a consequence of the Soviet invasion of Hungary.

August

29. Mussolini's remains are restored to his family and buried at Predappio, also the birthplace of the prime minister Adone Zoli.

September

25. Epidemic of "Asian" flu. Four hundred thousand people fall sick.

October

First issue of the weekly *Gente* comes out. It is published and edited by Edilio Rusconi, who has already achieved success with Rizzoli's *Oggi*. More glossy magazines are sold in Italy than anywhere else in Europe: the five most important are published in Milan, *Tempo*, *Epoca*, *Oggi*, *Gente* and *Domenica del Corriere*, with a total circulation of three million copies.

4. Moscow announces that it has launched the first artificial satellite into orbit. It is called Sputnik.

November

16. The summit of the Atlantic Alliance, attended by president Eisenhower of the United States, decides to install missile bases in Europe.

December

Women's clothing is exported to a value of 1,800 million lire. In 1950 it had been 45 million.

Daniel Bovet, a Swiss pharmacologist working in Rome, wins the Nobel Prize for Medicine.

22. Total nationalization of the telephone system.

Pininfarina designs the body of the *Flaminia* for Lancia, Bruno Munari the *Cubico* ashtray for Danese, Marcello Nizzoli the *Mirella* sewing machine for Necchi, Achille and Pier Giacomo Castiglioni the *Mezzadro* stool (Zanotta, 1970), Enzo Mari the game called *16 animali* for Danese and Ignazio Gardella the *Digamma* armchair for Gavina.

A kilo of bread costs 133 lire, of meat 1239. A pair of men's shoes over 5000 lire, the annual radio license 3450.

First issue of *Il Mobile Italiano*, edited by Carlo De Carli. It will cease publication in 1961.

A law is passed requiring equal pay for men and women.

At the movies, *A King in New York* by Charlie Chaplin, *Smultronstället* (*Wild Strawberries*) by Bergman, *Il grido* (*The Outcry*) by Michelangelo Antonioni, *Le notti bianche* (*White Nights*) by Visconti and *Le notti di Cabiria* (*The Nights of Cabiria*) by Fellini.

Pierre Cardin opens his fashion house.

Giangiacomo Feltrinelli publishes the first ever edition of Boris Pasternak's *Doctor Zhivago*. Alberto Arbasino publishes *Le piccole vacanze,* Pier Paolo Pasolini *Le Ceneri di Gramsci,* Italo Calvino *Il barone rampante* (*The Baron in the Trees*), Carlo Emilio Gadda *Quer pasticciaccio brutto de via Merulana* (*That Awful Mess on Via Merulana*), Elsa Morante *L'isola di Arturo* (*Arturo's Island*), Jack Kerouac *On the Road* and Indro Montanelli *Storia di Roma* (*History of Rome*).

At the 11th Triennale the *International Exhibition of Industrial Design*, organized by Gillo Dorfles, Leonardo Ricci, Alberto Rosselli and Marco Zanuso, is the last such event at the Triennali to be dedicated specifically to the theme.

The Situationist International is formed at Cosio d'Arroscia (Cuneo): its members include Giuseppe Pinot-Gallizio, Constan, Abdelhafid Khatib, Gilles Ivain, Guy Debord and Michele Bernstein.

Rome. One-man show by Alberto Burri at the Galleria l'Obelisco in which he presents his "combustions," i.e. works produced by burning wood with an oxyhydrogen flame.

Deaths of Leo Longanesi, Ottone Rosai, Humphrey Bogart, Erich von Stroheim, the trade unionist Giuseppe Di Vittorio, Gaetano Salvemini and the fashion designer Christian Dior.

1958

January

The *New York Times* carries a statement made by Enrico Mattei during a visit to Peking: "Italy may not recognize China, but she does recognize the 'Republic of Methanopolis.'" The newspaper reflects the growing irritation of the United States and the big oil companies known as the "seven sisters" with the independent commercial policy pursued by the ENI.

1. The treaties establishing the European Economic Community come into force.

21. Cardinal Alfonso Ottaviani accuses Catholic politicians who are ready to "open" to the left of betrayal.

February

Mila Schön makes her debut in fashion.

5. The Festival of Sanremo is won by Domenico Modugno with *Nel blu dipinto di blu*.

12. Debate in the Chamber on the meddling of the Vatican in Italian politics. Adone Zoli, the Prime Minister, says that, as a Catholic, he must take account "on the moral plane of teachings that emanate from a very high place."

13. The government puts the commune of Naples under a commissioner following grave irregularities on the part of Achille Lauro's administration.

20. French planes bomb a Tunisian village where Algerian freedom fighters had taken refuge: seventy-eight dead.

27. Milan. On via Osoppo, seven bandits assault and rob a security van of the Banca Popolare, without firing a shot. They make off with almost half a billion lire. All will be caught.

27. The Soviet occupying army leaves East Germany.

March

Maria Antonelli, pioneer of Italian fashion in the first shows organized by Bista Giorgini, launches a ready-to-wear line of her own.

1. The court in Prato censures Bishop Pietro Fiordelli for describing the couple Loriana and Mauro Bellandi as "public sinners and cohabiters" because they had only undergone a civil marriage.

14. Neo-Fascists and Communists come to blows while the Chamber grants legal status to the Volunteer Corps of Liberty.

20. Sugar Ray Robinson wins his fifth world title, in the middleweight class.

24. The magistrates' governing council is set up.

April

1. Milan. Systematic study of air pollution in the city gets under way, with observation and measurement posts and a "vertical" station run by the Brera Observatory and the public health office.

2. The "yellow" trade union of the Liberi Lavoratori ("Free Workers") wins the elections at Fiat.

May

Luigi Caccia Dominioni designs the armchair *Catilina* for Azucena.

Milan. The grand auditorium of the Conservatory is inaugurated.

1. The writer Danilo Dolci 's passport is confiscated for defamation of the government and the spread of biased information. In a speech made at Siena he blamed parish priests, the police and the representatives of the State for the backwardness of Sicily.

2. At the height of the election campaign, the Bishops' Conference reminds the faithful that they should vote "in accordance with the principles of the Catholic religion and the rulings of the Church."

13. The upper echelons of the French armed forces in Algeria demand the use of an iron fist against separatists and the guerrillas. Charles de Gaulle accepts the premiership and plenipotentiary powers. He will use them to put an end to the war and to concede self-determination to the Algerians.

25. General election. The DC recovers two percentage points, taking it to 42.3 per cent of the votes. In spite of the crisis caused by the Soviet invasion of Hungary, the PCI obtains almost 23 per cent. The PSI gains a point and a half and reaches 14.2 per cent.

June

5. The first Festival of Spoleto is held at the instigation of the composer Giancarlo Menotti.

15. In Hungary, Imre Nagy and Pál Meléter are shot for their revolt against the regime in October 1956.

15. Milan. At the Pinacoteca di Brera a madman slashes Raphael's *Marriage of the Virgin*.

July

2. Amintore Fanfani forms his second government: a two-party coalition of the DC and PSDI.

14. Iraq. Military *coup d'état* led by Abdul Kassem. King Faysal is killed and a republic proclaimed.

August

12. The atomic-powered submarine *Nautilus* passes underneath the North Pole from the Pacific to the Atlantic. She resurfaces at Portland.

20. The scandal of "God's banker," Giovanni Battista Giuffré, breaks. His ruin brings to light the connivance of politicians.

29. Ercole Baldini, a former winner of the Tour of Italy, wears the rainbow-striped jersey in the world road championship.

September

20. The era of brothels comes to a close. The Merlin law comes into force.

28. France. The Fifth Republic is born. De Gaulle is its president.

30. In the Senate, Minister of Defense Antonio Segni announces that the government has agreed to the installation of NATO medium-range missiles in Italy.

October

9. Death of Pius XII. He had been pope since March 2, 1939.

28. The conclave elects the patriarch of Venice, Angelo Roncalli, as pope. He takes the name of John XXIII.

November

5. *La dolce vita* in Rome: scandal of the dancer Aiché Nanà's striptease in a restaurant in Trastevere.

5. The price of the Fiat *500* is cut from 465 thousand lire to 395 thousand.

26. The *New York Times* derides Italian foreign policy.

December

Inauguration of the Torre Velasca designed by the BBPR studio, made up of Ludovico Barbiano di Belgioioso, Enrico Peressutti and Ernesto Rogers. The second B in the acronym stands for Gianluigi Banfi, who had died in a Nazi extermination camp in 1945.

7. The first section of the Autostrada del Sole, from Milan to Parma, is opened.

Rex-Zanussi brings Gino Valle's *Unirex* range of appliances into production.

At the jazz club "Santa Tecla," Milan rocks to the sound of Chuck Berry and celebrates the glories of the homegrown version. Ghigo Agosti sings *Coccinella non fa più la barboncella*. Giorgio Gaber and Enzo Iannacci, playing together in the duo "I Corsari," hold the field, along with Rob Nebbia and the Babby Luna. Ricky Gianco rocks up *Ciao ti dirò*, Clem Sacco sings *Oh mamma voglio l'uovo alla cocque.*

The National Chamber of Italian Fashion is established.

Carla Fracci becomes prima ballerina at La Scala.

Ten thousand hula hoops are sold in the space of a few days.

In the wake of Modugno's victory at the Festival of San Remo with *Volare*, the music publisher Guertler entrusts a song that he has on the backburner, *Come prima*, to the voice of his office boy Antonio Lardera. The pop singer Tony Dallara is born.

At La Scala, Gianandrea Gavazzeni has a success with *Assassinio nella Cattedrale*, Ildebrando Pizzetti's opera based on T.S. Eliot's *Murder in the Cathedral*. The director is Margherita Wallmann. The scenery and costumes are by Piero Zuffi.

Milan. November. Exhibition of Amedeo Modigliani's work at Palazzo Reale.

At the movies, Tati's *Mon Oncle* (*My Uncle, Mr. Hulot*) and Mario Monicelli's *I soliti ignoti* (*Big Deal on Madonna Street*).

In the bookstores, Giuseppe Tomasi di Lampedusa's *Il Gattopardo* (*The Leopard*, Strega Prize and a bestseller in Italy), Giovanni Testori's *Il ponte della Ghisolfa*, Vladimir Nabokov's *Lolita* and Graham Greene's *Our Man in Havana*.

Deaths of the playwright Guido Rocca, the sports journalist Emilio De Martino and the astronomer Giuseppe Armellini.

1959

January

Six hundred buyers crowd into the Sala Bianca of Palazzo Pitti in Florence for the 15th "High Fashion Show."

1. Victory of the revolutionaries led by Fidel Castro on Cuba. The dictator Batista flees.

   The mania for pinball machines worries the authorities: they are prohibited, with the symbolic destruction of 2000 machines.

4. The Christian Democrat politician Giuseppe Dossetti enters the priesthood.

15. At the PSI congress, the party's independent position with regard to the PCI is reasserted.

February

3. The climbers Cesare Maestri and Tony Egger conquer Cerro Torre in the Patagonian Andes.

16. Government of Antonio Segni.

March

Laura Aponte makes her debut at the Sala Bianca in Florence with a collection of knitwear. She has already found a market in the English-speaking countries.

14. The current known as the *Dorotei* (since it was formed at the convent of the Suore Dorotee in Rome) emerges within the Christian Democrat Party.

16. Aldo Moro is elected Secretary of the DC.

April

Nino Rota's *Il cappello di paglia di Firenze* is staged at La Piccola Scala.

The Dalai Lama escapes from Tibet following its occupation by China.

4. Vatican. The Holy Office confirms the excommunication of Communists and extends it to Socialists as well.

15. The first Italian nuclear reactor comes on line at Ispra.

May

Milan soccer team wins the soccer championship.

25. The British *Daily Mail* newspaper comments: "The level of efficiency and growth in the potential for production of Italy constitutes one of the economic miracles of the European continent."

June

24. Luigi Gedda, president of Catholic Action and leader of the anti-front movement in the 1948 elections, goes into retirement.

29. John XXIII issues his first encyclical *Ad Petri cathedram*. Its subject is ecumenism.

July

1. New rules of the road come into force.

August

7. President of the Republic Gronchi pardons Arnaldo Graziosi for the murder of his wife after fourteen years of imprisonment.

September

2. Khrushchev goes to the United States to meet President Eisenhower. It is the first time a Soviet premier has visited America.

7. Maria Callas and the Greek shipowner Aristotele Onassis make their love affair public.

13. The Soviet space probe Luna 2 reaches the moon.

28. Salvatore Quasimodo wins the Nobel Prize for Literature.

October

5. Florence. Judges order a search of the apartment of Ernesto Rossi, a leader of the antifascist and secular movements "guilty" of having mocked the kneeling of president Gronchi before the pope.

November

11. The prefect of Catanzaro annuls the award of the Crotone literary prize to Pier Paolo Pasolini's *Una vita violenta* (*A Violent Life*) on a technicality.

December

2. Fréjus. The Malpasset Dam collapses: 300 dead, 100 of them children.

7. In the North Atlantic Council, France opposes integration into NATO military forces.

   The tenor Mario Del Monaco receives 1355 telegrams of congratulation for his performance at the opening night of *Otello* at La Scala.

10. Award of the Nobel Prize for Physics to Emilio Segre.

11. The problem of the adulteration of foodstuffs is debated for the first time in the Chamber.

   The production of Checkov's *Platonov e gli altri* at the Piccolo Teatro in Milan marks the beginning of the artistic partnership between Valentina Cortese and Giorgio Strehler.

   New York. Frank Lloyd Wright's Guggenheim Museum is inaugurated.

Guglielmo Ulrich designs the *Trieste* chair for Saffa and Vittorio Gregotti, Lodovico Meneghetti and Giotto Stoppino the *Cavour* armchair for Sim.

Nanni Ricordi, heir of the dynasty of music publishers, and Franco Crepax discover and record the singer-songwriters Bindi, Lauzi, Paoli, Tenco, Gaber, Ricky Gianco, Iannacci and Maria Monti.

Opening of the first section of the Autostrada del Sole, from Milan to Bologna.

France. President de Gaulle recognizes the right of the Algerian people to self-determination.

Renata Tebaldi returns to La Scala, in the role of *Tosca*. She had abandoned the Milanese opera house in the mid-fifties, convinced that the directors were biased in favor of Maria Callas.

Milan. One-man show by Piero Manzoni, the "shit-in-a-can" artist, at the Galleria Azimuth.

Pino Pascali writes screenplays for television advertising spots.

On the big screen: Federico Fellini's *La dolce vita* and Billy Wilder's *Some Like It Hot*.

Books of the year: *Donnarumma all'assalto* by Ottiero Ottieri (Bagutta Prize), *La morte in banca* by Giuseppe Pontiggia, *La Gilda del Mac Mahon* by Giovanni Testori, *Il calzolaio di Vigevano* by Lucio Mastronardi, *Die Blechtrommel* (*The Tin Drum*) by Günter Grass, *The Naked Lunch* by William Burroughs, *La suora giovane* (*The Novice*) by Giovanni Arpino and *Il cavaliere inesistente* (*The Nonexistent Knight*) by Italo Calvino.

Deaths of the poet Vincenzo Cardarelli, the founder of the People's Party Don Sturzo, the painters George Grosz and Renato Birolli, the composer Ernst Bloch and the founder of the Catholic University Agostino Gemelli.

1960

January

Construction of the Kariba Dam on the Zambezi River commences. The contractors are Italian.

Eight out of a hundred Italians own an automobile, eighty-one out of a thousand a television set.

2. The "great champion" Fausto Coppi dies from an attack of undiagnosed malaria.

30. At the Festival of Sanremo, Tony Dallara and Renato Rascel win with *Romantica*.

February

Jacques Piccard's bathyscaphe *Trieste* reaches a depth of 11,521 meters in the Pacific Ocean.

13. First French atomic test in the Algerian desert.

20. The Liberal Party, led by Giovanni Malagodi, accuses the DC of wanting to dispense with centrism and withdraws its support for the government. Four days later, Prime Minister Antonio Segni hands in his resignation.

March

Irene Galitzine triumphs on the catwalk of the Florentine Sala Bianca with her "pajama palace" models.

3. Earthquake at Agadir in Morocco: ten thousand victims.

6. Brigitte Bardot becomes a mother.

21. South Africa. Police fire on anti-apartheid demonstrators at Sharpeville: forty dead.

26. Tambroni forms a single-party Christian Democrat government with the support of the MSI and the Monarchists.

April

The fashion designer Giovanni Fercioni celebrates a career spanning fifty years: the invitation is designed by Brunetta.

10. Inauguration of Brasilia, Brazil's new capital built from scratch in the middle of the country.

13. The Christian Democrat Adrio Casati, president of the Province of Milan, has the shooting of Luchino Visconti's movie *Rocco e i suoi fratelli* (*Rocco and His Brothers*) at the Idroscalo halted as he supposes it to be "not very moral and scurrilous."

May

Achille and Pier Giacomo Castiglioni design the *Sanluca* armchair for Gavina and the *Splügen Bräu* lamp for Flos, Roberto Menghi a polyethylene watering can for Pirelli and Richard Sapper the *Static* clock for Lorenz.

6. Princess Margaret of England marries the photographer Tony Armstrong-Jones.

18. The Vatican newspaper *L'Osservatore Romano* does not approve of the possible collaboration between the DC and PSI and reminds Catholic politicians that they should submit to the judgment of the ecclesiastic authorities.

The law which has excluded women from public posts since 1917 is declared unconstitutional.

June

Juventus wins the championship.

22. The Austrians refuse to submit the question of Upper Adige/South Tyrol to the International Tribunal at The Hague and decide to appeal to the UN.

28. General strike in protest against the congress of the MSI at Genoa, city of the Resistance, and against the Tambroni government. On the 30th, an antifascist march clashes with the police.

30. Leopoldville. King Baudouin of Belgium is present at the proclamation of the independence of the Congo. The country is immediately rent by tribal hatred.

July

1. End of Somalia's status as a United Nations trust territory, administered by Italy since 1950.

1. Marlene Dietrich sings in Berlin for the first time since she had gone into exile in 1931.

7. Reggio Emilia. Five people die during the repression of a street protest against Tambroni. The following day, four more demonstrators will be killed in Palermo.

17. Gastone Nencini wins the Tour de France.

18. A group of Catholic intellectuals, led by Leopoldo Elia, Pietro Scoppola and Beniamino Andreatta, sign an appeal against Neo-Fascist support for the government and the return to authoritarianism.

19. Tambroni hands in his resignation.

27. Amintore Fanfani forms his third administration, receiving the support of the center parties and an agreement to abstain from the Socialists.

August

19. Guido Carli is appointed governor of the Bank of Italy.

20. The new Leonardo da Vinci airport is opened at Fiumicino.

21. The comic and television presenter Mario Riva falls from the terraces of the Arena in Verona and dies ten days later.

25. The Olympics open in Rome. Italy will win thirteen gold medals. The most unexpected is Livio Berruti's in the 200 m.

September

7. At the Venice Film Festival, the award of the Golden Lion to André Cayatte's *Le passage du Rhin* (*Tomorrow is My Turn*) is disputed by those who thought it should have gone to Visconti's *Rocco e i suoi fratelli*.

17. Flooding in Northern and Central Italy: dozens of deaths and billions of lire in damage.

October

11. *Tribuna Politica* starts on television.

28. The ax of the public prosecutor in Milan, Carmelo Spagnuolo, falls on Antonioni's film *L'avventura*. He accuses it of obscenity. The director agrees to cut several sequences.

November

7. At the provincial and municipal elections, the PCI gains, the DC holds and the PSI falls back.

8. The Democrat John Kennedy wins the American presidential elections.

15. The Morelli-Stoppa theatrical company goes to the Quirinale to protest against the ban on performing Giovanni Testori's *Arialda*, accused of undermining "the basic principles of the family."

December

Congo. The leader of the Congolese national movement and prime minister at the time of independence, Patrice Lumumba, is seized by the soldiers of Colonel Joseph Mobutu and handed over to the secessionist forces of Moise Tshombe in Katanga.

15. King Baudouin of Belgium marries Fabiola de Mora y Aragón.

At Penne in Abruzzo, Brioni Roman Style opens a factory for the mass production of ready-to-wear men's clothing.

Bob Dylan sings *Blowin' in the Wind*, his most famous protest ballad.

The Milan-Serravalle section of the Autostrada dei Fiori is opened, completing the expressway.

Emilio Pucci patents the fabric he calls "Emilioform," a mix of helanca and silk shantung.

Milan. The Innocenti plant for production of the *A40* opens at Lambrate.

Four young lads in Liverpool form a pop group. They call themselves the Beatles.

Milan. At the Taverna Messico, on via San Giovanni sul Muro, the jazz musicians Basso, Valdambrini, Cuppini and Cerri (saxophone, trumpet, drums and guitar) hold an improvised jam session with Chet Baker, the great white trumpet player.

Gio Ponti's 127-meter-high Pirelli skyscraper soars above Milan.

Rome. At the Galleria La Salita, exhibition entitled 5 *pittori–Roma 60* ("5 Painters–Rome '60") with Franco Angeli, Tano Festa, Francesco Lo Savio, Mario Schifano and Giuseppe Uncini.

First manifesto of the *Nouveau Réalisme*, a movement created by Pierre Restany and joined by Klein, Arman, Hains, Spoerri, Raysse, Tinguely, César and Rotella.

In the bookstores, *La ragazza di Bube* (*Bebo's Girl*) by Carlo Cassola and *Il vizio assurdo* by Davide Laiolo.

The fashion world mourns the death of Salvatore Ferragamo, who leaves behind him 20,000 models of shoe and 350 patents, and of Franco Bertoli, pioneer of Giovanni Battista Giorgini's shows.

Deaths of Albert Camus, Adriano Olivetti, the historian Federico Chabod, the journalist Orio Vergani, the singer Fred Buscaglione and the actor Clark Gable.

Fifties

Fausto Coppi at the Stelvio Pass, 1953
(© Publifoto, Milan/Tino Petrelli)

Fiat presents their 600, January 1955
(© Publifoto, Milan)

Work on the first stage of the autostrada del Sole
(© Publifoto, Milan)

Emigrants at Milan Central Station, Milan 1959
(photo: Gruppo 66/Mario Finocchiaro)

John Cage during the television quiz Lascia o Raddoppia? *Milan, 26 February 1959*
(© Publifoto, Milan)

1961

January

20. John Kennedy enters the White House.

21. Milan is the first city in Italy to have a center-left administration, headed by the Social Democrat Gino Cassinis. The PSI has its own councilors.

February

At the Festival of Sanremo success, but no victory, for the singer-songwriters: Gino Paoli with *Un uomo vivo*, Pino Donaggio with *Come sinfonia* and Umberto Bindi with *Arrivederci*.

4. Rome. Trial for the Martirano crime; Raul Ghiani and Giuseppe Fenaroli will be sentenced to imprisonment for life.

8. Furio Cicogna is the new president of the Confindustria (Italian Manufacturers' Association). He takes over from Alighiero De Micheli.

March

Rome. Valentino dedicates twelve dresses in white satin to Jacqueline Kennedy at the last showing of his autumn-winter collection.

14. At its 34th Congress, the Socialist Party proposes, in a report by Secretary Pietro Nenni, entering the government in order to carry out structural reforms such as the nationalization of the electric power industry.

26. Centennial of the Unification of Italy. It is celebrated with an Expo in Turin.

April

12. The Soviet cosmonaut Yuri Gagarin makes the first orbital flight around the Earth aboard the Vostok capsule.

15. Attempted landing on Cuba by anti-Castro exiles, armed by the United States. It is the fiasco known as the "Bay of Pigs."

May

The Milan-Turin railroad line is electrified. After 103 years the steam locomotives go into retirement.

5. Alan Shepard is the American response to Yuri Gagarin: he makes a flight into space.

24. Failure of the discussions between Austria and Italy at Klagenfurt over the problem of Upper Adige. The summit between Foreign Ministers Bruno Kreisky and Antonio Segni at the end of January had also come to nothing. As would the bilateral talks held in Zurich on June 24.

30. The president of the Dominican Republic, Raphael Trujillo, is assassinated after thirty-one years in power.

June

3. Vienna. First meeting between Kennedy and Khrushchev: *détente* is still a long way off.

12. The tensions in Upper Adige lead to a series of attacks on electricity pylons.

13. Kennedy, during talks at the White House with Amintore Fanfani and Antonio Segni, gives his imprimatur to inclusion of the Socialists in the government.

July

An American U2 spy plane is shot down over the USSR.

Kennedy sends 15,000 "advisers" to Saigon, to assist the South Vietnamese armed forces.

11. Attacks by extremists from Upper Adige on the railroad system at Novara, Como and Verona.

15. John XXIII's encyclical *Mater et Magistra* ("Mother and Teacher"): the responsibilities of the Church toward the Third World, the working class and the new social problems.

16. Hans Stanek, Secretary of the Südtiroler Volkspartei, is arrested on suspicion of instigating the terrorist attacks in Upper Adige.

August

2. Construction of the Berlin Wall begins.

14. John XXIII appoints Cardinal Amleto Cicognani as Vatican secretary of state.

September

At the Venice Film Festival, Alain Resnais's *L'Année dernière à Marienbad* (*Last Year at Marienbad*) wins the Golden Lion.

9. At the Monza Grand Prix the Ferrari driven by von Trips, struck by Jim Clark, rears up and falls on the crowd: sixteen people are killed.

13. Conference of the DC at San Pellegrino in preparation for a center-left coalition.

24. **Organized by Cosmit, the Italian Furniture Show makes its debut in Milan.**

24. First peace march from Perugia to Assisi, organized by the advocate of nonviolence Aldo Capitini.

October

15. National census. The results show that there are 50,624,000 Italians.

15. Salvatore Gallo, accused of having killed his brother and given a life sentence in 1954, is declared innocent and released owing to the reappearance of his presumed victim.

20. Screening of Claude Autant-Lara's film *Tu ne tueras point* (*Thou Shalt Not Kill*) banned in Rome because it deals with conscientious objection.

November

5. Milan. The station of Le Varesine closes after sixty years. The first train leaves from the new Garibaldi Station at 5.14 a.m.

11. Kindu. Thirteen Italian aviators fall victim to the civil war in Congo. They were on a mission to transport food and medicines under the aegis of the UN.

21. The Christian Democrat Guido Gonella criticizes the television for "having introduced Togliatti and dancing girls into the heart of the family."

27. Self-criticism by Italian Communists over Stalinism and a demand for thorough de-Stalinization.

December

11. Jerusalem. Death sentence passed on Adolf Eichmann, mastermind of the "final solution," the genocide of Jews.

23. Railroad accident at Catanzaro: seventy-one victims.

Eighty-seven flights a week made between Milan and Rome.

Olivetti brings into production the *Space* office system, designed by the BBPR studio.

At the movie theaters, Ermanno Olmi's *Il posto* (*The Job*), Pier Paolo Pasolini's *Accattone*, Francesco Rosi's *Salvatore Giuliano*, Michelangelo Antonioni's *La notte* (*The Night*), Dino Risi's *Una vita difficile* and Vittorio De Sica's *La Ciociara* (*Two Women*).

Umberto Simonetta publishes *Lo sbarbato*, Gillo Dorfles *Ultime tendenze dell'arte oggi*, Nanni Balestrini *Il sasso appeso* and Leonardo Sciascia *Il giorno della civetta* (first translated as *Mafia Vendetta*, later as *The Day of the Owl*).

The monthly *Casa Novità* (now *Abitare*), edited by Piera Pieroni, commences publication.

Raffaella Curiel designs her first collection.

The Twist is all the rage at nightclubs and dancehalls.

At La Scala, Nino Sonzogno conducts the first Italian performance of Benjamin Britten's *A Midsummer Night's Dream*.

Piero Manzoni produces *The Artist's Shit* and, in a joint exhibition with Castellani at the Galleria La Tartaruga in Rome, presents his *living sculptures*, signing people's bodies and issuing them with certificates of authenticity.

Deaths of Mario Sironi, the Congolese politician Patrice Lumumba, UN Secretary General Dag Hammarskjöld, Gary Cooper, the actress Belinda Lee, Giovanni Treccani degli Alfieri, founder of the Istituto dell'Enciclopedia Italiana in 1925, and Ernest Hemingway, by his own hand.

1962

January

Naples. A majority at the congress of the Christian Democrats votes in favor of opening up to the Socialists.

February

Debut of the stylist Federico Forquet on the catwalk of the Sala Bianca in Florence.

5. Rome. Liz Taylor and Richard Burton fall in love on the set of the film *Cleopatra*.

7. Mining tragedy in the Saar. An explosion at a depth of 500 meters kills 284 miners.

9. Francis Cooper, pilot of the American U2 spy plane shot down over Soviet territory, is exchanged in Berlin for the Russian spy Rudolf Abel, who has been arrested in the United States.

18. A tidal wave takes the lives of six hundred people in Northern Europe.

20. The astronaut John Glenn is launched into orbit aboard the Apollo space capsule: his flight lasts for four hours and fifty-six minutes.

22. Amintore Fanfani forms his fourth administration. He will win a vote of confidence on March 10 with the backing of the DC, PSDI and PRI and the abstention of the PSI. It is the first center-left government.

March

Milan. The MIPEL, or International Leather Market, is held for the first time.

The government raises pensions by 30 per cent.

Two hundred and fifty knitwear manufacturers are operating in Carpi. By 1996 the number will reach two thousand.

Gino Valle designs the Solari display system for airports, Achille and Pier Giacomo Castiglioni the *Arco*, *Taccia* and *Toio* lamps for Flos, Joe and Gianni Colombo the *Acrilica* lamp for O-Luce, Gae Aulenti the ?*Sgarsul*? armchair for Poltronova, Marco Zanuso and Richard Sapper the *Doney* 14 television set for Brionvega.

April

Death of the thoroughbred Ribot, unbeaten at all the world's great racing tracks.

5. Work is completed on the Great St. Bernard Tunnel.

10. Sophia Loren wins an Oscar for her performance in Vittorio De Sica's *La Ciociara*.

May

Algeria is granted independence with the signing of the Treaty of Evian.

Stampede at the box office for *Dr. No*, the first movie based on the novels of the English writer Ian Fleming. Bond is played by Sean Connery.

6. At the ninth count, a center-right alliance elects Antonio Segni president of the Republic.

31. Collision at Voghera between the passenger train from Milan to Ventimiglia and a freight train: sixty-two dead.

June

2. Civil war in Venezuela. After two days, troops loyal to President Betancourt defeat the rebels.

18. The government drafts a law proposing the nationalization of electric power.

26. In an interview, the president of Fiat, Vittorio Valletta, openly supports the center-left alliance.

July

Valentino makes his debut on the catwalk at Palazzo Pitti, in the Sala Bianca: it is the last hour of the last day, but a triumph.

7. Resurgence of union activity among Fiat workers. Clashes with the police are largely provoked by young immigrant workers who do not belong to the union. Over 1000 people are arrested. Thirty-six will be given summary trials and sentenced to a maximum of one year and five months imprisonment.

10. Telstar is placed in orbit, permitting worldwide telecasts.

August

7. The Thalidomide scandal breaks. The drug recommended to pregnant women as a mild sedative turns out to have terrible consequences, resulting in the birth of babies without limbs.

14. The last 43 centimeters of rock in the Mont Blanc Tunnel are blown up.

24. Sue Lyon plays Lolita in the film by Kubrick based on Nabokov's novel. At the Venice Festival the spotlights are all on her.

October

1. *Panorama* comes out: at first a monthly, it will become a weekly in 1967 under the editorship of Lamberto Sechi, who will remain in charge until 1979.

11. John XXIII solemnly inaugurates the Ecumenical Council Vatican II.

20. South Tyrolean terrorists start to operate a long way outside the territory of Upper Adige: a bomb explodes in the checkroom of Verona station: one dead.

22. American naval blockade of Cuba to halt the installation of Soviet missiles. Khrushchev decides to withdraw them. On the same day the Communist Giovanni Ardizzone, demonstrating against the blockade in Milan, is killed in a clash with the police.

27. The president of ENI Enrico Mattei dies in a plane crash. Sabotage is suspected.

November

China attacks India. A short war ensues.

Publication of the first issue of *Diabolik*, "the spine-chilling cartoon strip" devised by the sisters Angela and Luciana Giussani.

3. Eugenio Cefis is appointed vice president of ENI.

27. The nationalization of electric power becomes law.

29. After eight weeks, Dario Fo and Franca Rame quit the television program *Canzonissima* in protest against continual intervention by the censors.

December

2. Enrico Berlinguer enters the leadership of the PCI.

21. The reform of the junior high school is finally passed, raising the school-leaving age to fourteen.

29. A law is approved imposing a withholding tax on stocks. The flight of capital abroad commences.

Over the year, 181 million working hours are lost to strikes.

The birthrate is 17 per 1000.

The Beatles record their first 45: *Love Me Do* and *PS I Love You*.

Luciano Foà founds the Adelphi publishing house.

The first issue of the magazine *Quaderni Piacentini* comes out.

The sculptor Giacomo Manzù finishes *The Door of Death* in St. Peter's.

Michelangelo Pistoletto produces his first *glass pictures*.

The Rolling Stones make their debut.

Books: Luciano Bianciardi's *La vita agra*, Piero Chiara's *Il piatto piange*, Maria Corti's *L'ora di tutti*, Giorgio Bassani's *Il giardino dei Finzi-Contini* (*The Garden of the Finzi-Continis*) and Aleksandr Solzhenitsyn's *One Day in the Life of Ivan Denisovich*.

On the big screen: Dino Risi's *Il sorpasso*.

Deaths of the poster designer and painter Marcello Dudovich, Enrico Mattei, the writers William Faulkner and Antonio Baldini and Marilyn Monroe.

1963

January

Milan. The winter is extremely harsh, with temperatures falling to 14·5°C below zero. The basins of the Navigli and the Idroscalo freeze.

24. Amintore Fanfani announces the installation of Polaris long-range missiles on Italian territory.

28. Carmelo Spagnuolo, public prosecutor in Milan, orders the seizure of Luis Buñuel's film *Viridiana*.

28. Francesco Lo Savio commits suicide.

30. Friuli Venezia Giulia becomes the fifth region with a special statute.

February

Rodolfo Bonetto designs the 152 timer for Veglia Borletti, Enzo Mari a perpetual calendar for Danese and Marco Zanuso the *Lambda* chair for Gavina.

1. The length of time served by conscripts in the army is reduced from eighteen to fifteen months.

8. General strike by industrial workers in solidarity with metalworkers negotiating their wage agreement, which will be approved on February 17, along with a recognition of company bargaining.

March

Debut of the fashion designer Walter Albini.

2. President of the Republic Segni makes Ferruccio Parri, Cesare Merzagora and Meuccio Ruini senators for life.

7. John XXIII gives a private audience to Nikita Khrushchev's daughter and son-in-law (Alexei Adzhubei, editor of *Izvestiya*). The visit is interpreted as sign of a thaw.

April

The furrier Carlo Tivioli makes his debut.

11. Pope John XXIII publishes the encyclical *Pacem in terris* ("Peace on Earth").

29. General election: the DC and PSI lose ground, the Liberals and Communists gain.

May

19. As conditions for entering the government, the PSI demands city-planning reform and the institution of Regional Administrations.

21. Milan soccer team wins the European Cup-Winners' Cup, beating Benfica in London. It is the first time an Italian team has won the championship.

25. The Quirinale entrusts Aldo Moro with the task of forming the new government. He will give up a month later.

June

3. John XXIII dies at 7.49 in the evening, carried off by a tumor of the stomach.

14. China criticizes the agreement between the British, Soviets and Americans to end nuclear tests. This marks a *de facto* break in the united front of the two Communist powers.

21. Cardinal Montini becomes pope on the third ballot and takes the name of Paul VI. Giovanni Colombo takes over from him at the head of the Milanese Curia, the largest in the world.

28. Saigon. Buddhist monks set fire to themselves to protest against the repression of their religion by South Vietnamese president Ngo Dinh Diem.

Inter under Angelo Moratti wins the championship: it is the team's third soccer championship since the war.

July

11. The stopgap government put together by Christian Democrat Giovanni Leone to hold the fort until the DC and PSI find an agreement is voted into office by both Chambers.

August

8. The Great Train Robbery in England. The thieves get away with £2,600,000, the largest haul ever made in the world up until that time.

31. The Social Democrats shoot from the hip on the National Committee for Nuclear Energy (CNEN), chaired by Felice Ippolito. Their true objective is to prevent the building of nuclear power plants.

September

Pino Lancetti's collection has a markedly military character and is lauded by the press.

12. To celebrate racial integration in American schools, 200,000 Blacks march on Washington.

29. Paul VI, as a mark of continuity with John XXIII, opens the second session of the Vatican Council.

October

10. Tragedy on the Vaiont River. A massive landslide on Mount Toc falls into the reservoir: the resulting wave overspills the dam and wipes out the village of Longarone. Death of 1989 people.

18. Germany has a new chancellor, Ludwig Erhard. Konrad Adenauer has handed in his resignation after fourteen years in power.

November

5. The government of Giovanni Leone resigns to allow the formation of a center-left coalition.

22. The president of the United States, John Fitzgerald Kennedy, is assassinated in Dallas.

December

Aldo Moro forms his new government, which will be voted in by the Senate on December 21.

10. Giulio Natta, professor of industrial chemistry at Milan Polytechnic, wins the Nobel Prize for his development of synthetic polymers

Milan. The Gratosoglio housing development, designed by the BBPR Studio, is opened: rows of ten-story buildings and seventeen-story highrises.

Palermo. The '63 Group is born. It includes Enrico Filippini, Alberto Arbasino, Edoardo ?Sanguineti?, Germano Lombardi and Umberto Eco.

Milan. At the Ospedale Maggiore, the heart surgeon Renato Donatelli installs artificial valves in a heart for the first time in Italy.

Italians own a total of one million six hundred thousand refrigerators. There were only half a million of them in 1958.

Unemployment remains below 500,000.

Milan. The Mario Negri Institute of Pharmacological Research is set up.

Reporting on a parade of furs by Jole Veniceni, Dino Buzzati records thirty-eight showstoppers. "It was," he writes, "a celebration in miniature of the 'economic miracle.'"

Luigi Santucci publishes *Il velocifero*, Carlo Emilio Gadda *La cognizione del dolore* (*Acquainted with Grief*), Natalia Ginzburg *Lessico famigliare* (*Family Sayings*), Primo Levi *La tregua* (*The Truce*, or *The Reawakening*), Alberto Arbasino *Fratelli d'Italia* and Ottiero Ottieri *La Linea Gotica* (Bagutta Prize).

On the big screen: Federico Fellini's *Otto e mezzo* (*8 1/2*), Ingmar Bergman's *Tystnaden* (*The Silence*), Luchino Visconti's *Il Gattopardo* (*The Leopard*), Francesco Rosi's *Le mani sulla città* (*Hands over the City*) and Dino Risi's *I mostri*.

Deaths of the cycling champion Learco Guerra, the singer Edith Piaf, the composer Paul Hindemith and the painters Francesco Lo Savio and Piero Manzoni.

1964

January

4. Paul VI makes a pilgrimage to the Holy Land.

12. The socialist left wing splits from the PSI and founds the PSIUP (Italian Socialist Party of Proletarian Unity). Its leaders include Lelio Basso, Vittorio Foa and Lucio Libertini.

26. The Republican Party expels one of its longstanding leading members, Randolfo Pacciardi, advocate of a presidential republic.

February

Mariuccia Mandelli, in art Krizia, makes her debut on the Florentine catwalk of Palazzo Pitti and wins the critics' prize.

New York. Kennedy Airport is besieged by a hundred thousand young people who have come to greet the Beatles.

In Ruanda-Urundi, shortly after the declaration of independence, the Hutu people massacre the Tutsi.

1. The sixteen-year-old Gigliola Cinquetti makes a splash at the Festival of Sanremo with *Non ho l'età* ("I'm not Old Enough").

22. Tightening of the purse strings by the Moro government to deal with the economic situation.

26. The outsider Cassius Clay wins the world heavyweight championship, beating Sonny Liston.

March

The drive against polio gets under way with the Sabin vaccine.

The stylist Rudy Gernreich sends the first topless model onto the catwalk.

14. Credit of one billion dollars from the USA to cope with the economic crisis.

April

Robbery on via Montenapoleone. A gang of Italian and French thieves blocks all the entrances to the street and clears out the showcases of the Colombo jewelry store.

Getulio Alviani designs the *Positivo*/*Negativo* fabric for Germana Marucelli.

May

14. Corleone. Arrest of the Mafia boss Luciano Liggio. He had been on the wanted list for sixteen years.

24. Lima. During a soccer game between Peru and Argentina, the disallowing of a goal leads to the death of 350 people.

June

The fifth steelworks is opened at Taranto: it is the biggest in Italy.

20. Pop Art makes its debut at the Venice Biennale. Robert Rauschenberg wins first prize.

22. Michele Straniero, the founder of Cantacronache, performs *Gorizia* in the *Bella ciao* show at the Festival of Spoleto. The song is antimilitaristic and Straniero is denounced for defamation of the armed forces.

25. An allocation of funds to State schools is defeated by the Chamber. The Moro government resigns. This marks the beginning of one of the most complicated and obscure crises in the history of the republic. They are the days of the so-called "Solo Plan" which provided, according to revelations made in 1967, for intervention by the carabinieri should the political crisis worsen. There was talk of a coup to prevent the Socialists returning to power.

27. Inter soccer team beats Real Madrid, winning its first European Cup-Winners' Cup and subsequently the Intercontinental Cup.

July

22. The long cabinet crisis is resolved, with a new Moro administration.

August

2. Incident in the Gulf of Tonkin. It is used as a pretext for the American decision to bomb North Vietnam.

7. President of the Republic Antonio Segni suffers an attack of thrombosis at a meeting with Moro and Saragat. He is temporarily replaced as head of state by the president of the Senate, Cesare Merzagora.

10. Paul VI publishes the encyclical *Ecclesiam suam*.

21. After eight days in coma, Palmiro Togliatti, secretary of the Communist party and known as "the Best," dies at Yalta. His place is taken by Luigi Longo.

September

The number of cars in circulation reaches 4,670,000. In 1954, there had only been 342,000.

3. South Tyrolean terrorism. Attack on the carabinieri barracks at Brunico: a lance corporal is killed.

9. The acknowledged head of the South Tyrolean extremists, Georg Klotz, is arrested in Austria.

October

Danese brings into production Bruno Munari's *Falkland* lamp and Carnielli Rinaldo Donzelli's *Graziella* bicycle.

4. The Autostrada del Sole is completed.

10. Tokyo Olympics: Italy will win nine gold, ten silver and seven bronze medals.

14. Fall of Khrushchev. He is replaced by Brezhnev.

November

Martin Luther King is awarded the Nobel Prize for Peace.

1. Milan. The subway line from piazzale Lotto to Sesto San Giovanni is opened. It has cost 45 billion lire. Work on the second line commences at Lambrate.

6. Lyndon B. Johnson wins the American presidential elections.

21. The Verrazzano-Narrows Bridge is opened in New York: spanning New York Harbor from Brooklyn to Staten Island, it is 2038 meters long and has twelve lanes.

December

6. Antonio Segni resigns as president of the Republic.

28. Giuseppe Saragat is elected head of state on the twenty-first ballot.

In the bookstores: *L'ombra delle colline* by Giovanni Arpino (Strega Prize), *Rien va* by Tommaso Landolfi (Bagutta Prize), *Il male oscuro* by Giuseppe Berto, *One-Dimensional Man* by Herbert Marcuse, *Herzog* by Saul Bellow and *Eléments de Sémiologie* (*Elements of Semiology*) by Roland Barthes.

At the movie theater: Pasolini's *Il Vangelo secondo Matteo* (*The Gospel According to Saint Matthew*), Sergio Leone's *Per un pugno di dollari* (*A Fistful of Dollars*), Teshigahara Hiroshi's *Suna No Onna* (*Woman of the Dunes*) and Carlo Lizzani's *La vita agra*.

Giovanni Gandini founds the comic-strip magazine *Linus*. Years later, the putative father of the periodical will become Oreste Del Buono.

Marco Zanuso and Richard Sapper design the *Algol* television set and *TS502* radio for Brionvega and the *4999* child's highchair for Kartell.

American Pop Art is given its first consecration at the 32nd Venice Biennale. Robert Rauschenberg wins the prize.

Milan. The fifth and last door of the cathedral is mounted. It has been made by the sculptor Luciano Minguzzi. After six centuries the building is complete.

Deaths of the Indian premier Jawaharlal Nehru, King Paul of Greece and the painter Giorgio Morandi.

1965

January

Florence. Parade of Italian fashion in the Sala Bianca at Palazzo Pitti. It is the last to be organized by Giovanni Battista Giorgini.

Beginning of the era of the "flower children," of the rebellion of the young.

Milan. With the official investiture of Joe Adonis and the founding father of the Milanese underworld Otello Onofri, Francis Turatello commences his rise through criminal ranks.

The number of telephone subscribers in Italy has risen to five million.

February

1. The lira is awarded the Oscar of currency.

11. Gian Maria Volontè and his theatrical company put on Rolf Hochhuth's *Der Stellvertreter* (*The Deputy*) in Rome, a play highly critical of Pius XII's passivity with regard to the extermination of the Jews. The performance is banned by the police.

21. Malcolm X, leader of the Black Panthers, is assassinated.

March

Gae Aulenti designs the *Pipistrello* lamp for Martinelli, Enzo Mari the *Atollo* fruit stand for Danese and Joe Colombo the *Elda* armchair for Comfort and the *Spider* lamp for O-Luce.

18. The Soviet cosmonaut Aleksei Leonov walks for ten minutes in the emptiness of space.

25. During the congress of the Republican Party, Secretary Ugo La Malfa launches the idea of a wages policy that envisages the start of concerted economic planning between the different parts of society.

30. Julie Andrews wins an Oscar for her performance in *Mary Poppins*.

May

Nino Cerutti entrusts Giorgio Armani with the design of the Hitman collections.

14. The surgeon Luigi Solerio successfully separates the Siamese twins Giuseppina and Santina Foglia at a hospital in Turin.

June

Karl Lagerfeld starts to work for the Fendi label.

Al-Fatah begins its guerilla warfare in Palestine.

6. Milan. The Beatles perform at the Vigorelli to an audience of 15,000.

18. Nino Benvenuti beats Mazzinghi and wins the world junior middleweight championship.

July

14. Felice Gimondi wins the Tour de France.

15. The Mont Blanc tunnel opens.

August

Revolt of the Black ghettoes in America. The suburb of Watts in Los Angeles is the scene of bloody repression by the police.

A new Indo-Pakistan war for the control of Kashmir.

26. South Tyrolean terrorists kill the carabinieri Ariu and De Gennaro at Sesto Pusteria.

30. Tragedy at Saas-Almagell in Switzerland, where the side of a glaciated valley falls onto the construction site of a dam: ninety-seven dead. Fifty-three of them are Italian immigrants.

September

The Benetton knitwear factory opens at Ponzano Veneto.

2. Luciano Lutring, known as the "machinegun soloist," is captured in Paris.

15. Helenio Herrera's Inter, after winning the championship and the Cup-Winners' Cup, brings home the second Intercontinental Cup.

21. Amintore Fanfani is elected president of the UN general assembly.

October

Roberto Capucci shows in Paris: in his collection, he uses plastic filled with colored water, glass fiber, Perspex, raffia and pebbles from the beach.

4. Paul VI travels to the United States. It is the first time a pope has visited the country. He makes a speech at the UN.

November

Ian Smith, Prime minister of Southern Rhodesia, makes a unilateral declaration of independence from Great Britain.

8. The financial newspaper *24 Ore*, founded in September 1946, takes over the paper called *Il Sole*, which has just celebrated its hundredth anniversary.

9. Blackout in New York. The power supply is cut off for twelve hours, from 5.24 in the afternoon until the morning after.

December

8. The Second Vatican Council closes.

Italian contractors commence work on the Aswan Dam in Egypt, moving the monuments of the pharaohs or raising them many meters from their original position.

Leopoldo Pirelli, who has actually been running the company since 1959, takes over from his father Alberto as president of the group. The eighty-three-year-old Alberto is made honorary president.

For the first time, the Bagutta Prize goes to a poet: Biagio Marin for *Il non tempo del mare*.

A joint exhibition is held to mark the opening of the Studio Marconi by Lucio Del Pezzo, Valerio Adami, Emilio Tadini and Mario Schifano.

The periodical *Edilizia moderna*, in publication since 1929, takes stock of the problems faced by design.

Over the year, investments are 35 per cent below 1963 and employment falls by 4 per cent.

Carlo Castellaneta publishes *Villa di delizia*, Paolo Volponi *La macchina mondiale* (*The Worldwide Machine*) and Vittorio Sereni *Gli strumenti umani*.

On the screen: *I pugni in tasca* (*Fist in His Pocket*) by Marco Bellocchio and *Io la conoscevo bene* by Antonio Pietrangeli.

Walter Bonatti is the first climber to make a solo ascent of the north face of the Matterhorn in winter.

Deaths of Winston Churchill, the painters Mario Mafai and Antonio Ligabue, the tenor Tito Schipa, former King Farouk of Egypt, the architect Le Corbusier, the fashion designer Remo Gandini, the expert on criminal law Francesco Carnelutti and Aldo Borelli, editor of the *Corriere della Sera* from 1929 to 1943.

1966

January

20. Indira Gandhi, daughter of Jawaharlal Nehru, is elected Prime Minister of India.

21. Aldo Moro resigns as head of the government.

February

3. The Soviet Luna 9 space probe lands on the moon. In June it will be joined by the American Surveyor.

14. Moscow tries the dissident writers Yuri Daniel and Andrei Siniavsky for "anti-Soviet propaganda through books published abroad." They are sentenced to five and seven years in a labor camp respectively.

15. Don Lorenzo Milani, parish priest of Barbiana in the Mugello, is cleared of charges of illegal apology of crime for defending conscientious objection in the columns of the Communist journal *Rinascita*.

24. Third Moro government: a coalition of the DC, PSI, PSDI and PRI.

March

Afra and Tobia Scarpa design the *Coronado* sofa for C&B Italia (now B&B Italia), Marco Zanuso and Richard Sapper the *Grillo* telephone for Siemens and Ettore Sottsass laminate furniture for Poltronova.

The Gemini 8 capsule and the Agena rocket link up in space.

1. After a voyage of 108 million kilometers the Soviet Venera 3 probe reaches Venus.

16. The public prosecutor's office charges three students at the Liceo Parini over an investigation of the sexual behavior of young people published in the school journal *La Zanzara*. One of them is a girl and is subjected to a physical examination.

22. *Rapprochement* between the Catholic and Anglican Churches: the archbishop of Canterbury meets Paul VI in Rome.

April

2. The students accused in the *Zanzara* case are acquitted but the attorney general in Milan appeals against the decision.

18. For the first time the Americans bomb Hanoi, capital of North Vietnam.

27. Clashes provoked by right-wing extremists at the faculty of Architecture in Rome. The Socialist student Paolo Rossi is killed.

30. First Eurodomus in Genoa.

30. Giovanni Agnelli is the new president of Fiat. He takes over from Vittorio Valletta.

May

The miniskirt, launched by Mary Quant, is all the rage.

4. Fiat sets up shop in the Soviet Union. The company will build a plant for the production of the *124* model, which will be called *Ziguli* in Russian.

15. Beginning of a strike by British dockworkers that will paralyze every port in the country for almost two months.

22. Daylight saving time is introduced for the first time since the war.

June

Artemide produces Vico Magistretti's *Eclisse* lamp, Olivetti Mario Bellini's video terminal TVC250 and C&B Italia the *Amanta* armchair, also designed by Mario Bellini.

A new dance is a hit at the dancehalls and nightclubs: the shake.

28. Military coup in Argentina, led by General Onganía.

July

The Chinese president Mao Zedong, at the age of 73, demonstrates his excellent state of health by swimming the Yangtze River.

7. Merger of Montecatini and Edison. Montedison is born.

9. Accident on the Mont Blanc cableway: two dead and eighteen wounded.

12. The law on dismissal for cause is finally approved.

19. Unauthorized construction becomes a tragedy at Agrigento: five housing developments are caught up in a landslip.

19. At the world soccer championships in Great Britain, Italy is eliminated by North Korea.

25. South Tyrolean terrorism heats up. Police officers Salvatore Cabitta and Giuseppe D'Ignoti are killed in a shootout.

August

The American presence in Vietnam, made up of 15,000 "advisers" in Kennedy's time, now runs to hundreds of thousands of soldiers.

18. The beginning of the cultural revolution in China. Mao Zedong and Lin Biao give the green light to the Red Guards.

September

9. Bomb attack on a barracks at Malga Sasso in Vipiteno: 2 dead. Responsibility for the outrage is claimed by South Tyrolean terrorists.

11. The Sardinian bandit Graziano Mesina escapes from the prison at Sassari where he was serving a sentence of twenty-four years.

October

30. Unification of the Socialists. The PSI and PSDI merge to form the Unified Socialist Party, PSU.

November

4. Flooding in Florence. Incalculable damage to the city and its artistic heritage. The bad weather also has serious effects in the Veneto, Friuli and Emilia Romagna.

28. Vittorio Valletta is made a senator for life by President of the Republic Saragat.

December

Filippo Melodia, accused of abducting his fiancée Franca Viola, is sentenced to eleven years in prison. Franca has rejected a shotgun wedding. For the first time in Sicily, a pernicious and age-old male-chauvinist culture starts to crack.

31. The problem of banditry in the Barbagia region of Sardinia worsens. At Ollolai, the eye witness to a crime, Francesco Pira, is murdered, along with his wife and small grandchild.

Milan. The owner of the Derby Club on viale Monterosa, Gianni Bongiovanni, shows himself to be an extraordinary discoverer of comic and cabaret talent: Andreasi, Cochi and Renato, Walter Valdi, Teo Teocoli, Massimo Boldi, Beruschi, Toffolo and Abatantuono. The success of the Derby Club has already triggered a surge in the popularity of cabaret in Milan, with the opening of Tinin Mantegazza's Cab 64, the Nebbia Club and the Ca' Bianca Club.

Milan. The San Carlo Hospital comes into operation. Its construction has taken four years and has cost twelve billion lire.

Among the books, Leonardo Sinisgalli's *Poesie di ieri*, Eugenio Montale's *Autodafé*, Dino Buzzati's *Il Colombre*, Salvatore Quasimodo's *Dare e avere* (*To Give and To Have and Other Poems*), Truman Capote's *In Cold Blood*, ?Gabriel Garcia Márquez's *Cien años de soledad* (*One Hundred Years of Solitude*)? and, posthumously, Mikhail Bulgakov's *Master i Margarita* (*The Master and Margarita*).

The magazine for men only, *Men*, comes out.

Milan. The Living Theatre makes its debut at the Teatro Durini.

Maestro Gianandrea Gavazzeni becomes artistic director of La Scala.

The best-selling record is *Michelle* by the Beatles. Among Italian singers, Gianni Morandi has a hit with *La fisarmonica* and Adriano Celentano with *Il ragazzo della via Gluck*.

At the movie theater: Pietro Germi's *Signore e signori* (*The Birds, the Bees and the Italians*), Pasolini's *Uccellacci e uccellini* (*The Hawks and the Sparrows*) and Gillo Pontecorvo's *La battaglia di Algeri* (*The Battle di Algiers*).

Thanks to the efforts of eight leading furniture manufacturers, the magazine *Ottagono* is founded. Its editor is Sergio Mazza.

Deaths of Elio Vittorini, Buster Keaton, the director Erwin Piscator and the sculptor Alberto Giacometti.

1967

January

25. The SIFAR scandal breaks (SIFAR was the acronym of the Defense Information Service, headed by the carabinieri general Giovanni De Lorenzo): hundreds of dossiers have secretly been compiled on politicians, trade unionists, prelates, businessmen and journalists, perhaps in preparation for a coup.

26. The singer-songwriter Luigi Tenco shoots himself after being left out of the final stage of the Sanremo Festival.

27. Tragedy at Cape Kennedy. A fire breaks out during a ground test of the Apollo capsule and the astronauts Virgil Grissom, Edward White and Roger Chaffee are killed.

February

The Cadette label, designed by Walter Albini and founded by Italo Clocchiati and Cristine Tichmars, makes a successful debut at Palazzo Pitti.

Milan. The West Orbital is opened, running from the Ghisolfa to the expressway for Genoa.

Emergence of an unfamiliar word: ecology. It was used by reporters to comment on the display of five thousand dirty handkerchiefs along Fifth Street in New York as a symbol of pollution in the city.

8. At La Sapienza University in Pisa students protest against the plan of university reform. Seven days later, students at Turin University occupy Palazzo Campana for the same reasons.

March

Marco Zanuso designs the *Lombrico* sofa for C&B Italia, Gio Ponti the *Pirellone* lamp for Fontana Arte, Joe Colombo the 4867 chair for Kartell and Anna Castelli Ferrieri sectional elements 4970-84, again for Kartell.

6. Svetlana Stalin, daughter of the deceased Soviet dictator, flees to the West.

28. Paul VI's encyclical *Populorum Progressio* ("The Progress of Peoples") is published: cooperation among peoples and the problems of developing countries.

April

Milan. Fiorucci opens its store on corso Vittorio Emanuele.

Demonstrations by young people all over Italy against the war in Vietnam. The "flower children" chain themselves to lampposts.

18. Nino Benvenuti beats Emile Griffith in New York to take the world middleweight title.

21. Coup by the colonels in Greece. King Constantine takes advantage of the situation.

May

4. Sardinian banditry assumes worrying proportions. Two police officers die after a shootout at a checkpoint on the road for Bitti.

7. The Ferrari driver Lorenzo Bandini is trapped in his burning car on the Grand Prix circuit at Montecarlo. He dies after seventy-two hours of agony.

10. An investigation of the SIFAR files by Lino Jannuzzi, published in the weekly *L'Espresso*, reveals the existence of a plan of sedition that was to have been set in motion on July 14, 1964. He accuses Giovanni De Lorenzo, commander of the carabinieri, and speaks of the involvement of Antonio Segni, president of the Republic at the time. The magazine will be sued for libel and will lose the action.

June

7. Six-Day War in the Middle East. Israel seizes the Arab part of Jerusalem, the West Bank and the Sinai as far as the East bank of the Suez Canal. The minister of defense Moshe Dayan appears on the covers of all the magazines.

13. Eugenio Montale is made a senator for life.

18. Graziano Mesina and his lieutenant Miguel Atienza are surrounded on the Supramonte by the "blue berets," the special corps of police set up to fight Sardinian banditry. In the resulting shootout two officers, Antonio Grassia and Pietro Ciavola are killed along, it is discovered a week later, with Atienza.

26. One of the twenty-seven new cardinals appointed by Paul VI is the bishop of Cracow, Karol Wojtyla.

July

Black rage explodes in America. Detroit is laid waste. The riots spread to other major cities in the United States.

8. The poet of the beat generation, Allen Ginsberg, is arrested in Italy for obscenity: he has read verses at the Festival di Spoleto that are held to have offended the common sense of decency.

August

1. The Catholic Church prohibits distribution of the catechism approved by the Dutch bishops.

September

25. Milan. After robbing a bank, the Cavallero gang escapes through the streets of the city, shooting as they go. A long pursuit follows. Three people are killed and twenty-two wounded.

October

10. Bolivia. Ernesto Che Guevara is captured and killed.

31. After fifteen days and fifteen nights of debate and filibustering, the Chamber passes the electoral law for the new regional councils.

November

The Fendi sisters "treat" furs as if they were casual wear.

17. Milan. Occupation of the Catholic University. Mario Capanna is expelled. It is the first student sit-in in Italy.

27. Mariano Rumor is confirmed as Secretary of the DC, now controlled by the *Dorotea* current.

December

2. First heart transplant. It is carried out by Christiaan Barnard on Louis Washkansky at the Groote Schuur Hospital in Cape Town, South Africa.

Poltronova brings into production Archizoom's *Superonda* sofa and Sottsass's *Kubirolo* sectional furniture, Zanotta the *Blow* armchair designed by De Pas, D'Urbino, Lomazzi and Scolari as well as Willie Landels's *Throw Away*, Piaggio the *Ciao* moped and Design Centre Angelo Mangiarotti's *Cub8*.

Potere Operaio comes out. It is edited by Oreste Scalzone, Franco Piperno and Antonio Negri. In July 1969 it will turn into a political movement.

Gucci designs a foulard for Grace Kelly. He calls it *Flora*.

In the bookstores, Desmond Morris's *The Naked Ape*, Milan Kundera's *Zert* (*The Joke*) and Régis Debray's *Revolution in the Revolution*.

On the big screen: Michelangelo Antonioni's *Blowup*, Luis Buñuel's *Belle de Jour* and Marco Bellocchio's *La Cina è vicina* (*China is Near*).

The musical *Hair* is staged in Broadway. It will be a worldwide success and an emblem of the youth of those years.

Autobianchi is taken over by Fiat.

Equipe 84 has a hit with the song *Ventinove Settembre*.

"Poor Art" is born with the exhibition *Arte Povera e Inspazio* at the Galleria Masnada in Genoa, organized by Germano Celant.

Deaths of Totò, Konrad Adenauer, Don Lorenzo Milani, Giordano Dell'Amore, rector of the Bocconi University and for a long time president of the Cariplo Bank, the painters René Magritte and Guido Tallone, the writer André Maurois, the conductor Victor de Sabata and the physicist Robert Oppenheimer, one of the fathers of the atomic bomb.

1968

January

Czechoslovakia. Alexander Dubcek becomes the new Secretary of the Communist Party and initiates a policy of reform and limited freedom. It is the beginning of the "Prague Spring."

Archizoom designs the *Safari* sofa for Poltronova and Pio Manzù the *Cronotime* clock for Ritz-Italora.

10. Beginning of student protest in Italy, inspired by the revolt of American youth against the war in Vietnam. The fuse is lit in Turin, with the occupation of Palazzo Campana, seat of the faculty of the Humanities. The next day, January 11, it is the turn of five faculties at the University of Padua. La Sapienza University in Pisa is occupied on the 17th. From the 23rd to the 27th, it is the turn of the faculties of Education, Architecture and Literature in Florence. On the 24th the protest spreads to Lecce, on the 25th to Siena and on the 31st to Trent (faculty of Sociology).

14. Earthquake in Sicily, in the valley of the Belice. The villages of Ghibellina, Montevago and Salaparuta are mortally wounded.

31. The Tet Offensive in Vietnam. The Vietcong and North Vietnamese troops besiege the American base of Khe Sanh, occupy the city of Hue, attack key points in the enemy lines and penetrate for a few hours into the suburbs of Saigon.

February

2. The protest spreads to the University of Rome.

6. Winter Olympics in Grenoble. Eugenio Monti wins two gold medals in the two- and four-man bobsleigh with Luciano De Paolis, Roberto Zandonella and Mario Armano. Franco Nones dominates the 30-kilometer cross-country and Erica Lechner the luge.

March

Valentino shows in Paris during the prêt-à-porter week. He will never regret his decision.

1. Rome. Fierce clashes at Valle Giulia between police and student protesters trying to occupy the faculty of Architecture: around 700 people are wounded.

5. High-school students join in the protest too. The first school to be occupied is the Liceo Parini in Milan.

11. The State University of Milan is occupied. Lectures are suspended, exams blocked.

16. The Neo-Fascists put up violent resistance to the protesters. In Rome, the secretary of the MSI Giorgio Almirante, Giulio Caradonna and other deputies barricade themselves in the faculty of Jurisprudence.

26. The Sardinian bandit Graziano Mesina is arrested close to his birthplace, Orgosolo. He is charged with many kidnappings.

April

4. The integrationist Black leader Martin Luther King is assassinated in Memphis.

11. Shots are fired from a pistol at the leader of the German student movement, Rudi Dutschke. He is seriously wounded in the head.

May

Silvio Berlusconi's Edilnord begins construction of the Milano Due residential district.

Designers, architects, artists and intellectuals occupy the Palazzo della Triennale, demanding a new charter. This marks the beginning of a long period of crisis.

10. The student revolt gets under way in Paris. The Sorbonne in Paris is occupied and barricades are raised against the police in the Latin Quarter. De Gaulle will dismiss the government and call new elections.

20. General election in Italy. The DC holds, the PCI gains. The united Socialists and Social Democrats take a nosedive: with respect to the results attained separately by the PSI and PSDI in 1963, a loss of 5.1 per cent in the Chamber and 5.4 per cent in the Senate.

26. Milan. The boxer Sandro Mazzinghi wins back the junior middleweight title, beating the South Korean Ki Soo Kim on points.

June

5. Sandro Pertini is elected president of the Chamber.

6. Robert Kennedy, campaigning for the presidential nomination in America, is assassinated in Los Angeles with three pistol shots fired by the Arab immigrant Sirhan Sirhan.

6. In *Rinascita*, Giorgio Amendola, leader of the Communist right, criticizes the "resurgence of extremist infantilism and outdated anarchist positions" in the student movement.

10. Rome. The Italian soccer team, managed by Valcareggi, wins the European championship.

11. Pier Paolo Pasolini's attack in poetry on the student protesters causes a sensation: "You have the faces of spoilt children/ […] / you are timid, unsure, despairing." Pasolini declares that he sympathizes with the police: "[…] they are sons of the poor, they come from the slums, whether those of the country or the city."

July

11. Giovanni Leone forms a new government.

29. Paul VI's encyclical *Humanae vitae* on birth control. The ban on artificial methods of contraception is confirmed.

August

Rome. The first pedestrian precinct in Italy is created in piazza Navona.

21. Czechoslovakia is invaded by the troops of the Warsaw Pact. The Prague Spring is crushed beneath the tracks of Soviet tanks.

25. Protests against the Venice Film Festival are staged by actors, directors and screenwriters like Cesare Zavattini, who occupy the Palazzo del Cinema at the Lido on the 28th. After eviction by the police, they stage a counter-festival.

September

Albania breaks with the USSR, leaves the Warsaw Pact and espouses Maoist ideology.

1. At Imola, Vittorio Adorni wins the world road cycling championship.

14. A group of dissenting Catholics stages a sit-in at the cathedral of Parma.

23. The Mexican police fire on demonstrators (mostly students) who have come out onto the streets of Mexico City on the eve of the Olympics to publicize their demands. It is a massacre.

October

17. At the 19th Olympics, held in Mexico City, the Black American athletes Tommy Smith and John Carlos climb the podium to receive their medals for the 200 meters and salute the crowd with their heads bowed and one first raised, sheathed in a black glove: the symbol of "black power."

20. Jacqueline Kennedy marries the Greek shipowner Aristotele Onassis.

November

3. Flooding in Piedmont. The area around Biella is the most badly affected.

6. The Republican Richard Nixon is the new president of the United States.

14. General strike calling for the reform of pensions.

19. The Leone government resigns. Saragat calls on Rumor, who forms a DC-PSI-PRI coalition and is voted in on December 23.

December

2. Avola. Strike of laborers to obtain equal pay in the province of Syracuse. Clashes take place with the police, who fire on the strikers: Giuseppe Scibilia and Angelo Sigona are killed. Solidarity marches are staged all over Italy, followed by skirmishes between the extreme left and the forces of order.

4. Birth of *L'Avvenire*, a Catholic newspaper created out of the merger of *L'Italia* and *L'Avvenire d'Italia*.

7. Led by Mario Capanna, a group of students protests against the luxury of the opening night at La Scala.

12. Turin. After a long crisis, the FIOM-CGIL is once again the biggest trade union at Fiat.

Gimmo Etro makes his debut in the furnishing fabrics sector. In 1983, he will open his first men's boutique on via Bigli in Milan.

Over the year, Feltrinelli publishes an Italian translation of Márquez's *A Hundred Years of Solitude*; Beppe Fenoglio's *Il partigiano Johnny* is brought out posthumously; Franco Basaglia publishes *L'istituzione negata* ("The Hopeless Institution"), attacking the psychiatry in use in madhouses: his arguments are to lead, some ten years later, to the passing of law 180 and the closure of the lunatic asylums.

The Teatro San Babila opens in Milan.

Casa Vogue comes out, first as a supplement to *Vogue* and then as an independent publication. The editor is Isa Tutino Vercelloni. Birth of the magazine *Rassegna: modi di abitare oggi*, edited by Adalberto Dal Lago; it will remain in publication until 1975.

At the movie theaters, Stanley Kubrick's *2001: A Space Odyssey* and Costa-Gavras's *Z*.

Protest by artists at the 34th Venice Biennale, led by Luigi Nono, Emilio Vedova and Gastone Novelli, which forces closure of the event.

Occupation of the Milan Triennale.

Publication of Ugo Mulas's book *New York Scene*.

Deaths of Salvatore Quasimodo, winner of the Nobel Prize for Literature, the painters Lucio Fontana and Pino Pascali, cosmonaut Yuri Gagarin, the first man in space, the writer Giovanni Guareschi and Padre Pio.

1969

January

Paris. The Vietnam peace negotiations open.

Carlo Scarpa designs the *Doge* table for Simon International and Marco Zanuso and Richard Sapper the *Black* television set for Brionvega.

8. Rome. The law year is given a counter-inauguration by judges, lawyers, law students and members of the trade unions of court officials who are demanding reform of the penal code.

16. Prague. The student Jan Palach sets himself on fire in Wenceslaw Square in protest against the Soviet invasion.

16. A circular from Fiorentino Sullo, Minister of Public Education, legitimizes the right of students to assembly in schools. A few days later, the Minister abolishes the examination between the fifth class of the gymnasium and the first class of the classical high school. In February, a decree law reforms the school-leaving exam: students are no longer required to take all subjects and the autumn re-sits are done away with.

19. The DC has a new Secretary, Flaminio Piccoli.

31. Viareggio. The twelve-year-old Ermanno Lavorini is abducted and killed. It appears to be a pedophile crime. A suspect, Adolfo Meciani, commits suicide in jail. The real culprits are youths of the far right: a kidnapping, which turns out badly, with the aim of raising funds for subversive activities.

February

Cairo. Yasir 'Arafat is named chairman of the Palestine Liberation Organization, or PLO.

Iva Zanicchi and Bobby Solo win Sanremo with the song *Zingara*.

Vico Magistretti designs the *Selene* chair for Artemide, Gaetano Pesce the *UP* padded furniture for C&B Italia and Rodolfo Bonetto the *Magic Drum* radio for Autovox.

3. Felice Riva, cotton industrialist and former president of the Milan soccer club, ends up in San Vittore prison following the bankruptcy of the Vallesusa cotton mill. Released, he will flee to Lebanon, staying there for almost fifteen years.

5. General and unified strike for the reform of pensions. The trade unions persuade the government to raise the average level of the pensionable wage to 74 per cent and introduce the sliding scale for pensioners as well.

6. Bologna. At the 12th Congress of the PCI, the left wing headed by Luigi Pintor, Aldo Natoli, Rossana Rossanda and Massimo Caprara challenges the soft line taken by the leadership in its criticism of the USSR over the invasion of Czechoslovakia. This is the group that will go on to found, with Lucio Magri, the newspaper *Il Manifesto*.

21. Aldo Moro proposes the so-called "strategy of attention" to the DC, which signifies taking account of the PCI and its less unbending positions with respect to the USSR, without dismissing them out of hand.

22. Rome. Ten university departments have been occupied for weeks. The rector closes them. The Minister asks for them to be reopened.

22. The occupation of the Marzotto plant at Valdagno comes to an end.

27. Richard Nixon makes an official visit to Rome. Students stage a demonstration against the war in Vietnam. Clashes with the police. One of the students occupying the university, Domenico Congedo, dies while trying to escape through a window from rockets launched by rightwing extremists.

March

Skirmishes between the Soviet and Chinese armies on the boundary between the two countries formed by the Ussuri River.

Debut of Rei Kawakubo's label "Comme des Garçons."

7. Golda Meir is elected Prime Minister of Israel.

11. Milan. Militants of the student movement, with Mario Capanna at their head, prevent Alberto Trimarchi, a professor of private law, from leaving his lecture room as he has refused to give a student who was insufficiently prepared for an examination his record book back. The faculty of Law is closed for a month.

26. The South Tyrolean terrorist Georg Klotz is given a sentence of twenty-three years.

April

9. Battipaglia. Two killed, Teresa Ricciardi and Carmine Citro, and 200 wounded at a demonstration protesting against the closure of a processing plant belonging to the State tobacco monopoly that degenerates into a riot. The demonstrators set fire to the City Hall and the police open fire.

11. General strike over the deaths at Battipaglia. Clashes and incidents in many cities, the most serious in Milan.

11. A revolt at the Nuove Prison in Turin sparks off others at San Vittore (Milan) and Marassi (Genoa), three days later. The cause is overcrowding.

11. Ciriaco De Mita comes to the fore in the DC and, at the convention of the party members, proposes a constitutional pact open to the Communist Party as well.

17. In Prague, Dubcek is sent into retirement by the pro-Soviet regime: he will get a job as a gardener. The new Secretary of the Communist Party is Gustav Husák, pro-Moscow but moderate.

25. Milan. Bombs, which the police blame on anarchists, at the Fiat stand at the Trade Fair (goes off and wounds five people) and at the Stazione Centrale (defused).

30. Cardinal Jean Villot is the new Vatican Secretary of state.

May

L'Orlando Furioso, a street theater performance, reveals the talent of the director Luca Ronconi and the Milanese actress Mariangela Melato.

Ettore Sottsass and Perry King design the *Valentine* typewriter for Olivetti, Giancarlo Piretti the *Plia* chair for Anonima Castelli and Joe Colombo the *Additional System* chairs for Sormani.

27. France. After eleven years in power, de Gaulle resigns after losing a referendum that he has himself called to validate his policies. He is succeeded by the Gaullist Georges Pompidou.

June

First issue of the monthly *Il Manifesto*, which will become a daily newspaper in 1971. Its promoters are accused of factionalism by the PCI.

2. Ten Italian engineers working for ENI are killed in the civil war between Nigeria and the Biafra secessionists.

9. Milan. Mario Capanna, Salvatore Toscano and Andrea Banfi, leaders of the student movement, are arrested for the "Trimarchi case," tried and given sentences of between three and thirteen months.

11. Conference of Communist parties in Moscow. Berlinguer, assistant secretary of the PCI, attacks the Soviet invasion of Czechoslovakia.

29. On the death of Arturo Michelini, Giorgio Almirante is elected Secretary of the MSI.

July

2. At the Arena in Milan, Paola Pigni sets a world record for the 1500 meters.

The right wing of the Socialist Party splits to create the Unitary Socialist Party (PSU). The earthquake has repercussions for the Rumor government, which is thrown into crisis and resigns on the 5th of the same month.

3. Turin. General strike against the high level of rent and evictions. Political groupings operating outside Parliament, with Lotta Continua ("Continuous Struggle") at their head, clash with the police: seventy wounded.

21. Man on the Moon. The Apollo 11 spacecraft takes Neil Armstrong, Michael Collins and Edwin Aldrin into orbit around the satellite. The Lunar Module detaches and lands. At 4.56 a.m., Italian time, Armstrong sets foot on the moon's surface. He is followed by Aldrin, while Collins has remained at the command of Apollo 11 in orbit. At the end of November, the Apollo 12 mission will take three more astronauts to the Moon.

31. For the first time, the CGIL, CISL and UIL take a unitary line over the wage agreement for metalworkers: 40 hours of work per week.

August

5. The conflict between Catholics and Protestants in Northern Ireland grows increasingly bloody.

6. Rumor forms his second government, a single-party Christian Democrat administration that receives the backing of the PSI as well as of the secessionists of the PSU.

8. Tens of thousands of hippies gather at Woodstock in the United States: psychedelic music is the latest wave in the ocean of rock.

9. Hollywood. Adepts of the satanic sect led by Charles Manson torture and kill Sharon Tate, actress and wife of the director Roman Polanski, and four of her guests. Sharon was pregnant.

15. The RAI (Italian Broadcasting Corporation) bans the song *Je t'aime, moi non plus* by Serge Gainsbourg and Jane Birkin from the radio program Hit Parade.

September

Formation of Lotta Continua, a group operating outside parliament led by Adriano Sofri.

11. Strike of metalworkers. It marks the beginning of the "hot autumn." The trade unions resort to strikes on a massive scale in the negotiations over the renewal of fifty national collective wage agreements.

23. CUBs (Unitary Grass-Roots Committees) encroach on union activity and inflame the situation. Pirelli suspends work for a day in two departments of the Bicocca plant where they have gained control.

October

18. The trade unions, with Luigi Macario, leader of the CISL metalworkers, acting as their mouthpiece, put forward the argument that wages are a "variable independent" of other factors in production.

22. After taking the European Cup-Winners' Cup by beating Ajax, the Milan soccer team, coached by ?paron? Rocco, plays Estudiantes for the Intercontinental Cup and wins.

24. Fiat takes over Lancia.

27. Pisa. Extra-parliamentary groups clash with the police: the student Cesare Pardini is killed.

30. *Potere Operaio*, organ of the extra-parliamentary movement of the same name ("Worker Power"), comes out with the headline "Yes to Worker Violence."

November

Gianni Rivera receives the Golden Football. It is the first time the award has been given to an Italian player.

9. The DC has a new Secretary, Arnaldo Forlani.

13. Union agreement at Pirelli. The workers win the right to assembly, department representatives and a production bonus.

19. Milan. Death of police officer Antonio Annarumma, struck by a metal bar thrown like a javelin at his four-wheel-drive vehicle during a clash between students and police at the tail-end of a trade-union march in support of the general strike over housing.

21. On the day of the funeral of Officer Annarumma, leaflets are distributed by a Committee for Public Defense. This is an attempt on the part of moderates to organize against extremism in the streets. In the meantime, the Neo-Fascists try to invade the university, controlled by the student movement.

30. Signing of the agreement between Italy and Austria over South Tyrol-Upper Adige.

December

Milan. The second line of the Metropolitana between piazza Caiazzo and Cascina Gobba is opened.

2. Rome. *Paradise Now*, the show staged by the Living Theatre, is accused of obscenity. The police ask the head of the company, Julian Beck, and his actors to leave Italy.

4. The Constitutional Court declares the provisions of Family Law that prohibit concubinage and adultery unconstitutional.

12. Milan. At 4.37 p.m. a device explodes at the head office of the Banca Nazionale dell'Agricoltura on piazza Fontana: sixteen dead and ninety wounded. Four days later, while undergoing interrogation over the outrage, the innocent anarchist Giuseppe Pinelli dies falling from a window of the police station.

16. Pietro Valpreda, dancer and militant anarchist, is arrested and charged with being the principal of the massacre in piazza Fontana, i.e. with having taken the explosive device into the bank. The lengthy legal proceedings will demonstrate that he had nothing to do with it.

21. After a four-month-long confrontation that has overheated relations with the unions, the national wage agreement of the metalworkers is settled.

The Missoni build their production facilities at Sumirago (Varese).

During the year, Elsa Morante publishes *Il mondo salvato dai ragazzini* (*The World Saved by Little Children*), Gillo Dorfles *Il kitsch. Antologia del cattivo gusto* (*Kitsch: The World of Bad Taste*) and Philip Roth *Portnoy's Complaint*.

Milanovendemoda, a show organized by the advertising agents and sales representatives of the clothing sector, acting together in the Assomoda association, is staged for the first time.

On the big screen, Luchino Visconti's *La caduta degli dei* (*The Damned*) and Dennis Hopper's *Easy Rider*, film-manifesto of a generation.

On the stage, Dario Fo's *Mistero buffo* ("*Comic Mystery*").

Zanotta brings into production the *Sacco* armchair designed by Piero Gatti, Cesare Paolini and Francesco Teodoro.

Deaths of General Dwight Eisenhower, former president of the United States, Ho Chi Min, president of North Vietnam, the philosopher Theodor Adorno, the architect Ludwig Mies van der Rohe, the writer Ivy Compton Burnett, the singer Natalino Otto and the journalist Irene Brin.

1970

January

The regional administrations are about to be created. The Chamber of Deputies approves a law on their funding.

John Lennon announces that he will cut off his hair and sell it in plastic bags for charity.

Joe Colombo designs the *Tube-Chair* armchair for Flexform and the *Alogena* lamp for O-Luce.

Nigeria. The central government crushes Biafra's attempt at secession, already exhausted by hunger.

February

Israeli planes bomb the outskirts of Cairo.

Milan. Dario Fo founds the theater group *La Comune*. It stages *Morte accidentale di un anarchico (Accidental Death of an Anarchist)* at the warehouse on via Colletta.

7. Cabinet crisis. The Christian Democrat and Doroteo Mariano Rumor resigns. On the 12th he is again entrusted with the task of forming a government, but gives up on the 28th owing to the impossibility of cobbling together the center-left alliance.

23. Milan. Opposite the San Siro stadium, Mayor Aniasi lays the foundation stone of the new Sport Hall, whose roof will collapse under the weight of snow in the winter of 1985. It will eventually be demolished in 1988.

March

Austria. Against all expectations, the Socialists win the elections. Bruno Kreisky becomes Chancellor. He will be reelected many times.

With the Montedoro label, the stylist Walter Albini proposes the *Uni-max* formula: uniformity of cut and color for men and women. In Florence he shows his "births, deaths and marriages" collection: eight brides in long pink dresses, eight widows in short black ones.

A hundred countries sign the Treaty on the Non-Proliferation of Nuclear Weapons. France, India, China, Israel and Brazil decline to join them.

Cambodia. The pro-American Lon Nol deposes President Sihanouk. Pol Pot's Khmer Rouge commence their guerrilla war. Two hundred thousand American students will march on the White House to protest against military intervention by the United States.

Andrea Valcarenghi founds the grass-roots magazine *Re Nudo*.

Vivienne Westwood opens the store *Let It Rock* at 430, King's Road in London: it sells records from the fifties and clothes inspired by the fashion of that period.

2. Merger of Pirelli and Dunlop. It will not last long.

12. Jane Fonda's support for the cause of Native Americans leads to the arrest of the actress who, together with representatives of various tribes, has peacefully taken possession of the military fort of Lawson and the surrounding lands claimed by the Indians.

24. The CGIL has a new Secretary: Luciano Lama.

29. After abortive attempts by Aldo Moro and Amintore Fanfani, president of the Republic Giuseppe Saragat once again gives the job of forming the government to Mariano Rumor, who succeeds in reassembling the center-left coalition and takes the oath of office, along with his ministers, at the Quirinale. He is Prime Minister for the third time.

April

Achille Castiglioni and Pio Manzù design the *Parentesi* lamp for Flos.

15. Renato Lombardi is elected president of the Confindustria. He takes over from the original president, Angelo Costa. The manufacturers' association approves a new and more open charter. It has been drawn up by a commission chaired by Leopoldo Pirelli.

23. Giacomo Mancini assumes, as the new secretary, the leadership of the Socialist Party.

May

Kenzo opens the *Jungle Jap* boutique in Paris.

The pop group Premiata Forneria Marconi makes its debut.

14. The Statute of Laborers protecting the constitutional rights and freedom of assembly of factory workers becomes law.

21. After the Senate, the Chamber also passes the law on the referendum.

29. Altiero Spinelli and Franco Maria Malfatti are appointed chairmen of the Executive Commission of the European Community.

June

Great Britain. The Labour Party is defeated at the elections. The Conservatives form a government headed by Edward Heath.

7. Voting for the regional administrations is held.

17. Milan. A Mafia summit is held on via Generale Govone. It is attended by Gerlando Alberti, Giuseppe Calderone, Tommaso Buscetta, Gaetano Badalamenti, Salvatore Riina and Salvatore Greco.

21. At the World Soccer Cup in Mexico, Italy reaches the final after an epic battle with Germany: 4-3 in extra time. It then loses to Brazil.

25. Protesting teachers block assignment of the term's marks and school-leaving exams.

July

Saint Tropez. Bonfire of bras at the Epi Plage: feminists declare that "the brassiere is an instrument of male slavery."

Guido Piovene wins the Strega Prize with his novel *Le stelle fredde*.

2. The Beatles record the song *Her Majesty*, dedicated to Queen Elizabeth.

6. The Rumor government falls.

6. The first "jumbo jet" takes off from Malpensa after its worldwide debut in London on January 21 on the New York route. The Alitalia Boeing 747 is also on its way to New York. It has 350 people on board. Almost 5000 gather to watch the takeoff of the giant airplane.

14. Revolt in Reggio Calabria against the choice of Catanzaro as regional capital. Clashes with the police and barricades. The railroad worker Bruno Labate, a member of the CGIL, is killed. The police headquarters is attacked on the 18th. Sabotage of the rails in the vicinity of Gioia Tauro on the 22nd results in the derailment of the Palermo-Turin train: six wounded. Exploited by the right (the leader of the Action Committee is Ciccio Franco), the revolt lasts for two months. Its slogan is "Damn anyone who gives in." On September 15 the offices of the PSI and the municipal tax office are set on fire. On the 17th Angelo Campanella dies in the clashes. Minister of the Interior Restivo gives a report at Montecitorio: thirteen bombings, thirty-three roadblocks, six attacks on the prefectural offices, four on the police headquarters, 231 wounded, 282 arrests.

16. Genoa. The magistrate Adriano Sansa prohibits bathing along the shoreline of the city because of pollution of the sea. In Milan and its province 449 industries are charged with polluting the environment.

25. Libya. Moammar Gadhafi orders confiscation of all the property of the former Italian colonists and their expulsion.

26. The singer Albano Carrisi marries Romina Power.

August

6. A new government is formed by the Christian Democrat Emilio Colombo. He wins votes of confidence in the Upper and Lower Chambers and, six days later, takes the oath of office before President Saragat.

25. Five hundred thousand young people invade the Isle of Wight in England for a pop festival: it is an orgy of mass nudism, of transgression.

27. Tightening of the purse strings to stem the rise in public expenditure. There is a shortfall of 450 billion lire. Increases in the price of gasoline, telephone calls and stamps for the driving license and passport and in some taxes.

30. Rome. The Casati murder. Camillo Casati, a marquis and descendant of a family with a long history of involvement in politics and culture, kills his wife Anna and her lover Massimo Minorenti. It is a crime of jealousy, after years of "orgies" which are described in detail in the media.

September

Strike of the marriage bed in the United States: women demand total equality of rights.

Milan. The Anteo is transformed into the Anteo art cinema: it is the third, after the Orchidea and Rubino. It is one way of reacting to the slump of interest in movies to which the following figures, from the United States, bear witness: 15 million moviegoers as compared with 87 million in 1947.

16. Palermo. The mafia abducts and kills the *L'Ora* reporter Mauro De Mauro.

October

Chile. The Socialist Salvador Allende is elected president of the country.

Egypt. After the death of Nasser, the presidency passes to Anwar Sadat.

Anticipating fashion by at least twenty years, Raffaella Carrà leaves her navel bare between bodice and pants on the TV program *Canzonissima*. It is a scandal.

2. Milan. Clashes in front of the Palalido during a concert by the Rolling Stones: thousands of young people want to enter but there is no room. The final toll is seventy arrests and tens of wounded.

5. Genoa. Sergio Gadolla is kidnapped by terrorists.

12. The Christian Democrat Vito Ciancimino is elected mayor of Palermo. Ten DC councilors do not vote for him because they suspect him of being a Mafioso. And subsequently Ciancimino will be indicted on this very charge.

16. Jordan. Civil war breaks out in Amman between Jordanians and Palestinians: the so-called "Black September."

31. The whole of Italy is "covered" by direct distance dialing.

November

The United States resumes bombing of North Vietnam with B52s.

5. Italy and China reestablish diplomatic relations.

23. Paul VI decrees that from January 1, 1971, cardinals over the age of eighty will no longer take part in the election of a pope and that bishops must retire at seventy-five.

25. Pietro Nenni is made a senator for life.

27. Manila. Attempt on the life of pope Paul VI while on a pastoral visit to the Philippines. A man tries to stab him.

December

1. Italy legalizes divorce. The law is finally passed by the Chamber with 319 votes in favor and 286 against.

7. Orders and countermands from Junio Valerio Borghese for a coup that will be uncovered months later.

   Milan. I *Vespri Siciliani*, conducted by Gianandrea Gavazzeni, opens the season at La Scala.

12. Milan. During a demonstration in memory of the massacre in piazza Fontana, the student Saverio Saltarelli dies, struck on the heart by a teargas bomb.

23. The Mafia boss Luciano Liggio is given a life sentence.

Livio Castiglioni and Gianfranco Frattini design the *Boalum* lamp for Artemide.

During the year, Camilla Cederna publishes *Pinelli, una finestra sulla strage*, Bobi Blazen *Note senza testo*, Raffaele Carrieri *Stella-cuore,* Jorge Luis Borges *El informe de Brodie* (*Dr. Brodie's Report*), Mario Lodi *Il paese sbagliato* and Alberto Vigevani *L'invenzione* (Bagutta Prize).

At the cinema, Elio Petri's *Indagine su un cittadino al di sopra di ogni sospetto* (*Investigation of a Citizen above Suspicion*), Bertolucci's *La strategia del ragno* (*The Spider's Stratagem*), Pasolini's *Medea* and Michelangelo Antonioni's *Zabriskie Point*.

In Milan Christo wraps the monument to Victor Emanuel II in the cathedral square and the one to Leonardo in front of La Scala. Exhibitions by Pistoletto at the Ariete and Mario Merz at the Lambert.

The exhibition *Amore mio* ("My Love"), organized by Achille Bonito Oliva, opens at Montepulciano. The work of a group of Italian artists with cultural, emotional and sentimental interests that buck the political trend of the moment turns the attention back to the subject. Bonito Oliva's *Territorio magico* ("Magical Territory") is published by Centro Di, Florence.

Poltronova produces the *Joe* armchair designed by De Pas, D'Urbino and Lomazzi, Valenti the *Hebi* lamp by Isao Hosoe, Gufram the *Pratone* by Giorgio Ceretti, Pietro Derossi and Riccardo Rosso and the Busnelli Gruppo Industriale the *Fiocco* armchair by G14 Progettazione.

Deaths of General Charles de Gaulle, Angelo Rizzoli Senior, the Egyptian president Gamal Abdel Nasser, the Portuguese dictator António de Oliveira Salazar, the poet Giuseppe Ungaretti and the philosopher Bertrand Russell.

Sixties

The Vajont disaster, Belluno,
12 October 1963
(© Publifoto, Milan)

Procession for the feast of
Corpus Domini, Milan 1967
(photo: Gruppo 66/Carlo
Cosulich)

The opening of the first line
of the Milan underground,
Milan 1964
(photo: Carlo Orsi)

Opening of the Prielli building
in Milan, 1960
(photo: Carlo Orsi)

May Day celebrations at
piazza Duomo, Milan 1968
(photo: Gruppo 66/Carlo
Cosulich)

The Rolling Stone concert
at the Palalido, Milan 1967
(photo: Gruppo 66/Carlo
Cosulich)

1971

January

The Italian population reaches 54 million.

Zanotta begins production of its _Quaderna_ tables designed by Superstudio; Robots _Abitacolo_ by Bruno Munari.

15. The parliamentary board of inquiry investigating the *"Solo"* plan and the attempted coup set up by the commander of the Carabinieri, Giovanni De Lorenzo, concludes with a majority opinion reporting nothing out of the ordinary, but asking for a shakeup in the Secret Service, while a minority (PCI and PSIUP) harshly criticizes De Lorenzo's actions.

February

Emilio Pucci designs the emblem for Apollo 15.

The outsider Nada wins the Festival of Sanremo with *Il cuore è uno zingaro e va.*

Uganda. General Idi Amin Dada takes power in what is to be a ruthless and bloody dictatorship.

4. Catanzaro. A bomb is set off during an antifascist march killing Giuseppe Malacaria, a blue-collar worker.

27. A revolt in Aquila against the designation of Pescara as the capital of the Abruzzi region. Political party headquarters are attacked and burned.

March

Gae Aulenti designs the _April_ armchair for Zanotta.

Switzerland. A referendum gives women the right to vote.

17. The newspaper *Paese Sera* publishes news about an attempted coup d'état by Junio Valerio Borghese, former commandant of the mini republic, *Decima Mas*. A battalion of forest rangers is involved. The news is confirmed by the Minister of the Interior, Franco Restivo. Borghese flees to Spain.

26. Mario Rossi, a militant in the red terrorist group *XXII Ottobre*, escaping on his motor scooter after robbing a messenger, Alessandro Floris, shoots and kills his victim when the latter gives chase. An amateur photographer captures the instant on film. It will be an image that becomes an emblem of the *anni di piombo* (years of bullets).

April

Three hundred French women, led by a host of luminaries from literature and the cinema, admit to having had abortions.

The Christian Democrat Massimo de Carolis, together with the royalist Adamo degli Occhi, lead a huge march of moderate Milanese, marking the birth of the "silent majority".

7. Simmenthal Milano wins the *Trophy of trophies* in basketball.

16. Libero Mazza, Prefect of Milan, issues a highly controversial report on what he calls the "extremist opposites".

28. *Il Manifesto*, newspaper of ultra-leftist Italian Communist Party dissidents, hits the newsstands.

May

Giovanetti comes out with the sofa _Anfibio_ by Alessandro Becchi and Skipper. Angelo Mangiarotti designs the tables of the _Eros_ series, later produced by Skipper.

3. Eugenio Cefis leaves ENI (Italian National Hydrocarbon Corporation) to become president of Montedison.

7. Genoa.The thirteen year-old Milena Sutter is kidnapped and her body later found in the Mediterranean. Lorenzo Bozano is sentenced to life in prison for the crime.

8. For the first time in its criminal history, the Mafia kills a magistrate: the district attorney of the Republic of Palermo, Pietro Scaglione.

11. Tiziana Minschi's divorce from her husband, Gianmaria Volontè, marks the twelfth such case heard by the Milan court after the enactment of the Fortuna-Baslini law legalizing divorce in Italy 3 months earlier. There are already over 3,000 cases pending.

17. The Milanese explorer Guido Monzino reaches the North Pole.

June

The Inter soccer club wins its eleventh *Scudetto*.

19. The anti-divorce front presents a petition bearing 1,370,314 signatures for a referendum to abrogate the new divorce law.

The hot summer weather triggers the explosion of the newest fashion craze: hot pants.

July

16. Henry Kissinger, American Secretary of State, steps into the spotlight laying the groundwork for a US-China reconciliation in Beijing.

August

15. The end of the gold standard; the international monetary standard had been in place since World War II.

28. The overloaded Greek ferryboat *Heleanna* catches fire off the coast of Brindisi: 200 die.

September

Issey Miyake emerges from the shadow of Laroche and Givenchy to debut in New York. This month also marks the debut of another Japanese stylist: Yojhi Yamamoto.

21. The Italian swimming championship ends in Milan. Novella Calligaris breaks 7 Italian records and 3 European records in the 400, 800 and 1500 meter freestyle.

October

7. The tax reform obtains final approval: tax-records office, single tax on individuals and corporate bodies. It will be enacted on January 1, 1974.

Vittorio Emanuele di Savoia and Marina Doria marry in Teheran.

19. Alberto Pirelli dies; he had been at the helm of the family company with his brother since 1965.

25. The People's Republic of China enters the United Nations; Taiwan exits.

29. The Mafia boss, Frank Coppola, is arrested in Rome.

November

Construction is begun on the nuclear power plant in Caorso. It will be inaugurated in 1977 but will never go into full operation.

8. The imposter nun Antonietta Pagliuca is arrested in Rome for abuse of underage guests at the Istituto Santa Rita.

23. The rector of the Milan Polytechnical University, Francesco Carassa, does not approve of the atmosphere and teaching methods at the school of Architecture. Its dean, Paolo Portoghesi, along with seven other teachers, is suspended by the Public Education Minister.

December

War between India and Pakistan. The adversaries accept a UN-sponsored cease-fire.

9. Both houses of the Italian Parliament unite to vote for the president. A successor to Giuseppe Saragat has to be chosen. The entire Christian Democratic party is backing Amintore Fanfani, but he will not win. It is not until Christmas eve, at the end of the twenty-third vote, that Giovanni Leone is elected with the deciding votes of the MSI (Italian Social Movement).

20. Turin: Gaudenzio Bono, managing director of FIAT, hands in his resignation. Umberto Agnelli takes over. The President is Gianni Agnelli.

Books of the year include: *Satura* by Montale; *The inventor of the horse* by Campanile; *Trasumar e organizar* by Pasolini; *Io e lui* by Alberto Moravia; *Group portrait with lady* by Heinrich Böll; *Varianti e altra linguistica* by Gianfranco Contini; *Love Story* by Erich Segal (12 million copies sold worldwide).

At the cinema: *Death in Venice* by Luchino Visconti; *A Clockwork Orange* by Stanley Kubrick; *La classe operaia va in paradiso* by Elio Petri; and *San Michele aveva un gallo* by the Taviani brothers.

Obituaries: Nikita Khrushchev; the probable successor to Mao Lin Piao; the cinema critic Filippo Sacchi; the actor Nino Besozzi; the designer Joe Colombo; the publisher Arnoldo Mondadori; Louis "Satchmo" Armstrong; Coco Chanel.

1972

January

15. Crisis for the government of Emilio Colombo. He is reappointed but has to give up. Andreotti also fails. The president is forced to recognize that there is no possible majority and to dissolve parliament.

23. Earthquakes in the Marches: 360 tremors ranging from 6 to 8 on the Mercalli scale. The people of Ancona are forced to evacuate.

February

Northern Ireland sinks into civil war between Protestants and Catholics: 13 die in Londonderry.

The home pregnancy test becomes available: laboratory exams are not necessary.

3. Italy wins two gold medals at the Winter Olympics in Sapporo, Japan: Gustavo Thoeni wins the giant slalom, Paul Hildgartner and Walter Plaikner win the two-man bobsled.

21. The American president Nixon and Mao Tse-tung meet in Beijing, ending 25 years of diplomatic separation.

March

The Milanese era in prêt-à-porter begins. Walter Albini leaves the Florentine catwalk in the Sala Bianca and shows five of his collections at Milan's Circolo del Giardino: 300 garments designed for Basile, Misterfox, Callaghan, and Escargot. Albini is soon followed by Krizia (at the Permanente), Rosita and Tai Missoni, Ken Scott, and Jean Baptiste Caumont.

A group of students of the Piccolo Teatro founds the Teatro dell'Elfo theater company in Milan. Its members include Gabriele Salvatores and Elio De Capitani.

3. Milan: The Red Brigades enter the terrorism scene by briefly kidnapping a Siemens executive, Idalgo Macchiarini.

4. Owners of the newspaper *Corriere della Sera* fire the director Giovanni Spadolini and turn over the helm to Piero Ottone.

8. International Women's Day: feminists march through the streets of Rome and Milan shouting *Tremate, tremate, le streghe son tornate* (Tremble, tremble, the witches are back).

15. The body of publisher Giangiacomo Feltrinelli is discovered beneath a high tension pylon in Segrate. An investigation concludes that he was blown up by the dynamite he was using to damage the electrical grid.

17. Enrico Berlinguer is elected Secretary of the PCI at the XIII Congress in Milan.

April

6. Vietnam: The Vietcong attack at An Loc. The Americans respond by increasing bombing in the north. Meanwhile, the Secretary of State, Henry Kissinger, opens negotiations for a peace treaty.

20. The Apollo 16 astronauts travel 2.5 miles on the lunar surface in their electric lunar rover.

22. Raffaele Mattioli, legendary president of COMIT, goes into retirement.

May

5. A DC8 flown by Alitalia crashes into Monte Pellegrino while attempting to land in Palermo: 112 die.

5. Franco Serantini, a twenty year-old anarchist, dies in prison of head injuries after being arrested during clashes at a rally of the rightist MSI.

8. Elections: The DC (Christian Democrats) hold their 1968 seats and the relative majority. The MSI makes gains. The PCI wins 27.1%. The PSI (Italian Socialist Party) drops below 10% for the first time.

17. Milan: The commissioner Luigi Calabresi, is killed in front of his house. It is the first individual killing for Italian terrorism.

26. **The show "Italy: The new domestic landscape", directed by Emilio Ambasz, opens at the Museum of Modern Art in New York. It marks the recognition of the success of Italian design.**

31. Peteano massacre. Five carabinieri, following up on an anonymous call, inspect a FIAT 500 abandoned near the Yugoslav border. The car explodes. Three of the five die. It is discovered that the terrorists are rightists led by Vincenzo Vinciguerra.

June

The Bologna-Bari expressway is opened.

Arflex begins production of the upholstered furniture *Strips* by Cini Boeri and Laura Griziotti. C&B Italia comes out with the upholstered furniture *Le Bambole* by Mario Bellini and entrusts the publicity to Oliviero Toscani.

9. The Vatican censures Giovanni Franzoni, abbot of the Roman Basilica of Saint Paul without the Walls, for taking a favorable position to the abolition of the Concordat and the modernization of the church.

26. Andreotti sets up a centrist government.

July

The Egyptian president Sadat breaks definitively with the Soviet Union, recalling all his technicians and military advisors from Moscow.

After his victory in the Giro d'Italia, Eddy Merckx also wins the Tour de France.

3. Death of Vittorio Mascheroni, composer of *Stramilano*, *Fiorin Fiorello*, *Addormentarmi così*, and *Il tango della Gelosia*.

24. The three major labor unions, CGIL, CISL, UIL, unite into a single federation.

August

Alfa Romeo builds southern Italy's largest automobile plant in Pomigliano d'Arco giving birth to Alfa Sud.

The Milanese Magistracy charges the neo-Fascists Franco Freda and Giovanni Ventura for the Piazza Fontana massacre (December 12, 1969).

Milan: The first automatic gasoline station goes into operation in Piazza Firenze.

Richard Sapper designs the lamp *Tizio* for Artemide, Gae Aulenti the armchair 4794 for Kartell.

September

Marino Basso wins the world road cycling championship.

26. Tragedy at the Munich Olympics. Palestinian terrorists break into the dormitory of the Israeli athletes in the Olympic village. In the ensuing fight, 2 Israeli athletes are killed, 2 escape and 9 are taken hostage. Sharpshooters shooting into the group fail tragically: the 9 Israeli athletes are killed along with 5 terrorists and a German policeman.

October

13. An Uruguayan airplane with 45 aboard crashes in the Andes. It takes rescuers two months to reach the site. The 16 survivors say they managed to live by eating the remains of the dead passengers.

November

Richard Nixon, Republican, wins the US presidential election.

14. The "Valpreda Law" is approved giving power to the investigating magistrate to grant provisory liberty to people held in prison for a long time awaiting trial.

December

15. A law is passed instituting civil service as an alternative to military service for conscientious objectors.

18. Milan: Mafia boss Luciano Liggio's men kidnap the businessman Pietro Torricelli, inaugurating a spate of kidnappings.

19. Maurizio Pollini's concert in the Sala Grande of the Milan Conservatory is interrupted. The pianist wanted to read a declaration of solidarity with North Vietnam, signed by such notables as Claudio Abbado, Bruno Bettinelli, Luigi Dallapiccola, and Luigi Pestalozza. The audience grumbled. Pollini leaves without playing a note.

Books published in 1972: *Invisible cities* by Italo Calvino; *Pigliamoci tutto* by Nanni Balestrini; *Paese d'ombre* by Dessì; and *La donna della domenica* by Carlo Fruttero and Franco Lucentini.

First issue of the magazine *Data*, founded by Tommaso Trini, comes out with a cover by Luciano Fabro.

Guido Ballo directs a large exhibition of works by Lucio Fontana at Milan's Palazzo Reale.

After a period of self-imposed exile, Giorgio Strehler returns to Milan's Piccolo Teatro with a staging of *King Lear*. Paolo Grassi is named superintendent of La Scala.

At the cinema: *The Godfather* by Francis Ford Coppola; *Il caso Mattei* by Francesco Rosi. Bernardo Bertolucci's *Last Tango in Paris* is pulled from movie theaters for offending public decency.

The Ralph Lauren trademark is born in the United States.

Obituaries: the writers Dino Buzzati and Yasunari Kawabata; the poet Ezra Pound; the industrialist Giovanni Falck; the painters Giuseppe Capogrossi and Roberto Crippa; the former US president Harry Truman; the *chansonnier* Maurice Chevalie; and the tailor Balenciaga.

1973

January

The population of Milan reaches 1,745,220.

1. The Value Added Tax (IVA) is imposed.

23. Peace in Vietnam. In Paris, Kissinger and Le Duc Tho sign an agreement ending the American intervention.

Milan: *Ambleto* by Giovanni Testori inaugurates the Teatro Pierlombardo founded by Franco Parenti and Andrée Ruth Shammah.

A clash between students and police in front of the Bocconi University dormitory results in the death of Roberto Franceschi of the Movimento Studentesco.

The European Community grows to nine with the entry of Great Britain, Ireland and Denmark.

February

8. A wiretapping scandal erupts; Giulio Andreotti and Enrico Berlinguer are among those whose calls are monitored.

March

12. Fluctuation in European currencies. The Italian lira and the British pound fluctuate more than the others and a thinly veiled process of devaluation acts as a propellant for exports.

April

Cassina introduces the armchair *Maralunga* by Vico Magistretti and the *AEO* by Archizoom/Paolo Deganello; Poltronova offers the mirror *Ultrafragola* by Ettore Sottsass; Gaggia presents the espresso machine *Baby* by Makio Hasuike; Driade comes out with the modular furniture *Oikos* by Antonia Astori; and Vortice proposes the electric fan *Ariante* by Marco Zanuso.

7. The extreme rightist Nico Azzi is wounded while trying to arm a bomb in the bathroom of an express train between Turin and Rome.

12. Milan: The policeman Antonio Marino is killed by a hand grenade thrown by a neo-Fascist in Via Bellotti.

13. Rome: In Primavalle, the house of a local exponent of the MSI is torched. His children, Virgilio and Stefano Mattei, 22 and 8 years old, are burned alive.

27. The Watergate scandal erupts in the US, implicating president Nixon. The *Washington Post* discovers and reports a spying ring that had been wiretapping Democratic party facilities during the US presidential campaign.

May

The New York Times reports that the Italian Christian Democratic Party received generous financing from the US government. Italian president Amintore Fanfani denies the allegations.

3. The Italian State reacts to attempts to destroy its television monopoly. A local station *TeleBiella* is closed and the new telecommunications regulations ban private cable TV.

17. On the anniversary of the death of Commissioner Calabresi, the Minister of the Interior, Rumor, unveils a memorial plaque in an inner courtyard of the police station in Via Fatebenefratelli. Gianfranco Bertoli, a professed anarchist whose figure remains shrouded in mystery, throws a bomb into the crowd killing 4 and wounding 46.

27. Marcello Fiasconaro breaks the world track record in the 800 meters. It is a year of laurels for Italian sports: Paola Pigni runs the world's fastest mile; Novella Calligaris is the champion in the 800 meter freestyle; Klaus Dibiasi outshines his competitors on the diving board.

28. The publishing group *Corriere della Sera* changes ownership. The only remnant of the Crespi family, who had owned all the shares, is Giulia Maria Mozzoni. The other two shares are taken up by Gianni Agnelli and the oil magnate Angelo Moratti.

June

Jonathan De Pas, Donato d'Urbino and Paolo Lomazzi design the clothes hanger *Sciangai*, later produced by Zanotta; Mario Bellini creates the calculator *Divisumma 18* for Olivetti.

1. Greece: George Papadopoulos, leader of the military government which seized power in a 1967 coup, decrees the end of the monarchy. King Costantino is already in exile.

12. The withdrawal of the Italian Republican Party from the majority causes the Andreotti government to fall. The XII Christian Democratic congress steers a political course back towards the center-left.

July

England passes a law forbidding corporal punishment in schools.

In Afghanistan, a military coup unseats King Mohammed Zahir Shah and institutes a republic.

9. Rome: Paul Getty, grandson of the world's richest man, is kidnapped by the n'Drangheta who cut off one of his ears to convince relatives to pay the ransom.

Mariano Rumor becomes Prime Minister with the help of votes from the Socialists.

24. To slow inflation, the government freezes rents and prices for mass consumption goods.

August

28. Cholera strikes in Naples. Seven die in five days. The Italian president, Giovanni Leone, visiting the sick at the Cotugno hospital makes the gesture of the cuckold (raised index and little fingers) to ward off misfortune. His indiscretion is captured on film by a photographer.

September

Perón returns to Argentina after a long exile and is named President of the Republic.

A poster by Oliviero Toscani for "Jesus Jeans" sparks a scandal. The advertisement shows a model's ample derriere squeezed into a pair of extremely risqué hot pants with the allusive text "Chi mi ama mi segua" (If any man love me, let him follow me).

3. Barcelona: Felice Gimondi wins the world road cycling championship.

11. Military coup in Chile led by General Augusto Pinochet. The Socialist president, Salvador Allende, dies in the fighting.

October

6. Egypt and Syria launch an attack against Israel on the Jewish Holy Day of Atonement, starting the Yom Kippur War. After initial difficulties, Israel holds its position in the Golan Heights and pushes across the Suez Canal. A cease-fire is declared on October 22. In support for Syria and Egypt the Arab countries reduce petroleum production and crude oil prices immediately rise. The consequences are disastrous for industrialized countries.

17. Indro Montanelli resigns from *Corriere della Sera* as a result of disagreement with the director, Piero Ottone, over the newspaper's orientation.

November

22. The Interior Ministry officially dissolves the extreme rightist organization *Ordine Nuovo* (New Order) founded by Pino Rauti.

23. Austerity measures are put in place to reduce petroleum consumption: lower speed limits; 11pm closing time for cinemas, theaters and television broadcasts; reduced street lighting; fixed office hours; ban on illuminated signs and car-free Sundays.

December

Madrid: The Spanish Prime Minister, Carrero Blanco, dies in a dynamite attack.

10. In Turin, the Red Brigades kidnap Ettore Amerio, personnel director for FIAT.

15. La Scala: Claudio Abbado conducts *Simon Boccanegra* by Verdi. The director is Giorgio Strehler.

17. Rome: Palestinian terrorists attack a Pan Am airplane departing from the Fiumicino airport for Beirut, killing 30. The terrorists then escape by taking 14 persons hostage and hijacking a Lufthansa jet to Kuwait, where the hostages are released.

Rosita and Tai Missoni win the Neiman Marcus Award, the Oscar of fashion. The ceremony takes place in Dallas, Texas.

Meditazioni sullo scorpione by Sergio Solmi, published in a Ricciardi edition by Raffaele Mattioli, wins the Bagutta prize.
Other publications of the year: the first book of Franco Loi's poetry in the Milanese dialect, *I cart*; *Pasque* by Andrea Zanzotto; *Sillabario* by Goffredo Parise; *Manuale di conversazione* by Achille Campanile; *Caro Michele* by Natalia Ginzburg.

The sculptor Marino Marini donates 150 of his works to the City of Milan.

Achille Bonito Oliva organizes *Contemporanea*, an international and interdisciplinary exhibition held in the garages of Villa Borghese at which foreign artists are invited to show their work for the first time in Italy.

A great year at the cinema: *Amarcord* by Fellini; *Shouts and whispers* by Bergman; *American graffiti* by George Lucas; *The blow out* by Marco Ferreri, *The discreet charm of the bourgeoisie* by Luis Bûnuel.

The magazine *Domus* dedicates its cover to the Milanese "spontaneous dressing" boutique You Tarzan, Me Jane of Chiara Boni and Annalisa Castellini.

Obituaries: Pablo Picasso; Anna Magnani; the cellist Pablo Casals; Carlo Emilio Gadda; and, the writer Guido Morselli.

January

Withholding taxes are instituted.

Austerity measures of the oil crisis impose early closing times on night clubs.

3. The Milan Bourse institutes its own stock market index: MIB.

13. Colonel Amos Spiazzi is arrested in Padua as leader of the *Rosa dei venti* (Compass rose), a rightist coup-plotting movement.

February

13. Alexander Solzhenitsyn, dissident writer, is expelled from the Soviet Union.

March

Tullen begins production of the scissors *Snips* by the Design Group Italia and Anonima Castelli comes out with the chair *Box* by Enzo Mari. Mari also proposes Autoprogettazione with Simon International producing several pieces.

11. Debut of Luca Ronconi at La Scala directing *The Valkyries*, conducted by Wolfgang Sawallisch.

14. The fifth Rumor government involves the three parties DC-PSI-PSDI (Christian Democrats-Italian Socialist Party-Italian Social Democratic Party).

April

18. The Red Brigades kidnap the magistrate Mario Sossi in Genoa. He is released 35 days later after the terrorist group XXII October is released on bail.

25. A leftist military coup topples the Salazar dictatorship in Portugal. It is known as the "revolution of the carnations."

May

12. Italians vote on a referendum that would abrogate the divorce law; the "noes" win with 59.3%.

16. Milan: In an apartment in Via Ripamonti, the Corleonese Mafia boss Luciano Liggio is arrested; he will never leave prison.

19. Valery Giscard d'Estaing is elected president of France.

28. Brescia: A bomb hidden in a garbage can goes off during a union rally against neo-Fascism in Piazza della Loggia, killing eight.

30. Gianni Agnelli is the new president of the industrial group Confindustria.

31. Milan: A monument to Mazzini by Pietro Cascella is inaugurated in Piazza della Repubblica.

June

17. The Red Brigades burst into an office of the MSI and kill Giuseppe Mazzola and Graziano Girolucci.

23. A new newspaper *Giornale Nuovo* is founded by Indro Montanelli.

July

12. Milan: Giulia Maria Crespi, the last member of the family who had once been the sole proprietors of *Corriere della Sera* since 1925, cedes ownership to the Rizzoli family.

10. Greece: The reign of the colonels, in power since 1967, falls as a consequence of the Turkish-Cyprus war following the deposition of Makarios.

August

The beaches are taken over by the Brazilian fashion called the "tanga".

4. A bomb explodes on the Italicus Rome-Munich train as it passes through the station at San Benedetto Val di Sangro between Florence and Bologna, killing twelve. The strategy of tension continues.

6. The Watergate scandal forces Richard Nixon to resign as president of the United States.

September

7. Mozambique becomes an independent state.

8. The first arrest of Renato Curcio, head of the Red Brigades, in Pinerolo. Alberto Franceschini is also taken. It will come out that the operation was made possible by an infiltrator, Silvano Girotto.

24. A switchboard operator of Edilnord, a business belonging to the then unknown construction entrepreneur Silvio Berlusconi, delivers a brief newscast from the studios of *Telemilano Cavo*, inaugurating the era of Berlusconi TV.

October

Milan: The Boschi-Di Stefano art collection, comprising nearly two thousand works (including works by Sironi, Funi, Carrà, Martini, Morandi, and the Corrente painters) is donated to the city.

8. An arrest warrant is issued for the financier Michele Sindona, accused of fraudulent declaration of bankruptcy. Giorgio Ambrosoli is named liquidator of the Banca Privata di Sindona.

15. A Red Brigade hideout is discovered in Robbiano di Mediglia, near Milan. The terrorist Roberto Ognibene shoots and kills the carabiniere Felice Maritano.

November

The United Nations invite the PLO and Arafat to discuss the Palestinian issue. Israel withdraws in protest.

14. A large feminist march takes place in Rome.

December

5. The galaxy of red terrorism becomes more populous with the sudden arrival on the scene of *Autonomia Operaia* (workers' autonomy), who kill the carabiniere Andrea Lombardini during an attempted robbery of an armored car.

Giorgio Armani, after having long worked under Hitman di Nino Cerruti, comes out with the first collection of men's fashion to bear his name.

Elsa Morante publishes *La Storia*; Paolo Volponi *Corporale*; Gianni Celati *Le avventure di Guizzardi* (winner of the Bagutta Prize); Alexander Solzhenitsyn *The Gulag Archipelago*.

At the cinema: *The night porter* by Liliana Cavani; *Il fiore delle Mille e una notte* by Pasolini.

Gianni Versace designs the first collection, Complice, by Arnaldo Girombelli.

Obituaries: the writers Aldo Palazzeschi and Guido Piovene; the singer Alberto Rabagliati; the film directors Pietro Germi and Vittorio De Sica; the actor Gino Cervi; the painter Umberto Lilloni; the first man to fly across the Atlantic, Charles Lindbergh; and a legendary cyclist, Eberardo Pavesi.

1975

January

10. The Radicals Gianfranco Spadaccia, Adele Faccio and Marco Pannella claim responsibility for organizing the illegal Abortion and Sterilization Information Center which, in Florence, is directed by doctor Giorgio Canciani.

24. The Neo-Fascist terrorist Mario Tuti shoots at the carabinieri who are attempting to arrest him at his home in Empoli. Two die: Leonardo Falco and Giovanni Ceravolo. Tuti escapes. He is later arrested on the Côte d'Azur by the French police after a shoot out.

27. The trial begins in Catanzaro against Freda, Ventura, Giannettini and Valpreda for the Piazza Fontana massacre of 12 December 1969.

February

Women's prêt-à-porter by Giorgio Armani at Milan's Carminati restaurant in Milan, located in Piazza Duomo. A smashing success.

Gustav Thoeni wins the World Cup downhill skiing championship for the fifth time.

4. Great Britain: Margaret Thatcher unseats Edward Heath to take over leadership of the Conservative Party.

18. Renato Curcio, founder of the Red Brigades, escapes from the prison of Casale Monferrato with the help of a commando unit led by his wife, Margherita Cagol.

March

6. The Italian Parliament approves lowering the age of majority from 21 to 18 years old.

April

4. Claudio Abbado conducts the world premiere of Luigi Nono's opera *Al gran sole carico d'amore*, directed by Jurj Ljubimov.

13. Civil war breaks out in Lebanon between Christians and Muslims. Over ten thousand die in the first year.

16. Milan: The Neo-Fascists of Avanguardia Nazionale kill eighteen year-old Claudio Varalli, militant of Movimento Studentesco.

The Giorgio Armani trademark is born. Sergio Galeotti is the stylist's associate.

22. The new family rights bill is approved. It grants equal rights and responsibilities to spouses regarding children, shared property and the right of women to keep their maiden names. It also abrogates separation by fault and any distinction between legitimate and natural children.

29. The nineteen year-old Sergio Ramelli, rightist militant, is bludgeoned to death by a commando unit of extraparliamentarians (extremists not recognized by their party).

30. The Viet Cong enter Saigon. The Viet Nam war is over.

May

Milan: Reversal after the electoral victory of the left: a social-communist government will be instated thanks to the "conversion" of two centrists.

Giulia Maria Crespi, together with the architect Renato Bazzoni and the Brera Institute superintendent Franco Russoli, founds the Fund for the Italian Environment (FAI).

21. Institution of the Reale Law on public order: a tightening of regulations regarding release on bail, introduction of judicial arrest and greater discretion on the part of the police in the use of firearms.

The budding Punk movement takes as its point of reference for fashion the London boutique "Sex" in King's Road opened by Vivienne Westwood and Malcom Mclaren.

June

Milan: The leftist student Alberto Brasili is stabbed to death by 5 Neo-Fascists in Piazza San Babila.

The Suez Canal is opened to shipping traffic. It had been closed since the Middle East war of 1967.

4. The carabinieri surround a farmhouse in Arzillo (Alessandria) where the Red Brigades are holding hostage the industrialist Vittorio Gancia. Mara Cagol dies in the shoot out; Renato Curcio escapes.

16. The Italian Communist Party nearly ties with the Christian Democrats in regional elections: 33.4 to 35.3.

July

1. Cristina Mazzotti is kidnapped in Brianza. The eighteen year-old is killed even though her ransom was paid. Her father later dies of sorrow.

August

Greece: George Papadopoulos and the colonels responsible for the 1967 military coup are sentenced to die. Their sentences will be commuted to life imprisonment.

September

Niki Lauda wins the Formula One for the first time behind the wheel of a Ferrari.

30. The Circeo crime. Three young "*pariolini*" (Romans), Angelo Izzo, Gianni Guido and Andrea Ghira, torture and rape nineteen year-old Rosaria Lopez and seventeen year-old Donatella Colasanti for two days in a villa in the Circeo zone near Rome. Rosaria dies. Donatella is closed in the trunk of a car and abandoned in a street of Rome, but survives.

October

29. The string of killings among rightist and leftist extraparliamentarians goes on. Sixteen year-old Mario Zicchieri, militant in the Youth Front, is shot to death with a rifle in front of a Roman office of the Italian Social Movement.

November

2. Pier Paolo Pasolini dies in Ostia, killed by seventeen year-old Giuseppe Pelosi.

10. The Osimo Treaty closes the issue of Italy's eastern borders.

13. Doretta Graneris, together with her boyfriend, kills her own family: grandparents, father, mother and brother.

19. Roberto Calvi becomes president of the Banco Ambrosiano. On July 15 he was admitted to Licio Gelli's P2 lodge.

20. The dictator Francisco Franco dies in Madrid. He was 83 years old and had been in power since 1939. The monarchy returns and Juan Carlos ascends the throne.

Teuco begins producing the *Tonda* shower booth, designed by Fabio Lenci and Giovanna Talocci; Cassina comes out with the upholstered pieces *Sit Down* by Gaetano Pesce.

December

10. The poet Eugenio Montale wins the Nobel Prize for Literature.

30. Parliament passes a drug law that makes a clear distinction between dealers and users. The latter are not punished if caught possessing a "small quantity" of drugs.

The first Lombardy television station is founded: *Telealto Milanese*, founded by Renzo Villa, and two years later, *Antenna 3*.

First IdeaComo exhibition, a trade fair for the Como silk industry.

Giacomo Manzoni composes *Per Massimiliano Robespierre*, his third opera.

Gianni Brera publishes *Storia critica del calcio italiano*; Gavino Ledda *Padre padrone*; Renzo De Felice *Mussolini, il duce. Gli anni del consenso 1929-1936*.

The punk groups Sex Pistols and The Clash are all the rage.

At the cinema: *Nashville* by Altman; *Salò, or the 120 days of Sodom* by Pasolini; *The recital* by Angelopulos.

Obituaries: Aristotle Onassis; Chiang Kai-Shek; the former emperor of Ethiopia, Hailé Selassié.

1976

January

14. Newsstands see their first issue of *La Repubblica*, the newspaper founded and directed by Eugenio Scalfari. It looks like a long shot. But slowly over the years it will become Italy's most important newspaper in the second half of the twentieth century.

18. Renato Curcio, leader of the Red Brigades, is arrested along with his companion, Nadia Mantovani.

29. The *Corte di Cassazione* (Supreme Court of Appeal) issues the final verdict on Bertolucci's *Last tango in Paris*: it is forbidden to show it in Italy and the existing copies have to be burned.

February

The Lockheed scandal erupts: the American company had bribed politicians and military officials to increase demand for their Hercules C130 transport aircraft.

4. Piero Gros wins the gold medal in the special slalom at the winter Olympics in Innsbruck.

5. An exhibition at Milan's Castello Sforzesco, organized by Gae Aulenti, celebrates the centenary of the *Corriere della Sera*.

12. The fifth Moro government in Italy. It is pure Christian Democratic, with the support of the Social Democrats.

March

Military coup in Argentina. Perón's widow, Isabelita, is driven from power. General Videla assumes the presidency.

Zoran, nom d'art of Ladircobic Zora, creates his first collection, characterized by radical minimalism.

14. Carlo De Benedetti is the new managing director of FIAT.

17. Aldo Moro consults with the Communist Party Secretary, Berlinguer, on the question of what to do about the crisis of the Italian lira.

After his apprenticeship with Cardin and Patou, Jean-Paul Gaultier debuts with his own collection at the prêt-à-porter shows in Paris.

18. The Christian Democrats elect the leftward-leaning Benigno Zaccagnini as party Secretary.

April

Pol Pot and the Khmer Rouge impose a dictatorship in Cambodia that, in the name of revolution, causes at least one and a half million deaths.

May

5. Edgardo Sogno, a decorated fighter from the antifascist Resistance in Italy, is arrested by the investigating magistrate who is looking into an attempted coup. Two years later, Sogno is acquitted. But in a posthumously published interview he admits the substance of the charges against him.

6. Earthquake in Friuli: almost one thousand dead and entire towns destroyed. New tremors of the same intensity return in early September.

9. Germany: The terrorist Ulriche Meinhof hangs herself in a Stuttgart prison.

June

8. Genoa: The Red Brigades kill the attorney general Francesco Coco and his body guards, the carabinieri Giovanni Saponara and Antioco Dejana.

15. Enrico Berlinguer, in an interview in *Corriere della Sera*, states that the PCI does not want Italy to leave NATO, recognizing the positive function of the alliance.

17. South Africa: Rioting in the Soweto ghetto in Johannesburg leaves 176 dead.

21. Elections: The Italian Communist Party fails to overtake the Christian Democrats, who retain the relative majority with 38.7% of the votes, 4% more than the Communists who nevertheless gain 7.3% over the electoral results of 1972. The appeal of Indro Montanelli worked: "Plug your noses, but vote for the DC." The Socialists are in crisis, led by Francesco De Martino. The new government is pure DC, presided over by Giulio Andreotti who also managed to obtain the abstention of the PCI. This is a politically historical achievement. The dialog between Catholics and Communists is remembered as the "historic compromise."

25. The Constitutional Court removes all obstacles to local television stations. It is the first chink in the wall of the state television monopoly.

July

The Lefebvre case: The French bishop is suspended *a divinis* by the Holy See for refusing to accept and put into practice the innovations of the Vatican II Council.

4. Israeli blitz at the Entebbe airport in Uganda where Palestinian terrorists had landed a hijacked El Al airplane. All the hostages are freed and all the terrorists are killed.

9. Gaetano Amoroso and two other young leftists are knifed by extreme rightist youths. Amoroso dies three days later. On the 29th, a commando unit of Prima Linea (Front Line) kills Enrico Pedenovi, MSI provincial councilor.

10. At 12:40 p.m., a cloud containing highly toxic dioxins rises from the ICMESA reactor in Seveso. Hundreds of families are forced to leave their homes and workplaces. The decontamination will take years. Six months after the event the first health effects are observed: chloracne and vision problems.

10. The magistrate Vittorio Occorsio is killed by militants of the Neo-Fascist movement Ordine Nuovo.

15. Rome: Bettino Craxi is elected party Secretary of the Italian Socialist Party by the central committee in a meeting at the Hotel Midas.

17. Montreal Olympics. Two gold medals for Italy: the diver Klaus Dibiasi; and Fabio Dal Zotto in individual fencing.

22. Guido Carli is the new president of Confindustria.

August

6. Rome has its first non-Christian Democratic mayor in the history of the Italian Republic: the art scholar Giulio Carlo Argan, elected as an independent from the rolls of the PCI.

September

8. Michele Sindona is arrested in New York.

October

30. Lotta Continua, in a general assembly, decrees its own dissolution.

November

2. The Democrat Jimmy Carter wins the US presidential election, beating Gerald Ford.

30. The Social Democrat Mario Tanassi and the Christian Democrats Mariano Rumor, several-time Prime Minister, and Luigi Gui, several-time minister, are charged in the Lockheed bribery scandal by the Investigating commission headed by Mino Martinazzoli.

December

Milan: Maria Jesi donates her husband Emilio's collection of Italian art from the 1930s and 40s to the Pinacoteca di Brera.

7. Members of the Autonomia movement crash the inaugural evening of La Scala: Verdi's *Otello* conducted by Carlos Kleiber.

13. Milan: Emanuela Trapani, the sixteen year-old daughter of a cosmetics mogul, is kidnapped. The Vallanzasca clan holds her hostage for 41 days in an apartment in Via Alessi. In the period from 1974 to 1983, 103 people are kidnapped in Milan.

15. In a shoot-out in Sesto San Giovanni (Milan), the Public Security marshal Sergio Bezzega, the vice chief of police Vittorio Padovani and the Red Brigadist Walter Alasia lose their lives.

Enzo Mari and Giancarlo Fassina attach their names to the lamp system *Aggregato* for Artemide.

The Brazilian architect Oscar Niemeyer creates the Palazzo Mondadori in Segrate (Milan).

At bookstores: *Il sesto angelo* by father Davide Maria Turoldo; *Amica mia nemica* by Nelo Risi; *Porci con le ali* by Lidia Ravera and Marco Lombardo Radice, presenting the hugely successful cross-section of the world of youth.

Achille Bonito Oliva's *L'ideologia del Traditore* ("The Ideology of the Traitor") is published by Feltrinelli, Milan.

The silver screen is graced with *Casanova* by Fellini; *Novecento* by Bertolucci; *Barry Lyndon* by Kubrick; *Star Wars* by Lucas; and *In the realm of the senses* by Oshima.

Obituaries: Luchino Visconti; Alberto Mondadori (in 1958, breaking away from his father's publishing house, he founded *Il Saggiatore*); the kinetic artist Alexander Calder.

1977

January

11. Prague: A group of intellectuals sign a declaration demanding the reinstatement of civil rights. The initiative is brutally suppressed by the Communist regime.

20. Paolo Grassi, founder of the Piccolo Teatro in Milano and superintendent of La Scala, is nominated president of RAI.

21. The Chamber of Deputies passes a law decriminalizing abortion.

February

17. At the University of Rome, Luciano Lama, secretary of the CGIL labor union, is booed and hissed by university radicals during a speech.

24. RAI begins broadcasting in color.

March

5. Rome: Members of the Autonomia movement and the Movimento Studentesco march in protest of the sentencing of Fabrizio Panzeri for moral support in the killing of the extreme rightist student Mikis Mantakas. The situation deteriorates into urban guerrilla warfare with the police.

11. Bologna moves onto center stage of youth protest with clashes between Autonomia and the police, who were summoned by the rector of the Ateneo after an attack on militants of the Catholic activist group Comunione e Liberazione. A youth from Lotta Continua, Pier Francesco Lo Russo, dies. Radio Alice, mouthpiece for the Autonomia movement, is closed and its factotum, Francesco Berardi, nicknamed "Bifo", flees to France to escape arrest.

People begin to talk about a construction entrepreneur with a thing for television and the fight against the RAI monopoly: Silvio Berlusconi.

As written on the walls in Italy, the name of the Interior Minister, Francesco Cossiga, becomes KoSSiga in a reference to the German SS.

April

2. Milan: Police arrest Francis Turatello, king of underground gambling dens and cocaine trafficking. He will be killed in prison on August 17, 1981. The vacant position in organized crime will be filled by Angelo Epaminonda.

14. Eugenio Cefis, considered the most powerful man in Italy, resigns as president of Montedison and retires to private life.

21. Rome: In a confrontation with the police in San Lorenzo, a group of Autonomia members shoot and kill the officer Settimio Passamonti.

23. After long being ostracized, Dario Fo is allowed back on television in *Mistero Buffo*.

28. The Red Brigades strike in Turin in the lead up to the first important trial against the terrorist organization, killing the president of the Order of Lawyers, Fulvio Croce. On May 3 the trial has to be postponed because the people's judges are afraid to accept the position.

May

Cassina produces the chair *Cab* by Mario Bellini and the bookcase *Nuvola Rossa* by Vico Magistretti, who also designs the lamp *Atollo* for O-Luce.

12. Rome: The Radicals march against and in spite of the ban on all demonstrations handed down by the Interior Ministry. The police open fire. Nineteen year-old Giorgiana Masi is killed.

14. In Via de Amicis in Milan, during a clash with the police, leftist extremists level their guns. The Brigadier Antonio Custrà is felled. Investigations will reveal that those holding the pistols were young students.

June

Spain: The first free elections after almost forty years of Franco's dictatorship. The centrists for Suarez are victorious. The Socialist Party of Gonzalez is second.

2. Milan: The Red Brigades shoot at the legs of the director of the newspaper *Giornale*, Indro Montanelli, in via Manin. In Genoa the day before, the same fate fell to Vittorio Bruno, director of the paper *Secolo XIX*; the next day in Rome it will be Emilio Rossi's turn, director of TG1 (RAI 1 Television Newscast).

July

1. Fire fight between carabinieri and the terrorist group NAP: the terrorist Antonio Lo Muscio is killed. Maria Pia Vianale and Franca Salerno are wounded and arrested.

14. A total blackout lasting twenty-four hours in New York City is made all the more dramatic by widespread panic and looting.

August

The carabinieri raid the beaches but they are powerless to stop it: the topless is "in".

15. The war criminal, Herbert Kappler, commandant of the SS in Rome in 1944 and responsible for the mass killings of the Fosse Ardeatine, escapes from the Celio military hospital.

September

4. Francesco Moser wins the world road cycling championship.

18. Back from vacation, the Red Brigades pick up their guns again, shooting in the legs or otherwise wounding: Nino Ferrero, editor of the newspaper *Unità*; the Christian Democrat Publio Fiori (November 2); the Alfa Romeo executive Aldo Grassini; and the CEO of FIAT, Pietro Osella (November 10).

20. Twenty-five thousand youths from Autonomia, Movimento Studentesco, and Lotta Continua gather in Bologna to protest repression. They beat each other senseless but march together and many raise their hands in the sign of the P 38.

30. Neo-Fascists kill the Lotta Continua militant Walter Rossi. Revenge is taken in Turin the next day in an assault on the bar *Angelo Azzurro* believed to be a hangout of rightist extremists. Molotov cocktails are thrown into the bar setting it on fire and burning to death the student worker Roberto Crescenzio.

October

Niki Lauda wins his second world title behind the wheel of a Ferrari.

18. Alleged suicide of the heads of the Baader-Meinhof gang, Andreas Baader, Gudrun Ensslin and Jan Carl Raspe, in a Stuttgart prison.

21. Franco Di Bella takes over management of *Corriere della Sera* from Piero Ottone.

21. Moscow: In a speech commemorating the anniversary of the Soviet revolution, Enrico Berlinguer talks about the Italian Communist Party's vision for a socialist society: a non-ideological state, a plurality of parties. Ugo La Malfa interprets the speech as a "distinct political turning point" and proposes that the PCI enter the government.

November

16. The vice director of the newspaper *La Stampa*, Carlo Casalegno, is shot four times. The Red Brigades claim responsibility. Casalegno will die on November 29.

21. Franco Di Bella succeeds Piero Ottone at the helm of *Corriere della Sera*.

30. The poet Sandro Penna wins the Bagutta Prize for *Stranezze*.

Woody Allen's film, *Annie Hall*, introduces the oversize pants and shirt style designed by Ralph Lauren for Diane Keaton in her role as Annie Hall.

The Floriani Foundation begins its activity of cancer research and treatment.

The credenza *Sheraton* for Acerbis International is designed by Lodovico Acerbis and Giotto Stoppino. Fila introduces *Tratto-Pen* designed by Design Group Italia.

The inflation rate reaches 21.8 percent.

Zegna begins its "tailor made" service.

At the cinema : *That obscure object of desire* by Luis Bunuel; *The mirror* by Andrei Tarkovskij; *Un borghese piccolo, piccolo* by Mario Monicelli; and, a box office record, *Saturday night fever.*

The magazine *Modo* publishes its first issue. The director is Alessandro Mendini.

The Hungarian Rubik invents his brain-teasing cube; a huge success all over the world.

Renzo Piano and Richard Rogers design the Beaubourg in Paris.

Inauguration of the Centre Pompidou in Paris, designed by Renzo Piano and Richard Rogers.

Obituaries: Charlie Chaplin; Roberto Rossellini; Elvis Presley; Maria Callas; Bing Crosby; the conductor Leopold Stokowski; and the Brera superintendent Franco Russoli.

January

Victims of Red Brigade terrorism: the head of FIAT surveillance at the Cassino plant, Carmine De Rosa; the police officer Stefano Dionisio; the notary Gianfranco Spighi; the magistrate Riccardo Palma.

7. Rome: Two Fronte della Gioventù militants, Franco Bigonzetti and Francesco Ciavatta, are killed by leftist terrorists in front of an MSI office.

24. Luciano Lama, secretary of the CGIL, says he is ready to go before workers with his support for a policy of "not marginal but substantial" sacrifices.

February

Milan: After 6 years of work, the Garibaldi-Cadorna stretch of the subway line 2 goes into operation.

28. Aldo Moro, before the assembly of the Christian Democrat parliamentary groups, supports the policy of "opening up" to the Communist Party..

March

The Milan Trade Fair hosts the first Modit exhibition with 50 exhibitors: the idea was Beppe Modenese's who joins it with the catwalks of the Milano Collezioni. Contemporaneously the eighteenth Milanovendemoda exhibition opens.

The architect Gianfranco Ferré debuts as a stylist. He chooses the Milan hotel Principe di Savoia as the backdrop for his fashion show. Gianni Versace, after designing the collections for Gallagham, Genny, Complice and Alma, goes out on his own and shows his works at the Permanente in Milan.

11. Giulio Andreotti is in his fourth government: it is pure Christian Democrat with the support of the Socialists, the Communists and the Republicans.

16. Aldo Moro is kidnapped by the Red Brigades, who machine gun and kill his five-man escort: Oreste Leonardi, Domenico Ricci, Francesco Zizzi, Raffaele Iozzino and Giuliano Rivera.

29. At the Turin congress of the Socialist Party, their forty-first, Craxi and his fellow party members opt for a softer line than the firmness chosen by the Christian Democrats and the Communists regarding the Moro kidnapping and the possibility of negotiating hinted at by the Red Brigades. Craxi is reelected party Secretary.

April

11. More killings by the Red Brigades: in Turin, the prison guard Lorenzo Cotugno and, nine days later, a guard at the San Vittore prison, Francesco De Cataldo.

22. Appeal from Pope Paul VI to the "people of the Red Brigades" for the release of Aldo Moro.

May

9. The Red Brigades leave Aldo Moro's lifeless body in the trunk of a red Renault 4 parked in Via Caetani in Rome, symbolically near the office of the PCI in Via Botteghe Oscure and that of the DC in Piazza del Gesù.

10. Francesco Cossiga resigns as Minister of the Interior.

10. Law 180, which abolishes segregation in insane asylums and was vigorously fought for by the psychiatrist Franco Basaglia, receives final approval.

Alessandro Mendini designs the *Poltrona di Proust* for Alchimia. Alias produces the chair *Spaghetti* by Giandomenico Belotti.

21. Another victim of Red Brigade terrorism: the head of the anti-terrorism unit in Genoa, Antonio Esposito. Fifteen days later, the Red Brigades kill the marshal of the prison guards, Antonio Santoro.

29. The new abortion law is promulgated in the *Gazzetta Ufficiale* (Official Bulletin).

June

15. The Italian president Giovanni Leone is forced to resign over rumors connected to the Lockheed scandal (bribery associated with supply of Hercules transport aircraft), which will never be completely unraveled, and accusations of tax evasion and irregular real estate transactions.

Flou begins production of *Nathalie*, a bed by Vico Magistretti; Cinelli introduces its mountain-bike *Rampichino* by Paolo Erzegovesi; Caproni Nizzola comes out with the sail plane *Calif A-21 S* by Carlo Ferrarin and Livio Sonzo.

July

Milan's La Scala opera house celebrates its two-hundredth birthday with the superintendent Carlo Maria Badini at the helm.

8. At the sixteenth vote, the socialist Sandro Pertini is elected president of the Republic.

27. The rent control law passes.

August

Ideological question and answer session between Berlinguer and Craxi on the "third way" between real socialism and social democracy, a thesis upheld by the Communist party Secretary in an interview with *La Repubblica*. The secretary of the Italian Socialist Party counterposes the "libertarian and pluralistic" tradition of socialism à la Proudhon, a nineteenth century French theorist and author of the essay-manifesto *What is property*.

6. Giovanni Battista Montini, better known as Pope Paul VI, dies at Castelgandolfo. He had been elected on July 21, 1963.

26. At the third vote count, white smoke: the patriarch of Venice Albino Luciani is the new Pope. He chooses the name of John Paul I.

September

Versace makes his debut in men's fashion, with a show at his atelier in Via Spiga.

13. Milan: Arrest of the leftist terrorist Corrado Alunni.

17. At Camp David, with the mediation of the American president Jimmy Carter, Israel (premier Begin) and Egypt (president Sadat) sign a peace treaty. The Israelis withdraw from Sinai, seized in the war of 1967.

28. Pope John Paul I dies of a heart attack. His Papacy lasted just 34 days.

The stylist Enrico Coveri debuts at the Cour Carré of the Louvre.

October

1. Milan: Arrest of Lauro Azzolini and Franco Bonisoli, leaders of the Red Brigades. They are taken by surprise in a hideout in Via Montenevoso by the men of general Carlo Alberto Dalla Chiesa. Two years later, in the same apartment, in a hidden chamber sealed off with dry wall, some letters are found written by Aldo Moro during his captivity and not released by the Red Brigades; some see the circumstances as being highly suspicious.

10. More killings by leftist terrorists: in Rome, they shoot the magistrate Gerolamo Tartaglione and the next day, Prima Linea kills the criminologist Alfredo Palella.

16. The Polish cardinal Karol Woityla, archbishop of Krakow, is elected Pope. He is the first non-Italian pontiff since 1523.

November

3. A new terrorist group, Guerriglia Comunista, kills the twenty-seven year-old Maurizio Tucci. Five days later the Formazioni Comuniste Combattenti claim responsibility for killing Fedele Calvosa, chief district attorney of the Republic in Frosinone, his driver Luciano Rossi and his bodyguard Giuseppe Pagliei. On December 15 Guerriglia Comunista moves back into the spotlight boasting two bodies: those of the prison guards Salvatore Lanza and Salvatore Porceddu from the Turinese prison Le Nuove.

Looking beyond the suggestions from the catwalks, young people spontaneously adopt the preppy style, a street fashion inspired by the wardrobe of American prep school students from the 50s: kilt, blazer, tweed.

Giorgio Strehler stages *The Tempest* by Shakespeare at the Milan's Piccolo Teatro.

Alliance between Giorgio Armani and the Gruppo Finanziario Tessile, between creator and manufacturer.

The Arnoldo and Alberto Mondadori Foundation is established.

At the cinema, it is the year of the debut of Nanni Moretti with *Ecce Bombo*, the film that will become the manifesto of a generation, and Ermanno Olmi's masterpiece *L'albero degli zoccoli*.

Obituaries: Federico Patellani, a master of photo-reporting.

1979

January

24. Genoa. Guido Rossa, blue collar worker for Italsider and union delegate, is killed by the Red Brigades: this is his punishment for having reported Giuseppe Berardi who was passing out Red Brigade literature in the factory.

29. A commando unit from Prima Linea assassinates the judge Emilio Alessandrini.

March

At the Academy Awards ceremonies, the top film is *The Deerhunter*, starring Robert De Niro and Christopher Walken.

20. The journalist Mino Pecorelli, director of *OP*, a newspaper with sources in the secret services, is killed by a hit man in Rome.

April

The first Walkmans, invented by Sony, arrive on the shelves. Milan: The Teatro Nazionale, inaugurated on December 20, 1924 with *La cena delle beffe*, by Sem Benelli, goes back to its old vocation of staging plays.

7. Toni Negri, professor at the University of Padua, is arrested and charged with "armed insurrection against the state."

22. Four young Roman hoodlums set fire to the Somalian Mohammed Ajala, who usually slept in the open in Piazza Navona.

May

Pietro Mennea breaks the world record in the 200 meters. His record will hold for 17 years.

3. The Red Brigades attack the office of the Roman committee of the Christian Democrats. The police officers Antonio Mea and Pietro Olianu are killed.

June

Milan: A Fausto Melotti exhibition at the Palazzo Reale and, at the Rotonda della Besana, a retrospective on Umberto Milani's work.

Giuseppe Saronni wins the Giro d' Italia and the Milan soccer club wins the *Scudetto* by three points over an absolute outsider, Perugia.

4. Early political elections. The PCI loses four percentage points. The DC and the PSI hold their positions.

10. The first European elections substantially confirm the results of the political elections.

15. Over 60 thousand young pop fans gather on June 15 at the Milan Arena for a concert dedicated to Demetrio Stratos, singer in the group *Area* who died the day before in New York.

20. The Communist Nilde Jotti is the first woman to be elected president of the Chamber of Deputies. Amintore Fanfani is reelected president of the Senate.

July

The Strega literary prize goes to Primo Levi for *La chiave a stella*.

11. In Milan, in Via Morozzo della Rocca, Giorgio Ambrosoli, liquidator of the Sindona banks, is killed by the Mafia.

13. Terrorist killings continue. In Rome, the Red Brigades shoot to death the colonel of the carabinieri Antonio Varisco. Five days later, in Turin, Prima Linea kills the bartender Carmine Civitate, in whose bar the militants of Lotta Armata (Armed Struggle), Barbara Azzaroni and Matteo Caggegi, were killed. On September 21, Prima Linea strikes again claiming responsibility for the murder of Carlo Ghiglieno, planning chief for FIAT. In November, the Red Brigades start shooting again in Rome and Genoa, killing the police officer Michele Granato, the carabinieri Vittorio Battaglin and Mario Tusa, and the Public Security marshal Domenico Taverna. In December, another police officer joins the fallen: the marshal Mariano Romiti.

21. The Mafia eliminates the head of the Palermo mobile squad, Boris Giuliano. One month later they kill Cesare Terranova, magistrate and PCI representative in the Chamber of Deputies for two legislatures.

August

At the Venice Film Festival, which had not yet reinstated the prizes, the critics pick *La luna* by Bernardo Bertolucci, *Il prato* by the Taviani brothers, *Ogro* by Gillo Pontecorvo and *Escape from Alcatraz* by Don Siegel.

3. Francesco Cossiga is elected Prime Minister.

September

24. After a shoot out, Prospero Gallinari, one of the top men in the Red Brigades, is wounded and captured.

25. Craxi, in an article in *Avanti!*, proposes constitutional reform, starting with the presidential republic.

October

8. Fiat fires 61 workers accusing them of violence in the factory. The strike called to demonstrate solidarity fails.

November

3. Milan: Massacre in the trattoria *La Strega di Moncucco*: the killers of the Mafia boss Epaminonda burst into the restaurant to rub out a man in the Turatello clan and also kill seven bar patrons, unwitting witnesses to the crime.

December

1. The Bagutta Prize is won by Giovanni Macchia for *L'angelo della notte*.

6. The installation on Italian territory of Pershing and Cruise missiles is approved by the Chamber of Deputies.

27. Coup in Afghanistan. The pro-Soviet Babrak Karmal seizes power. Six divisions of the Soviet army enter the country.

The logo of the Regione Lombardia, designed by the graphic artist Pino Tovaglia, wins the Compasso d'oro prize.

At the bookstores: *Il galateo in bosco* by Andrea Zanzotto; *Se una notte d'inverno un viaggiatore* by Italo Calvino; *Centuria* by Giorgio Manganelli (Viareggio prize); *Storia di Tonle* by Mario Rigoni Stern (Bagutta and Strega prizes). Scheiwiller publishes, under the direction of Dante Isella, *Alalà al Pellerossa* by Delio Tessa and Adelphi puts out the first volume of the works of Pessoa translated by Antonio Tabucchi.

The first edition of Ideabiella in Cernobbio: exhibition of high quality drapery fabrics.

At the cinema: it is the year of *Apocalypse now* by Francis Ford Coppola; *Prova d'orchestra* and *La città delle donne* by Federico Fellini

Kartell puts into production the stools 4822-4844 by Anna Castelli Ferrieri; Anonima Castelli the chair Vertebra by Giancarlo Piretti and Emilio Ambasz; B&B the sofa Diesis by Antonio Citterio and Paolo Nava; Zanotta the table Cumano by Achille Castiglioni.

Achille Bonito Oliva puts forward his theories about the Italian *Transavanguardia*, the name he gives to the movement represented by Enzo Cucchi, Sandro Chia, Francesco Clemente, Mimmo Paladino and Nicola De Maria.

Obituaries: the architects Pier Luigi Nervi and Gio Ponti; Ugo La Malfa, Secretary of the Republican Party and founding father; the Milanese composer Nino Rota, Oscar winner for the music to *The Godfather*; the humoristic cartoonist Giaci Mondani.

1980

January

6. The president of the Sicilian Regional government, Santi Mattarella, is killed by the Mafia.

8. The Red Brigades kill the police officers Antonio Cestari, Rocco Santoro and Michele Tatulli. Other casualties of leftist terrorism during the year include: Vittorio Bachelet; the Christian Democrat Nino Amato; Paolo Paoletti, director of ICMESA; William Vaccher; the magistrate Guido Galli; the journalist Walter Tobagi; Renato Briano, the managing director of Marelli; Francesco Mozzanti, CEO of Falck; the general of the carabinieri Enrico Galvaligi; the magistrate Nicola Giacumbi; and the carabinieri Pietro Cuzzoli and Ippolito Cortelessa.

11. Florence: Rossana Cavigli gives birth to healthy sextuplets.

February

The 53 year-old Jesuit Carlo Maria Martini is ordained archbishop of the Milan diocese.

6. The Chamber of Deputies approves an antiterrorism decree by a very wide margin: it is the law on the so-called *pentiti* (penitents turned police informers).

14. The Venice Carnival is reborn: 50 thousand people in costume.

18. The Red Brigadist Patrizio Peci is arrested: for the first time there is the feeling that leftist terrorism can be defeated.

22. The NAR, an extreme rightist clandestine movement, kill the nineteen year-old student, Valerio Verbano, in Rome.

March

2. A scandal involving bets on soccer matches is discovered.

4. The Italcasse scandal involving illicit financing to industry results in 48 arrest warrants.

25. In El Salvador, the bishop Oscar Arnulfo Romero is assassinated by rightist commando unit as he is celebrating mass in the cathedral.

April

The Frejus alpine highway tunnel and the Venice-Trieste expressway are inaugurated.

Gae Aulenti designs the *Tavolo con ruote* and, with Piero Castiglioni, the lamp *Parola* for Fontana Arte.

5. The second Cossiga government, supported by the Christian Democrats, Socialists and Republicans.

10. Mass exodus of Cubans towards Florida.

14. The film *Kramer vs. Kramer*, starring Meryl Streep and Dustin Hoffman, wins four Oscars.

17. The British flag is lowered in Rhodesia, which becomes an independent state with the name Zimbabwe.

25. The US attempt to free 50 hostages held since November 4, 1979 by Islamic students who attacked and invaded the American embassy in Teheran fails before it gets off the ground. A helicopter collides with a transport aircraft killing several members of the rescue team.

May

18. Black uprising in Miami triggered by the acquittal of four white police officers who killed a black man.

23. Carla Gravina awarded at the Cannes film festival for her role in the film *La Terrazza* by Ettore Scola.

June

The Inter soccer club wins its twelfth *Scudetto*.

Bernard Hinault wins the Giro d'Italia.

12. Sergio Zavoli is named president of RAI.

25. Bob Marley gives a concert in San Siro stadium before an audience of 100 thousand: the stadium is devastated.

27. A DC9 operated by Itavia explodes in flight over Ustica: 81 dead. Twenty years later the case has still not been fully resolved, even though it now appears almost certain that the plane was hit by a missile.

July

5. Björn Borg wins Wimbledon for the fifth time in a row.

19. The 22nd Olympic Games open in Moscow, boycotted by the United States under Carter and by other countries in protest over the Soviet invasion of Afghanistan. Italy wins three gold medals in track and field: Mennea in the 200 meters, Sara Simeoni in the high jump and Maurizio Damilano in the 20 kilometer walk.

27. Reza Pahlevi, the Shah of Iran, dies in exile in Cairo.

August

2. A rightwing terrorist attack at the Bologna train station. A bomb in the waiting room kills 85 and wounds 200.

14. The political-unionist star of Lech Walesa rises in Poland.

Aldo Rossi designs the *Cabina dell'Elba* for Molteni, Giorgio Giugiaro the *Panda* for FIAT, Kita the armchair *Wink* for Cassina, Paolo Piva the sofa *Alanda* for B&B Italia.

September

John Cassavetes, for his film *Gloria* and Louis Malle for *Atlantic City* share the prize at the Venice Film Festival.

20. Nissan and Alfa Romeo sign an agreement that will be aborted on September 30. Berlusconi's television station, *Canale 5*, begins broadcasting.

October

3. The career of Muhammed Ali ends on the canvas in Las Vegas after a bout with Larry Holmes.

10. Earthquake in Algeria: 20 thousand dead.

14. Forty thousand FIAT workers march through the streets of Turin in support for their company.

15. The Iran-Iraq war begins.

18. Forlani forms a new government after Cossiga steps down.

November

16. Paris: The philosopher Louis Althusser confesses to having strangled his wife. He is in a precarious psychological state.

20. The Beijing government tries the "Gang of Four", headed by Mao's widow, the 66 year-old Jiang Qing.

23. Earthquake in Irpinia and Basilicata: over 5 thousand dead and 300 thousand left homeless.

December

Ettore Sottsass, Andrea Branzi, Barbara Radice, Marco Zanini, Michele De Lucchi, Martine Bedin, Matteo Thun, Aldo Cibic and others found "Memphis". The name comes from the Dylan song "Stuck inside of Mobile with the Memphis blues again", listened to again and again that evening at Sottsass's home.

3. The Red Brigadist Susanna Ronconi is arrested in Florence.

8. New York: John Lennon is shot and killed by a deranged fan.

12. The Red Brigades kidnap Giovanni D'Urso, magistrate at the apex of the prison system. He is released on January 15, 1981.

Inflation peaks at 21.7 percent.

The first issue of *Gap Casa* comes out. It is directed by Francesco Buffa di Perrero.

At the cinema: *Berlin Alexanderplatz* by Rainer Werner Fassbinder; *Manhattan* by Woody Allen; *Kagemusha* (golden palm award at Cannes) by Akira Kurosawa; *La terrazza* by Ettore Scola.

Umberto Eco's *The Name of the Rose* is a worldwide bestseller.

Achille Bonito Oliva founds "Aperto" ("Open"), the section dedicated to young artists at the Venice Biennale, and publishes *La Transavanguardia italiana*, Politi Editore, città?.

Obituaries: Josip Broz Tito; Pietro Nenni; the Italian communists Giorgio Amendola and Luigi Longo; the actors Peppino De Filippo, Romolo Valli, Peter Sellers, Tino Buazzelli, Steve McQueen and Milly, the cycling champions Gastone Nencini and Jean Robic; the painter Oscar Kokoschka; the diretor Alfred Hitchcock; the philosophers Eric Fromm and Jean Paul Sartre; the writer Gianni Rodari; and the Brazilian composer Vinicius De Moraes.

Seventies

*The election of Enrico Berlinguer as secretary of the PCI, 1972
(photo: Roby Schirer)*

*Aldo Moro with Benigno Zaccagnini. Aldo Moro was killed by Red Brigades, 9th May 1978
(photo: Roby Schirer)*

*Pier Paolo Pasolini is murdered at Ostia, 2nd November 1975
(© Publifoto, Milan)*

*Claudio Abbado
(© Teatro alla Scala Lelli & Masotti)*

*Feminist demonstration in Milan
(photo: Roby Schirer)*

1981

January

Cassina introduces the armchair *Sindbad* by Vico Magistretti.

20. Ronald Reagan, fortieth president of the United States, takes up residence in the White House.

20. After 444 days of captivity, 52 American diplomats are freed by the Teheran regime.

February

5. Valerio Fioravanti, rightist terrorist, takes part in the fatal ambush of the carabinieri Enea Condotto and Luigi Maronesi.

24. Madrid. While the Parliament is assembled for a vote of confidence on the Calvo Stelo government, Lieutenant Colonel Antonio Tejero of the Civil Guard bursts into the chamber to begin an attempted coup by Franco supporters that will fail mainly because of King Juan Carlos's firm commitment to democracy.

27. The Soviets prevent Giancarlo Pajetta from speaking at the 26th congress of the Soviet Communist Party. He is being censored for his criticism of the invasion of Afghanistan.

March

On the Paris catwalks the Japanese country style debuts with Yohji Yamamoto, Issey Miyake and Rei Kawakubo. The American fashion daily "W:W:D" speaks of the "Hiroshima beggar look."

In Milan, 55% of the sons and 34% of the daughters still live with their parents at the age of 25 and over. The phenomenon is dubbed the *famiglia lunga* (long family).

1. Milan. Car-free Sunday for the ecological revival of the city.

15. Milan. At Teatro Lirico the world premiere of Karlheinz Stockhausen's *Donnerstag aus Licht*, directed by Luca Ronconi, with scenography and costumes by Gae Aulenti.

17. Licio Gelli's villa in Castiglion Fibocchi (Arezzo) is searched, opening up the scandal of the secret Masonic lodge, P2.

April

4. Mario Moretti, head of the Red Brigades, is arrested in Milan.

May

5. Northern Ireland. Bobby Sands, British deputy and member of the IRA, dies after a hunger strike lasting 66 days,.

10. François Mitterand is elected president of the French Republic.

13. Rome. Mehmet Alì Agca attempts to assassinate pope John Paul II in piazza San Pietro.

19. Riccardo Muti debuts at La Scala conducting *Così fan tutte*, directed by Strehler.

20. Roberto Calvi and several of his Banco Ambrosiano collaborators are arrested on the order of the Milan Public Prosecutor's Office. In July he is sentenced to 4 years in prison, fined 15 billion lire and released from San Vittore prison.

The Red Brigades kidnap and kill Giuseppe Taliercio, director of the Montefibre company of Marghera.

June

13. In Vermicino, a town near Rome, a 6 year-old child, Alfredino Rampi, falls into a well. He survives three days but the numerous and at times heroic attempts made to rescue him are all in vain. The drama is televised live and the president of the Italian Republic, Sandro Pertini, spends hours and hours on the scene.

18. The Republican Giovanni Spadolini is the first non-Christian Democrat named Prime Minister since the Second World War.

20. Alberto Cavallari succeeds Franco Di Bella to become the new director of *Corriere della Sera*.

July

23. The Red Brigades free Renzo Sandrucci, whom they had held captive for 47 days.

29. Britain's Prince Charles marries Diana Spencer.

August

12. Death of Angelo Moratti, petroleum magnate and president of the Inter soccer club.

September

Milan: Ettore Sottsass designs the bookcase *Carlton* for Memphis.

26. The Italian president, Sandro Pertini, nominates Eduardo De Filippo senator for life.

October

The city of Milan honors the graphic artist Brunetta with a series of exhibitions titled "The people who made Milan great."

6. A commando unit of "Muslim Brothers" assassinates Egyptian president Anwar Sadat during a military parade in retribution for the Camp David peace accord.

8. A group of Socialist intellectuals led by Tristano Codignola, Enzo Enriquez Agnoletti and Franco Bassanini are expelled from the Socialist Party by Secretary Bettino Craxi, who is consequently accused of applying tyrannical methods.

November

16. The 10th congress of the CGIL labor union reconfirms Luciano Lama as Secretary.

December

2. Coup d'etat by general Jaruzelski in Poland.

17. The Italian Communist Party Secretary Enrico Berlinguer declares, "The socialist societies of the East have exhausted their propulsive capacity for renewal."

17. The Red Brigades kidnap the American NATO general James Lee Dozier in Verona. He will be freed on January 28, 1982 in Padua by a carabinieri SWAT team (NOCS).

The Armani Emporium makes its debut.

In the bookstores: *Chronical of a Death Foretold* by Gabriel Garcia Márquez, *La caduta dell'America* (The Fall of America) by Allen Ginsberg (translated into Italian by Fernanda Pivano), *Poesie* by Biagio Marin, *Il tramonto dell'ideologia* by Lucio Colletti.

At the cinema: *Predators of the lost Ark* by Steven Spielberg, *La tragedia di un uomo ridicolo* (The Tragedy of a Ridiculous Man) by Bernardo Bertolucci, *La notte di San Lorenzo* by the Taviani brothers, *Anni di piombo* by Margarethe von Trotta.

Obituaries: the poets Sergio Solmi and Nobel Literature prize winner Eugenio Montale.

1982

January

Mondadori, Perrone and Caracciolo found the television network *Retequattro*.

Edilio Rusconi establishes the television network *Italia*.

In Poland a decree is issued outlawing the political union movement Solidarity.

27. The mayor of Milan, Carlo Tognoli, inaugurates a grand exhibition of the 1930s: paintings, architecture, design and publishing.

March

La vera storia by Luciano Berio is on La Scala's playbill.

5. The rightist terrorist Francesca Mambro is captured after a robbery that cost the life of a passerby, the seventeen year-old Alessandro Caravellani.

21. After the Rome team suffered defeat at the hands of Bologna in a match for the soccer championship, ultras fans of Rome set a train car on fire; thirteen year-old Andrea Vitone dies in the blaze.

April

2. War in Malvinas islands.

30. Pio La Torre, deputy and Sicilian regional Secretary of the Communist party, is killed by the Mafia.

May

Anonima Castelli introduces the chair *Penelope* by Pollock and Artemide presents the lamp *Callimaco* by Sottsass.

2. The Christian Democrats elect Ciriaco De Mita party Secretary.

6. The Ferrari driver Gilles Villeneuve dies in an accident during a test run at the Zolder track in Belgium.

27. Five centuries after his arrival in Milan, the city celebrates Leonardo da Vinci with a two-year series of exhibitions.

June

6. Israel invades Lebanon.

18. The bankrupt Roberto Calvi is found dead under Blackfriars Bridge in London. His secretary, Graziella Corrocher, commits suicide in Milan by jumping from a window of the Banco Ambrosiano in via Clerici.

July

The *Corriere d'Informazione*, an afternoon edition of *Corriere della Sera*, issues its last copy. It had its period of maximum splendor in the 1950s with Gaetano Afeltra at the helm.

The Nuovo Banco Ambrosiano is founded under the leadership of president Giovanni Bazzoli. The bailout was made possible by a pool of 7 banks.

11. The Italian national soccer team, trained by Bearzot, wins its third world title in Madrid.

28. The president of the Institute of Religious Works, the Vatican bank, monsignor Paul Marcinkus, receives a subpoena for aggravated fraud in connection with the case of the Banco Ambrosiano, which is subjected to a compulsory settlement.

September

VIDAS is founded, an association of volunteers for the care of the terminally ill.

3. The general of the carabinieri Carlo Alberto Dalla Chiesa is assassinated in Palermo together with his young wife, Emanuela Setti Carraro.

Ferré designs his first men's wear collection.

October

1. The era of Helmut Kohl begins in Germany with the defeat of the Social Democrat Helmut Schmidt.

9. A Palestinian commando unit attacks the Roman synagogue. A two year-old child is killed.

16. The Lebanon militia, allies of Israel, break into the Palestinian refugee camps of Sabra and Chatyla on the Western outskirts of Beirut and massacre hundreds: mainly women, children and the elderly.

November

10. Death of the Soviet leader Leonid Brezhnev. He is succeeded by Yuri Andropov, former KGB head.

December

The city of Milan approves the municipal rain link "Il Passante". It will be eighteen years before the first section is completed.

1. Amintore Fanfani, taking over from Spadolini, forms his fifth government.

30. The council of ministers passes measures raising taxes by 6.75 trillion lire.

***Time* magazine dedicates its cover to Giorgio Armani.**

At the bookstores: *Sillabario 2* by Goffredo Parise, *Stella variabile* by Vittorio Sereni (Viareggio Prize), *Se non ora, quando?* by Primo Levi, *1934* by Alberto Moravia, *Vita breve di Katherine Mansfield* by Pietro Citati (Bagutta Prize).

The professional collaboration begins between Giuliano Benetton and Oliviero Toscani. It will produce the world's most provocative and controversial publicity campaign under the insignia of the United Colors of Benetton.

At the cinema: *Storie di ordinaria follia* by Marco Ferreri, *On Golden Pond* by Mark Rydell, *Eccezzziunale... veramente* by Carlo Vanzina.

The international exhibition *Avanguardia Transavanguardia* directed by Achille Bonito Oliva takes place at the ancient Roman walls.

Obituaries: Grace Kelly, princess of Monaco; the authors Giuseppe Prezzolini and Louis Aragon; and Riccardo Bauer, antifascist and father of the Italian Republic.

1983

January

Ente Moda Italia is founded to promote Italian fashion abroad.

6. The Fiat Uno debuts in Orlando, Florida.

24. The trial for the Moro killing concludes with thirty-two life sentences. The convicts include the top echelons of the Red Brigades, Mario Moretti, Prospero Gallinari, and Barbara Balzarani.

25. The Mafia kills the Assistant Public Prosecutor of the Republic of Trapani, Ciaccio Montalto.

February

Six hundred and seventy-four computer-related companies operate in Milan.

18. Angelo Rizzoli is arrested, marking the end of a publishing empire.

March

Eight Oscars for the film *Gandhi* by Richard Attenborough. Steven Spielberg receives three for *E.T.*, including one for special effects going to the Italian Carlo Rambaldi.

18. Umberto II di Savoia, last king of Italy, dies in Geneva.

May

Pope John Paul II comes to Milan in the first papal visit in 565 years.

The Roma soccer club wins its second *Scudetto*.

3. Gino Giugni, "father" of the Workers' Statute, is wounded by the Red Brigades.

June

Alberto Salvati and Ambrogio Tresoldi design the armchair *Miamina* for Saporiti. Pallucco relaunches the *1936* tables by Mario Asnago and Claudio Vender. Alessi puts into production its *Tea Kettle with Melodic Whistle* by Richard Sapper.

3. The Italian health authorities report that in October 1982, two people died in Italy of AIDS. It is the first alarm.

9. Second mandate for Margaret Thatcher in her landslide electoral victory.

16. Anti-Camorra operation with hundreds of arrests: the "Tortora" case begins.

27. The Christian Democrats hit an all-time low in Italian elections: 32.5%.

July

29. A car bomb with 220 pounds of TNT kills the magistrate Rocco Chinnici in Palermo.

August

Bradyseism in Pozzuoli.

4. For the first time in Italian history a Socialist, Bettino Craxi, is named Prime Minister.

21. Manila. The historical leader of the Philippine opposition, Benigno Aquino, is shot to death upon landing in Manila after three years of exile.

September

The government has to cope with a deficit of 140 trillion lire in its finance act.

Ten years after the military coup in Chile, resistance to the Pinochet regime grows.

1. Soviet missiles down a South Korean airliner which was off-route and in USSR airspace: 269 dead.

October

21. **The 13th ICSID (International Board of Industrial Design Firms) convention opens, held in Milan for the first time, organized together with ADI (Industrial Design Association) and ASSAREDO (Italian Association of the Furniture and Furnishings Industry).**

25. American forces land in Grenada to quell an attempted coup.

30. After seven years of military dictatorship, the Argentineans return to the ballot box to elect the candidate from the Radical party, Raul Alfonsin.

The stylist Franco Moschino makes his debut with a provocative collection. He will die at a young age in 1994.

November

The Nobel Peace Prize goes to Lech Walesa, leader of the Solidarity movement in Poland.

An exhibition, "Professione reporter", tells the story of Italy from 1934 to 1970 through the images of Vincenzo Carrese's *Publifoto*.

16. The Italian House of Deputies approves the installation of Cruise missiles at the Comiso base.

Fontana Arte puts into production the lamp system *Scintilla* by Livio and Piero Castiglioni; Memphis inaugurates the chair *First* by Michele De Lucchi, and Flexform introduces the sofa *Max* by Antonio Citterio.

In the bookstores: *Tutte le poesie* by Giorgio Caproni; *Mr. Palomar* by Italo Calvino; *Rosales* by Mario Luzi; *Ancient Evenings* by Norman Mailer; *La conchiglia di Anataj* by Carlo Sgorlon; *La rovina di Kash* by Roberto Calasso; *Nel grave sogno* by Giovanni Raboni.

At the cinema: *Zelig* by Woody Allen; *And the Ship Sails On* by Fellini; *Prénom Carmen* by Godard; *Colpire al cuore* by Gianni Amelio.

The *Galleria del Costume* (Palazzo Pitti) is inaugurated in Florence under the direction of Kirsten Aschengreen Piacenti.

Obituaries: Umberto Terracini, one of the founders of the Italian Communist Party; the poet Paul Géraldy; the dressmaker Germana Marucelli; and the journalist, author and humorist Giovanni Mosca.

1984

January

8. The 14th Winter Olympics are inaugurated in Sarajevo.

20. In Mexico City, Francesco Moser breaks through the 50 km barrier to become cycling's new one hour recordman.

February

14. The Craxi government sets up the sliding wage scale with a decree law that cuts three of the twelve cost-of-living increases planned for 1984.

March

The Swedish film director Ingmar Bergman wins the Best Foreign Film Oscar for *Fanny and Alexander*.

4. Two students from Verona, Marco Furlan and Wolfgang Abel, are arrested and charged with having killed priests and prostitutes, and autographing their crimes with the signature "Ludwig".

31. The peace mission ends in Lebanon. The Italian paratroopers return home.

April

16. Giovanni Spadolini is reconfirmed as Secretary of the Italian Republican Party.

May

The Juventus soccer club wins the *Scudetto*.

The Naples soccer club acquires Diego Armando Maradona from Barcelona for 15 billion lire.

9. Luigi Lucchini is the new president of Confindustria.

June

Aldo Rossi designs the espresso maker *Conica* for Alessi.

10. The Secretary of the Italian Communist Party, Enrico Berlinguer, dies after being taken ill during a rally.

17. Piero Ostellino succeeds Alberto Cavallari as director of *Corriere della Sera*.

Enzo Tortora is elected European deputy for the Radical Party.

July

The hoax of the fake Modigliani sculptures. Three youths sculpt them and throw them into the river that flows through Livorno. When they are found a good portion of Italian art critics declare them to be authentic.

Los Angeles summer Olympics: Italy wins 14 gold medals.

18. The Italian president Pertini names Carlo Bo and Norberto Bobbio senators for life.

August

At the Pesaro Festival, *Viaggio a Reims* by Rossini: conductor Claudio Abbado, scenes by Gae Aulenti, directed by Luca Ronconi.

September

The fashion designer Cinzia Ruggeri shows off a liquid crystal garment at the Milan Triennale.

25. Michele Sindona lands at Malpensa airport after ten years on the run. His future holds a prison sentence and a poisoned cup of coffee.

29. The information revealed by the ex-Mafioso turned State's witness (*pentito*) Tommaso Buscetta lead to the arrest of 366 presumed Mafiosi.

October

4. The RCS publishing house, Rizzoli-Corriere della Sera, is taken over by Gemina, a finance company controlled by Fiat and Mediobanca.

12. Ignazio and Rosario Di Salvo, Sicilian tax collectors, are arrested for collusion with the Mafia.

16. The last parting blow of the Italian state television monopoly. Judges in Rome, Turin and Pescara order the blackout of *Canale 5*, *Retequattro* and *Italia 1*. The Craxi government issues a decree granting authorization to broadcast in the absence of a law regulating television broadcasting. The decree will not pass the House. It is reintroduced and approved in early 1985.

29. Milan. Arrest of the crime boss Angelo Epaminonda, a.k.a. the *Tebano*. The information he reveals lead to the arrest of dozens of members of the Milanese Mafia.

31. Assassination of Indira Gandhi, Prime Minister of India.

November

6. Ronald Reagan wins reelection to the US presidency by a landslide.

December

1. Milan. Mass "Love in" in Piazza Scala during a student demonstration against the sexual violence law.

3. Bhopal catastrophe: toxic gas escaping from a Union Carbide plant in India kills two thousand people.

10. Carlo Rubbia wins the Nobel Prize for Physics.

23. A bomb rips through the Naples-Milan express train as it passes through San Benedetto Val di Sambro between Florence and Bologna, killing 15 and injuring 130.

B&B Italia begins production of the small armchair *Nena* by Sapper and the wardrobe system *Sisamo* by the Studio Kairos. Magis creates the stepladder *Step* by Andries Van Onck and Tisettanta introduces the system *Metropolis* by Antonio Citterio.

Milan has the world's largest gay discotheque. It is located in Isola and called *Nuova Idea*, with two dance floors: one for ballroom dancing and the other for rock.

A Mediobanca survey of a large sample of private businesses reveals that from 1982 to 1984 there was a transformation from a deficit of 1.5 trillion lire to a surplus of over 1.6 trillion lire.

Inflation is at 10 percent.

The 17th Triennale honors the *Great Designers*.

Milan. Palazzo Citterio is inaugurated with a exhibition of works by Alberto Burri. It is an extension of the Pinacoteca di Brera that will later be closed.

In the bookstores: *La casa sul lago della luna* by Francesca Duranti; *La donna delle meraviglie* by Alberto Bevilacqua; *The Unbearable Lightness of Being* by Milan Kundera; *L'angelo della notte* by Giovanni Macchia (Bagutta Prize).

The Castello di Rivoli opens in Rivoli (Turin).

The exhibition *Terrae Motus* opens at Villa Campolieto in Ercolano under the direction of the Lucio Amelio Foundation.

Obituaries: the poet and critic Raffaele Carrieri; Eduardo De Filippo; the actor Tino Scotti; the film director François Truffaut.

1985

January

5. The Red Brigades kill the NOCS agent Ottavio Conte

13. Milan has a record snowfall of 50 centimeters.

24. Walter Reder, ex Major of the SS, responsible for the mass killing at Marzabotto, is freed from the Gaeta penitentiary. In Graz, Austria, he is received with almost military honors.

February

A prolonged famine wreaks death across Sudan, Ethiopia and Chad.

9. Pippo Baudo hosts the Festival of Sanremo and gives it new life. The group *Ricchi e Poveri* win with their song *Se mi innamoro*.

11. The US dollar climbs past the 2,000 lire mark for the first time.

March

Dolce & Gabbana debut during the week dedicated to Milanese prêt-à-porter.

Enzo Mari designs the chair *Tonietta* for Zanotta. Pagani and Perversi create the bookcase *Hook System* for Joint.

10. A new and relatively young—with respect to the usual Soviet geriocracy—president takes power in the USSR: Mikhail Gorbachev.

Nicola Trussardi puts on a fashion show at Milan's Stazione Centrale; the stylist uses platform 20 as his catwalk.

25. The film *Amadeus* by Milos Forman wins eight Oscars.

27. The economist Ezio Tarantelli is killed by leftist terrorism on its last legs.

30. Milan. A huge riot erupts in piazza San Babila between punks and *paninari*. The police intervene and detain 200 youths.

April

2. An attempt on the life of judge Carlo Palermo in Trapani. Two children and their mother, Barbara Rizzo, are killed.

11. Death of Enver Hoxha, Stalinist dictator of Albania.

23. The pope deplores the broadcast in Rome of the Jean Luc Godard film *Je vous salue Marie*.

30. Television debut of Renzo Arbore's *Quelli della notte*; it is an immediate hit.

May

6. The new tilting train *Pendolino* is introduced.

25. Three thousand die in a Bangladesh cyclone.

29. The final match of the Champion's League Cup at the Brussels Heysel stadium. Liverpool fans attack the Juventus fans; thirty-eight people die in the ensuing brawl.

June

3. The new concordat is ratified. Prime Minister Bettino Craxi and Cardinal Casaroli are its creators.

10. The referendum to abrogate the sliding pay scale decreed by the Craxi government fails to pass: 54.3% against 45.7%.

12. Spain and Portugal join the European Economic Community.

21. Milan. The king of rock, Bruce Springsteen, drives the fans wild at San Siro stadium.

24. Francesco Cossiga is elected president of the Italian Republic at the first vote.

July

7. Boris Becker wins the Wimbledon tennis trophy.

13. The big names of rock 'n' roll sing for 16 hours in a benefit concert for the starving in Africa.

19. Tragedy in Val di Fiemme. The Stava tailings dam gives way: 268 people are caught and buried in the onrushing mud.

20. The Italian lire is devalued by 8 percent.

28. The Mafia assassinates the commissioner Giuseppe Montana in Palermo. Nine days later they kill the vice president of Mobile, Antonio Cassarà.

August

1. The Bari court of appeals acquits all the defendants in the piazza Fontana massacre case. Sixteen years after the event, the justice system is still groping in the dark.

South Africa. Uprising in the black ghettos.

26. A Greenpeace boat is deliberately sunk in Auckland, New Zealand. It was getting ready to set sail for Mururoa, the islands where the French were preparing nuclear tests. Suspicion falls on Mitterand's secret services, and the Minister of Defense, Charles Hernu, resigns.

September

A US-French expedition discovers the wreck of the Titanic on the floor of the Atlantic.

6. At the Venice Film Festival, the Golden Lion prize for an outstanding career goes to Federico Fellini.

9. The so-called "monster of Florence" kills two French campers, Nadine Mauriot and Michel Kravechvili.

19. An earthquake in Mexico City kills thousands.

October

7. Palestinian terrorists commandeer the Italian cruise ship *Achille Lauro* as it sails from Alessandria to Port Said. A wheelchair-bound passenger is pushed overboard and drowns.

10. Sigonella crisis. The Craxi government refuses to turn over to the Americans the Palestinian terrorist Abu Abbas and four of the *Achille Lauro* hijackers whose Egyptair flight is forced to land at the Sigonella military base in Sicily by American fighter planes.

November

10. Garry Kasparov unseats the world chess champion Anatoly Karpov.

12. The first heart transplant in Italy is carried out in Padua. The surgical team is headed by Vincenzo Gallucci.

16. The students return to the streets. One hundred thousand march in Rome for modernization of the schools.

19. The first meeting between Reagan and Gorbachev takes place in Geneva.

December

1. The journalist Mino Damato, during a television program that he conducts, walks barefoot over hot coals.

27. Palestinian terrorists attack the check-in counters of the Israeli airline El Al with machine guns and hand grenades; thirteen people are killed.

The Police Station has granted 61,605 visas to immigrants from outside of the European Community and estimates that there are some 35,000 illegal aliens present in the province of Milan.

Dante Isella edits the critical edition of the poetry of Delio Tessa, *L'è el dì di Mort, alegher! De là del mur e altre liriche*.

Fontana Arte begins production of the *Teso* bookcase and tables by Renzo Piano. Vittorio Gregotti projects Bicocca area in Milan.

In the bookstores: *Gli occhi di una donna* by Mario Biondi (Campiello Prize); *Vita standard di un venditore di collant* by Aldo Busi; *L'uomo che guarda* (The Voyeur) by Alberto Moravia; *Rinascimento privato* by Maria Bellonci.

An exhibition of about thirty young artists is opened in Milan in the abandoned Brown Boveri factory. The show is presented by Manuela Gandini and Giò Marconi, who will create the structure of the new generation emerging in Italian art galleries.

Obituaries: the "father of divorce" Loris Fortuna; the sculptor Fausto Melotti; the orchestra conductor Antonino Votto; the historian Fernand Braudel; the writers Italo Calvino, Riccardo Bacchelli, Anna Banti, Heinrich Böll and Elsa Morante; the actors Rock Hudson, Simone Signoret, Orson Welles, Yul Brinner and Francesca Bertini; Sergio Galeotti, Armani's right-hand man; and Marc Chagall.

1986

January

The thirty year dictatorship of the Duvalier family comes to an end in Haiti.

28. Aerospace disaster: the US space shuttle Challenger explodes in flight with seven astronauts aboard.

February

7. Six years before the *Tangentopoli* scandal, the president of the Milan Chamber of Commerce, Piero Bassetti, in an interview for the newspaper *La Repubblica* on the city's big projects, on hold like the municipal rail link from the Garibaldi train station to piazza della Repubblica, says: "I have the impression that this whole debate on the areas, on their planned use, on the Portello, on the office district bears witness to the subordination of politics to the ritual problem of the feeding trough: how you control the contracted work and who controls it. Hence the paralysis. Depending on how you organize the method you organize the theft."

10. The Red Brigades kill the former mayor of Florence, Lando Conti.

25. President Marcos flees the Philippines.

26. Gorbachev announces the politics of openness: *glasnost*.

28. The historical leader of the CGIL, Luciano Lama, steps down as Secretary of the union.

March

A big night at the Academy awards for *Out of Africa* by Sidney Pollack.

17. The scandal of methanol-containing wine: the first deaths in Milan.

22. Michele Sindona, sentenced to 15 years in prison, dies after drinking a cup of poisoned coffee, sharing the fate of Gaspare Pisciotta, lieutenant and killer of the bandit Giuliano.

April

Tod's shoes of Diego Della Valle introduces moccasins characterized by a sole in relief with 133 small rubber protuberances.

The Naples court of appeals acquits Enzo Tortora of the charges of collusion with the Camorra.

The Milan Trade Fair has 2,980 exhibitors and nearly 2 million visitors.

2. Terrorist attack on a TWA flight from Rome to Athens.

13. A historical occurrence at the Rome synagogue: Pope John Paul II and Rabbi Elio Toaff pray together.

15. The Americans bomb Tripoli in reprisal against what they consider the guiding nation of international terrorism. Libya launches two missiles aimed at the Italian island of Lampedusa but they do not reach their target.

28. A radioactive cloud rises from the Soviet nuclear reactor at Chernobyl; great alarm in Europe.

June

Michele De Lucchi and Giancarlo Fassina design the *Tolomeo* lamp for Artemide.

Argentina wins the world soccer championship.

Moreno Argentin is cycling's world road racing champion.

July

18. Agreement is reached between the Italian government and the unions on a code of self-regulation in transportation strikes.

September

26. Moser beats the old record of the hour set at Oersted by 39 meters, riding 48,543 meters in 60 minutes.

23. It costs Fiat 3 billion dollars to buy back the stocks that they had sold to Libya in 1976.

October

9. Raul Gardini and the Ferruzzi Group become the majority shareholders of Montedison.

November

Milan. The Braidense library celebrates its 200th year.

6. Fiat buys Alfa Romeo.

10. After ten years in office, Carlo Tognoli is no longer mayor of Milan.

December

The Musée d'Orsay (project by Gae Aulenti) is inaugurated in Paris.

7. Riccardo Muti triumphs at La Scala inaugurating the musical season with Verdi's *Nabucco*, and regales the audience with an encore of *Va pensiero*. He is the new musical director of the opera house.

10. Rita Levi Montalcini wins the Nobel Prize for Medicine.

The earth has five billion human inhabitants.

19. Gorbachev frees the dissident Sakharov from confinement.

Luceplan introduces the lamp *Costanza* by Alberto Meda and Paolo Rizzatto. B&B presents the sofa *Sity* by Citterio.

Milan. Giorgio Strehler inaugurates the Teatro Studio.

Reinhold Messner climbs Lhotse (8,516 m) without oxygen. It is his sixteenth Himalayan peak over 8,000 meters.

In the bookstores: *Tutte le poesie* by Vittorio Sereni; *Il pianeta azzurro* by Malerba; *Family dancing* by David Leavitt.

At the cinema: *Ginger and Fred* by Fellini; *La famiglia* by Scola; *Speriamo che sia femmina* by Monicelli; *Mission* by Roland Joffé; and *Platoon* by Oliver Stone.

Corrado Levi organizes *Il Cangiante*, consecrating some of the artists who participated in the exhibition at the Brown Boveri factory. Marco Mazzucconi, Stefano Arienti, Pierluigi Pusole, Bruno Zanichelli are among the invitees.

Obituaries: Alfredo Binda, cycling legend; the actors James Cagney and Cary Grant; the writers Simone de Beauvoir, Luis Borges, Goffredo Parise and Piero Chiara; the film directors Otto Preminger and Vincent Minelli; the sculptor Henry Moore.

1987

January

The number of industrial employees in Milan, 349 thousand in 1971, has now fallen to 178 thousand. There are 238 thousand employed in the private service sector: commerce, banking, insurance, finance, hotels and software, a market where Milan is Italian leader with 30 thousand operators.

2. Alfa Lancia is launched with share capital of 1.5 trillion lire.

February

12. Ugo Stille is named director of *Corriere della Sera*, succeeding Piero Ostellino.

March

Genny of Ancona produces the prêt-à-porter collection for the Paris debut of Christian Lacroix, who has seven years as director of the *maison* Patou under his belt.

3. Bettino Craxi resigns after presiding over the longest lasting government in the history of the Italian Republic. Amintore Fanfani is the electoral minister.

8. Mike Tyson wins the world heavyweight boxing championship.

April

In Milan, 26 women out of one thousand bring children into the world.

Silvio Berlusconi, acquiring most of the shares possessed by the editors, becomes the majority shareholder of the newspaper *Il Giornale*, founded and directed by Indro Montanelli.

20. The economist Federico Caffè disappears, never to be found again.

May

The Naples soccer club wins the championship. A banner turned to face the cemetery says: "*Guaglià, che ve siete persi*" [Hey folks, if you only knew what you missed.]

Margaret Thatcher is elected to a third term as British Prime Minister.

Persian Gulf. An Iraqi missile hits a US warship killing 38.

14. Milan's Piccolo Teatro is 40 years old; the event is celebrated with the 1,560th rendition of *Arlecchino, servitore di due padroni*, interpreted by Ferruccio Soleri.

28. A nineteen year-old German, Mathias Rust, lands his private plane in Moscow's Red Square after evading Soviet radar. It is a slap in the face: the Defense Minister, Sokolof, loses his post.

June

Massimo Josa Ghini designs the *Dinamic* seat series for Moroso; Cini Boeri and Tomu Katayanagi come out with the *Ghost* armchair for Fiam; Rossi introduces the chair *Milano* for Molteni and Alberto Meda the *Light-Light* chair for Alias.

A law is passed entitling men to "paternity leave" if they have to care for a newborn child.

14. Italy goes to the ballot box and confers victory on the Socialists and the Christian Democrats. The porno star Ilona Staller "Cicciolina" is elected to Parliament on the Radical ticket. Giovanni Goria is the new Prime Minister.

July

NASA detects the hole in the ozone for the first time.

18. Flooding in Valtellina. A landslide buries the villages of Morignone and Sant'Antonio Morignone. Fifty-three people die and fifteen hundred are left homeless.

September

The East German president Honecker visits Bonn for political talks: a first.

October

19. Wall Street loses 22.6% in one day. "Black Monday" drags down stock markets all over the world.

November

Gaetano Pesce designs the *Feltri* armchairs for Cassina.

A referendum closes down all nuclear power plants in Italy and strips magistrates of immunity from civil liability.

Adriano Celentano emcees the television program *Fantastico*, preaches and asks his audience to turn off and turn their back on their television sets.

Antonio Maccanico becomes president of Mediobanca.

December

12. In Washington, Reagan and Gorbachev sign the first treaty regulating missiles in Europe.

14. Gianfranco Fini is the new party Secretary of the Italian Social Movement (MSI), taking the reins from Giorgio Almirante.

31. The dollar is worth 1,169 lire.

Tecno launches the *Nomos* tables by Foster; Bruno Gecchelin designs the *Shuttle* spotlights for Guzzini; Edilpro puts into production the modular living unit *Mapi* by Pierluigi Spadolini; Luceplan presents the lamp *Lola* by Alberto Meda and Paolo Rizzatto.

At the cinema: *The Last Emperor* by Bernardo Bertolucci; *Full Metal Jacket* by Stanley Kubrick.

Obituraries: the painters Renato Guttuso and Andy Warhol; the writers Carlo Cassola, Giovanni Arpino, Marguerite Yourcenar and, by suicide, Primo Levi; the singer Claudio Villa; the guitarist Andrés Segovia; the actors Danny Kaye and Rita Hayworth.

1988

January

The COBAS union calls a transportation strike.

Milan. The publisher Gabriele Mazzotta establishes a foundation in memory of his father Antonio.

The Red Brigades kill the senator Roberto Ruffilli, De Mita's right-hand man.

February

1. Unemployment in Italy is at 12.3 percent.

The Festival of Sanremo is won by Massimo Ranieri with the song *Perdere l'amore*, which strikes a tender chord with fifty year-olds.

25. Alberto Tomba wins the gold medal in the giant slalom at the Calgary winter Olympics.

March

10. Sergio Pininfarina is the new president of Confindustria.

18. Two hundred thousand women march in Rome for equal opportunity and the enactment of a law against sexual violence.

April

12. Bernardo Bertolucci's *The Last Emperor* wins nine Oscars, including best film and best director.

13. The first De Mita government.

May

Laura Biagiotti holds a fashion show in Beijing, marking the Chinese debut of Italian fashion.

The Milan soccer club under Arrigo Sacchi wins the *Scudetto*. It is the 11th time the team in the black and red jerseys has won the trophy, but it is the first time in nine years.

8. Mitterand beats Chirac to be reelected president of the French Republic.

15. As promised by Gorbachev, theSoviet troops with draw from Afghanistan.

June

13. The Vatican Secretary of state, Agostino Casaroli, meets Gorbachev at the Kremlin. It is the first time a high ranking Vatican representative is officially received in Moscow.

21. The central committee of the Italian Communist Party elects Achille Occhetto party Secretary, replacing Alessandro Natta.

July

The Standa department store chain changes owners: the Ferruzzi Group leaves and Berlusconi's Fininvest steps in.

7. An oil platform in the North Sea explodes: 187 die.

23. A cloud of toxic sulfur dioxide rises from the ACNA plant in Cengio, Valle Bormida.

28. The *pentito* Leonardo Marino accuses Adriano Sofri, former leader of Lotta Continua, Giorgio Pietrostefani and Ovidio Bompressi of the Calabresi murder.

August

1. The kidnappers of the Aspromonte zone in Calabria free a young boy, Marco Flora, after 17 months of captivity.

14. Enzo Ferrari dies in Modena just a few months after his ninetieth birthday.

20. Cease-fire in the Iran-Iraq war after eight years of conflict and a million casualties.

28. Tragedy for the Italian acrobatic fighter plane team, the *Frecce Tricolori*, in Ramstein, Germany. Three airplanes collide in flight: one crashes into the spectators killing dozens along with the pilot.

30. The Italian State Council makes religion class obligatory in schools.

September

Ermanno Olmi, with his film *La leggenda del santo bevitore* (The Legend of the Holy Drinker), wins the Golden Lion at the Venice Film Festival.

2. At the Seoul summer Olympics, Gelindo Bordin wins the marathon and Ben Johnson, winner of the 100 meter dash, is disqualified for doping.

November

8. Ronald Reagan's vice president, Republican George Bush, is elected president of the United States.

December

7. Fifty thousand die in an earthquake in Armenia.

22. A terrorist bomb explodes aboard a Pan Am jumbo jet in flight over Lockerbie, Scotland: all 259 passengers and 11 people on the ground are killed.

Kartell introduces the chair *Dr. Glob* by Philippe Starck. Edra produces several sofas by Zaha Hadid.

The architect Aldo Rossi wins the international Pritzker prize. A large exhibition will be dedicated to him at the Beaubourg in 1991.

At the cinema: *Who framed Roger Rabbit?* brings new technical mastery to the mix of human actors and cartoons; *The last temptation of Christ* by Martin Scorsese, a film that will displease the Vatican Curia; and *Compagni di scuola* by Carlo Verdone.

In bookstores: *Foucault's Pendulum* by Umberto Eco.

The Luigi Pecci Contemporary Art Center opens in Prato, the first Italian museum of contemporary art built ex novo.

Obituaries: Marisa Belisario, manager of Italtel; the actors Paolo Stoppa and Marta Abba; the politicians Giorgio Almirante and Giuseppe Saragat; the musicologist Massimo Mila; the jazz trumpet player Chet Baker; Enzo Tortora.

1989

January

Protests in Bagnoli (Naples) over the threatened closing of Italsider.

February

14. The writer Salman Rushdie is sentenced to death in absentia by the fundamentalist Iranian regime for "offenses to the Muslim sentiment" contained in his book *The Satanic Verses*.

17. The 18th congress of the Christian Democrats elects Arnaldo Forlani to the post of party Secretary.

March

Prada, time-honored maker of handbags and leather goods, makes its debut in women's wear.

Giuseppe Tornatore wins the best foreign film Oscar for *Nuovo Cinema Paradiso*.

April

15. Ninety-five fans are crushed to death by the throng at the Sheffield soccer stadium.

19. Students and youths occupy Tienanmen square in Beijing demanding liberty and democracy. In the night between June 3 and 4, many will be killed by the tanks of the Chinese armed forces.

May

General strike against health care "tickets," which have spelled the end of the era of free medicine.

June

Florence. At the Pitti Immagine Uomo exhibition, the first fashion show in the West of the Russian stylist Slava Zaitsev.

The Barbie doll is thirty years old.

An extended drought in Lombardy. Novenae in the churches to bring rain.

The Inter soccer club of Giovanni Trapattoni, Matthäus, Brehme, Serena, and Diaz wins the *Scudetto*, with a record number of points in an 18-team championship.

3. Death of the Ayatollah Khomeini.

12. The mother of kidnap victim Cesare Casella goes to the Aspromonte zone in Calabria to move public opinion.

18. Solidarity wins the first free elections in Poland since 1947. The Socialist societies of Eastern Europe have their days numbered.

20. An attempt on judge Giovanni Falcone's life fails.

July

Enzo Mari designs the *Tappeto volante* bed for Interflex. Meda and Rizzatto create the lamp *Titania* for Luceplan. Magistretti comes up with the wardrobe *Shigeto* for De Padova.

14. France celebrates the two-hundredth anniversary of the Revolution.

The Adriatic sea is clogged with algae blooms for the second summer in a row.

October

17. Earthquake in San Francisco kills 63 and leaves 14 thousand homeless.

24. The new Italian penal code goes into force.

November

9. In response to the constant trickle of émigrés leaving the country from all quarters, East Germany opens its borders. The crowd breaks down the Berlin Wall.

13. Occhetto proposes to change the name of the Italian Communist Party and to found a new party.

17. The Czechoslovakians defy police repression and drive out the Communist government. Dubcek and Havel emerge triumphant.

27. The trial begins of Sofri, Pietrostefani and Bompressi for the Calabresi murder.

29. Gorbachev visits Rome and Milan; it is a great personal triumph.

December

3. Bush and Gorbachev are in Malta for a summit.

7. Riccardo Muti inaugurates the season at La Scala with *I Vespri siciliani* by Giuseppe Verdi, directed by Pierluigi Pizzi.

14. After sixteen years of military dictatorship, Chileans go to the polls to elect as president the Christian Democrat Patricio Alwin.

20. The US marines invade Panama and oust the dictator Noriega.

23. The Romanian dictatorship implodes. The satrap Nicolae Ceausescu is summarily executed along with his wife Elena.

Gianfranco Ferré is named artistic director of Dior, taking the place of Marc Bohan.

At the cinema: The last Fellini film *The Voice of the Moon*; *Palombella rossa* by Nanni Moretti and *Women on the Verge of a Nervous Breakdown* by Almodovar.

Piero Castiglioni designs the lamp system *Sillaba* for Fontana Arte; Mario Cananzi and Roberto Semprini the sofa *Tatlin* for Edra; King Kong Production the tray *Girotondo* for Alessi.

La grande sera by Giuseppe Pontiggia arrives in bookstores. The novel *Volevo i pantaloni* by Lara Cardella is a big hit.

The exhibition *La lingua morta della scultura* (*The dead tongue of sculpture*), directed by Achille Bonito Oliva, is inaugurated at the Isabella Ryban Foundation in New York.

Obituaries: the painters Salvador Dalì and Mino Maccari; the actors Franco Parenti and Silvana Mangano; the poet Antonio Porta; the publicist Dino Villani (creator of the Miss Italia pageant); the ex Secretary of the Christian Democrats Benigno Zaccagnini; the writers Leonardo Sciascia and Cesare Zavattini; Cesare Musatti, father of Freudian psychoanalysis in Italy; the pianist Vladimir Horowitz; the film director Sergio Leone; the physicist Edoardo Amaldi; the orchestra conductor Herbert von Karajan; the actress Bette Davis

1990

January

Florence. Palazzo Strozzi hosts the exhibition *Roberto Capucci: L'Arte nella Moda*, organized by Pitti Immagine Corporate.

2. The Italian Statistics Institute ISTAT discloses that the cost of living in Italy has increased by 6.6 percent.

February

24. Death of the former Italian president Sandro Pertini. He is buried in his hometown, Stella, in the hills near Savona.

March

The Italian Communist Party congress accepts the proposal of Secretary Achille Occhetto. A constituent phases in the launching of a new party in tune with the Socialist International.

April

21. After over 25 years, Verdi's *Traviata* is staged again at La Scala. Muti challenges the orphans of Maria Callas with a young singing team: Tiziana Fabbricini and Roberto Alagna. It is a triumph.

29. The Naples soccer club wins its second *Scudetto*.

May

Zanotta produces the multifunctional object *Joy* by Achille Castiglioni.

6. The Italian Communist Party loses approximately 6 percent in the administrative elections, falling to 23.2. The Socialists gain 2 percent. The Christian Democrats hold their ground. The northern League and the Veneto League gather, in some Northern provinces, 20 percent of the vote. In Milan, the Northern League gets 11 members into Palazzo Marino (city hall) and 15 into the Pirellone (regional government).

May

Cellular telephones make their appearance.

2. The first guilty verdict for Adriano Sofri, Giorgio Pietrostefani and Ovidio Bompressi, accused by the police informer (*pentito*) Leonardo Marino of the Calabresi murder.

June

Carlo Fontana is the new superintendent of La Scala.

The third Milan subway line is inaugurated, creating the first direct link between the northern and southern zones of the city.

4. The world soccer championship begins at the San Siro stadium with a match between Argentina and Cameroon. Among the 85 thousand spectators there are 5 chiefs of state, including Italian president Francesco Cossiga. Diego Maradona is on the field. The stadium was expanded and roofed, but it will turn out that the lack of air damages the playing turf. Italy will take third place.

6. Gianni Bugno arrives in Milan to win the Giro d'Italia.

August

Boris Yeltsin wins the free elections in Russia to become president.

Raul Gardini invites 1,200 people to the launching of the *Moro* in Venice. The sailboat will compete in the Americas' Cup.

2. Iraq invades Kuwait. On November 29 the UN Security Council will issue an ultimatum to Saddam Hussein: he must withdraw his troops by January 15, 1991 or face war.

7. A young woman, Simonetta Cesaroni, is knifed to death in Via Poma in Rome. The murder will go unsolved.

September

14. In Milan, the garbage crisis enters its third day. The municipal waste authority, AMSA, has filled the available landfills to capacity and has no solution for the thousands of tons of accumulating municipal wastes.

October

The street style "grunge" is born, with people dressing in layers like onions.

The movement of capital from Italy abroad is liberalized.

Compact disks are introduced onto the market.

There are approximately 200 thousand doctors in Milan. In 1950 there were 4,016; in 1960, 6,513; in 1970, 7,749; and in 1980, 12,784.

3. Germany is reunified after 45 years of separation.

15. Mikhail Gorbachev is awarded the Nobel Peace Prize.

23. The Gladio case erupts. It is a secret paramilitary structure created in 1951 in preparation for a possible invasion by Soviet troops.

November

The oarsmen Carmine and Giuseppe Abbagnale win the world championship for the sixth time.

Christie's of New York auctions a van Gogh painting for 99 billion lire.

22. Margaret Thatcher, British Prime Minister, loses the election and her power.

December

Fleur Jaggy wins the Bagutta literary prize with *I beati anni del castigo*. Mario Soldati is president of the panel of judges.

Valentino celebrates his thirty years of work in Milan and Rome.

A survey reveals that out of 100 Milanese, 10 never read a newspaper other than the sports pages, 25 never read a periodical, 33 have neither bought, borrowed or been given a book over the course of the last year.

Gianni Versace debuts in the world of Paris haute couture.

At the cinema: *Dances with Wolves* by Kevin Costner; *L'aria serena dell'Ovest* by Silvio Soldini.

"Design Diffusion News" is founded under the direction of Alberto Maria Prina. Philippe Starck designs the citrus press *Juicy Salif* for Alessi.

Bestseller: *Io speriamo che me la cavo*, an unusual book presenting a collection of third grader's writings from an elementary school in Arzano. Franco Fortini publishes *Estrema ratio*.

The American stylist Tom Ford is commissioned by Gucci to design its women's prêt-à-porter collections.

Obituaries: Sergio Brighenti, star of trotting races; Felice Musazzi, leader of the comedy team *I Legnanesi*; the actors Greta Garbo, Ava Gardner, Aldo Fabrizi and Ugo Tognazzi; the Polish film director Tadeus Kantor; the composers Leonard Bernstein and Luigi Nono; the writers Giorgio Manganelli and Alberto Moravia; the poet Giorgio Caproni.

Eighties

*Attempted assassination
of Pope John Paul II, Rome
13th May 1981
(© Publifoto, Milan)*

*Earthquake in Irpinia,
23rd October 1980
(© Publifoto Notizie,
Milan/Vincenzo Coronati)*

*Fall of the Berlin Wall,
9th November 1989
(photo: Carlo Orsi)*

*Riccardo Muti at Teatro
alla Scala, Milan 1986
(photo: Carlo Orsi)*

1991

January

Somalia. The bloody civil war between tribes continues. President Siad Barre flees the country.

16-17. The Gulf war. Iraq is bombed. On 24th February ground forces enter the war in operation "Desert Storm."

17 During the night US, British and Italian forces bomb Iraq. The Gulf war, aimed at forcing Saddam Hussein to withdraw from Kuwait, begins.

The USSR sends troops into the rebellious republics of Latvia and Lithuania.

31. The final congress of the Italian Communist Party: the Democratic Left party is founded. Achille Occhetto is elected Secretary.

February

8. The Constituent Congress of the Lega Nord is held in Pieve Emanuele. Umberto Bossi becomes Secretary.

20. The Yugoslav Federation collapses, Croatia and Slovenia declare their independence. The first conflicts will begin in March.

South Africa. President De Klerk announces that apartheid will be abolished by June.

The Warsaw Pact is dissolved.

Georgia proclaims its independence from the USSR.

March

Enrico Baleri designs the *Mimì* chair for Baleri Italia, Luca Meda designs the bookcase *Piroscafo* for Molteni, Rou Azafd designs the armchair *Soft Big Easy* for Moroso.

3. Biblical exodus of Albanians to Italy.

11. The Moby Prince disaster off the shore of Leghorn: the ship rams into an oil tanker, bursts into flames and 141 people die.

At the Triennale Cosmit organises the exhibition *Mobili Italiani 1961-1991. Le varie età dei linguaggi*, under the supervision of Pierluigi Cerri and Claudia Donà.

12. A five-party government led by Andreotti is formed.

A long battle begins between CIR under De Benedetti and Fininvest under Berlusconi for control of Mondadori.

The population of Milan is 1,367,733. This decrease is at its apex with a drop of 45 per thousand: in 10 years the city has lost 300,000 inhabitants.

The Fondazione Milano per la Scala is founded: among other things it will contribute to financing a performance when the theatre is obliged to cut its budget.

May

7. During an official visit to the USA the Italian President Francesco Cossiga calls for a reform of the Italian Presidency. It is one of his strongest criticisms.

11. An economic package of 15 thousand billion lire is passed to cover the budget deficit.

21. India. Ex-Prime Minister Gandhi Rajiv Gandhi is assassinated, his mother Indira Gandhi had also been assassinated for political motives.

Sampdoria soccer team wins its first championship.

June

2. Indro Montanelli turns down a nomination as a life-senator. Giovanni Agnelli, Giulio Andreotti, Francesco De Martino and Paolo Emilio Taviani accept.

Tremendous eruption of the volcano Pinatubo in the Philippines.

9. 95,6 % of the electorate are in favour of the repeal of multiple preferences on the ballot paper.

July

10 . Rome. The Olgiata murder case. Alberica Filo della Torre is murdered. The case is an unsolved mystery.

August

19. A coup by conservative communists against Gorbachev fails. In December the USSR is dissolved, Gorbachev resigns. The Soviet flag is removed from the domes of the Kremlin.

20. Twenty thousand Albanians disembark on the coast of Puglia.

25. Gianni Bugno wins the world professional road championship in Stuttgart.

September

14. A maniac with a hammer damages Donatello's *David* in Florence.

October

26. The National Anti-Mafia Division is founded.

November

8. After the dissolution of the USSR and the Warsaw Pact, the Nato summit in Rome sets out new objectives and strategies.

14. The daily newspaper *L'Indipendente* is founded under the editorship of Riccardo Franco Levi. It will have a short golden era under Vittorio Feltri.

Confrontation between president Cossiga and the Supreme Judiciary Council. Cossiga threatens to resort to police intervention if the agenda for the meeting on the 20th of December is not modified. The magistrates back down.

25. Brescia. In the early administrative elections the Lega Nord becomes the number one party winning 24% of the votes.

December

3. A nation-wide magistrates strike against the continuous attacks from the Italian president Francesco Cossiga.

4. Cocer (The carabinieri central representative council) expresses support for the Cossiga's criticisms of the institutions. Parliament is on the alert.

6. The Democratic Left calls for the impeachment of president Cossiga for attacking the constitution.

7. La Scala opens with Wagner's *Parsifal* conducted by Riccardo Muti.

15. Constituent congress of Rifondazione Comunista.

Versace entrusts his advertising campaign to photographer Herb Ritts who chooses the very best top models: Linda Evangelista, Naomi Campbell and Cindy Crawford.

Books: *Anche le formiche nel loro piccolo s'incazzano* by Gino and Michele, *Il Provinciale* by Giorgio Bocca (Bagutta Prize winner), *Parola di Giobbe* by Giobbe Covatta, *La strada per Roma* by Paolo Volponi (Strega Prize winner).

Cinema: *The Sheltering Sky* by Bernardo Bertolucci and *Ultrà* by Ricky Tognazzi.

Deaths: the actors Salvo Randone, Renato Rascel, Yves Montand, and Walter Chiari; the writers Natalia Ginzburg, Vasco Pratolini, Mario Tobino and Graham Greene; the musicians Miles Davis and Gino Negri; the sculptor Giacomo Manzù; the painter Gianni Dova; the inventor of the Polaroid Edwin Land and the director Frank Capra.

1992

January

15. The EC recognises the independence of Croatia and Slovenia.

Seven-year-old Farouk Kassam is kidnapped in Porto Cervo by Sardinian bandits.

18. Milan. Piero Borghini is elected mayor of Milan by a multi-party majority: DC, PSI, PSDI, PLI, Lega pensionati, Lega nuova, Unità riformista. Independent technicians are given seats in the City Council.

20. Democrat Bill Clinton takes office at the White House in place of outgoing president George Bush.

23. Francesco Cossiga resigns from the Christian Democrat Party.

February

2. Parliament is dissolved and new elections are called.

7. In Maastricht, the twelve member countries of the European Community sign a treaty that is a further step towards the European Union.

8. At the winter Olympics in Albertville Italy wins four gold medals: Alberto Tomba (giant slalom), Deborah Compagnoni (super-G), Stefania Belmondo (30 km cross-country), Josef Polig (combined).

17. Milan. The arrest of Mario Chiesa, chairman of the Pio Albergo Trivulzio, marks the start of "Mani pulite " corruption investigation. The names of public prosecutor Francesco Saverio Borrelli and substitute public prosecutors Colombo, Davigo and Di Pietro come more and more into the public limelight.

March

The Los Angeles race riots break out.

2. Civil war in Bosnia between Muslims and Serbs. Sarajevo is under attack from Serbian artillery. A siege begins that will last over a thousand days: 1251 victims of bombs and snipers.

12. In Sicily Salvo Lima, head of the Andreotti faction, is assassinated by the Mafia.

31. Gabriele Salvatores wins the Oscar for best foreign language film with *Mediterraneo*.

April

5-6. In the general elections the three main parties DC, PCI and PSI suffer severe losses.

The first signs of the breakdown of the traditional party system are seen with the advance of Lega Nord which becomes the number two party in Lombardy winning 80 seats between the Chamber of Deputies and Senate.

22. First notices of judicial investigation and first arrests in the "Mani pulite" investigations.

25. Head of State Francesco Cossiga announces his resignation on television two months before the end of his term of office.

May

The Milan City Council buys the Jucker collection, which is principally composed of futurist works.

Raul Gardini's *Moro di Venezia* qualifies for the final stage of the America's Cup but is defeated by *America Cube*.

23. The Capaci murders. The magistrate Giovanni Falcone who symbolises the struggle against the Mafia, his wife Francesca Morvillo and three bodyguards are killed in a bomb attack on the Punta Raisi-Palermo motorway.

25. Oscar Luigi Scalfaro is elected president on the sixteenth count.

31. Carlo Azeglio Ciampi, the governor of the Bank of Italy, states that Italy's participation in the European Union is at risk due to public debt and inflation.

Ferrari launch their 512T with Pininfarina bodywork.

June

A group of Italian scientists working in a laboratory under the Gran Sasso mountain see the neutrinos produced in the sun for the first time.

28. Socialist Giuliano Amato forms a four-party government with DC, PSI, PSDI and PLI.

July

10. Amato's government, which was given a vote of confidence in the first days of the month, passes a budget of 30,000 billion lire with taxes on homes, current accounts, bank deposits, increases in stamp duty on driving licences and passports and a partial revision of the pension system.

14. Pope John Paul II undergoes an intestinal operation.

19. Palermo anti-Mafia judge Paolo Borsellino and five bodyguards die in a Mafia bomb attack.

25. Barcelona Olympics: Italy wins six gold medals.

August

13. Television system reform: national broadcast licences are awarded to the three Rai channels, the three Mediaset channels, Videomusic, Telemontecarlo and Rete A.

September

2. Paolo Mieli becomes the editor of *Corriere della Sera* leaving *La Stampa* his position there is taken by his vice-editor Ezio Mauro.

6. Gianni Bugno wins the world cycling championship for the second time.

6. Mafia boss Giuseppe Madonia is arrested.

11. Camorra boss Carmine Alfieri is arrested.

17. Ignazio Salvo is shot in a Mafia rubout.

17. Further fiscal measures introduced by the government. Amato's measures courageously levy the sum of 93,000 billion lire.

October

12. Mino Martinazzoli is elected as Secretary of the Christian Democrat party.

23. The Court of Cassation overrules the conviction of Sofri, Bompressi and Pietrostefani for the Calabresi murder.

November

Democrat Bill Clinton is elected president of the United States.

December

United Nations intervention in Somalia.

10. The ex-secretary of the PSDI party and Minister for Public works, Franco Nicolazzi, is convicted for the "carceri d'oro" (golden prisons) scandal.

15. Bettino Craxi is served with his first notice of judicial investigation.

Achille Castiglioni designs the armchair *Polet* for Interflex, Metis (Claudio Valent and Marinella Patetta) design the *Nobi* lamp for Fontana Arte and Luca Scacchetti the *Hydra* seat for Poltrona Frau.

Michele De Lucchi designs the *Philus* computer for Olivetti.

Almost 14% of the population of Milan (just over 190,000) are single.

Conservative Premier John Major announces the separation of Prince Charles and Diana.

GDP is at 1.4% in real terms. In 1989 it was 2.8%.

The novel *Petrolio* by Pier Paolo Pasolini is posthumously published.

Cinema: *Basic Istinct*, *Malcolm X* by Spike Lee, *Morte di un matematico napoletano* by Mario Martone. *Il ladro di bambini* by Gianni Amelio is awarded a special prize at the Cannes Film Festival.

The Catholic Church presents its new Catechism.

Deaths: the graphic designer Max Huber, the painter Bruno Cassinari, Fr. Ernesto Pisoni, successor to Carlo Gnocchi at Pro Juventute and editor for many years of the Catholic daily *L'Italia*, Marlene Dietrich, the writer Carlo Bernari, flautist Severino Gazzelloni and journalist Gianni Brera. Giulio Carlo Argan and Giuliano Briganti also died.

1993

January

"Mani pulite" investigations become increasingly broad and thorough: notices of judicial investigation are served to leading members of the Socialist and Christian Democrat parties.

15. Cosa nostra boss Totò Riina is arrested in Palermo.

16. Pietro Pacciani, suspected of being the monster of Florence, is arrested.

February

Widespread resignations in the Amato government due to "Mani pulite", the most clamorous of which are Claudio Martelli, Minister for Justice, and Francesco De Lorenzo, Health Minister.

11. Craxi resigns as Secretary of the Socialist Party.

26. A car bomb explodes in the underground garage at the World Trade Center, the Twin Towers in New York. It is presumed that it was planted by Islamic extremists: seven people are killed.

March

The traditional dress of Chassidim Orthodox Jews inspires Quirino Principe men's wear design for Krizia.

5. The Conso Law on Tangentopoli is introduced. It is considered as a slate wipe and the president refuses his signature.

15. A further spate of notices of judicial investigation to politicians and entrepreneurs involved in payoffs, contract rigging and misappropriation of funds for international co-operation.

25. The Senate passes the new law for the direct election of mayors.

27. Giulio Andreotti is served with a notice of judicial investigation. The accusations are very serious: connivance and conspiracy with the Mafia. He will be acquitted in 2000.

April

2. Red Brigade founder Renato Curcio is granted leave of absence from prison after serving 17 years.

19. The country calls for radical institutional reform in a referendum.

28. Carlo Azeglio Ciampi forms a new government without party consultation: it is a technical cabinet. He is the successor to Giuliano Amato, who courageously dealt with the State deficit.

29. The Chamber of Deputies votes against authorisation to investigate on Craxi.

May

3. Andreotti surrenders his parliamentary immunity.

19. Nitto Santapaola, considered to be the boss of the Mafia in Catania, is arrested.

21. Ciampi's government passes a bill amounting to 12,000 billion lire of cuts. Italy is preparing for the Euro.

27. A Mafia bomb destroys the Torre dei Pulci in Florence; the Uffizi Gallery is also damaged: there are five victims.

June

5. Milan. Direct elections of the mayor. The Lega candidate Formentini is installed in Palazzo Marino.

10. Authorisation to investigate on Andreotti: the judiciary suspects him of instigating the Pecorelli murder.

22. The health scandal erupts. Ex-minister De Lorenzo is thought, on the declarations of a turncoat, to be at the centre of the affair.

July

War in Bosnia.

20. Ex chairman of ENI Gabriele Cagliari who was involved in Tangentopoli commits suicide in San Vittorie prison, Milan.

21. Raul Gardini, ex president of Montedison, commits suicide in his Milanese home.

27. A Mafia bomb explodes at the Contemporary Art Pavilion in Milan (a policeman, three firemen and a North African immigrant are killed) and also in Rome at San Giovanni Laterano and at San Giorgio al Velabro.

August

English designer Chipperfield designs *Monolith* for B&B; Newson designs *Tv-Chair* for Moroso, Vico Magistretti designs the bed *Tadao* for Flou.

4. The Chamber of Deputies passes an imperfect majority electoral law.

Financier Sergio Cusani is tried in the "Mani pulite" trials.

September

6. Workers at ENI protest against redundancies.

27. Health scandal. A search at the home of Duilio Poggiolini, president of the Commissione unica dei farmaci, uncovers property worth 300 billion lire.

October

American scientists Hall and Stillman clone a human embryo for the first time.

The Società Umanitaria di Milano (the Humanitarian Society of Milan), founded in 1893 on a legacy from the banker Moisè Loira, celebrates its hundredth year.

4. Boris Yeltsin uses force to silence parliamentary opposition.

5. Pope John Paul II publishes the encyclical *Veritatis splendor.*

November

23. At a press conference in Casalecchio (Bologna) Silvio Berlusconi announces his entry into politics and states that if he were among the Roman electorate he would vote Gianfranco Fini for mayor. This marks the first step in the "rehabilitation" of the MSI.

December

5. At the local elections the centre-left wins 47 city councils, the Lega 24, MSI 11. Rutelli becomes mayor of Rome and Bassolino becomes mayor of Naples.

7. The Lega gets caught up in Tangentopoli because of 200 million lire accepted as funding by Alessandro Patelli, the executive secretary.

21. Sofri, Bompressi and Pietrostefani are acquitted in the Calabresi murder trial.

Italian stylists on the catwalk in Peking.

The Giuseppe Verdi Symphony Orchestra, an orchestra exclusively formed of young people, is founded in Milan. In 1999 it will have its own concert hall in corso San Gottardo in the former cinema Massimo.

The telematic stock exchange trading system is launched.

Eritrea declares its independence.

Rabin and Arafat shake hands at the White House in the presence of president Clinton. The gesture marks a step forward in the slow, difficult peace process.

Inflation is at 4.2%, the lowest in the last 25 years, but unemployment is at 11%.

In Holland the law no longer prosecutes doctors who practice euthanasia.

Renzo Piano designs the *Lingotto* lamp for Guzzini, Pietro Arosio designs the *Mirandolina* chair for Zanotta, Antonio Citterio and Low design the *Mobil* drawer-unit for Kartell.

Cinema: *Schindler's List* and *Jurassic Park* by Steven Spielberg, *Il grande cocomero* by Francesca Archibugi.

Books: *La breve passeggiata* by Alberto Vigevani, *Bagheria* by Dacia Maraini.

"The cardinal points of Art" is the theme of the Venice Art Biennale under the direction of Achille Bonito Oliva, who formulates the concepts of multiculturalism, transnationalism and multimediality for the first time together.

Deaths: Albert Sabin, who discovered the vaccine for polio, Aldo Ravelli (agent on the stock exchange for many important Milanese families known as "il banchiere rosso"; Rudolf Nureyev, the tennis player Ashe, skiing champion Zeno Colò, the writers Giovanni Testori and Anthony Burgess, the actress Audrey Hepburn, jazz musician Dizzie Gillespie, Federico Fellini and King Baudouin of Belgium.

1994

January

13. The Ciampi cabinet resigns.

Indro Montanelli, editor of *Il Giornale* owned by the Berlusconi family, leaves the paper in disagreement with Silvio Berlusconi's decision to enter politics, "to play the field."

22. Alleanza Nazionale is founded.

26. Marco Luchetta, Alessandro Ota and Dario D'Angelo, a journalist, an operator and a television technician, die in war ridden Mostar, Bosnia.

February

6. Berlusconi unveils *Forza Italia*, his political movement.

9. The European Parliament passes a document opposing discrimination against homosexuals.

10. The Polo delle Libertà is founded, a centre right electoral alliance.

13. Winter Olympics at Lillehammer. Italy wins seven gold medals, the most important are Manuela Di Centa (15 and 30 km cross-country) and Deborah Compagnoni (giant slalom).

March

Spielberg's *Schindler's List* wins seven Oscars.

20. Journalist Ilaria Alpi and cameraman Miran Hrovatin are killed in an ambush in Mogadishu.

27. General elections with a majority system: the centre right win with 45.9% of the votes against 32.9% for the progressives.

April

Architect Ettore Sottsass is celebrated with an exhibition at the Beaubourg in Paris.

The Sistine Chapel is reopened after lengthy restoration.

A million people die in Ruanda when the Hutu tribe takes revenge on the Tutsi tribe.

28. "Mani pulite". The trial of Sergio Cusani, Raul Gardini's right-hand man, for financial irregularities comes to an end. Cusani is sentenced to eight years imprisonment. At San Vittore he strives to raise public awareness on the issues of Italian prisons.

May

Israeli premier Rabin and PLO president Arafat sign an agreement on Palestinian autonomy.

Milan soccer team dominates the European soccer scene winning the *scudetto* and Champions League.

In the World Cup, held in the United States, Italy reaches the final and plays against Brasil. Baggio misses a decisive penalty kick. Italy is second. This period marks the end of Maradona's career, he tested positive for doping: cocaine.

Peking: Laura Biagiotti opens the first Italian boutique in China.

Pulp Fiction by Quentin Tarantino wins the Palme d'Or at Cannes.

1. Ayrton Senna dies on the Imola circuit.

6. In Bariloche, Argentina, an American television reporter tracks down Erich Priebke, the Nazi officer that took part in the ardeatine caves massacre.

9. Nelson Mandela is elected president of South Africa marking the real end to apartheid.

11. Berlusconi forms a new government.

24. The following politicians are charged with involvement in the "Montedison Affair": Forlani, Craxi, Cirino Pomicino, Umberto Bossi, La Malfa, Altissimo, Martelli and De Michelis.

June

Florence. Under the supervision of Ted Polhemus and Roberto Grandi the exhibition *Supermarket of Style* for Pitti Immagine is held, it deals with spontaneous fashion and street fashion.

13. Massimo D'Alema is elected Secretary of the PDS, winning over Walter Veltroni. He becomes the successor to Achille Occhetto.

September

At the Venice Film Festival *Before the rain* by Milcho Manchevski and *Vive l'amour* by T'sai Ming-Liang are awarded with a Leone d'Oro.

12. Two hours of street fighting in Milan between police and young members of the Social centres.

October

Stephan Janson is hailed as the rising star of Italian prêt-à-porter.

Helmut Kohl is elected Chancellor of Germany for the fifth consecutive term.

8. Italy becomes the world volleyball champion.

16. Writer and Nobel prize winner Nagib Mahfuz is knifed in Cairo by Islamic extremists.

16. With a referendum Finland decides to apply for entry into the European Union.

26. Israel and Jordan sign a peace agreement.

November

Swiss cyclist Rominger breaks the hour record.

6. Floods in Piedmont.

12. Bill Gates buys the Hammer Codex by Leonardo da Vinci.

21. Thirty Nato bombers attack the Bosnian Serb airport of Ubdina; it is the most large-scale operation by the Atlantic Alliance in Bosnia.

22. Silvio Berlusconi is served with a notice of judicial investigation while he chairs a United Nations conference on crime in Naples.

December

6. Antonio Di Pietro, a leading figure in the "Mani pulite" investigations resigns from the judiciary.

10. Rabin, Peres and Arafat are awarded the Nobel Peace Prize.

11. Russian President Boris Yeltsin orders the invasion of the rebel republic of Chechnya. Guerrilla forces take root.

22. Berlusconi's government is forced to resign thanks to an about-turn by the Lega.

Arad creates the *Book-Worm* bookcase for Kartell.

Jean Nouvel designs the table *Less* for Unifor and Philippe Starck creates the *Lord-Yo* chairs for Driade.

Umberto Veronesi founds the European Oncology Institute in Milan.

The Channel tunnel is inaugurated.

Under the supervision of Luigi Settembrini and Germano Celant the exhibition *Italian Metamorphosis* takes place at the Guggenheim museum in New York.

Maurizio Cattelan exhibits rubble for the PAC with the title *Made in Italy*.

Deaths: Burt Lancaster, Jacqueline Kennedy, the leader of the rock group Nirvana Kurt Kobain, Jerry Rubin, one of the founding members of the hippie movement, Wanda Osiris, the writers Paolo Volponi, Domenico Rea, Charles Bukowski and Elias Canetti, philosopher Karl Popper, singer-songwriter Domenico Modugno, actors Massimo Troisi and Giulietta Masina, playwrights Eugène Jonesco and John Osborne.

January

There are 299,772 companies operating in Milan.

9,500 Italians (0.016% of the population) declare an annual gross income of over 500,000,000 lire.

2. Ex-dictator of Somalia Syaad Barre dies exiled in Lagos.

12. Pope John Paul II is in the Philippine on a pastoral visit.

16. Japan hit by an earthquake: 4,000 die and 250,000 are left homeless.

20. Scandal in Europe over HIV-infected blood.

Two Islamic kamikaze terrorists attack a group of people waiting for a bus in Natanya on the outskirts of Tel Aviv: 19 die.

22. The O.J. Simpson trial opens in Los Angeles: he is accused of killing his wife and an acquaintance of hers.

23. At a Congress in Fiuggi, Alleanza Nazionale decides to relinquish their fascist nostalgia.

24. Lamberto Dini presents his government to the Chamber of Deputies and wins a vote of confidence.

28. More than twenty years after the end of the war an agreement between Vietnam and the United States is signed at Hanoi.

30. The Algerian government is kept under macabre pressure by Islamic fundamentalists. 38 are killed when a bomb explodes outside the Central Police Station in Algiers.

February

Paolo Zani designs the *Riga* lamp for Candle, Antonio Citterio creates the *Florence* armchair for B&B Italia, Carlo Batoli designs the *Breeze* chair for Segis.

4. The statue of the Madonna at Civitavecchia weeps blood. Crowds flock to pray.

9. A burst of machine-gun fire kills television operator Marcello Palmisano in Mogadishu.

14. The Letten Park drug ghetto experiment in Zurich fails. The authorities that had approved the experiment order its closure.

16. The Ulivo, a centre-left alliance, is founded.

March

The film *Forrest Gump* wins seven Oscars.

The United Nations contingent withdraws from Somalia, two years of attempts to bring peace to the country have failed.

6. The death penalty is reintroduced in the state of New York.

11. Thousands are killed in Burundi in the civil war between the Hutu and Tutsi tribes.

14. An episode of racial intolerance in Pisa: two Romany children are injured by a bomb while they are begging at traffic lights.

15. Tomba wins the World Alpine Skiing Cup.

20. Terrorist nerve gas attack in the Tokyo underground: 10 victims.

27. Maurizio Gucci is murdered in via Palestro, Milan.

28. Director Michelangelo Antonioni wins a Career Oscar.

29. The Texas Senate passes a law allowing reduced jail sentences for sexual criminals who accept castration.

29. The Papal encyclical *Evangelium Vitae* reaffirms the church's condemnation of abortion.

April

2. Ethnic massacres resume in Ruanda.

28. The armed forces are called in to halt the illegal immigration of Albanians in Puglia.

May

Campeggi manufacture the *Kenia* fold-up chair designed by Vico Magistretti, Montina produce the *Cramer* chair by Konstantin Grcic and Giorgetti the *Nyri* drawer unit by Chi Wing Lo.

Underground by Kusturica is awarded a Palme d'or at the Cannes Film Festival.

Commemorations for the fiftieth anniversary of the end of the Second World War.

Nato intensifies punitive raids in Bosnia.

A decimating Ebola virus epidemic breaks out in Zaire.

7. Jacques Chirac is elected president in France ending a long period of Socialist supremacy.

8. Pension reform.

28. The Lega leader Bossi opens the Northern Parliament in Mantua.

28. In the local government elections in Spain, Aznar's right-wing party wins in 10 out of 13 regions.

June

South Africa abolishes the death penalty.

In Italy the birth rate is in decline, the number of deaths outweighs the number of births.

11. In a referendum on the reordering of television channels Berlusconi's arguments are upheld.

15. In Chechnya at the battle of Budennovsk the separatists keep the Muscovite troops in check.

26. The United Nations celebrate their first fifty years.

29. The Russian space station Mir docks with the space shuttle Atlantis.

July

The Strega literary prize is awarded to the late Maria Teresa Di Lascia for *Passaggio in ombra*.

Spaniard Miguel Indurain wins his fifth consecutive Tour de France.

12. Greenpeace protest against the French nuclear experiments in Mururoa.

18. Teenage despair over the break-up of the boy-band "Take That".

25. Islamic fundamentalist attack in the Paris metro: four die.

August

Mike Tyson resumes his boxing career.

16. Schumacher signs a contract with Ferrari.

21. Six are killed in a car bomb attack in Jerusalem.

September

9. Vietnamese film *Cyclo* wins at the Venice Film Festival.

24. Arafat and Peres sign a treaty marking the second phase of Palestinian autonomy.

26. At the United Nations an accord is reached between Serbs, Croats and Muslims on peace in former Yugoslavia.

October

Fashion designer Tom Ford relaunches the Gucci image.

Michael Schumacher wins his second world title, for Benetton.

Irish poet Seamus Heaney wins the Nobel Prize for Literature.

November

Cinema regains popularity. Cinemas are reopened or enlarged in Milan: Plinius (5 screens), Gloria (2 screens), Ducale (4 screens) and Anteo (3 screens).

Bill Gates becomes the richest man in the world: 12.9 billion dollars.

4. Israeli premier Yitzhak Rabin pays with his life for having sought peace. He is assassinated in Tel Aviv by a Jewish fundamentalist.

December

The Italian national volleyball team wins the World Cup in Tokyo.

Robert Altman's provocative film *Prêt-à-porter* is set in the fashion world.

Susanna Tamaro's novel *Va' dove ti porta il cuore* reaches sales of 2 million.

At the Triennale, exhibition *45/63 Un museo del disegno industriale in Italia* is supervised by Manolo De Giorgi.

The Sandretto Re Rebaudengo Foundation is opened at Guarene d'Alba (Cuneo).

Deaths: Jonas Salk who discovered the vaccine for polio, Alberto Burri, Edda Ciano, actresses Paola Borboni, Lana Turner and Ginger Rogers, the inventor of tranquillisers Henri Laborit, pianist Arturo Benedetti Michelangeli, poet Stephen Spender and the many times over motoring champion Manuel Fangio, actor Dean Martin, sculptor Francesco Messina, directors Louis Malle and Nanni Loi and cartoonist Hugo Pratt.

1996

January

The Dini cabinet resigns.

First elections held in the autonomous Palestinian territories: victory for Yasser Arafat.

8. François Mitterand, president of France for 14 years, dies aged 80.

23 Mario Chiesa, from whom the whole "Mani pulite" affair began, is finally sentenced to 5 years and 4 months. He will be assigned to social services.

29. The Fenice Opera House in Venice is burnt down.

February

An oil tanker is wrecked on the Welsh coast spilling 70,000 tons of crude oil into the sea causing an ecological disaster.

World Skiing Championships on the Spanish Sierra Nevada: Alberto Tomba, Isolde Kostner and Deborah Compagnoni win gold medals.

23. Diego Curtò, ex president of the civil court is sentenced to 4 years for corruption.

March

3. A further step forward is taken in the Middle East peace process. At Sharm el Sheikh the PLO recognises the state of Israel and Israel in turn recognises the Palestinian's right to a sovereign state.

6. The *Corriere della Sera* reaches its 120th year. It was founded in 1876 with a circulation of 3,000 copies. The staff consisted of three editors, one clerk and an office boy.

14. Noto Cathedral, a jewel of Sicilian baroque, collapses.

20. "Mad cow" in Britain. The virus is also contagious for humans.

April

For the fourth time running Yuri Chechi is world champion in gymnastics.

The daily newspaper *Il Foglio* is founded. The editor is Giuliano Ferrara.

19. Changing of the guard at Pirelli. Leopoldo Pirelli leaves the post of president to Marco Tronchetti Provera, already holder of the important post of managing director.

21. The Ulivo wins the general elections. Romano Prodi is asked to form a government. The stock exchange is euphoric and gains 4.9%.

Ferragamo buys a majority share in Emanuel Ungaro.

24. Vincenzo Torriani, patron of the Giro d'Italia from 1946 to 1992,0 dies.

May

Secrets and lies by Mike Leigh wins the Palme d'or at the Cannes Film Festival.

Milan soccer team becomes Italian champion for the fifteenth time, their fourth championship in five years and what is more two weeks before the conclusion.

The right wins the general elections in Israel. Benjamin Netanyhau leader of the Likud forms the government.

20. Mafioso Giovanni Brusca, who was responsible for the Capaci murders, is arrested in Agrigento, the police force exults.

June

Florence. *G.A. Story*, an exhibition-show by Bob Wilson tells the story of Giorgio Armani's work.

July

Half a million young people take part in the Love Parade in Berlin.

15. Three years after the bomb attack in which five people lost their lives, the PAC (Contemporary Art Pavilion) reopens in via Palestro, Milan.

16. Stock exchange crash, the super-Deutschmark crushes the lire, the market closes at –2.16% losing 19,000 billion lire in two days.

September

First edition of the Florence Fashion Biennial. In seven exhibitions the affinities, the mutual influences, the creative relationships between fashion, art, design, photography, cinema, architecture and communication are explored. The artistic directors are Luigi Settembrini, Germano Celant and Ingrid Sischy.

Denny Mendez is the first coloured girl to be elected Miss Italia.

English cyclist Chris Boardman sets a new record for the hour: 56.375 km.

Michael Collins by Neil Jordan wins a Leone d'oro at the Venice Film Festival.

15. Lega Secretary Umberto Bossi calls for the independence of Padania.

October

20. Milan. The Biblioteca Ambrosiana reopens after seven years of restoration financed by Cariplo.

November

6. Bill Clinton is re-elected president of the United States.

December

12. Milan. A human chain is formed around the Law Courts in solidarity with the magistrates investigating into "Mani pulite".

17. Kofi Annan, a diplomat from Ghana, is elected Secretary General of the United Nations.

Philippe Starck designs the *Miss Trip* chair for Kartell, Achille Castiglioni designs the *Fucsia* lamp for Flos and Riccardo Baimer creates the *La leggera* chair for Alioo.

A study by two university economists reveals that one inhabitant of Milan in three is poor: 385,000 inhabitants have difficulty making ends meet, while 17,000 families live under constant threat of eviction.

Ferré leaves the creative board of Dior, his place is taken by John Galliano.

Turnover in the fashion world in billions of lire: 1,820 Armani, 1,200 Fendi, 1,007 Valentino, 1,250 Ferré, 1,189 Prada, 804 Gucci.

There are 213 voluntary organisations in Milan: it is estimated that there are 48,600 people involved in no profit activities.

Milan. There are 7,161 inhabitants per square kilometre. 44.3% live in rented accommodation, while over 51% own their home.

The Milan Trienniale organises the exhibitions *Design Italiano '63-'72* and *Design Italiano '73-'95* under the supervision of Andrea Branzi.

The leader of the Lega, Bossi, launches the motto: independent Padania.

Mediobanca celebrates fifty years of activity.

Giovanni Soldini wins the Atlantic crossing from Plymouth to Newport.

Deaths: Wally Toscanini, singer Luciano Tajoli, poets Josif Brodskij and Dario Bellezza, writer Marguerite Duras, director René Clement, comedian Gino Bramieri and actor Marcello Mastroianni.

January

Rosita and Tai Missoni hand over control of their label to their daughter Angela.

At the Sestrière world Championships Deborah Compagnoni wins the slalom and giant slalom (she already holds two Olympic medals and a world championship) and Isolde Kostner triumphs in the Super-G.

2. Spain's Miguel Indurain ends his cycling career having won the Tour de France five times and the Giro d'Italia twice.

12. The Milan-Rome Pendolino super-train derails entering Piacenza. Eight people are killed.

13. The US Supreme Court discuss the Paula Jones case, the young woman accuses president Clinton of sexual harassment.

14. A group of young people, including the Furlan brothers, are accused of throwing stones off a motorway flyover and a subsequent death in Tortona.

17. Milk producers block the entrance to Linate airport in Milan in protest against fines imposed by the EU for having surpassed limits in milk production.

February

19. Deng Xiao Ping dies in Peking aged 93.

28. Revolt in Albania. Military arsenals are looted, in April a left-wing coalition wins the elections.

March

25. *The English Patient* by Anthony Minghella wins nine Oscars.

28. Trying to make a ship carrying Albanian refugees change route, the Italian corvette *Sibilla* rams the ship and 87 people die.

April

5. Milan. A bomb explodes at Palazzo Marino: little damage is done.

15. 200 die when fire breaks out among pilgrims' tents in Mecca.

23. Ferruccio de Bortoli is nominated editor of *Corriere della Sera*.

May

9. Marta Russo is murdered at Rome University.

10. A squad of Lega Veneta members occupy St. Mark's Square in Venice with a rudimentary armoured car, they barricade themselves in the bell tower.

11. Milan. Gabriele Albertini is elected mayor on the second ballot winning against the left-wing candidate Aldo Fumagalli.

13. Tony Blair prohibits the use of pocket calculators in primary school.

Enrico Baleri and Denis Santachiara design the pouffe *Tatino*, *Tatone* for Baleri Italia, Newson the table *Io* for B&B, Starck designs the *Caadre* mirror for Fiam.

17. Revolt in Zaire, Mobutu leaves after 32 years of absolute power. Kabila takes power (he will be assassinated in January 2001) and restores the country's old name: Congo.

23. Juventus win their 24th championship.

27. Moscow orders the dismantling of the missiles aimed at Europe.

June

Pitti Immagine Uomo at the Stazione Leopolda in Florence, the exhibition *Faces - 500 faces* photographed by Oliviero Toscani.

After 14 years of restoration Galleria Borghese reopens in Rome.

2. After the left win the elections in France socialist Jospin is asked to form a government.

5. Photographic evidence of Italian soldiers torturing prisoners in Somalia appears on the weekly magazine *Panorama*.

8. Ivan Gotti wins the Giro d'Italia.

28. Disastrous weather in Northern Italy with floods and landslides: three people die.

July

1. As agreed Great Britain return Hong Kong to China.

1. Toni Negri, the ideological leader of Autonomia operaia, returns to Italy from France. He will have to serve a five year jail sentence.

12. The remains of Ernesto Che Guevara found in Bolivia are brought to Cuba.

22. **Designer Gianni Versace is murdered in front of his home in Miami. Lady Diana and Elton John are present at his funeral which takes place in Milan Cathedral.**

25. Brazilian soccer star Ronaldo arrives in Milan and is cheered by thousands of delirious Inter fans when he appears at a window in via Durini.

27. German Jan Ulrich wins the Tour de France.

August

7. At the Athens World Championships, Anna Rita Sidoti wins the 10 km walking race.

24. At the youth celebrations in Paris pope John Paul II asks the forgiveness of Protestants for the Huguenot massacre of 1572.

26. Carl Lewis withdraws from competitive sport. He had won nine Olympic gold medals.

28. The musical film on the Mafia *Tano da morire* is shown at the Venice Film Festival.

31. Lady Diana and her partner Dodi Al Fayed die in a car accident in Paris.

September

The Spice Girls are latest phenomena of the teenage music world.

The Teatro alla Scala Foundation is set up to replace public management. Private donations amount to 28 billion lire.

Japanese film *Hana-bi* wins a Leone d'Oro at the Venice Film Festival.

5. Mother Teresa of Calcutta dies.

23. Algerian fundamentalists carry out a massacre in Benthala: 250 men, women and children are brutally murdered. The victims of the civil war amount to 81 thousand.

26. Earthquake in Umbria and the Marche: 11 die, hundreds are injured and damage to the artistic heritage is enormous.

27. Bob Dylan sings at the Eucharistic Congress in Bologna and the pope mentions his song *Blowing in the wind* during the homily.

October

Bilbao. The museum designed by architect Franck Gehry is inaugurated.

Following family tradition Jacques Villeneuve wins the Formula One World Championship. Max Biaggi becomes world motorcycling champion for the fourth time running in the 250 category.

2. **Prêt-à-porter fashion shows in Milan. Many collections are inspired by Lolita.**

31. 11 die in a fire in the hyperbaric chamber at the Galeazzi Institute in Milan.

November

7. 68 die when an Islamic squad attacks a group of tourists at Luxor in Egypt.

16. The centre-left holds its own in some important Italian cities: Bassolino in Naples, Rutelli in Rome and Cacciari in Venice are all re-elected on the first count.

December

10. Dario Fo is awarded the Nobel Prize for Literature.

19. The independent milk producers trade unions withdraw from their "siege" of Rome: They had brought their mascot, the cow Carolina, as far as St. Peter's Square.

Kartell produce the *FPE* chair by Ron Arad; Gervasoni produce the *Otto* system by Paola Navone; Luceplan produce the *Blow fan* by Ferdi Giardini.

Minimalia supervised by Achille Bonito Oliva (Venice '97, Rome '98, New York '99, PS1) examines the Italian minimal movement from Giacomo Balla to the most recent generations.

During the year the television programme *Striscia la notizia* never falls below an audience of 9 and a half million.

Noteworthy successes in cinema during the year were *Full Monty* by Peter Cattaneo, *Ovosodo* by Paolo Virzì, the Iranian film *Taste of Cherry* by Kiarostami, *Richard III* by Al Pacino and *Everyone says I love you* by Woody Allen. 1996-'97 record box-office takings in Italy had been Leonardo Pieraccioni's film *Il ciclone* reaching almost 70 billion lire.

Deaths: director Marco Ferreri, Giovanni Alberto Agnelli heir to the Fiat empire, composer Fiorenzo Carpi, directors Fred Zinnemann and Giorgio Strehler, journalists Franco Di Bella and Camilla Cederna, Tina Lattanzi the Italian voice that dubbed Greta Garbo, the beat poet Allen Ginsberg, actors Robert Mitchum and James Steward, pop artist Roy Lichtenstein, trainer Helenio Herrera, the historical leader of French communism George Marchais.

1998

January

2. Massacre at the hands of Islamic fundamentalists in Algeria: 412 die in a single night.

9. Experiments for Dr. Luigi Di Bella's cancer cure are approved.

Florence. The exhibition *Il motore della Moda* is held at the Stazione Leopolda.

10. **Hdp buy the Valentino fashion house for 540 billion lire.**

21. The Lewinsky scandal. American president Bill Clinton is accused of having had sexual relations with White House intern Monika Lewinsky.

Pope John Paul II visits Cuba and meets Fidel Castro. His papacy is about to enter its twentieth year.

22. Cesare Romiti is no longer president of Fiat having reached the maximum age limit.

24. Christian Ghedina from Cortina wins the awesome Kitzbühel downhill race.

26. Mozart's *Così fan tutte* staged following the notes of the late Strehler, opens the Nuovo Piccolo Teatro di Milano, designed by Marco Zanuso.

February

3. During a practice flight an American Airforce plane severs the cable of a cableway at Cermis in the Alps near Trent causing the death of 20 people.

18. At the London summit the World Bank issues the figures on world poverty: 3 billion people in the world are living on less than two dollars a day.

March

At the Academy Awards the film *Titanic* wins eleven Oscars.

2. Censorship calls a halt to *Totò che visse due volte* by Ciprì and Maresco. Ten days later censorship is finally abolished.

6. Serbia commences "ethnic cleansing" against he Albanian majority in Kosovo.

11. **For security reasons the Parisian magistrature blocks an Armani fashion show in a marquee at Saint Sulpice: it is feared that there could be attacks because of resentment for the invasion of Italian fashion in Paris.**

15. With the document "We Remember, a Reflection on the Shoah (Holocaust)," the Catholic Church admits its passive attitude regarding the Holocaust during the war.

21. Antonio Di Pietro founds the political movement L'Italia dei Valori.

April

Massimo Morozzi designs the upholstered *Cubista* for Edra, Marc Newson the *Io* table for B&B Italia.

Bill Clinton also atones for the United States speaking in Uganda: "We erred. Before becoming a nation the United States exploited slavery."

14. A peace agreement is signed in Northern Ireland between Protestants and Catholics.

26. A much-disputed victory of Juventus over Inter opens the way to their twenty-fifth championship victory.

27. The stock exchange crashes: Milan closes at –6.42 %.

May

Italy enters the Euro.

5. Floods in the Campania region. The entire areas of Sarno and Quindici are covered by a huge slide of mud: 147 victims.

11. India, after over twenty years, resumes testing nuclear weapons. On 28th Pakistan answers with five tests.

14. Revolt in Jakarta. President Suharto resigns a week later. He had been in power since 1966.

24. *La vita è bella* by Benigni wins the Grand Prix at Cannes.

June

Florence. Stazione Leopolda. *1968-1998 exhibition. Stile in progress - 30 years of "L'Uomo Vogue".*

War between Ethiopia and Eritrea.

Nanni Moretti returns to the big screen in *Aprile*.

Gigi Simoni's Inter wins its third UEFA cup beating Lazio in Paris.

1. **After 16 years of success and expansion, Pietro Marzotto leaves the presidency of the Marzotto Group.**

20. At the summit in Tokyo the seven most industrialised countries in the world discuss the Japanese economic crisis.

29. **At Milano Collezioni Uomo, mayor Gabriele Albertini accepts to pose wearing a pair of cashmere briefs by Valentino.**

July

The Sahara is advancing. Aided by the hole in the ozone layer, desertification threatens 145 million inhabitants of Sahel and 67 million in North Africa.

Enzo Siciliano wins the Strega Literary Prize with *I bei momenti*.

12. Paris. France beats Brazil 3 to 1 thus winning the World Cup.

14. Milan. Director Luca Ronconi is nominated director of the Piccolo Teatro.

17. In St. Petersburg a reparative state funeral is held for Tsar Nicolas II and his family who were assassinated during the Russian Revolution.

18. Using the anticoagulant Epo as a doping substance costs Richard Virenque and his team their expulsion from the Tour de France.

28. Experimentation of the anti cancer cure concludes negatively, Dr. Di Bella disputes the results.

August

2. Marco Pantani triumphs in the Tour de France after having won the Giro d'Italia.

7. Kenya. Bomb attack at the US embassy in Nairobi and at Dar-es-Salam in Tanzania: 137 victims.

13. Milan. By order of deputy mayor Riccardo De Corato, a million lire fine is to be imposed on clients who block the traffic while haggling with prostitutes.

23. Russian president Boris Yeltsin changes the head of government yet again: he recalls formerly sacked Victor Chernomyrdin.

September

Gianni Amelio is awarded a Leone d'oro in Venice for the film *Così ridevano*.

France, in Bordeaux, Maurice Papon, ex official of the Vichy republic is tried for joint responsibility in the deportation to Germany of 1600 Jews.

23. At the Herriot hospital in Lyon the first hand transplant is performed.

27. Germany. The Social Democrats win the elections. The helm is passed to Gerhard Schroeder.

October

17. Ex-dictator of Chile Pinochet is arrested while being treated in a clinic in London.

21. Romano Prodi leaves Palazzo Chigi. Massimo D' Alema takes over as neo-Premier, the first post-communist leader to take the post.

25. The international Airport of Malpensa 2000 is opened.

29. Aged 77, John Glenn, a pioneer astronaut, takes part in a mission on board the space shuttle *Discovery*.

November

13. Leader of the Kurdish resistance Ocalan lands in Italy fleeing from the Turkish secret services.

December

11. Two panettone cakes of the brands Motta and Alemagna are poisoned with rat poison by the Animal Liberation Front.

19. Bill Clinton is incriminated for perjury and obstruction of justice in the Sexgate affair.

31. The Euro is born in Brussels with the approval of fixed exchange rates between the 11 countries admitted.

Denis Santachiara designs the armchair-sofa *Gummy* for Campeggi.

The Milan stock exchange closes the year with a revaluation of 41%.

Spielberg's film *Save Soldier Ryan* is a success.

Deaths: Frank Sinatra, the graphic designer Bruno Munari, singer-songwriter Lucio Battisti, writer Anna Maria Ortese, German Industrial car manufacturer Ferdinand Porsche, Vatican foreign minister Agostino Casaroli, mezzosoprano Lucia Valentini Terrani, Japanese director Akira Kurosawa, art historian Federico Zeri and Richard McDonald, founder of the fast food chain, painters Mario Schifano and Gino De Dominicis.

1999

January

Firenze. Pitti Immagine Uomo organises the exhibition *Volare. L'icona italiana nella cultura globale* at the Stazione Leopolda: installation by Achille Castiglioni, Gianfranco Cavaglià and Italo Lupi.

Milan. Twelve homicides within the first three weeks of the year: the issue of security comes to the fore again.

Nato presents an ultimatum to Serbia but ethnic cleansing is intensified in Kosovo.

February

Milanese navigator Giovanni Soldini wins the Around Alone regatta, a solitary race around the world held every four years. He even lengthens his route to save French competitor Isabelle Autierre who is drifting without sails.

The leader of the "Mani pulite" investigation, Francesco Saverio Borrelli, is appointed Attorney General. His second Gerardo D'Ambrosio takes his post at the public prosecutor's office.

Mikhail Gorbachev takes part at the Sanremo Festival.

7. King Hussein of Jordan dies.

15. The village of Valtur in the Austrian valley of Parnaum is swept away by avalanches and snowslides.

March

Philippe Starck designs the *Cadre* mirror for Fiam Italia, the *La Marie* chair and *Gnomes* stool for Kartell.

3. A US study reveals that the last decade has been the hottest in the millennium.

22. *La vita è bella* wins three Oscars: one for Benigni as best leading actor.

24. Nato bombs Belgrade and Milosevic's army in reprisal for the massacres in Kosovo.

April

14. Fire in the Mont Blanc tunnel: 45 die.

19. Berlin. The new Reichstag is inaugurated.

May

A new wave of terrorism. A terrorist squad kills Massimo D'Antona, a university professor and consultant to the Minister Bassolino for issues related to employment, in Rome.

The government changes in Israel: Ehud Barak, leader of the Labour coalition, wins the elections and takes the place of Benjamin Netanyhau.

Leonardo's *Last Supper* is reopened to the public after restoration.

13. Carlo Azeglio Ciampi is elected president on the first count.

14. A gang of 12 bandits holds up a security van in via Imbonati, Milano, forcing their way through with machinegun fire. A guard is killed. The bandits will all be arrested within a few months. Many of them are ex-members of Prima Linea.

June

European elections. Forza Italia and the Bonino list (8.5%) score a great success in Italy.

10. Belgrade accepts the United Nations peace plan. The Balkan war comes to an end.

July

After having recovered from cancer, Lance Armstrong wins the Tour de France.

Petrol surpasses 2000 lire.

16. John John Kennedy, son of the late president, dies in a crash at the controls of his own plane, his wife Carolyne Besset and sister-in-law die with him.

Prada buys 75% of Church, the historical English shoe label and, together with Bernard Arnault, the Roman fashion house Fendi.

August

Yeltsin appoints Vladimir Putin as head of the Russian government.

Earthquake in Turkey: 15,000 die.

Military service comes to an end. The professional armed forces are instituted by law.

13. The Russian armed forces attack the Islamic rebels in Dagstan and Chechnya.

30. After a referendum calling for the independence of East Timor from Indonesia, 20,000 Catholics are killed in a massacre.

September

Giulio Andreotti is acquitted of both charges: being the instigator of the Pecorelli murder and connivance with the Mafia.

At the Venice Festival *Not one less* by Chinese director Zhang Yimou wins the Leone d'Oro.

15. Romano Prodi is appointed president of the European Commission.

October

Austria. The xenophobic right led by Joerg Haider is the real winner of the general election.

Valentino Rossi becomes world motorcycle champion in the 250 class.

November

Milan. The age gene is discovered by researchers at the European Oncology Institute.

Sofri, Pietrostefani and Bompressi, sentenced to 22 years for the murder of Luigi Calabresi, are freed. They are granted a revision of their trial.

December

Seattle. The World Trade Organisation Congress is threatened by a mass demonstration by anti-globalisation movements.

The beatification of Padre Pio in St. Peter's.

Plagued by bad health and scandals Russian President Yeltsin resigns. Putin takes the helm.

25. Pope John Paul II opens the Holy door in Saint Peter's marking the opening of the Jubilee.

Box is born: Manuela Cifarelli is the editor.

The Minister for the Environment invites municipalities to close city centres to traffic on Sundays as a measure to "cut down" pollution.

Moroso present the *40/80* armchair by Achille Castiglioni and Ferruccio Laviani.

Franco Raggi designs the *Flute* lamp for Fontana Arte; Alberto Meda and Paolo Rizzato design the *Partner* bookcase for Kartell.

Seven mystery novels by writer Andrea Camilleri are among the ten best-selling books of the year.

"Dappertutto" is the theme of the Venice Biennale under the direction of Harald Szeemann, and takes up a large part of the Arsenal that had never before been open to the public.

Palma Bucarelli dies, she was legendary curator of the Galleria Nazionale d'Arte Moderna in Rome from 1945 to 1975.

Deaths: The King of Morocco Hassan II, singer-songwriter Fabrizio De André, editors Giulio Einaudi and Vanni Scheiwiller, Biki Leonardi Bouyeur, stylist Nicola Trussardi, director Stanley Kubrick, violinist Yehudi Menuhin, television presenter Corrado Mantoni, writer Mario Soldati and Leo Castelli.

January

Moroso put the sofa *Victoria & Albert* by Ron Arad into production, Edra produce the *Air One* armchair by Ross Lovegrove and Luceplan produce the *Agaricon* lamp also by Lovegrove.

In a University laboratory in Oregon Tetra, a cloned monkey is born, it is the second cloned animal. The first was the sheep Dolly born in the Biotechnology Institute in Edinburgh.

18. Illicit funding of his party ruins the political career of ex German Chancellor Helmut Kohl who admitting his responsibility is forced to resign from politics.

20. Ex Secretary of the Socialist party and ex Premier Bettino Craxi dies a victim of diabetes and kidney cancer in Hammamet, he was the first socialist to lead a government in Italian history. He was under investigation for several counts in the "Mani pulite" inquiries which marked the end of his political career.

February

The law on *par condicio*, which regulates political propaganda in television and electoral publicity, is passed.

In Iran, moderate Mohammad Khatami wins the elections: it is seen as a possible step towards the return of democracy in the country.

March

American Beauty by Sam Mendes wins five Oscars.

Spain. The centre-right Popular Party led by José Maria Aznar wins the elections with a landslide victory over the socialists.

New Zealand. Off the coast of Auckland, Prada's *Luna Rossa* enters the final but is beaten by the New Zealanders on *Black Magic*.

8. Ash Wednesday, in *Instrumentum laboris* the pope continues his self-criticism of the church asking for forgiveness for the crusades, religious wars, the inquisition, the burning of heretics, forced conversions and the persecutions of the Jews.

John Paul II visits Jerusalem.

April

A public bid by Prada, already owning 75% of the company, for the privileged shares in the German label Jil Sander is successful. Prada thus gains complete control of the fashion house.

The mapping of the human genome, the exact sequence of genes, is completed. New frontiers in medicine are opened.

The centre-right wins the regional elections. Massimo D'Alema's government resigns. The Ulivo appoints Giuliano Amato to Palazzo Chigi.

11. **Milan. Cosmit presents the exhibition *Stanze e segreti* projected by Luigi Settembrini at the Rotonda della Besana: supervised by Achille Bonito Oliva.**

12. In a serious accident soccer champion Ronaldo damages a tendon and cannot play for Inter in the championship. Ronaldo had just returned after being out of action for five months because of the same injury to the same knee.

May

Israeli troops withdraw from South Lebanon after 22 years of occupation.

Lazio soccer team wins its second championship.

4. Gino Bartali dies in Florence.

June

The presidents of the two Koreas meet at Pyongyang. After half a century there are signs of a thaw.

Cease-fire between Eritrea and Ethiopia. An agreement is signed in Algeria.

Stefano Garzelli wins the Giro d'Italia.

At the European soccer championship final France beats Italy.

July

5. A French Concorde bursts into flames immediately after takeoff from Roissy and crashes into a hotel near the airport: 113 are killed. All Air France Concords are grounded.

8. Gay pride march in Rome amid heated controversy over its coincidence with the Jubilee.

August

28. A visit by ex-defence minister, the falcon Ariel Sharon, to the al-Aqsa compound in Jerusalem sparks off a new and more intense Intifada in Israel and the occupied territories. The peace process is blocked.

September

Sidney Olympics. Italy wins 13 gold medals with unexpected success in swimming.

The pope proclaims the beatification of Pius IX and John XXIII, two antithetic leading figures of the Catholic Church.

October

Elections in Yugoslavia. Slobodan Milosevic loses to Vojislav Kostunica.

9. In Suzuka in Japan, Schumacher wins for Ferrari in Formula One, their first victory in 21 years.

15. Weeks of floods, landslides, bursting rivers in Valle d'Aosta, Piedmont, Lombardy and finally Liguria. Billions of lire in damage and 25 victims.

November

7. Controversial and chaotic elections in the USA. Gore has more popular votes but Bush has more electoral votes. For a month disputes and appeals divide the US.

December

13. The US Supreme Court awards the victory to Bush.

Philippe Starck designs the sofa *Bubble Club* for Kartell, the Cerri & Associati Studio design the fold-up *Donald* chair for Poltrona Frau and Paolo Rizzato the *Flexus* sofa for Alias.

Russian nuclear submarine *Kursk* cannot surface from the depths of the Barents Sea. Moscow refuses the help of Western countries. 118 die.

Perù. President Fujimori wins the elections again, protests are widespread due to evident vote rigging. But a pay-off scandal forces him to flee.

The centre-left coalition chooses Rutelli as their probable candidate as Premier for the 2001 elections.

President Ciampi pardons Alì Agca who attempted to assassinate the pope.

The film *Pane e tulipani* by Silvio Soldini meets with both critical and public success.

The Ministry for cultural heritage approves the central office for architecture and contemporary art.

The collection of *Arte Povera* opens at Rivoli Castle.

Deaths: Vittorio Gassman, president of Mediobanca Enrico Cuccia, Mafia turncoat Tommaso Buscetta, Walter Matthau, director Roger Vadim and Charles Schulz, the "father" of Linus.

Nineties

*Ex President of Italy
Sandro Pertini dies. Rome,
24ᵗʰ Feburary 1990
(photo: Carlo Orsi)*

*Judge Giovanni Falcone is
killed in the Capaci attack,
23ʳᵈ May 1992
(Olympia/Renato Bencini)*

*Senator Giulio Andreotti
is served with a notice
of judicial investigation.
Rome, 27ᵗʰ March 1993
(photo: Roby Schirer)*

*The Luna Rossa crew,
Auckland, New Zealand,
March 2000
(photo: 77/Carlo Borlenghi)*

*Milan. Immigrant street
vendor
(photo: Roby Schirer)*